Pan-Asianism and the Legacy
of the Chinese Revolution

Pan-Asianism and the Legacy of the Chinese Revolution

VIREN MURTHY

The University of Chicago Press
Chicago and London

The University of Chicago Press, Chicago 60637
The University of Chicago Press, Ltd., London
© 2023 by The University of Chicago
All rights reserved. No part of this book may be used or reproduced in any manner
whatsoever without written permission, except in the case of brief quotations in
critical articles and reviews. For more information, contact the University of Chicago
Press, 1427 E. 60th St., Chicago, IL 60637.
Published 2023
Printed and bound by CPI Group (UK) Ltd, Croydon, CR0 4YY

32 31 30 29 28 27 26 25 24 23   1 2 3 4 5

ISBN-13: 978-0-226-82798-8 (cloth)
ISBN-13: 978-0-226-82800-8 (paper)
ISBN-13: 978-0-226-82799-5 (e-book)
DOI: https://doi.org/10.7208/chicago/9780226827995.001.0001

Library of Congress Cataloging-in-Publication Data

Names: Murthy, Viren, author.
Title: Pan-Asianism and the legacy of the Chinese Revolution / Viren Murthy.
Description: Chicago : The University of Chicago Press, 2023. |
    Includes bibliographical references and index.
Identifiers: LCCN 2022061325 | ISBN 9780226827988 (cloth) |
    ISBN 9780226828008 (paperback) | ISBN 9780226827995 (ebook)
Subjects: LCSH: Takeuchi, Yoshimi, 1910–1977—Political and social views. |
    National characteristics, East Asian. | Nationalism—East Asia—History—
    20th century. | Imperialism—Public opinion. | Capitalism—Public opinion. |
    Intellectuals—East Asia—Attitudes. | East Asia—History—20th century. |
    East Asia—Intellectual life—20th century. | China—Public opinion.
Classification: LCC DDC320 .M87 2023 | DDC 320.54095—dc23/eng/20230105
LC record available at https://lccn.loc.gov/2022061325

♾ This paper meets the requirements of ANSI/NISO Z39.48-1992 (Permanence of Paper).

Contents

Introduction
Pan-Asianism in the Short Twentieth Century 1

1 Asia as Pharmakon
The Early Constitution of Asia as Resistance 16

2 The Critique of Linear Time
Pan-Asianism in Early Twentieth-Century China 50

3 Asia as Anticapitalist Utopia
Ōkawa Shūmei's Critique of Political Modernity 80

4 Takeuchi Yoshimi, Part I
Rethinking China as Political Subjectivity 110

5 Takeuchi Yoshimi, Part II
Pan-Asianism, Revolutionary Nationalism, and War Memory 136

6 Wang Hui
Contemporary Pan-Asianist in China? 192

Epilogue
Pan-Asianism, the Chinese Revolution, and Global Moments 214

Acknowledgments 221
Notes 225
Bibliography 253
Index 267

INTRODUCTION

Pan-Asianism in the Short Twentieth Century

In the past few years, discussion in the public sphere of the rise of Chinese and Asian capitalism has been ubiquitous. Xi Jinping's recent plan to connect much of Asia and the West by means of reviving the ancient Silk Road has been viewed as both a possible alternative to a world economy dominated by the West and a potential threat to other countries in the region. Thus, it is not surprising that in recent decades, a turn toward analyzing pan-Asianism from various scholarly and popular perspectives has occurred. Most scholarly works have refrained from making sweeping claims about the nature of pan-Asianism and have restricted themselves to a specific period, such as interwar and wartime Japan.[1] Popular books, however, have tended to be programmatic and quick to draw overly broad conclusions. Each of these approaches provides a different window into pan-Asianism. On one hand, academic works have given us a detailed analysis of how lesser-known intellectuals have thought about pan-Asianism in specific political contexts. On the other hand, works written for wider audiences have raised awareness of the stakes in studying pan-Asianism. The latter often argue that pan-Asianism could be a wave of the future, sweeping us toward a world beyond Western domination. Indeed, one of the main reasons for the turn toward pan-Asianism in both the academic and popular literature is the thriving economies in East Asia, such as Japan and the other "Asian Tigers" (Korea, Singapore, Taiwan) and, more recently, the so-called rise of China. Consequently, political analysts have turned to pan-Asianism in an attempt to explain why China, India, and Japan in particular have become powerful capitalist countries and to help the world prepare for a shift of power from the West to the East. There is much to be said for such an approach, but it fails to comprehend the tensions between what many twentieth-century pan-Asianists envisioned for the future and what has actually transpired. That is to say, historically, pan-Asianists' vision of the future was fundamentally different from both the world we see around us today and a future we might imagine.

One can generally define pan-Asianism as involving claims about the geographical and cultural unity of Asia. Indeed, a major tension in pan-Asianist discourse concerns how one relates culture to geography—and for this reason, the boundaries of Asia might differ. However, more important is the idea that Asian nations because of certain cultural or geographical characteristics could transform the world. At the heart of their vision was the notion of a unity of Asian nations, of weak nations becoming powerful, and of the Third World confronting the "advanced world" on equal terms. But there was more: pan-Asianists envisioned a future beyond both imperialism and capitalism.

After the Russian Revolution and especially after World War II, pan-Asian thinkers produced complex, productive, and potentially problematic syntheses of the ideal of Asian unity, Third Worldism, and socialism. These syntheses remain meaningful today because capitalism and imperialism continue to dominate our world and because a vision of a world beyond has subsisted.

The postwar public intellectual and pan-Asianist Takeuchi Yoshimi (1910–1977) claimed that pan-Asianism is notoriously difficult to define and cannot be treated as a category that transcends its conditions.[2] He believed that the meaning of pan-Asianism emerges from its context. Using this as a point of departure for examining how various thinkers mobilized the concept of Asia, we can immediately see that the evolution of pan-Asianist thought has been mediated by ideas of anti-imperialism, socialism, and subjectivity, as well as the dialectic between radicalism and conservatism.

This book examines prominent twentieth-century Japanese and Chinese pan-Asianists to bring to the fore such issues, especially as they cluster around strategies for resisting imperialism and struggling for a different future. This book combines academic and popular approaches. Following academic discussions of pan-Asianism, I closely read specific pan-Asian texts to reveal their internal logic as it relates to larger historical contexts. However, like popular books on pan-Asianism and the rise of Asia, my project is not limited to narrowly defined periods. This book teases out a pan-Asian critique of capital, which pan-Asianist thinkers used in different ways to critique the history they found themselves in the midst of from the early twentieth century to the present.[3]

As Chinese and Asian capital has become more pervasive, people increasingly have engaged in the discourse of the "rise of China." However, by examining twentieth-century pan-Asianism, we can pose a more fundamental question: What precisely does it mean to "rise"? As China and Asia become more powerful and influential, one must ask whether this really challenges the existing power structures across the world or whether we are merely seeing the replacement of Western capitalist powers by Eastern capitalist powers. While the rise of China is not the specific subject of this book, looking through the lens of pan-Asianist thought we see different images of China, especially as China became socialist. This transformation of China signaled a fundamental shift in pan-Asianist discourse, especially in Japan, but more widely as well.

The overarching themes mediating pan-Asianism throughout the twentieth century are also the themes of this book: the definition of pan-Asianism, the problem of the critique of capitalism in twentieth-century pan-Asianism, the sublated nineteenth century and Hegel, and finally, the issue of war memory. All the chapters deal with these themes to different degrees. For example, pan-Asianists from Okakura Tenshin (1863–1913) to Sun Yat-sen (1866–1925) to Ōkawa Shūmei (1886–1957) each expressed some of the basic tenets of pan-Asianism and its attendant critique of imperialism and capitalism. However, Takeuchi Yoshimi is unique because, during the postwar years, he constantly confronted the legacy of the war as he resuscitated a pan-Asianism inspired by Chinese literature and revolution. In many ways, his reading of the Chinese Revolution sublates and synthesizes the different concerns of the pan-Asianists described in the earlier chapters of this book. Throughout this book, I use the term "sublate," which translates *aufheben* in Hegel's philosophical writings. As Hegel explains: "The German '*aufheben*' . . . has a twofold meaning in the language: it equally means '*to keep*,' 'to preserve,' and 'to cause to cease,' or 'to put an end to.'"[4] Hegel points out that when something is sublated it loses its immediacy and becomes part of a larger process. Takeuchi and the various people I discuss in this book take up previous notions of pan-Asianism in this manner and make them part of the movement toward a better world beyond imperialism and capitalism. But pan-Asianism also sublates various other concepts, such as individualism, making them moments of a movement toward a better future.[5]

Each of the protagonists discussed in those chapters confront capitalism in different ways and to differing degrees envision processes of radical political and social transformations. After 1917 and especially after 1949, socialist revolution in Asia became a reality, and Takeuchi rethinks the legacy of pan-Asianism through that lens. Examining pan-Asianism from the early twentieth century to the present reveals how the legacies of pan-Asianism and the Chinese Revolution mutually determine one another.

4   INTRODUCTION

Expanding the Spatial and Temporal Boundaries of Pan-Asianism

In the past few decades, numerous works have tackled the problem of pan-Asianism, and most of those have informed the narrative that follows here. Eri Hotta's *Pan-Asianism and Japan's War*,[6] for example, focuses on a specific period and examines how the Japanese government mobilized pan-Asianism in the service of Japanese imperialism. Cemil Aydin and Craig A. Smith each go beyond a Japan-focused paradigm by placing Japan in relation to anti-Western discourse in other places in Asia. Aydin's book *The Politics of Anti-Westernism in Asia*[7] juxtaposes pan-Asianism with pan-Islamism, allowing the author to go beyond a narrative that merely associates pan-Asianism with its most familiar institutional embodiment, namely Japanese imperialism. Somewhat echoing Takeuchi Yoshimi, he notes the dual nature of Japanese pan-Asianism as somehow embodying an anti-imperialist ideology while making use of imperialist propaganda. Bringing in the Islamic perspective shows how the ideals of anti-Westernism resonated well beyond Japan and consequently spoke to more fundamental issues of global inequality. Smith has recently published a thoroughly researched work, *Chinese Asianism*, which deals with both Chinese pan-Asianists and Japanese influences on them. Smith's work is different from most texts on pan-Asianism because the book focuses on China rather than Japan. Consequently, like Aydin, he shows how the specter of Japanese imperialism mediates our understanding of pan-Asianism, while simultaneously underscoring the significance of pan-Asianism beyond the well-known Japanese use of the ideal of Asian unity during the war.[8] Smith offers a typology of pan-Asianisms that include "Confucian Asianism, racial Asianism, civilizational Asianism, socialist Asianism, pan-Asian liberation Asianism, China-centric Asianism [and] Japan-centric Asianism."[9] This book deals with most of these pan-Asianisms and notes a liberatory impulse in many of these pan-Asianisms. In other words, even if a particular pan-Asianism stresses civilization, culture, or race, it does not do so merely for the sake of these categories but rather promises a better future through the vehicle of the nation-state. For this reason, Smith points out that pan-Asianism always intersects with nationalism. He describes Prasenjit Duara's work as showing that "Asianism is a discourse based on civilization, which has its roots in the nation-validated discourse of Civilization, which has led to the conflation between Asianism and the nation."[10] I agree with Smith that nationalism is an essential part of pan-Asianism. However, part of pan-Asianism's power lies in gesturing toward transnational unity. This is why in the same article that Smith cites, Duara writes, "we must recognize that the ideological relations between nationalism and civilization require some separation of the two."[11] So, rather than the discourse of civilization causing or leading to a conflation of civilization and nation, I read Duara to be making the following point: nations almost always require a supplemental narrative to legitimate themselves, and discourses of civilization often perform this role. Consequently, religious or philosophical discourses such as Confucianism, Buddhism, Christianity, or socialism/Marxism serve to ground the nation by pointing to something more universal. In this process, some national narratives may conflate civilization and nation; however, if this conflation is complete, the narrative of civilization will lose much of its legitimizing force. It could appear to be a principle only legitimate for this particular nation. Therefore, civilization will generally tend to transcend the nation, thus forming its normative ground. At the same time, this tension between civilization and nation makes national narratives unstable and allows for competing visions of community within a nation.

Duara's work revolves around the question of transcendence. He notes that the civilizational discourses themselves not only transcend the nation but also necessarily follow narratives of transcendence. He contends that Asian philosophies and religions tend to emphasize a dialogic notion of transcendence as opposed to absolute visions of transcendence. The former posits not an absolute outside the temporal world but one within it. As we will see in the discussion of Hegel in chapter 1, this model of transcendence implies that the finite is not separate from the infinite. Duara argues that the remnants of such Asian worldviews could point toward a better world, especially with respect to a sustainable ecosystem. In this way, Duara anticipates what I call "back-to-the-future" narratives.[12] He writes: "The goal of this work is to identify traditions in Asia that have been consonant with global imperatives in the Anthropocene—when humans have begun to significantly affect nature and the environment—not only by revealing different attitudes and ideals regarding nature (and other subjugated entities) but also by showing us different methods and techniques of self-formation that can link the personal to the social and the universal to counter the consumerism and nationalism of our times."[13] Like many of the proponents in the book, Duara advocates returning to past traditions to envision a future beyond capitalism and "the nationalism of our times."

With respect to this book, the end of Duara's sentence, "the nationalism or our times" is crucial and brings with it a question concerning nationalisms from another time. Pan-Asianists have always been nationalists, but I would stress they attempt to connect nationalism to transnational unity and eventually universal goals.[14] Consequently, the book is about the legacy of a period where the nation was conceived as part of a movement toward a universal

6 INTRODUCTION

vision of human emancipation. This is the space in which pan-Asianism and Third Worldism come together. In a recent book on Chinese Muslims in the Japanese empire, Kelly A. Hammond links pan-Asianism in a helpful manner: "In other words, the idea of what 'Asia' meant throughout the 1950s and 1960s was once again reenvisioned and repackaged to reflect the particular postwar, postcolonial moment, but its new fashioners drew heavily from the imperial formation and vocabulary of the Japanese empire."[15] Both Asia and the Third World during the 1950s and 1960s were connected to an alternative future beyond both Soviet-style socialism and Western capitalism. Takeuchi Yoshimi brings these different types of pan-Asianism together.

Pan-Asianism as a "Back-to-the-Future" Narrative

Although Takeuchi contended that pan-Asianism was impossible to define, he did affirm that it involves the "intention of solidarity of countries of Asia—be it as an instrument of invasion or not."[16] This book draws on this point but brings out additional presuppositions underlying the idea of pan-Asianism.

Takeuchi aimed to sublate the geographical moment of pan-Asianism to make way for solidarity. In this way, geography becomes an idea, which is a moment in an anti-imperialist movement. Intellectuals from other parts of East Asia rallied around the idea of Asia to promote unity in their struggle against imperialism. Western nations had imposed the category of "Asia" on other nations to promote imperialism, but intellectuals from Asia turned this category on its head and launched a counterattack against one of the conceptual conditions of imperialism: Eurocentrism. However, imperialism functioned in another way to unite Asia beyond the Western appellation, since Asian solidarity became defined precisely by the nations that were imperialized. In this case, acts of being imperialized and resisting imperialism could determine whether a nation was part of Asia or not. For this reason, Sun Yat-sen conceived of Japan as moving in and out of Asia, depending on its relation to other nations.

As I mentioned above, many pan-Asianists believed that the unity of Asia rested on more than mere geography and that Asian identity did not merely emerge from being subjected to imperialism. They also invoked culture, which became part of the struggle against imperialism. This is clear in much of the pan-Asianism of thinkers from Okakura Tenshin to Zhang Taiyan (1869–1936) to Ōkawa Shūmei, who argued that Asian culture is superior to that of the West and often explicitly connected Asian culture with socialism against Western capitalism. This critique could be called conservative because it embodied attempts to preserve Asian traditions against the onslaught of

Westernization and imperialism.[17] However, this focus on the past was by no means simple, and it brought with it another central tenet of pan-Asianism: the culture of Asia could be the basis on which to build a better future beyond capitalist modernity. I call this configuration a "back-to-the-future" narrative, since it entails the idea that creating a better future requires going back to the past. This narrative demonstrates the overlap between conservative and radical thought in pan-Asianism. Pan-Asianism clearly had both of these tendencies, which as we will see, were embodied in particular thinkers.

The Short Twentieth Century

The difference between my approach to pan-Asianism and that of many popular accounts becomes clear from the following comment by Kishore Mahbubani in his book *Can Asians Think?* He asserts that Asia "lost most of the 20th century—even much of the second millennium, while Europe and later America shot ahead in human achievements, colonised the globe and took control of the world economy. The picture looked very different at the turn of the last millennium. China was reaching towards new heights under the Song dynasty."[18] This statement is illuminating, but it downplays the challenges to capitalism and colonization in the twentieth century. This is partly because after the Cold War and especially by the 2000s, the end of the world became easier to imagine than the end of capitalism.[19] This constrains how one envisions and evaluates Asia. Pan-Asianism appeared differently in a world where an alternative to capitalism was on the table—as it was precisely during the "short twentieth century." In using the term "short twentieth century," I follow the English Marxist Eric Hobsbawm and the Chinese critical theorist Wang Hui (b. 1959) in understanding this "century" not as a quantitative marker that ended after 1999 but instead as ending at the point where hope for a socialist future faded away.[20] Hobsbawm contended that the twentieth century began with the First World War and ended with the fall of the Soviet bloc in 1989. Arguing from the standpoint of China, Wang Hui claims that the twentieth century began in 1905 and ended in 1976 when Mao Zedong died and Chinese socialism transformed. Pan-Asianism also changed as what Wang calls the "end of China's short twentieth century" drew near. By the mid- to late 1970s, several different factors emerged, including the rise of neoliberalism, the end of the Cultural Revolution, the death of Mao, China's opening and reforms, and a global mistrust of socialism, all of which predated the collapse of the Soviet regime. Pan-Asianism would not be the same after these changes. The bulk of this book therefore focuses on some of the ways pan-Asianism was imagined during the twentieth century.[21]

This focus transposes Wang's concept to a milieu to which he might object, since he highlights the Chinese and Russian experiences, which directly involved socialism, while I use his periodization to situate Japanese intellectuals, some of whom were associated with the very imperialism that pan-Asianism attacked. This brings us to the problem of the institutional form of pan-Asianism: it had had only one, namely the imperialistic and fascist structures of wartime Japan. This caused many postwar intellectuals to become disheartened with calls for Asian unity. Takeuchi Yoshimi (1910–1977), the subject of chapters 4 and 5, vociferously attempted to resurrect pan-Asianism during the postwar period and find radical potential in the project of Asian resistance even after it had been discredited by the war.

However, like the other pan-Asianists discussed in this book, Takeuchi wrote of an alternative to global imperialism and capitalism. After World War II, he combined creatively prewar pan-Asian critiques of capitalism with the ideals of Mao's revolution. Because his standpoint of critique was an idealized form of Mao's China, he had difficulties responding to the Cultural Revolution and the questioning of Maoism. Takeuchi died one year after Mao; together their deaths implied the end of a certain style of pan-Asianism. This marked the end of the short twentieth century.

Hegel and the Sublation of the Nineteenth Century in the Twentieth

In his recent work, Wang Hui contends that the twentieth century represented a break from the nineteenth because it went against the liberal ideals that began with the French Revolution and were carried on by thinkers in Europe.[22] This narrative is important for pan-Asianism as well because as a form of anti-colonial thought, pan-Asianism defies the Eurocentrism of the nineteenth century. G. W. F. Hegel's work is crucial here because he both distilled the Eurocentric position and also provided resources to construct an alternative. Chapter 2 explores how Hegel constructed Asian nations as lost in immediacy, lacking space for subjectivity. In other words, in Asian nations, people immediately followed the norms set by the community without subjective reflection, or what Hegel called the "moment of negativity." Hegel turns Asia into a moment of a historical movement toward freedom, and we shall see how pan-Asianists respond by making Hegel into a moment of their own vision of history, which has goals similar to Hegel, namely the reconciliation of individual and communal freedom. In each of these cases, being a moment implies being a logically necessary element or stage that is sublated in a larger process. For example, in Hegel's view, Asia or the Orient entails ethical substantiality without individuality. This is what he calls "theocracy." In later stages of history, people mediate this substantiality, which is then mediated by individual subjectivity and freedom. Pan-Asianists, in turn, believe that the abstract individuality of the West itself must be sublated into a moment so that we can attain true freedom, which is not divorced from ethical life.

Many Japanese and Chinese pan-Asianists read Hegel, but my purpose here is not to argue that he influenced them. Rather, I contend that Hegel's conceptual framework clarifies some of the strategies that pan-Asianists employed. The most obvious strategy, central to all of the chapters, but especially chapters 1 and 3, and inherent in the thinking of Okakura and Ōkawa and others, was to posit Asian communal forms, drawing on Confucianism and other philosophies, against the abstract, disembedded individuality of the West. This is especially significant in the context of Hegel, since Hegel is equally critical of abstract individuality and devoted his *Philosophy of Right* to outlining the institutional conditions under which people could realize a freedom that combined community and individuality (substance and subject in Hegel's terms). From this perspective, pan-Asianists could be seen as attempting to carry out the Hegelian project.

The critique of abstract individuality returns us to the critique of capitalism, which pan-Asianists expressed as the blind pursuit of individual interest that manifested itself in the global arena as imperialism. This critique of capitalism, through affirming older forms of community, had the danger of eliminating subjectivity, as we will see most clearly in the case of wartime Japan and Ōkawa's works, discussed in chapter 3.

Postwar Japan presents another scenario. There Takeuchi Yoshimi affirmed a new type of subjectivity in China and Asia more generally. This turned the tables on the Hegelian narrative by contending that it is actually the West that lacked subjectivity, rather than Asia. The father of modern Chinese literature, Lu Xun, and Mao's Chinese Revolution become key rallying points that Takeuchi uses to demonstrate the unique subjectivity of China. In chapter 4 we will see that Takeuchi launched this narrative in the interwar period, when he continued a radical subjectivity by examining the Chinese experience. This new conception of subjectivity would be part of his vision for an alternative world during World War II, in which he believed Japan played a crucial role. Takeuchi thus supported what we would call right-wing pan-Asianism in the interwar period. Most prewar and interwar pan-Asianists fled from pan-Asianism during the postwar period, but Takeuchi continued on by developing his ideas of both subjectivity and pan-Asianism during the postwar era, which would force him to come to grips with issues such as memory and revolution.

Between Revolution and War Memory

Takeuchi's attempt to rescue pan-Asianism from leftist criticism during the postwar era involved two different gestures. He attempted to synthesize prewar Japanese pan-Asianism and the Chinese revolutionary experience. However, at the same time he realized that, given Japan's history of imperialism during the war, any dream of Asian unity had to involve doing justice to the problem of war memory and war responsibility. He argued that part of the project of rethinking Japanese subjectivity in the postwar era would have to involve what he called the "generalization" of the war experience. This would be especially important for the younger generation, that is, those who were very young during or were born after World War II. This memory would be key to transforming subjectivity and preparing the way for pan-Asian unity.

Pan-Asian unity in Takeuchi's view would continue Sun Yat-sen's idea of a nationalism that prepared the way for a different future. After 1949, he believed that Mao and revolutionary China embodied this ideal and based his criticism of the Japanese Communist Party on this position. Much of this discourse has contemporary relevance because at least since the 1980s, postcolonial theorists have criticized Marxists for being Eurocentric. Here again, however, the short twentieth century comes into play. Although Takeuchi's critique of the Marxists mimics that of later postcolonial critics, he wrote during a time when many still held a general belief in the possibility of socialism, which influenced his vision of anticolonial nationalism and transnational resistance to imperialism.

Furthermore, affirming Asian nationalism and the possibility of a world beyond capitalism has a fundamentally futural dimension. The right and left shared this vision, and because Takeuchi grasped this similarity, in his writings he linked prewar proimperial pan-Asianists, such as Ōkawa Shūmei, with Mao's radical revolutionary vision. This element of Takeuchi's thought is especially important for us today, given the rise of right- and left-wing populisms, both of which are dissatisfied with the present world. The point is not that we should support Trump, Abe, or Modi but that Takeuchi's reflections on the history of pan-Asianism underscore why people might be drawn to such figures because they appear as alternatives to the capitalist or neoliberal status quo. The Japanese case is interesting in this context because Japan's wartime leaders and propagandists were more anticapitalist in their rhetoric than any of the right-wing populist leaders today. However, they used anticapitalist rhetoric to mask the development of a fascist and imperialist form of capitalism.

The whole pan-Asianist experience raises the question of how an Asian or Third World country (we will see how these two terms came together during the postwar period) could pose alternatives to the capitalist imperialism that emerged in the West. In Takeuchi's view, China, and especially the 1949 Revolution, affirmed that an Asian way to the future was possible. In particular, the revolution suggested that one did not have to follow the Western path to industrialism and offered an alternative to orthodox Marxism, which contended that modernization was essential for socialism and progress. All of the pan-Asianists discussed in this book questioned the linear model of development based on the West and posed the question of whether being a "late developer" or being incorporated into the global capitalist system late opened the possibility of bypassing capitalism through another form of revolution.

From this perspective, the history of pan-Asianism can be seen as a footnote to Marx's famous letter to the Russian populist Vera Zasulich, where he contends that one can draw on earlier forms of community to construct socialism and that one does not need to first go through capitalist industrialization.[23] Of course, part of the reason this appealed to pan-Asianists was that Asian nations were in a global capitalist world and had already been confronted with capitalism in the form of imperialism. For such nations, pan-Asianism was a solution that combined the struggle against imperialism with the construction of socialism.

Takeuchi believed that Mao effected this combination and that the Cultural Revolution—with its emphasis on politics rather than economic growth—could be regarded as the culmination of the socialist movement. However, for Takeuchi, this also marked the beginning of the decline of China's socialist twentieth century. In chapter 5, we will see that Takeuchi slowly became pessimistic about the future of socialism in China and admitted that he could not foresee what the future would hold. This brings us to a situation not very different from our own current moment, where people are unclear about whether China represents a rising hegemon, an alternative to the West, or both. I will return to this issue of the status of pan-Asianism in our current moment in chapter 6 by examining the recent writings of the contemporary Chinese critical theorist Wang Hui.

The book as a whole poses two questions for us today: Is a narrative of an "Asian" alternative still relevant as a means of seeking an alternative to capitalism? And in what ways can we continue the dialogue between pan-Asianism/Third Worldism and Marxism? While the chapters do not explicitly answer this question, they do interpret pan-Asianist thought with our present situation in mind. In a world where capitalism is increasingly facing crises, these questions are becoming increasingly pressing.

Chapter Outlines

Chapter 1, "Asia as Pharmakon: The Early Constitution of Asia as Resistance," lays the groundwork for the rest of the book by examining the Japanese intellectual who might be considered the paradigmatic anti-pan-Asianist, Fukuzawa Yukichi (1835–1901), and one of the first transnationally recognized pan-Asianists, Okakura Tenshin. Both sides of this divide can be contextualized in relation to Hegel and, in particular, his conception of history as the progress of subjectivity. Hegel described the Orient as bereft of subjectivity, and though Fukuzawa was probably not very familiar with Hegel, he outlined a similar trajectory of civilization. In Fukuzawa's philosophy, the growth of civilization and subjectivity is fundamentally connected to capitalism, which in turn becomes a fulcrum that can be used to understand debates across Asia. From a Japanese perspective, the key shift in Fukuzawa's discourse concerns the radical demotion of China and the simultaneous elevation of Western civilization. Pan-Asianism was a response to this discourse and the attempt to put forward a legitimate Asian alternative. For this reason, pan-Asianist discourse often returns to the subject of China. This chapter uses Okakura to outline this basic response, which is an Asian version of romantic anticapitalism.

Chapter 2, "The Critique of Linear Time: Pan-Asianism in Early Twentieth-Century China," continues themes from the preceding chapter in a Chinese context. Chinese intellectuals often took Japan as a model for the future. Many of them adopted a version of Fukuzawa Yukichi's vision of progress, placing the West ahead of Asia. The Chinese reformer Kang Youwei (1858–1927) stands apart from Fukuzawa in key ways, since Kang himself outlined a socialist vision of the future while offering an evolutionary vision of the world and placed Asia behind the West. This is clearly evident in how he situated India, which represented a vision of a future to avoid. His revolutionary contemporary Zhang Taiyan (1869–1936) was initially supportive of the Japanese path as well but ended up constructing a pan-Asian vision that was critical of Japan and promoted unity between India and China. Li Dazhao (1889–1927) also embraced this idea of a pan-Asian alternative to the path Japan was following at the time. This chapter ends with a discussion of Sun Yat-sen's famous essay of 1925, which affirms pan-Asianism but potentially delinks the idea of "Asia" from geography. Sun notes that Japan can either be in Asia or not depending on whether it follows an imperialist path. More significantly, he claims that after the 1917 Revolution, Russia became part of Asia. This statement is important because it suggests that the idea of Asia is more than merely geographical and underscores the connection between pan-Asianism and socialism.

Chapter 3, "Asia as Anticapitalist Utopia: Ōkawa Shūmei's Critique of Political Modernity," focuses on Ōkawa Shūmei, one of the foremost propagandists for the Japanese state during World War II. Of all the pan-Asianists discussed in this book, Ōkawa came closest to giving his pan-Asianism an institutional form by supporting the wartime Japanese government, eventually being identified as a Class-A war criminal during the Tokyo war crimes tribunal. His vision of Asia is especially significant because he constructed an unusually inclusive vision of Asia, which included the Arab world and at times even the Jews. Moreover, his critique of Eurocentrism and support for anticolonial movements in India became an important, if controversial, legacy for later pan-Asianists such as Takeuchi Yoshimi. This chapter analyzes Ōkawa's key texts, showing how he mobilized Indian philosophy along with heroic visions from Chinese history in order to create a fascist vision of Asia; the chapter also argues that this fascist vision responded to real problems of capitalist modernity, including global unevenness and the alienation of people from politics.

Chapter 4, "Takeuchi Yoshimi, Part I: Rethinking China as Political Subjectivity," examines how Takeuchi constructed a new theory of subjectivity, which would inform his vision of pan-Asianism. Whereas Hegel had defined the Orient as lacking subjectivity and being drowned in the substantiality of community, Takeuchi turns this on its head by arguing that it is precisely Asia that has a subjectivity that is more radical than the West's. He does this largely through an innovative reading of the famous Chinese writer Lu Xun (1881–1936). During the prewar and interwar periods, Takeuchi supported Japan's war as part of the pan-Asianism project. For this reason, he provides a key bridge in pan-Asianist thought from the prewar to the postwar periods, because unlike many other pan-Asianist intellectuals, he did not reject pan-Asianism after World War II but rather attempted to rethink it in a new context and bring it into dialogue with other movements, such as Third Worldism.

Chapter 5, "Takeuchi Yoshimi, Part II: Pan-Asianism, Revolutionary Nationalism, and War Memory," presents a detailed examination of the place of Takeuchi's pan-Asianism in his overall thought, including his theory of nationalism, revolution, and war memory. In Takeuchi's famous essay "What Is Modernity?," written in 1948, he combats Eurocentrism by rethinking the 1911 Revolution. In doing so, he envisions an alternative Asian modernity based on the Chinese experience. "What Is Modernity?" was written only a few months before the Chinese Revolution of 1949, and Takeuchi's interpretation of China overlaps with that of Mao. The essay contains the kernel of Takeuchi's vision of China and Asia as resistance. In it, Takeuchi begins to formulate how weak countries on the periphery can break free from the capitalist world system. This chapter also examines how Takeuchi reacted to the larger movement of decolonization that emerged in the 1950s and 1960s, including the famous 1955 conference in Bandung.[24] In this regard, Takeuchi's vision of Asia developed in relation to the idea of socialism in underdeveloped or late-developing countries, which paradoxically connects his vision with the West and the Enlightenment. Toward its end, the chapter also examines Takeuchi's famous essay "Asia as Method," in which he claims that the task of Asia is to take ideas of the West, such as equality, to a higher level. Takeuchi died in 1977, and by then the type of pan-Asianism discussed in this book had come to an end. By the late 1960s, with the outbreak of the Cultural Revolution in China, Takeuchi was becoming less optimistic about the future of China and Asia. The death of Mao changed the terrain of pan-Asianism and began what we might call an age of leftist melancholy. It also marked the end of the short twentieth century.

Chapter 6, "Wang Hui: Contemporary Pan-Asianist in China?," explores the future of pan-Asianism in the midst of leftist melancholy and continues to trace the dialogue between pan-Asianism and Marxism that pan-Asianists from Okakura to Takeuchi had begun. Much of Takeuchi's thinking hinged on a particular interpretation and evaluation of the Chinese Revolution. Chapter 6 asks how such ideas might fare in China today. To answer this question, the chapter presents an examination of the political writings of Wang Hui. Wang Hui revives Third Worldism, Asian unity, and revolution in an unfavorable historical context, namely when the Chinese Revolution and socialism in general appear to have been a failure. Wang attempts a double maneuver where, on the one hand, he uses the Chinese revolutionary past to criticize the present and, on the other, he points out the links between Mao's China and China today.

Considering China's rise, one wonders whether pan-Asianism—especially the Chinese Revolution—has won a pyrrhic victory. Two decades into the twenty-first century, one can again speak of the rise of Asia and a China that invokes Mao's legacy. Some might even say that Takeuchi Yoshimi's pronouncements have come true, and China has emerged victorious. However, given the extent to which capitalism mediates everyday life in China, this victory seems fraught with paradoxes at best. It appears that the future of socialism will depend on reviving resistance arising from pan-Asianism at another level. While such a project must be inspired by the past, it is a task for the future.

The epilogue situates the goals of pan-Asianism in relation to the logic of capitalist automation and questions the idea of the global. If we follow

Takeuchi and Wang Hui in bringing together pan-Asianism with socialism, then we need to reflect critically on both the continuities between the twentieth and twenty-first centuries and the possibility of a postcapitalist world. Capitalist automation is an issue that most pan-Asianists have overlooked, but going forward it will be crucial for the project of creating a postcapitalist world. This is because the logic of productivity partially explains the twin nemeses of pan-Asianism—imperialism and capitalist expansion—but also constantly drives capitalism into crisis. This itself is one of the factors that could pave the way to a world beyond proletarian labor, but this path should not be understood in a linear manner.

1

Asia as Pharmakon:
The Early Constitution of Asia as Resistance

During the late nineteenth and early twentieth centuries, China and Japan were drawn into the global capitalist system of nation-states and saw their status in the world forever transformed. In many Asian nations, a vision of the world with China at the center was replaced with one where the West colonized the non-West. The emergence of the idea of Asian unity and pan-Asianism must be understood in this context. "Asia" was at first viewed negatively when it emerged in the West, as the writings of Hegel and other philosophers clearly show. Some Japanese modernist scholars, such as Fukuzawa Yukichi, adopted this denigration of the East and advocated "leaving Asia." Others, including Okakura Tenshin (1863–1913), the Japanese art critic and one of the first pan-Asianists, resisted this view. Examining the tensions between Fukuzawa's and Okakura's respective positions provides a window into the primal origins of pan-Asianism.

Asia at this time became a sort of pharmakon—a poison that could actually be a radical cure.[1] Fukuzawa and others viewed Asia as an obstacle to fighting colonialism and forming an independent state. Okakura, on the other hand, saw in Asia the possibility of resisting colonialism and creating an alternative world.

A number of scholars have examined the production of the idea of Asia and the West as an issue connected to geographical imagination and Western imperialism.[2] However, the connections among imagined geographies, the nation-state, and global capitalism include temporal dimensions as well. The unevenness associated with colonial domination itself stems from differences in space, time, and power. States in certain regions may exert an influence over those in others. More fundamentally, states are born into a world with power differentials. At the turn of the twentieth century, North

Atlantic states dominated those on the periphery of the global capitalist system. Because these imperialist countries forced peripheral nations to adopt capitalism, these weaker countries were described as "late" developers. The temporal adjective "late" suggests an already fixed grid for historical development, conceptualized by those in power to such an extent that even those on the periphery tended to accept the appellation "late." This lateness, however, is connected to another temporal category, which becomes central after the development of capitalism, namely productivity—more efficient production through the use of technology and science. Given the combination of the international competition between different embodiments of capital and the geopolitical tensions between nation-states, unevenness is connected not only to a difference in military power but also to the productivity of the enterprises in a given nation. Indeed, imperialism is inevitably connected to the expansion of capitalism and the opening of markets in foreign nation-states.

In the above context, two competing visions of Asia emerged. Fukuzawa accepted the terms of development laid down by the West and advocated leaving Asia. Okakura, on the other hand, believed in an Asia that could twist free from Western domination precisely because it had a different philosophical and cultural base. Both sides sought to break free from Western domination, but the proponents of pan-Asianism made a further point. Anticipating postcolonial theory, they criticized the notion of linear time, challenging Western models of development and advocating for an alternative. Already in this early conflict about Asia there was a tension between those struggling to carve out a place within the existing world—perhaps akin to the contemporary Chinese government's attempt to become a strong capitalist state—and those fighting to create a different world. Fukuzawa represented the former camp and Okakura the latter.

Because Fukuzawa's idea of linear progression echoed Hegel's argument about Asia in his *Philosophy of History*, I begin with a discussion of this text. Hegel's skewed analysis of the Orient introduced some concepts that pan-Asianists would later mobilize in favor of an Asian alternative. This is partly because Hegel's analysis of Asia is couched in a larger critical vision of the modern world, which has relevance beyond his specific judgments. I focus on an opposition that Hegel makes between substantiality (or community) and negativity (or subjective activity), which he connects to individual and, eventually, collective agency. In the rest of this chapter, and in some of the ensuing chapters, we will encounter pan-Asianists echoing Hegel's theory of the state-substantiality and his theory of negativity as a means to promote Asia.

Hegel himself theorized the Orient as enveloped in substantiality without negativity. And several thinkers in Asia attacked substantiality and affirmed the other side of the above antinomy—subjectivity or negativity. Fukuzawa Yukichi's critique of Asia reflects this perspective. Okakura Tenshin, however, attempted to lay out a new synthesis between substantiality and negativity through a discussion of art. Given the alienation present at the heart of modernity, the substantiality that Hegel associated with Asia could be seen as a positive. Why should we not return to that substantiality in some form? Indeed, Okakura gestured in this direction when he attempted to resist the rationalism and teleology of Hegel by drawing on different sources and, in what process, rethinking the significance of Asia.

Hegel on Asia/the Orient: Lands without Subjectivity

Criticism of Hegel for his teleological view of Asia is commonplace today. Prasenjit Duara argues that Hegel's philosophy of history encapsulates a notion of history as linear that legitimates the nation-state and imperialism.[3] Mark Driscoll has developed this criticism more recently.[4] Driscoll writes: "Hegel is confident that the trajectory of the (white) World Spirit is indexed precisely to historical progress; for the first time the 'strides forward' of Europeans colonize every part of the earth."[5] Criticism in this vein uses Hegel as a foil or a vision of Asia that we must overcome. Others might attempt to excuse Hegel because his knowledge of Asia was insufficient. However, no matter how one qualifies one's judgment, using Hegel as a foil goes against Hegel's own warnings about simply negating that which we find inadequate before we move on to something else.[6]

Moreover, Hegel's own interest in the Orient was not superficial. In a recent edited volume collecting Hegel's works on India, Rimina Mohapatra and Aakash Singh Rathore show that Hegel was more or less obsessed with the Orient and with India in particular.[7] Moreover, Hegel himself underscored similarities between his own work and concepts such as substantiality and other ideas in Indian and "Oriental" philosophy. For example, in the *Encyclopaedia Logic*, he exclaims that the "Oriental intuition of the unity of substance forms the foundation of all genuine further development."[8] At the same time, perhaps because of the similarities he saw, he criticized Indian philosophy for its lack of negativity. This critique appears not only in his remarks on Indian philosophy but also in his treatment of Spinoza and of Jewish philosophy. The problem, according to Hegel, is that all of these philosophies grasp the absolute without mediation, thus degenerating into a night in which all cows are black. In other words, in these philosophies, there is no room for particularity or individuality; everything is subsumed under the night of the absolute such that one cannot see the particularity of any single thing (cow). In what follows, we will see how views similar to Hegel's visions of Asia were used by pan-Asianists to open spaces for a critique of Eurocentrism.

Hegel partially opens such a space himself, since his negative reading of Asia, or the Orient, began by recognizing Asia's autonomy. Following Voltaire and others, Hegel attempted to break from religious histories that began with the Israelites. Hegel, however, goes further and criticizes texts by Friedrich Schlegel and G. F. Creuzer that connected Oriental and Christian histories.[9] As Susan Marchand has argued, Schlegel, Creuzer, and other German Orientalists showed that the roots of Christian culture lay in the East.[10] From this perspective, they romantically hoped to revive Christian culture by returning to its Eastern—especially Indian—roots. Hegel rethought China and the Orient to combat this romanticism and eventually came to devalue Asia in his work. However, his response also offered a perspective from which to view Asian histories as independent from those of Europe.

By separating Asia and Europe, Hegel retained the possibility of different historical trajectories. However, to complete his own partially romantic project, he then had to bring Asia and Europe together under a universal theory. In this regard, his remarks are especially relevant for this chapter and beyond because whether they explicitly refer to him or not, many critics and advocates of Asia were aware of some version of Hegel's theory. Scholars in favor of Western-style modernization (e.g., Fukuzawa), though not often mentioning Hegel, still reproduced a similar evolutionary narrative. This suggests that Hegel grasped something fundamental about the modern world, to which both sides of the Asia debate had to respond. Moreover, despite Hegel's overall negative evaluation of Asia, his narrative of Asia contained many positive elements that figure in later visions of pan-Asianism. Indeed, pan-Asianists throughout the twentieth century attempted to synthesize what Hegel would call "substantiality" or "ethical life and individuality." The latter would, of course, be characterized as Western, while the former was associated with the East or Asia.

Before we delve into Hegel's writings on the Orient, we should make a few remarks about his idea of *Geist*, or spirit, which provides some of the conceptual conditions for separating the Orient from the Occident, or East from West. In Hegel's first published book, *Phenomenology of Spirit* (1807), he writes of spirit as entailing a way of life that includes beliefs, norms, and practices. These ensembles are not static nor are they free of constraints, which means they might morph into other conceptual and practical ensembles (other forms of spirit, or *Geist*). Hegel presupposes this framework when writing about the Orient.

Hegel discusses the Orient in a number of works, but I will focus on the *Lectures on the Philosophy of History* because this work deals with the themes of substantiality and negativity, which I will use to illuminate the opposition between Fukuzawa and Okakura. Hegel's *Lectures on the Philosophy of History* begins with the Oriental world and posits a linear evolutionary path of the sort that Fukuzawa later describes and modifies. But, according to the *Philosophy of History*, what is it that the countries in the Oriental world lack, and what do they have? Hegel contends that they lack subjectivity and freedom, but they have a type of ethical life he believes would be further developed by the West: "The Oriental world has as its closest principle, the substantiality of ethical life [*Subtantialität des Sittlichen*]. We have the first example of the subjugation of an arbitrary will, which is merged in this substantiality."[11]

Although Hegel considers the Oriental world primitive from an evolutionary perspective, we immediately see something necessary and positive in Oriental society, the "substantiality of ethical life." Ethical life (*Sittlichkeit*) is of course a key concept in Hegel's *Philosophy of Right*, where he outlines the criteria for what he believes is a just society. One can begin to see Hegel's point with respect to the problem of the family and its values.[12] The Orient begins with *Sittlichkeit*, but ethics does not allow a place for individuality. *Sittlichkeit* refers to the ethical constraints on individual or abstract freedom, which are eventually institutionalized in the modern world and thus make way for a more robust idea of freedom that encompasses communal obligations. In particular, the modern world brings together the substantiality associated with ethical life, which we find in the Oriental world and also in the Greek world, with individuality or subjectivity.[13]

In Hegel's view, although the Oriental world has the substantiality of ethical life, it lacks subjectivity.

> Since Spirit has not yet attained interiority [*Innerlichkeit*], it wears the appearance of spirituality still involved in the conditions of Nature. Since the external and the internal, Law and Moral Sense [*Einsicht*], are not yet distinguished—still form an undivided unity—so also do Religion and the State. The Constitution generally is a Theocracy, and the Kingdom of God is to the same extent also a secular Kingdom as the secular Kingdom is also divine.[14]

The association of theocracy with Asia emerges here as not the negation of interiority but the absence of interiority. The negation of interiority is precisely what occurs in the just state that Hegel describes in the *Philosophy of Right*. Indeed, in the *Philosophy of History*, we see the same trajectory from substantiality to the negation of substantiality through interiority and then finally a negation that reconciles these two moments, which allows for the expression of freedom within community. This means that negation is already there in substantiality but is forgotten. Hegel explains: "Since substance has been defined as the truth of the particular things that are sublated and extinguished in it, absolute negativity has effectively already been posited as its determination, and absolute negativity is itself the source of freedom."[15] Hegel argues that in the concept of substance there is already negativity, but this negativity has itself been negated, and consequently we have the image of pure substance, which is opposed to concrete individuals. Recall that this is a problem not just for the Orient but also for pantheistic philosophers such as Spinoza.

In the Oriental case, because awareness of negativity and interiority is lacking, there is no autonomy with respect to what Hegel calls "moral sense" or "insight." Because Orientals do not distinguish between individual insight or subjectivity and objective substance, they do not have religion in the modern sense, as a sphere separate from politics. According to Hegel, the Orient has a theocracy, where religion and the state form an undivided unity. The subject is always already interpolated in such a way that negativity is precluded.

This lack of interiority or negativity keeps the Orient static and makes it such that the substantiality of community does not progress. With the Greek world we begin to see signs of subjectivity, but this characteristic becomes clearer in the Christian world. Hegel explains this point most clearly when he discusses the Crusades, which he describes as a turning point in history:

> Christendom found the empty Sepulchre, but not the union of the Secular and the Eternal; and so it lost the Holy Land. It was practically undeceived; and the result which it brought back with it was of a negative kind: viz., that the definite embodiment which it was seeking, was to be looked for in Subjective Consciousness alone, and in no external object; that the definite form in question, presenting the union of the Secular with the Eternal, is the Spiritual self-cognizant independence of the individual. Thus the world attains the conviction that man must look within himself for that definite embodiment of being which is of a divine nature: subjectivity thereby receives absolute authorization, and claims to determine for itself the relation [of all that exists] to the Divine. This then was the absolute result of the Crusades, and from them we may date the commencement of self-reliance and spontaneous activity. The West bade an eternal farewell to the East at the Holy Sepulchre, and gained a comprehension of its own principle of subjective infinite Freedom.[16]

Hegel connects the power of the negative to both interiority and subjectivity. Unlike in the East, Christianity and the West feature a transcendence of immediate objectivity and a focus on "the spiritual self-cognizant independence of the individual." In Christianity, the Holy Land is gone, and all that is solid melts away. At this point, subjectivity is thrust back upon itself. Consciousness becomes reflexive and subjectivity absolute. To find the divine

22   CHAPTER ONE

requires looking within rather than looking outward. This is the point at which the West becomes conscious of itself as free and leaves the East. Note that this geographical move begins with a turn inward.

But this is just the beginning of a long journey, and this infinite self will become entangled in numerous antinomies. Hegel constantly seeks to reconcile the secular with the eternal and also the subjective with the objective.[17] For our purposes, more important than his proposed reconciliation is his description of the contradictions, which animates discussions of pan-Asianism and also pervades our present day.

He describes these contradictions at length in his *Lectures on Fine Art*:

> Now this opposition does not arise for consciousness in the restricted sphere of moral action alone; it emerges in a thorough-going cleavage and opposition between what is absolute and what is external reality and existence. Taken quite abstractly, it is the opposition of universal and particular, when each is fixed over against the other on its own account in the same way; more concretely, it appears in nature as the opposition of the abstract law to the abundance of individual phenomena, each explicitly with its own character; in the spirit it appears as the contrast between the sensuous and the spiritual in man, as the battle of spirit against flesh, of duty for duty's sake, of the cold command against particular interest, warmth of heart, sensuous inclinations and impulses, against the individual disposition in general; as the harsh opposition between inner freedom and the necessity of external nature, further as the contradiction between the dead inherently empty concept, and the full concreteness of life, between theory or subjective thinking, and objective existence and experience. These are oppositions which have not been invented at all by the subtlety of reflection or the pedantry of philosophy; in numerous forms they have always preoccupied and troubled the human consciousness, even if it is modern culture that has first worked them out most sharply and driven them up to the peak of harshest contradiction. Spiritual culture [*geistige Bildung*], the modern understanding, produces this opposition in man which makes him into an amphibian [*zur Amphibie macht*], because he now has to live in two worlds which contradict one another.[18]

Hegel's use of the term "amphibian" is peculiar because the passage discusses contrasts, such as those between concrete and abstract, along with the infinite and the finite. However, for our purposes, the literal meaning of "amphibian," a creature living on both land and water, is also relevant. In his *Philosophy of World History*, Hegel explains that land involves people "in an infinite multitude of dependencies, but the sea carries [them] out beyond these limited circles of thought and action."[19] In that text he associates the sea

ASIA AS PHARMAKON

with subjectivity and the infinite but also with plunder and commerce. Land, contrarily, is connected to dependency and finitude.

As we will see, Okakura and later Wang Hui (see chapter 6) drew on this opposition in arguing for an Asian alternative. However, in his *Lectures on Fine Art*, Hegel discusses oppositions such as the finite and the infinite as constituting the human condition, and consequently we are all amphibious. Some of these contradictions may have existed since the beginning of history. After all, Plato had already made a distinction between the universal forms and individual entities. Hegel contends, however, that contradictions such as those between abstract laws and individual phenomena, or between inner freedom and external nature, become more intense and generalized in people's experience during the modern period. In the modern world, we do not just distinguish between universal and particular; we actually live as both particular and universal. We can find examples of this opposition around the world. T. J. Clark offers the examples of Manet's *Olympia* and other paintings that express alienation and lack of reconciliation, which suggest that he, Manet, was responding to the predicament described above.[20]

Hegel contends the contradictions mentioned above became heightened because of modern changes in education and culture (*die neuere Bildung*). We can extend Hegel's insights by invoking Karl Marx and György Lukács to show how these contradictions are also mediated by capitalism and the state. According to Lukács, in capitalist society, people must live in two worlds, an interior world of desires and experience and an exterior world where the course of events might frustrate the élan of the interior. He attempted to ground this split in relation to the experience of workers in the factory who have desires but face an unpredictable world of machines and markets.[21] Freedom is presupposed by the market and to some extent the factory; however, in a capitalist world, it turns into its opposite. To sustain their freedom, workers must sell their labor power and come under both the organized yoke of the capitalist in the factory and the capricious workings of the market. In other words, what Marx calls the "despotism of the factory" and the "anarchy of the market" together serve to undermine the freedom presupposed by the capitalist system.[22]

The capitalist market and factory correspond to what the French philosopher and social theorist Jacques Bidet identifies as the two structures of modernity—namely market and organization[23]—which work together to produce estrangement. "Organization" is a broad term that should be understood to include what Louis Althusser called the "ideological state apparatuses," including, for example, schools and families.[24] It is at this point that we can return to the problem of education, or *Bildung*. As Terry Pinkard explains, "Modern individuals were educated, as it were, to hold fast to the set of dispositions and habits that came in tandem with the new world of nuclear families rather than clans, of economic production now fully severed in principle from the economy of the household, and of the practical unavoidability of constitutionally ordered political arrangements to cope with this."[25]

The examples of institutions Pinkard mentions already embody some of the contradictions to which Hegel alluded. For example, people experience an affective intensity in the nuclear family that they constantly feel is lacking in the market. This is precisely because economic production has been severed from the household, which still reproduces labor power. Consequently, the affective intensity of the family now appears negated by the cold calculating logic of the capitalist market. Finally, constitutionally ordered political arrangements, which in Hegel's view were to reconcile the above contradiction, have not been able to do so. Rather, political structures often appear alien to people whose lives are largely dependent on their roles in a capitalist market or civil society. In late nineteenth-century China and Japan, the institutions Pinkard mentions were in the process of emerging, especially with respect to the modern state and the capitalist market.

A fundamental aspect of pan-Asianism was an attempt to save Asia from the alienation that characterized Western societies by drawing on Asian traditions. This was Okakura's position to a certain degree, and as we shall see in chapter 3, Ōkawa Shūmei also attempted to overcome the fragmentation and alienation of civil society by returning to Asian traditions. However, we must understand pan-Asianism in light of its nemesis, namely early versions of modernization theory. In the late nineteenth century, many Asian intellectuals engaged in a Hegelian-like critique of the Orient. Put simply, many prewar thinkers' evaluation of Asia was connected to whether they emphasized the substantiality of community or the negativity of freedom. If for Hegel philosophy implied the negation of Asia, then Fukuzawa's thinking went a step further and turned this into an Asian self-negation. Fukuzawa outlined a world in which Asia did not completely embrace freedom but needed to do so to avoid colonization. Just as Hegel narrated a moment when the West left the East through turning inward, after the Meiji Restoration, Fukuzawa encouraged Japan to act autonomously and thus leave Asia.

Fukuzawa Yukichi: From Evolutionary Civilization to Leaving Asia

The Meiji Restoration of 1868 marked not only a major break in Japanese history but also a rupture that had ramifications throughout Asia. The primal scene of the Meiji Restoration and Japan's entry into global capitalist modernity is usually taken to be the arrival of Commodore Matthew Perry in Edo (now Tokyo) Bay with his Black Ships in 1853. This scene is also one of the key spaces where the concept of Asia was born. In the year following Perry's demand that Japan open its ports to trade with the United States, Japanese elites saw themselves confronted with a global capitalist world characterized by imperialism. They reacted in two different ways, both of which mirrored Hegel's distinction between substantiality and negativity. One side of the response is usually referred to as "civilization and enlightenment" (*bunmei kaika*), which refers to the turn toward the West and an emphasis on subjectivity. But civilization/enlightenment also implies a linear vision of history, which could be in tension with individual subjectivity. Fukuzawa Yukichi, who actively promoted civilization and enlightenment, emphasized subjectivity and an evolutionary narrative. Given how the Western powers were dominating China and encroaching on Japan, many elites distanced themselves from China and hoped to learn from the West. The presence of the Western imperialist powers changed the dynamic between Japan and China and encouraged an enlightenment narrative associated with the West. At the same time, others took on an anti-imperialist stance that advocated "revering the emperor and expelling the barbarian [*sonnō jōi*]." This second side appears conservative insofar as it advocates a return. "Revering the emperor and expelling the barbarian" could be described as a return to substantiality—a longing to return to a prior prereflective form of community based on affective intensity. At the same time, because it harbored the idea of resistance, this movement of return also had a negative dimension. That is, it sought to negate imperialism.

The Meiji Restoration inaugurated a radically new society that embodied both spatial and temporal contradictions. The term "amphibious" is apt here but only in a limited sense: social change was brought about through external force. Perry's ships crossed the ocean, bringing with them the imperatives of capitalism. The resistance this generated was, however, aroused out of a particular land and culture. This tension, which is discussed throughout this book, stemmed from the spatiotemporal strategies of the Meiji Restoration, but it also gave rise to pan-Asianism.

The temporal dynamic of the Meiji Restoration was a combination of the "emperor strikes back" and "back to the future." The term "restoration" implies a return, specifically a return of the emperor, but at the same time the Meiji Restoration is considered a watershed marking the beginning of modern Japan.[26] Consequently, bringing back the emperor was a call to go back to the future, so to speak—to modernize. The emperor that returned had never previously existed but nonetheless symbolized the past. This double temporality of the Meiji Restoration expresses the amphibious time of the modern nation-state. On the one hand, the nation-state had to appear new to show that it was better than all earlier forms of community—which it did by invoking ideals associated with capitalism and the ocean, which entailed ideas of the Enlightenment[27] that were now internalized by Meiji intellectuals—but, on the other hand, the nation-state needed to show its connection to the past to legitimate its identity through affirming land-related culture, especially in the form of the nation.

The nation, consequently, had to be simultaneously both new and old. Nationalists narrated this opposition by affirming past communities along with a vision of progress, which usually entailed economic development. To the extent that the latter was associated with capitalism, it was premised on negativity and free subjects, who nonetheless had to submit to the laws of wage labor, the market, and the nation-state. The destructive nature of capitalist development constantly puts the legitimacy of the nation and capitalist ideology into crisis. Pan-Asianism responded to this crisis, which is why it often returns to narratives of community and the nation.

The early response to this capitalist crisis has recently been depicted in *The Last Samurai*, a book describing the 1877 Satsuma Rebellion—the most serious resistance to Meiji Restoration—led by Saigō Takamori.[28] Although Saigō has become a favorite among conservatives, he is also associated with pan-Asianists. Saigō wanted a return of the emperor in a way that did not result in Japan being pushed toward an Enlightenment future.[29] Enlightenment is also used in the Japanese context as *kaika*, to which I am also referring. The opposition between the Enlightenment and revering the emperor/expelling the barbarian was not unique to Japan but found in many Asian nations struggling against imperialism. For example, writing about Chinese intellectual currents about thirty years after the Meiji Restoration, the historian Li Zehou claimed that Chinese intellectuals in the late Qing dynasty (1644–1912) were caught between the dual imperatives of the Enlightenment and saving the nation.[30] While saving the nation might be different from bringing back the emperor, both were connected to the formation of the nation-state, which implies the temporality of return and community.

Within this larger contradiction, although individual thinkers made different choices with respect to Asia, Fukuzawa Yukichi's perspective was particularly influential. Fukuzawa viewed history as evolutionary and placed China and other Asian nations behind the more "civilized" Western nations. In his well-known *Outline of a Theory of Civilization*,[31] published in 1875, shortly after the Meiji Restoration, Fukuzawa replaced China with Japan as the center of Asia. This transposition represented a radical shift in the framework in which civilization was evaluated. Looking at this shift historically, until the Meiji Restoration, Japan had for the most part defined itself in relation to China and Chinese culture, especially Confucian culture. During much of the imperial period, spanning from 220 BCE to 1911, China considered itself the center of an informal international gift economy or tribute system—a highly ritualized system of exchanges between the Chinese imperial court and leaders of other Asian nations. Although Japan was for the most part not integrated into this system, Chinese culture was still hegemonic. In Japan, the birth of "Asia" as a category was connected to the fall of this earlier conception of the centrality of China. After all, whether or not one thinks of China as the center of Asia, the concept of Asia itself implies a world of nation-states beyond the tribute system at which China was the center.

A key factor in the decentering of China in Japanese eyes was the series of defeats China suffered at the hands of Western and Japanese imperialism, beginning with the Opium War (1839–1842). Fukuzawa contended that China had been ousted from the center and replaced by the West, which embodied a new form of civilization. In this context, he rethought the pasts of Asia, China, and Japan.

Fukuzawa connected the idea of Asia to spirit:

> If scholars read widely into the histories of the world and compare Asia and Europe, and they inquire into the points in which the two areas of the world differ—without going into such things as their geographies and products, their ordinance and laws, their technical skills and technical backwardness . . . they will definitely discover a certain spiritual entity behind these respective differences. This entity is difficult to describe. But when it is nourished it grows to embrace the myriad things of the earth; if repressed or restrained, its external manifestations will also vanish. It is in constant motion, advancing or retreating, waxing or waning. It may seem a will-o'-the wisp apparition, but if we look at its real manifestations within present-day Asia and Europe, we can clearly see it is not illusory. If we wish to attach a name to this entity, we might call it the ethos of a nation's people. In regard to time we call it the trend of the times [*jisei*]. In regard to the persons we call it the human mind. . . . It is this spirit of civilization that makes Asia differ from Europe.[32]

Although Fukuzawa had no serious engagement with Hegel, he used the term "spirit" (*seishin*) to analyze the difference between Asia and Europe. At first, Fukuzawa seems to separate geographies and products from spirit but then notes that spirit "embraces the myriad things of the earth," which suggests its connection to material things. Fukazawa distinguishes between surface phenomena, such as clothing and hairstyles, which some might mistake for civilization, and that which generates civilization, which is the spirit or ethos of a nation. With respect to time, this spirit becomes the trend of the times (*jisei*), which suggests a movement, similar to Hegel's perspective about spirit's movement in history.

With these concepts, Fukuzawa shows how Asia is behind, but following numerous Western scholars, he lays down the foundation for pan-Asianism by showing that the concept of Asia is coherent. This spirit of civilization holds both nations and regions together despite superficial differences. Although Fukuzawa will eventually connect civilization to the wealth and power of a nation, he notes that this spirit cannot be measured at the level of commodities: "It cannot be bought or sold."[33] Spirit combines space and time to show difference between Asia and the West.

Fukuzawa divides the past into three periods—primitive, half-civilized, and civilized—which are spatiotemporal categories. In this narrative, the temporal is logically prior to the spatial. These categories are not merely pasts or presents of any particular country; they are universal, and all countries must go through these stages. However, at a lower level of abstraction in history, segments of time are geographical since primitive, half-civilized, and civilized refer to different parts of the world. The past or primitive society refers to places such as Africa and Australia and the civilized to regions such as the United States and Western Europe. The half-civilized category is perhaps the most interesting for our purposes since it is represented by Asian nations. Within the Asian nations, China and India are unable to move out of the past, but Fukuzawa avers that Japan has more potential to follow the civilized countries.

Fukuzawa, like Hegel, categorized societies into levels of civilization, based largely on the concept of autonomy, which is connected to a certain type of knowledge. Each of the levels, from barbarian to civilized, represents a different degree of autonomy from nature. While Fukuzawa did not go as far as Hegel in outlining a free society, he constructed a similar narrative of freedom in his categories of civilization. For example, in the primitive stage, people do not produce book learning, and each member of society is "unable to be the master of his own situations; he cowers before the forces of nature."[34] Nature here appears as a type of absolute past, or a time out of history, out of self-conscious actions. The second level, the semicivilized Asian stage, is an in-between state and therefore more complex. At this stage, people do write books and form stable communities. However, they do not devote themselves to practical learning; they do not question and are not able to think originally. "There are accepted rules governing society, but being oppressed by custom, they could never form rules in the true sense [*kisoku no tai wo nasazu*]."[35] At this second stage, rather than being slaves of nature, people become slaves of custom, which forms a type of second nature. This is an aspect of what Hegel means by substantiality and *Sittlichkeit*. Fukuzawa uses the term "oppressed" (*attō*), which literally implies that the force of the past is so great that it weighs down on the present. Because people are oppressed by the past, their rules are often trumped by custom. To some extent, this is reminiscent of Confucius's dislike of litigation and his praise of informal mechanisms,[36] which Fukuzawa conceives of as custom and as a hindrance. Thus, autonomy implies being liberated from nature, which is a type of absolute past, and from the past that human beings have created, that is, history congealed as custom, which acts as a second nature.

> In the highest stage, the civilized, people's spirits enjoy free play and are not credulous [*wakudeki*] of old customs. They act autonomously and do not have to depend upon the arbitrary favor of others. They cultivate their own virtue and refine their own knowledge. They neither idolize the old nor become complacent about the present. Not resting in small gains, they plan great accomplishments for the future. They move forward without going back. They achieve their goal and do not stop. Their path of learning is not vacuous; it has indeed discovered the root of invention. Their industrial and business ventures prosper day by day to increase the source of human welfare.[37]

The temporal metaphors here are crucial. Unlike people in the second stage, civilized people are not stuck in the customs of the past. They are able to negate them and move toward the future. Here the past appears as a burden that hinders the present from moving into the future. Fukuzawa first describes the future as an open space, but this space is immediately filled with industrial production and wealth, which imply the development of capitalism. Indeed, the movement of civilization, like capitalism, appears to revolutionize everything and break free from the past.

However, this revolutionary force is not the whole story, as capitalism requires the nation-state to enforce the laws of the market and thereby ensure its legitimacy. A narrative of the nation served to position Japan as the leader of Asia in a world dominated by Western civilization and capitalism. In this narrative, the Chinese past is used, by contrast, to legitimate the Japanese shogunal system as being closer to the West. Moreover, Japanese Shinto myths invoked the emperor to establish the continuity of the nation. Fukuzawa explains the despotism of China, as opposed to a slightly more open position in Japan, by referring to the existence of Japanese feudalism, which was still obliquely connected to the Chinese *fengjian*/feudal system, or the system that existed before the Qin emperor unified China.

I say that China has endured as a theocratic autocracy over the centuries, while Japan has balanced the element of military power against the element of theocracy. China has had but one element, Japan two. If you discuss civilization in these terms, China has never once changed and thus is not equal to Japan in her development. It is easier for Japan to adopt Western civilization than for China.[38]

Even in what is an evolutionary view, the past returns here to open a space for negativity or subjectivity. Fukuzawa contends that the separation of military power and theocratic power, which is characteristic of Chinese *fengjian*/feudalism, allows a certain amount of freedom from substantiality, which, without negativity, would lead to theocracy. He argues that China before the unification by the Qin emperor in 221 BCE had room for freedom because there was no overarching unity between theocracy and military power. This is why, during the Spring and Autumn (771–476 BCE) and Warring States (475–221 BCE) periods, there were the hundred schools of philosophy, including Confucianism, Daoism, and Legalism, all vying for power. But, Fukuzawa argued, after the unification of China in 221 BCE, it moved to a system of theocratic autocracy. Fukuzawa provided an explanation for how China became a despotic state. In 1875, when Fukuzawa looked back at history, the failure of the Nara (710–794) and Heian (794–1185) periods to consolidate a long-lasting imperial system and the triumph of the shogunal system appeared positive since they moved Japan closer to the West.[39] Fukuzawa thus believed the tension between the military shogunal forces, and the Japanese regime of the emperor allowed a space for freedom in which the future could be created.

But Fukuzawa's critique of Confucianism and centralization would eventually extend beyond to China. By the late 1890s, Fukuzawa feared that the Meiji government might erase the difference between the theocracy and military power in the figure of the emperor. Moreover, to reinforce the new form of imperial power created by the Meiji Restoration, the Meiji government made use of Confucianism, especially its concept of loyalty. In other words, the Meiji government singled out loyalty to the emperor as one of the most important facets of Confucianism. Fukuzawa's autobiography, published in 1899, suggests that his critique of Confucianism concerned Japan as well as China:

> The true reason for my opposing the Chinese teaching with such vigor is my belief that in this age of transition, if this retrogressive doctrine remains at all in our young men's minds, the new civilization cannot give its full benefit to this country. In my determination to save our coming generation, I was

prepared even to face single-handedly the Chinese scholars of the country as a whole.[40]

Fukuzawa here notes the importance of what he views as a period of tradition and the contest between progress and retrogression. He attacks Confucianism, which stands in for much of Asia, in order to save Japan.

Earlier I suggested that Fukuzawa was concerned about the use of Confucianism to support a new form of imperial rule. However, he still saw a role for the emperor in his vision of Japan's future. Indeed, another way Fukuzawa distinguished between China, Asia, and Japan was by contrasting the continuity of the Japanese imperial line with the discontinuous Chinese system, which experienced a series of regime changes and at times even experienced a situation where the majority of Han Chinese were governed by non-Han rulers, such as when the Manchus ruled China from 1644 to 1911. In Fukuzawa's view, the continuity of the imperial line in Japan expressed an identity on a more abstract level, which he associated with the national polity (*kokutai*), a key concept in the emperor-centered Meiji nation-state.[41]

Fukuzawa reintegrated aspects of Chinese and Japanese discourses about the past to situate Japan in Asia in relation to the West. Consequently, he had to reconcile any gesture toward a return with a future of national unity compatible with the modern nation-state inaugurated by the Meiji Restoration. Fukuzawa expressed two attitudes toward the past. He highlighted freedom from the past, and he also pointed to an indeterminate space in which the future could be created. However, he underscored the continuity among past, present, and future in a community represented by the national polity. The two perspectives on history and the past that Fukuzawa outlined express the contradictory project of building a national capitalism in a world of imperialism. Nationalists had to stress the continuity of the nation through time and also its unity through time. However, modern capitalism presupposes that people are free from the state and able to sell their labor power in the market. Capitalism conditioned much of the intellectual content during the Meiji period (1868–1912) but did not present itself as a determinate social form; rather, it was naturalized. Capitalist competition, occurring both nationally and transnationally, also implied increasing productivity through technological innovation, which as we have seen was one of the major characteristics of Fukuzawa's concept of civilization.

Fukuzawa articulates an early formulation of the thesis that Benjamin Schwartz saw in Yan Fu, the late Qing liberal theorist and translator.[42] Schwartz argued that in countries that entered the global capitalist system late, liberal intellectuals tended to see freedom as a means to make the country wealthy and powerful, which points to capitalism and the nation-state. Fukuzawa evidenced this tendency when he claimed that Western nations became powerful precisely because of their high level of civilization and freedom. But as Schwartz adumbrates, this kind of attempt to justify freedom with reference to power is both particular and universal. Both Japan and China entered the global capitalist system late, and consequently the nation-state became crucial for fighting imperialism. From another perspective, Fukuzawa, Yan Fu, and many other Japanese and Chinese intellectuals identified a global tension between capital and the nation-state. As Marx explains in *Capital*, a society based on the exchange of market commodities requires that laws and contracts be backed by the state, of which the dominant form became the nation-state.[43] Thus the tension between the past and the future aspects of historical narratives reproduced the opposition between capital, which stressed the freedom of an unencumbered individual who makes contracts, and the nation-state, which places the atomized individual back into an imagined community with ostensibly deep roots in the past.

In Fukuzawa's scheme, Asia appears to trail Europe, but this did not necessarily mean he was advocating that Japan leave Asia and join Europe. For this reason, pan-Asianism cannot mean merely uniting with other Asian countries since one could advocate this while still following the example of the West. For example, although Fukuzawa is known for advocating leaving Asia, initially he hoped to collaborate with the late Qing general and diplomat Li Hongzhang (1823–1901) to resist the West. In addition, he hoped to help Korea's enlightenment. Tsukiashi Tatsuhiko contends that initially Fukuzawa believed that the Korean coup of 1884 could enable Korea to become independent and civilized. During this coup, a number of pro-Japanese activists in Korea attempted to overthrow the Korean dynastic system and replace it with a regime modeled on the Meiji system. As president of Keio University, Fukuzawa even welcomed pro-Japanese reformers such as Kim Ok-kyun (1851–1894) to Japan. He had two reasons for wanting the Korean coup to succeed. First, he believed that a weak Korea would make Japan vulnerable to imperialist attack. As he put it, a stone house is not safe from fire as long as a wooden house stands next to it. A second and more sentimental reason was that Korea reminded him of what Japan was like twenty or thirty years earlier, before the Meiji Restoration.[44] The failure of the Korean coup in 1884 contributed to Fukuzawa's disappointment with Asia, and after that he began calling for Japan to leave Asia.[45]

In 1885 Fukuzawa published the editorial "Leaving Asia," which amounts to a complex negation, or complete negative evaluation, of Asia and can be read as squarely taking aim at a past world where China was the center. We can also conceive of this negation of Asia as itself a reaction to any moves to unite Korea and China in order to negate imperialism. Fukuzawa's editorial again brings Confucianism into the picture:

> In this live theater, through which civilization is constantly renewed, to speak of education is to talk about Confucianism; the mission of schools is said to be that of benevolence, justice, ritual propriety and wisdom, but this is all merely the trappings of appearance, from beginning to end, lacking insight into the principles of truth. It is like a person who has cast off all morality and refines only his cruelty and want of honor, all the while remaining arrogant and lacking any inclination towards self-reflection.[46]

Fukuzawa thus reiterates his critique of Confucianism but ends up returning to a Hegelian theme: a lack of self-reflection. The problem Fukuzawa identified here is not just abstract; there are concrete consequences, the most important being the loss of sovereignty. Fukuzawa invokes the problem of colonialism and unevenness to make his argument for leaving Asia:

> Though Japan stands in . . . Asia, our national spirit has moved onto Western civilization from the Asiatic old-fashioned traditions. However, unfortunately we have two neighbors, China and Korea. Both of these nations have maintained the Asiatic traditional manners of life for many years as well as Japan, but they are indeed similar to each other and entirely different from Japan, though I do not know exactly whether their race or their lineage and education are different from ours. Though they must be well-informed about the current civilization in world-wide communication networks, both of these nations never try to reform their personal and national conditions and hold firm to their old-fashioned traditions from a thousand years ago.[47]

At this point, writing for a general audience, Fukuzawa connects the ability to stand apart from tradition—or what Hegel attributes to subjectivity—even more clearly with the West and associates tradition and the past with Asia. However, as in *Outline of a Theory of Civilization*, Japan emerges as a country in Asia that is already leaving those geographical boundaries. Although Fukuzawa describes China and Korea as representing those who are stuck in their traditions despite wide networks of communication, Fukuzawa's own stance is neatly embodied in the popular maxim of the Chinese government in the mid-1990s: "moving toward the world [*zou xiang shijie*]." Finally, this passage highlights a key point in the imagining of Asia, namely that race is not an essential component. Rather, Asia and the West are distinguished by the presence or absence of reflection and the ability to negate one's tradition. In this way, Fukuzawa provides an archetypical model of evolutionary thought that positions Asia as inferior to Europe. Okakura Tenshin

34 CHAPTER ONE

and others would attack this model in the process of constructing their own pan-Asian ideals.

Okakura Tenshin and Asia as Resistance

Okakura Tenshin also drew on Hegelian themes, but he did so to oppose "leaving Asia" and to emphasize Asia as positive. Although Fukuzawa's theory of civilization placed Asia in the middle of an evolutionary timeline, by the late nineteenth century a number of scholars were reacting against the ideal of modernity or Western civilization. Okakura attempted to show that Asia was united in culture and art. In this he stood apart from Fukuzawa, who emphasized the centrality of science. Given Okakura's positive evaluation of Asia, he is usually thought of as the dialectical opposite of Fukuzawa. Against this interpretation, Urs Mathias Zachman points out that Fukuzawa and Okakura were united in their concern for Japan's national sovereignty.[48] We can add that they shared a geographical image of the world in which Asia was united. This was a belief they shared with Hegel and other nineteenth-century philosophers. However, Fukuzawa and Okakura took significantly different positions with respect to teleology and Western culture.

Paradoxically, Okakura had a much more Western-style education than did Fukuzawa, but he ended up being more critical of Western culture. This should be understood historically in relation to both his personal life and the wider global context. In fact, the formation of his thought suggests that his ideas about pan-Asianism were fundamentally mediated by the West, and it is perhaps this mediation that allowed Okakura to proclaim, "Asia is one."

Okakura Tenshin was born in 1862, and so, unlike Fukuzawa, his early years were spent amid the tumult of the Meiji Restoration. His father was a samurai in Yokohama. We could say that his father and his female guardian represent two opposite sides of this restoration.[49] After the Meiji period, his father left the samurai calling to become a businessman. In this he was representative of the nationwide shift from samurai culture to the market. Becoming a businessman meant moving to a market-oriented ideology, which stressed the exchangeability of everything.

However, another figure represented what Hegel called the "the immediate substantiality of spirit" found in the family.[50] Okakura's mother died when he was eight. But even before this, his father had hired a female guardian, Tsune, a middle-aged woman. It was Tsune who raised Okakura in his early years. Tsune was from a family loyal to the emperor and consequently critical of Enlightenment culture. Her family stressed the importance of samurai

ASIA AS PHARMAKON   35

culture, and partly because of this influence, Okakura appeared to favor the project of expelling the barbarian (*jōi*), which he was also taught in school.

In his early years, Okakura's formal education was primarily Western. As a businessman, his father recognized the potential of international trade through Yokohama, a treaty port, and wanted his son to learn English above all else, and Okakura did learn English from missionaries. As a result, by the age of eight, Okakura still could not read a single Chinese character. Consequently, his father eventually sent him to a nearby temple, where he studied Japanese and classical Chinese.[51]

After graduating from a school run by missionaries, Okakura left Yokohama in 1873 because his father had quit the silk business and opened an inn in Tokyo. In 1875, he passed the entrance exam to the Tokyo School of Foreign Learning (Tokyō kaisei gakkō), which in 1877 combined with the Tokyo Medical School to become Tokyo University. Tokyo University aimed to educate students in Western learning and hired foreign teachers, among them, Ernest Fenollosa (1853–1908), an American philosopher who had an enormous influence on Okakura.

Fenollosa taught the philosophies of Hegel and Spencer to students at Tokyo University, and both of these philosophers had an impact on Okakura. Fenollosa was also interested in Japanese art, although the Meiji state generally favored Western art over Japanese art, which it considered representative of an obsolete regime. This judgment rested on a belief in the temporality of progress espoused by Fukuzawa and other Meiji thinkers.

Despite his ideological differences with the Meiji elite, Okakura still hoped to get a job in the Meiji government, perhaps because it would provide a steady income. In 1880, he had initially planned to write a graduation thesis on the state and finish it about two weeks before the deadline. Fate intervened, however. He got into a quarrel with his wife, and she burned the thesis. In less than two weeks he wrote a completely different one titled "The Theory of Art," a subject that would make it difficult for him to get a high-level position in the bureaucracy. From that point onward, Okakura devoted his life to the realm of culture and art, a platform from which he would deal with politics.

After graduation, Okakura found a lower-level government job in the Ministry of Education, dealing first with music and later with fine art. In both realms, he struggled against administrators and a Meiji state that promoted Western art and music. By the early 1880s however, a slow turn back toward Japanese art had begun. This partially resulted from the need of the nation-state for a narrative of national continuity. Fenollosa also contributed to this reevaluation of Japanese art with his lecture "An Explanation of Truth in Art," presented at a club in Tokyo in 1882.[52] In his lecture, Fenollosa praised traditional Japanese art as superior to Western art. He associated Japanese art with the spiritual, while asserting that Western art was materialistic. This turned Hegel's judgment on its head. Like Hegel's negativity, in Fenollosa's formulation, spirituality transcends materiality. Yet the issue here is not reason but rather how Japanese art went beyond the mechanistic nature of Western art. Fenollosa hoped to take Hegel further and create a new synthesis between Eastern and Western art, with the East, led by Japan, representing spirituality. Although Okakura does not often engage with Hegel explicitly, we find that he invokes Hegelian themes in ways similar to Fenollosa.

In the 1880s and 1890s, Fenollosa's ideas were well received not only by Okakura but by the Meiji elite in general. This may have been partly because Fenollosa's idea of combining Japanese spirituality with Western technique resonated with older elites who supported the late Tokugawa idea of combining Japanese morality with Western technology.[53] The Tokugawa shogunal regime learned about Western technology, and elites began considering ways to preserve Japanese culture while adapting Western technology. Indeed, for some, learning about Western technology was a way of preserving Japanese culture. Moreover, developments in the mid- and late Meiji era provided other social and political reasons to struggle against the dominance of materialism. By the 1890s, the material was connected to capitalism, whose darker side had become apparent and was associated with the West. For example, by the 1890s, an increasing number of industrial workers in Tokyo and other cities had become the source of significant political agitation.[54] Similarly, inequalities were noticeably increasing in Japanese urban centers. In response to these changes, several leftist parties emerged, including the Socialist Party organized by Katayama Sen (1859–1933), a Christian socialist of the Meiji period. Socialism could be described as an internal critique of the West that often drew on premodern religious and philosophical sources.

However, such critiques did not always confront the problem of imperialism or the domination of the West. Fenollosa's work, and especially Okakura's writings of the early twentieth century, would fill this gap in ways that Katayama and Fukuzawa, as well as others, could not. Even though Fukuzawa's work can be seen as a response to imperialism, it was not really a critique of imperialism since Fukuzawa called on Japan to compete within an imperialist system. He emphasized negativity or subjectivity, which, as we have seen, Hegel invoked to argue that Asia was static. Following Fenollosa, Okakura used similar categories but defended Asian ideals pointing the way to a better future.

Okakura's confrontation with the idea of the West and Asia was mediated by his study of Indian philosophy and a trip to India. Through the connections of Josephine MacLeod, a wealthy American devotee of the Indian philosopher Swami Vivekananda (1863–1902), Okakura traveled to Bengal and elsewhere in India for a few months from 1901 to 1902.[55] MacLeod introduced Okakura to the philosophy of Vivekananda, which he incorporated into his own thought. After Vivekananda's speech at the World's Parliament of Religions in Chicago in 1893, he became extremely well known, and this probably increased Okakura's interest. At this meeting, Vivekananda's main aim was to demonstrate the oneness of all religions. He attempted to overcome Hinduism's division into castes and develop a universal religion based on Advaita Vedanta. Vivekananda transposed the metaphysical notion of Advaita, literally "non-duality," onto geography to create a cosmopolitan religion. In short, the transcendence of the self and the abolition of distinctions in Advaita philosophy were analogous to the transcendence of individual religions.

Okakura appropriated this structure in Vedantic thought to discuss Asia. But he brought geography into a system that had long before posited an abstract universality. At the World's Parliament of Religions, Vivekananda presented to the world, especially Europe and America, a philosophy that was universal but had roots in India. Okakura underscored the Asian dimension of this universality even more clearly and even gestured toward alternate forms of universality. From this perspective, the definition of "Asia" entails a sense of struggle and politics.

In the opening lines of Okakura's *Ideals of the East*, published in 1901, he declared:

> Asia is one. The Himalayas divide, only to accentuate, two mighty civilizations, the Chinese with its communism of Confucius, and the Indian with its individualism of the Vedas. But not even the snowy barriers can interrupt for one moment the broad expanse of love for the Ultimate and Universal, which is the common thought-inheritance of every Asiatic race, enabling them to produce all the great religions of the world, and distinguishing them from those maritime peoples of the Mediterranean and the Baltic, who love to dwell on the Particular, and to search out the means, not the end of life.[56]

In Okakura's analysis, Asia moves from unity to opposition to a deeper unity but does not proceed dialectically. At first, we are presented with the opposition between substantiality and individuality. Indeed, the Vedas had long been associated with the interiority of contemplation, while Confucianism emphasized community. But this difference, Okakura declared, is superficial. It is within Asia that Okakura found the distinction between negativity-subjectivity and substantial community. This passage shows that in his thinking, Asia was not only about geography or physical boundaries. Even the snowy barriers of the Himalayas could not stop a fundamental movement, the unity of Asia, and the overcoming of superficial oppositions. For Okakura, Asia was not a geographical region but a place of love for the universal. This love manifested itself in a variety of ways, producing each of the great religions. Here again the idea of amphibiousness arises. Maritime peoples are engaged in trade and conquest and are thus concerned with the particular and with means rather than ends. The significance of Asia lies in its ties to the land, which unleash its ability to resist and eventually sublate maritime culture.

Okakura's juxtaposition of Asia as continental and the West as maritime is of course linked to Japan's experience with the Black Ships and colonialism. The ocean represents imperialism, whereas the people of Asia were sedentary. However, his vision was also connected to his political involvement in India. In the late nineteenth and early twentieth centuries in Bengal, a group of radical intellectuals and anticolonial freedom fighters supported violent mass movements. Okakura was involved with these intellectuals. In his notes during this period, he explained that the British had enslaved the Indians and then continued the theme of separating the maritime regions from Asia by underscoring the problem of imperialism, which he connected to philosophical differences and then later to capitalism.

> The glory of Europe is the humiliation of Asia. The march of history is a record of the steps that lead the West into an inevitable antagonism to ourselves. From their very outset, the restless maritime instincts of the Mediterranean and the Baltic, born of chase and war, of piracy and pillage, stood in strong contrast to the continental contentment of agricultural Asia.[57]

Okakura shows how Asia was drawn into a zero-sum game. Europe could not become glorious without invading Asia. To explain this, he further elaborates on the distinction between the maritime and the continental. The maritime is connected to a history of pillage and imperialism, and this in turn is linked to a particular conception of freedom: namely the idea of individuals pursuing an infinite amount of goods.

Okakura is reacting to the manner in which Western imperialism constantly encroached on the continent through maritime power. In 1904, around the time Okakura was constructing his vision of Asia as landed power, the British geographer Halford Mackinder wrote an influential tract about the importance of controlling the land. He comments:

> But the land power still remains and recent events have again increased its significance. While the maritime peoples of Western Europe have covered the

ASIA AS PHARMAKON

ocean with their fleets, settled the outer continents, and in varying degree made tributary the oceanic margins of Asia, Russia has organized the Cossacks, and emerging from their northern forests, has policed the steppe by setting her own nomads to meet the Tartar nomads.[58]

As Alfred McCoy explains, for Mackinder "'the final geographical realities' of the modern age were land power versus sea power."[59] Mackinder sees Russia as the pivot of history, and this might be perceived differently from the standpoint of an East Asian nation. Nonetheless, his comments capture a fundamental orientation of Western European foreign policy. In a later essay, he articulates this by saying "Who rules the Heartland commands the World-Island."[60] Although Mackinder does not deal extensively with the ideological justification for imperialism, we know that maritime imperialists use the concept of freedom to justify their exploits. Hegel's view of the Orient as lacking negativity/subjectivity can be understood as, perhaps unintentionally, justifying such imperialism and relegating continental Asiatic states to spaces where people lack subjectivity.

Okakura theorizes land and water from the standpoint of Asia and anti-imperialism. The consciousness of maritime imperialism gave rise to a subjectivity of resistance. This resistance required a synthesis of land and ocean, forcing people to redefine terms such as "freedom" so that they were no longer monopolized by the West.

> The West has often accused the East of a lack of Freedom. Truly we have not that crude notion of personal rights guarded by mutual assertion—that perpetual elbowing through the crowd—that consistent snarling over the bones, which seems to be the glory of the Occident. Our conceptions of liberty are far higher than these. With us it lies in the power to complete the individual idea within itself. The true infinity is the circle and not the extended line. Every organism implies a subordination of parts to a whole. Real equality lies in the due fulfillment of the respective function.[61]

Okakura makes a number of important points here. First is the importance of cultural difference or, in Hegel's terms, different forms of spirit. The reason scholars of the West saw only a lack of freedom in Asia was that they failed to understand that Asia possesses a different type of freedom. Okakura later explains that in the West, freedom implies "the projection of individual enjoyment," while in Asia it consists of "the harmony of an interrelated life."[62] The projection of individual enjoyment amounts to "snarling over bones" and animality, which is connected to the glory of the West and the downfall of Asia. According to Okakura, this freedom eventually leads to imperialism, but he also contrasted this abstract freedom to the more concrete experience of Asia. Western and maritime freedom represents a linear infinity because based on this idea, people strive for an infinite amount of goods and are never satisfied. He contrasted this linear infinity with the circle. By juxtaposing the circle and the line, Okakura turned the tables on a Hegelian distinction between good and bad infinity, represented by the circle and the line respectively.

In his *Science of Logic*, Hegel contends that "bad infinity" implies an unending sequence, and it is generated by a worldview that radically separates the infinite from the finite.[63] On one side is an unending line, and on the other lies finite things—and an absolute gulf lies between them. Linear infinity corresponds to an abstract infinity that has no larger purpose. In Hegel's logic, the concept of the infinite begins a transition from quality to quantity. Marx clearly picked up on the quantitative dimension. The quantitative, Marx asserts, is indifferent to quality. Hence both exchange value and money are indifferent to the qualitative dimension of commodities.[64] In the quote above, Okakura points to an infinite drive to increase one's commodities, including resources to produce commodities, which results in plunder.

However, Hegel's point is that the infinite that stands against the finite cannot really be infinite because it is limited by the finite. Consequently, the true infinite, what Hegel calls "affirmative infinite," cannot be separate from the finite; it is to be found within the finite. Affirmative infinity is "bent back upon itself, its image becomes a circle."[65] Hegel believed this to be present only in Christianity, but in fact it can be found in many Chinese philosophies, including Daoism, Buddhism, and Confucianism. Because it is not separate from the finite, this infinite could be characterized as a circular movement—the constant transformation of the finite as itself expressing the infinite. However, this transformation of the finite beyond itself is not blind but involves a purpose. Expressed in political terms, freedom involves the infinite of subjectivity, while connecting it to the concrete goal of creating a harmonious whole, including both communities and nature, which are both mediated by an organic holism. The danger in Okakura's holism is of course that it appears to involve subordination, though he tries to offset this with a description of community. We find Asia precisely within community, which implies a freedom different from the abstract freedom of the Enlightenment. In his essay "The Awakening of the East" (published posthumously in 1939) Okakura explains:

> The sweet tolerance of the East grants freely what the most aggressive demands fail to obtain in the West. In spite of its apparent restraint, Eastern life is more conducive to individuality than Western, whose uniformity and

competition stamp mankind with the cheap monotony of machine-made goods. Our poorest enjoys his pipe of leisure under the evening tree, where he discusses village politics.[66]

Okakura describes the West as unable to overcome a major antinomy of modernity, namely the opposition between individuality and cheap monotony, while the East, or Asia, might provide a solution. Up to this point, we have not seen Okakura discuss capitalism explicitly, and his critique of capital is fragmentary. This has led Mark Anderson to conclude that we should not think of late Meiji cultural resistance to imperialism as entailing a critique of capitalism. In his chapter dealing with Okakura, Fenollosa, and numerous contemporaries, he writes: "While their thought is an important critique of scientific reason, it does not challenge the logic of capital in any significant way."[67] Anderson continues to show how such resistance to imperialism could justify the accumulation of Japanese capital and forced cultural homogenization. This point anticipates part of my argument in chapter 3. However, I would characterize Okakura's critique as a challenge to capitalism that was finally unsuccessful. In other words, unlike Anderson, I take seriously Okakura's critique of capitalism because he attacks many of its key building blocks, including the abstract individual and, as we shall see below, a certain profit motive. We must understand such challenges and those found in the even more right-wing ideology of Ōkawa Shūmei (which we will discuss in chapter 3) as serious confrontations with capitalism even if they eventually supported its more authoritarian forms. Japanese imperialist ideologues could use such ideology because Okakura and others often associated capitalism with the West.

In Okakura's view, although the West emphasizes individuality and the pursuit of desire, the structure of society turns this ethos upside down. Individuals become cogs in the machine, an expression Max Weber would use a couple of decades later. In 1921, Weber wrote, "Rational calculation . . . reduces every worker to a cog in this bureaucratic machine and, seeing himself in this light, he will merely ask how to transform himself into a somewhat bigger cog."[68] Although Okakura did not theorize a tie between becoming a cog and both the capitalist market and organization, he did see a connection between a modern society based on market exchange and the problem of life itself (Western life) being stamped with the cheap monotony of machine-made goods. He suggested that once a society becomes capitalist, no aspect of society is left untouched by its effects.

He continues this vaguely Marxist critique in other places in the same essay. As we have seen, the maritime West follows another path: "Their pride was built of contempt for the helpless who were yoked to their wagons of luxuries."[69] Here, rather than an interconnected web of duties, we have wagons of luxuries, which suggests superfluous wealth. Okakura further specifies that the problem has to do with money. He points out that "the modern spirit flies from God to gold."[70] Just as the modern is connected to the maritime and the West, the transition Okakura speaks of is from religion to commerce. Here, gold serves as money—or the universal equivalent. Indeed, Okakura's point runs counter to Marx's often-cited line in the *Communist Manifesto*:

> The bourgeoisie, wherever it has got the upper hand, has put an end to all patriarchal, feudal and idyllic relations. It has pitilessly torn asunder the ties that bound man to his "natural superiors" and has left no other nexus between man and man than naked self-interest, than callous cash payment. It has drowned the most heavenly ecstasies of religious fervor, of chivalrous enthusiasm, of philistine sentimentalism in the icy waters of egoistical calculations.[71]

Here Marx represents religion and the idyllic as artifacts of a past that have been swept away by capitalism. Okakura takes this point to a new level and echoes Marx's later point about money becoming like a god in capitalist society. In short, Okakura describes a world where capitalism has become a religion.[72] In an essay published about one year after the Japanese victory in the Russo-Japanese War, Okakura takes this line of reasoning further and makes the connection to Marxism more explicit.

> In spite of the vaunted freedom of the West, true individuality is destroyed in the competition for wealth, and happiness and contentment are sacrificed to an incessant craving for more. The West takes pride in its emancipation from mediaeval superstition, but what of that idolatrous worship of wealth that has taken its place? What sufferings and discontent lie hidden behind the gorgeous mask of the present? The voice of socialism is a wail over the agonies of Western economies—the tragedy of Capital and Labor.[73]

Several elements in this passage are reminiscent of Marx. First is the problem of incessant striving for wealth. Although Okakura uses the term "wealth," the context of his remarks suggests that he is actually discussing what Marx would call "value" or "abstract wealth." He juxtaposes happiness and contentment—which as we have seen, he associated with Asia—to the craving for more. Consequently, he implies that a desire for wealth is not merely about procuring items for use or personal satisfaction but of simply getting more.[74] While this could refer to a psychological condition of wanting more for its own sake, this is itself often connected to the logic of capital, which entails that capitalists create surplus value. Okakura mentions gold, but again this is not merely material wealth but also abstract wealth. While one can only have a certain amount of concrete wealth, abstract wealth in the

ASIA AS PHARMAKON

form of money or credit can be endlessly accumulated. This becomes the bad infinity of value, which stands separate from all concrete things. Because of this separation, the craving for more money is similarly independent of one's physical level of satisfaction. In Meiji Japan, society had already established the beginnings of a capitalist market, where money as a representative of abstract wealth, the god of commodities,[75] was becoming predominant.

But perhaps more importantly, the passage continues with the mention of labor and capital and also socialism. By underscoring capital, Okakura supports the interpretation that wealth was akin to exchange value or even capital. That is, capital seeks to increase money rather than producing goods for consumption. He then mentions labor, which is the key to Marx's critique and points to socialism as a cry against the injustices of capitalist society.

In short, Okakura couched his arguments for pan-Asianism in a narrative that overlapped with Marx insofar as he criticized capitalism for promoting a religion of money and recognized the relevance of socialism. Echoing Marx, Okakura saw this as a global process:

> But with a hunger unsatisfied by its myriad victims in its own broad lands, the West also seeks to prey upon the East. The advance of Europe in Asia means not merely the imposition of social ideals which the East holds to be crude if not barbarous, but also the subversion of all existing law and authority. The Western ships which brought their civilization also brought conquests, protectorates, ex-territorial jurisdiction, spheres of influence, and what not of debasement, till the name of the Oriental has become a synonym for the degenerate, and the word "native" an epithet for slaves.[76]

Okakura was aware of the myriad problems associated with capitalism as a global process. It was, he argued, the commercialism of capitalism that made it such that "the very life of the West depends on finding markets for her goods."[77] Here, without explicitly stating it, Okakura implies capitalism, since he speaks not only of the logic of the market but also of a larger logic that involves social organization and imperialist expansion. While markets have existed periodically throughout history, capitalism represents a particular logic that combines markets with a specific form of organization and generalized commodity production. Okakura gestures toward this point when he asks, "What chance has individualised Eastern trade against the sweeping batteries of organized commerce?"[78] By stressing cooperation, Okakura's comment again overlaps with Marx's description in *Capital* of the trajectory of capital,[79] that is, capitalism eventually involves increasingly organized factories and labor in order to increase efficiency. This process is part of what Moishe Postone calls the "treadmill dynamic,"[80] whereby capitalist competition compels

44 CHAPTER ONE

factories to constantly increase production, thus cheapening the time and money needed to make one particular commodity. Okakura makes the same point: "Cheapness and competition, like the mitrailleuse under whose cover they advance, now sweep away the crafts. The economic life of the Orient founded on land and labor and deprived of a protective tariff through high-handed diplomatic action, succumbs to the army of machine and capital."[81] The cheapening of commodities is a result of the treadmill dynamic of capitalist production, which spread across the globe. However, Okakura warned against thinking of this process as simple. Capital does not just offer cheaper commodities to Asian nations. In fact, given global inequalities, quicker production in one part of the world does not necessarily mean that goods will be cheaper when converted to Asian currencies. Perhaps more importantly, demand for such goods may not be sufficient, or the societies in the East might try to stop foreign goods from entering their domestic markets, which might not be capitalist. It is at this point the mitrailleuse, that is, a volley gun or a gun with multiple sling-shot barrels, enters to force capital onto Asian nations. This begins a process that neither the Occident nor the Orient can control and one that undermines the fabric of life in Asia. This is where land and labor succumb to the army of the machine and capital. When Okakura mentions labor in the above passage, he refers to it as the general capacity to produce use-values, rather than the commodified abstract labor in capitalism. He sees the earlier forms of labor and trade replaced by labor as capital, which leads to religious fervor being drowned in the icy waters of egoistical calculation and the religion of money. In other words, in precapitalist societies, labor is not merely in the service of capital but connected to the land and ritualistic practices.

But Okakura's approach contains two differences from the Marxist paradigm, at least as it is usually understood. First, when Okakura mentions land, he is concerned mainly with imperialism. While Marx did not avoid the question of imperialism, most Marxists before Lenin did not place it at the center of their theory. Second, most Marxists would consider the drowning of older forms of religious fervor as progress. As such, labor becomes subsumed under capital and consequently controlled by machines. In contrast to Marx and many others, Okakura considers religious fervor and the bonds between human beings as potentially subversive of these icy waters and commodity fetishism that promote imperialism.

Okakura contends that anti-imperialism meant a reenchantment of the world and a return to Asian traditions and art: "Competition stamps mankind with the cheap monotony of machine-made goods," and therefore Eastern life, by contrast, is more conducive to individuality. Here we get a sense of

Okakura's aesthetic sensibility and his interest in music. Note that he speaks of a monotony that is cheap. Monotony implies a repetition of the same tone again and again, a bad infinity, which can never amount to art or music. This is the cultural complement to the seriality that dominates life in capitalism, a world in which quantitative differences prevail. By using the term "cheap," Okakura attempts to show that we are dealing with something that is merely quantitative, and in this way he juxtaposes the cheap monotony of the West to the harmony of Asia.

Okakura contrasts the harmony of the Asian village with the "naked self-interest" of capitalism. The village appears premodern, but it enjoys participatory politics, or at least its members have the freedom to discuss politics. Thus, he writes, "Our poorest enjoys his pipe of leisure under the evening tree, where he discusses village politics." In short, following the above logic, Okakura also invokes a past in order to go back to a future, so to speak, in which Asia represents a new universality. Continuing a theme from *Ideals of the East*, Okakura connects Asian harmony to communism: "Eastern society is wondrously beautiful in its harmony of interrelated duties. The land furnished occupations and the ideals of the Commonwealth, where each component formed and welded the integral whole. The Oriental sovereign, a projection of the parental idea, and the centralising force in the total scheme, was not more or less important than the various factors of communism."[82]

Socialist movements such as the Christian socialism of Katayama Sen were present in Japan and elsewhere in East Asia, and for them, communism represented a possible future rather than the past. Okakura embraces this ideal but at the same time links communism with Confucian-like ideals, such as harmony and interrelatedness. Once again, he turns Hegel on his head. What Hegel considered to be Oriental despotism was, in Okakura's eyes, an Eastern type of freedom and harmony. In other words, while Okakura, like Hegel, was interested in synthesizing freedom and community, he barely mentions either the institutions that Hegel singled out or his evaluation of civilizations around the world.

Moreover, returning to Hegel's own description of the antinomy of modern life, including the struggle relating to universality and particularity and related oppositions, Okakura seemed to stand opposite both Hegel and Fukuzawa. Although Hegel was perhaps the most thorough critic of one-sidedness, he vehemently denied that some type of religious or aesthetic feeling could produce freedom and community, instead affirming the role of reason (*Vernunft*). In Okakura's formulation, it is at once art and the idea of Asia that emerge as fulcrums of resistance. This is why the subtitle of *Ideals of the East* is "the Spirit of Japanese Art," which suggests that it is in art that ideals lie.

46   CHAPTER ONE

Given Okakura's background and his role in promoting the study of art history in Japanese universities, his focus on art is not surprising. However, we get a sense of his motivation for connecting art with the essence of Asia when he discusses the difficulties of grasping the history of Japanese art.

> Any history of Japanese art ideals is, then, almost an impossibility, as long as the Western world remains so unaware of the varied environment and inter-related social phenomena into which that art is set, as [if] it were a jewel. Definition is limitation. The beauty of a cloud or a flower lies in its unconscious unfolding of itself, and the silent eloquence of the masterpieces of each epoch must tell their story better than any epitome of necessary half-truths. My poor attempts are merely an indication, not a narrative.[83]

Unlike the philosophy that Hegel recommends, Okakura extols the silent eloquence of art. The actual movement of the material must be grasped in a way that cannot be represented. Thus Okakura follows the anti-Hegelian trend of the late nineteenth and early twentieth centuries. We might learn something about Okakura's point of view by considering Friedrich Schelling's homage to art: "Philosophy to be sure reaches the highest level, but it brings only, as it were, a fragment of man to this point. Art brings the whole man, as he is, to that point, namely to a knowledge of the highest of all, and in this rests the eternal difference and the miracle of art."[84] Like Okakura, Schelling associates thinking with fragmentation. It is because of this fragmentation that Okakura speaks of half-truths. From this perspective, Okakura continues in a romantic mode. Art has a power that goes beyond mere intellect. In particular, art involves a harmony that eludes thought, but this harmony might nonetheless be important for politics. However, as we have seen above, the problem of concealment persists. A history of art is impossible as long as the West dominates and makes Asian contexts invisible. As a result, even Asians cannot see their history and consequently do not perceive the unity of Asia.

Toward the end of his essay "The Awakening of the East," Okakura underscores how breaking free from Western hegemony is the precondition for understanding Asian unity. "The spell of white prestige must be completely broken that we may learn our own possibilities and resources."[85] Okakura's task was precisely to break this spell, which required both a rejection of false ideologies of universalism and also a recognition of mediation by the West, especially in language and technology.

> Our sad experience in international complications has warned us that the ties of blood between them are always thicker than that milk of humanity and justice which might draw them to us.

ASIA AS PHARMAKON   47

> Their very language, in which I am enabled to appeal to you, signifies the
> unification of the East. It reaches from the Kuriles to Cape Comorin, from the
> sea-ribbed coast of Cambodia to the rippled verdure of Crete, carrying the cry
> of a common resurrection.[86]

Okakura rejects the false universalism of the West, which covers up the relations of bloodshed or racism that characterize it. Against this abstract universality of the West, which obscures concrete power relations and the promise of the traditions of Asia mentioned above, Okakura calls for a unity that both implies nationalism and goes beyond it. Indeed, this will be a characteristic of pan-Asianism many years after Okakura's time. Theorists of nationalism have pointed out the importance of communication—which requires language—for nationalism. In this case, it is actually the language of the West, which goes beyond indigenous languages such as Chinese and Japanese, that provides the mediation required to create unity for Asia. English, a European language that came to Asia through imperialism, ends up being one of the means through which Asia can become conscious of itself. It is through this language that a common experience of being dominated surfaces. Indeed, Okakura attempts to bring out this domination and show that it needed to be changed. Hegel's and Fukuzawa's respective works describe this domination to some extent, but they do not characterize it as an injustice. Rather, such imperialism is legitimated through an evolutionary narrative. To counter this, Okakura speaks of a resurrection, which begins with a battle cry that returns to challenge linear narratives of history throughout the twentieth century.

On the important subject of the intersection of nationalism and Asianism, Okakura's explanation of why Japan should lead the rest of Asia overlapped with that of Fukuzawa. In particular, like Fukuzawa, Okakura highlighted Japan's history of unbroken sovereignty but also the legacy of the Asian past.

> It has been, however, the great privilege of Japan to realize this unity in com-
> plexity with special clearness. The Indo-Tartaric blood of this race was itself
> a heritage which qualified it to imbibe from the two sources, and so mirror
> the whole of Asiatic consciousness. The unique blessing of unbroken sover-
> eignty, the proud self-reliance of an unconquered race, and the insular isola-
> tion which protected ancestral ideas and instincts at the cost of expansion,
> made Japan the real repository of the trust of Asiatic thought and culture.[87]

In Okakura's telling, the unbroken line of sovereignty attested to Japan's ability to consistently resist imperialist aggression, while other Asian nations did not fare as well. This again shows how pan-Asianism should be understood not as a movement to directly transcend the nation but as a counternarrative of the nation looking toward another world. Here we see that both Fukuzawa and Okakura responded to a world of global capitalist imperialism but in different ways. As we have seen, Okakura believed that Japan was a carrier of Asian culture and that this validated its role as leader, as evident in his statement that "Japan is a museum of Asiatic Civilization; and yet more than a museum, because the singular genius of the race leads it to dwell on all phases of the ideals of the past, in that spirit of living Advaitism which welcomes the new without losing the old."[88]

But Japan was more than a museum: it kept the past while moving toward the future, preserving its traditions while becoming modern and absorbing Western technologies. In Okakura's description, Japan accomplished the dual tasks of the nation-state by being both old and new. This is what he called "living Advaitism," since like the Advaita Vedanta, Japan could manifest an unchanging substance, and then, like Hegel, it could put this substance in motion in history. Japan shows how Asia could simultaneously change and remain the same.

This involved a period of struggle against the West, but as in the Asianisms to come, there was a messianic moment, a turn toward the future. Toward the end of "The Awakening of the East," Okakura writes of how the peoples of Asia could follow Japan in becoming independent:

> Why should not the four hundred millions of China and the three hundred millions of India be armed to stay the further transgression of the predatory West? Why should not the Mohammedan empires be moved to their glorious Jihad? . . .
>
> And a mighty Asiatic peace shall come to clothe humanity with universal harmony. And Europe shall receive the blessing of Asia given with a freer if firmer hand.[89]

The hope for pan-Asianism lies not in war but in a mission for peace. Borrowing from Vijay Prasad's description of the 1950s and 1960s, we could say that, for Okakura, armed anticolonialism was connected to hopes for a peaceful world beyond capitalism and imperialism.[90] In the twentieth century, this legacy was controversial; however, the problems amid which such hope emerged would continue after Okakura's time and still remain with us today.

Conclusion

We have seen how Fukuzawa and Okakura each developed one aspect of Hegel's philosophy. Fukuzawa followed Hegel's notion that history is evolutionary and constructed a vision of Asia as something Japan must overcome or leave. He created a narrative that explains why Japan was both in Asia and yet, unlike China, could follow the West. Okakura resisted this narrative and became an archetype of pan-Asianism. He drew on something similar to what Hegel calls "substantiality" or the "immediacy of community" but did so to argue that Asia also had a different type of freedom. This encompassed an alternative to both capitalism and imperialism and would be an emblem of pan-Asianism for the rest of the twentieth century. We will now turn to early twentieth-century Chinese pan-Asianists, who adopted some of Okakura's arguments while at the same time warning people about the danger of Japanese imperialism.

2

The Critique of Linear Time:
Pan-Asianism in Early Twentieth-Century China

Fukuzawa Yukichi and Okakura Tenshin began a debate that would have ramifications across Japan's boundaries and especially in China. Given that Japanese intellectuals questioned the concept of history as progress, which placed Europe at the center as they confronted imperialism, it is not surprising that other countries on the periphery of the global capitalist system followed suit. In China, we find the same split between those who supported modernization based on the Western model and those who challenged this model and pointed to an Asian alternative. However, Chinese and other peoples in Asia who sought an alternative to the European model of society also felt the need to modify the Japanese vision of Asian unity. Even before Japan realized its imperial project, Okakura Tenshin and Fukuzawa Yukichi both placed Japan at the center of Asia despite their differences. On the other hand, Chinese intellectuals such as Zhang Taiyan and Sun Yat-sen conceived of a pan-Asianism that went beyond the Japanese experience.

The following sections examine three Chinese intellectuals who not only criticized the belief that time is linear but also challenged the Japanese interpretation of Asia. The early twentieth-century anti-Manchu revolutionary Zhang Taiyan (1869–1936) explicitly attacked the notion of linear time and also briefly organized for the cause of pan-Asianism. Li Dazhao (1889–1927) and Sun Yat-sen (1866–1925) later produced their own forms of pan-Asianism. Sun in particular was well received in Japan. All these versions of pan-Asianism had as their historical background the Japanese victory in the Russo-Japanese War of 1904–5 and its global impact. One might think that Japanese and Chinese pan-Asianists would have been united based on their commitment to a critique of global capitalist imperialism and their visions of an alternative. However, the geopolitical situation, and in particular, the

THE CRITIQUE OF LINEAR TIME   51

tensions between Japan, China, and Korea, constantly bedeviled pan-Asianist projects. This chapter describes the tension in the Chinese discourse between outlining an Asian alternative to the West and the more specific problem of overcoming conflicts within East Asia.

Modernity and Evolutionary Thinking in the Late Qing

In the late nineteenth and early twentieth centuries several discourses echoed Fukuzawa Yukichi's theory of civilization, which served as the backdrop for the ideas of advocates of pan-Asianism in China. We have seen that both Okakura's and Fukuzawa's thinking about Asia involved a narrative of nationalism, calling on the peoples of Asia to establish continuity while encouraging them to enter the modern world and resist imperialism. In China as well, some intellectuals followed Fukuzawa in adopting an evolutionary model of progress. After China's losses in a series of wars, including the Sino-Japanese War of 1895, Kang Youwei (1858–1927), Liang Qichao (1873–1929), and other reformers formulated plans for strengthening China so that it could compete in the global capitalist system of nation-states. They each at times considered the Meiji Restoration as a model for China to follow in its quest to eventually emerge victorious in global competition.

The ultimate goal of such competition was to overcome the global capitalist world of international struggle. Indeed, perhaps even more than Fukuzawa, Kang and other reformers were amphibious intellectuals. They were schooled in traditional Chinese thought and even passed the civil service examination in order to serve in the government. However, as China tumbled into a crisis related to oceanic imperialism, Kang and other reformers called for modernizing China. Unlike Japanese liberal intellectuals, they inhabited a world in which the older dynastic system still existed and along with it the possibility of carrying out reform from within premodern political structures. During the late nineteenth and early twentieth centuries, perhaps the most salient intellectual debates in China concerned whether to modernize the imperial system from within or overthrow it. Moreover, these reformers and modernizers often drew on China's classical texts in order to construct a plan for the future. Perhaps the most significant plan was embodied in Kang Youwei's *The Great Unity* (*Datong shu*), which projected a Confucian-inspired socialist utopia in which ownership would be communal and the world would be unified and free of conflict. This would be a world that transcended divisions between land and ocean or colonized and imperialist.

However, this utopia could only be reached after struggle and social evolution. Kang proposed a theory of a racially divided world in which the whites were most evolved. He was nonetheless able to legitimize the Chinese nation and the yellow race from a civilizational perspective by arguing that the white race evolved so successfully because Europeans implemented Confucian principles. Kang then asserted that Chinese had an obligation to revive Confucian principles and develop their own nation so as to be able to compete in the international arena.

However, Kang Youwei also inherited the project of New Text Confucians, who redefined Chinese identity in cultural terms in order to legitimate the Manchu ruler in China and allow for decentralized control of Tibetans and Mongolians. In this context, the reformers' narrative of the nation went beyond race and tended toward a transnational understanding of China, especially regarding its domestic situation. In their view, being Chinese was not a question of race; rather non-Chinese could become Chinese if they practiced Confucian rituals and music. Since Kang stressed the unity of the empire, rather than invoking race, as was done in earlier dynasties such as the Ming (1368–1644), he mobilized a narrative of imperial continuity from the Qin (221–206 BCE) and Han (202 BCE–220 CE) dynasties onward. This raised the issue of the tribute system, which reached much of what we now call Asia. From this perspective, it was not merely Tibet and Mongolia that fell under the umbrella of China but also Vietnam, Thailand, and Korea, all of which would become parts of what people would later call Asia.

The traditional Chinese notion of empire, or "all under heaven" (*tianxia*), was typically understood to include places subject to the tribute system and did not draw a clear distinction between inside and outside. Those who were not Chinese were barbarians, but they could become Chinese by following Confucian rituals. This was naturally the policy that various late Qing Confucians promoted in times of ethnic crisis. However, given the numerous defeats that China suffered at the hands of foreign countries in a series of wars and invasions after the Opium War in 1842, Chinese intellectuals had to reconceive their presence in a world in a way that went beyond the tribute system. In particular, many of the places that were formerly part of the tribute system began to be colonized by foreign powers. In Kang's words, "now our country is in a period when countries mutually struggle; it is not the time when the empire is closed off. During the period when countries mutually struggle, knowledge about politics, technology, literature and crafts can all be set up side by side and those who are behind will become extinct."[1]

Kang took the West as a model but also sought to understand the struggle of countries in Asia to become modern. In 1899, during a period of exile, he ventured to India: "First, after residing in Penang for years, my health has been badly affected by the heat and humidity. I would like to move to the snowy mountain in India. Second, India is the most ancient nation in the world. Its long history and its mixture of India's old system and the British new system may serve as a good reference for China."[2] Kang would of course be surprised by the climate when he arrived in India, but the second part of his reaction, concerning the amphibious or hybrid nature of India, reflected the situation in other nations in Asia such as Japan, which also were faced with straddling old and new temporalities. In other words, despite his admiration of India, its significance stemmed from its showing a path that one should not travel. Before his trip to India, Kang made a comment that encapsulates his vision of history: "Formerly, India was a celebrated nation in Asia, but she stuck to her traditions without changing and so during the Qianlong reign (1736–1795) the British organised a company with capital of 120,000 ounces of gold to carry on trade with India and eventually subjugated the five parts of India."[3] In this passage, Kang contends that the British could colonize India because it clung to its past or traditions without implementing reforms. The basic manner in which he portrays India does not change, but his reasons do. In a letter to Liang Qichao, Kang compared India and Japan in order to explain why China should follow the Japanese path and not opt for local autonomy in the provinces.[4] From this perspective, while the goal for Kang remained modernization, he underscored the historical specificity of Asia, which unlike the West would not be conducive to a federal model. He chose India in this case since it was representative of societies, including China, that faced the threat of colonization.

The emphasis on the similarity between China and India did not amount to a call to unite with India. On the contrary, like Fukuzawa, Kang warned that China must not follow India's path. Kang's remarks on India should be understood in the larger context of views of time, influenced by Yan Fu's (1854–1921) extremely influential translation of Thomas Huxley's *Evolution and Ethics* (*Tianyan lun*) in 1897.

While revolutionaries disagreed about political projects and strategy, in the early nineteenth century they generally shared a similar conception of time. As we shall see, initially radical revolutionaries such as Zou Rong (1885–1905) proposed similar views of evolution, but eventually some of the more vocal proponents of revolution, including Zhang Taiyan, Sun Yat-sen, and the Marxist Li Dazhao, would eventually develop visions pan-Asianism. Advocates of the revolutionary overthrow of the Qing dynasty were in the minority until a series of events raised doubts about the viability of modernizing China under the Qing empire. But the real turning point came in 1900, when the Boxer Rebellion broke out and the Qing government failed to deal with both the mystical martial artist rebels and the foreign powers that came to

54   CHAPTER TWO

suppress them. The encroachment of Western armies in China led to serious concerns that China would be carved up like a melon if the Qing remained in power. In this context, it is not surprising that the revolutionaries were initially more Western-centric and modernist than the reformers and only later turned toward Asia. Moreover, Zhang Taiyan around this time endorsed unity between Chinese and Japanese based on their being the same race and culture (*tongwen tongzhong*).

The Revolutionary Continuation of the Reformers' Critique of Tradition

Kang and other reformers had an evolutionary view of history, and we might wonder why these apparently more radical revolutionaries supported an ostensibly conservative critique of modernity and a return to traditions as a way not to confront the West but to gesture to an alternative beyond the imperialist world. This was not always the case, and early revolutionaries such as Zou Rong, and even Zhang Taiyan, who became one of the first Chinese pan-Asianists, initially affirmed an evolutionary vision of history taking the West as a model. Zou's and Zhang's revolutionary writings are relevant to our story because they took an evolutionary perspective, perhaps even more than Kang Youwei and the other reformers. Their discourse, however, was not incompatible with pan-Asianism.

This radical evolutionary perspective was connected to a nationalism that aimed to overthrow the Qing. Unlike the reformers, who advocated a larger vision of culture that encompassed the Manchu rulers of the Qing dynasty, revolutionaries such as Zou Rong emphasized the distinction between the Han and Manchu "races," which would potentially shrink the boundaries of China. Zou was clearly arguing for nationalism against any trace of empire. One of the narratives for the superiority of a Han nation over a Manchu empire was that the Han nation was more modern and could survive in a Western-dominated world, meaning that modernity itself was associated with the West.

Zou was younger than early reformers such as Kang Youwei and represented a new wave of revolutionary thought that was encapsulated in a famous pamphlet, *The Revolutionary Army*, published in 1903. In this work, Zou brought together revolution, evolution, and Westernization. References to Western thinkers pervade Zou's pamphlet. In his self-written preface, Zou notes that he believed "in the great thinkers, Rousseau, Washington and Walt Whitman."[5] Moreover, it is perhaps strange to find that one of the most famous revolutionary tracts of early Chinese nationalism begins with a sentence that advocated cleansing "ourselves of 260 years of harsh and unremitting pain, so that . . . the descendants of the Yellow Emperor will all become Washingtons."[6]

This is an excellent example of the modernizing tendency of nationalism threatening to negate any sense of temporal continuity. The references to Washington and Rousseau reveal that Zou considered revolution to be a global process and not merely a Chinese phenomenon. Zou's gloss on the concept of revolution stresses this global dimension:

> Revolution is the universal principle of evolution. Revolution is a universal principle of the world [*shijie zhi gongli*]. Revolution is the essence of the struggle for survival or destruction in a time of transition. Revolution follows heaven and responds to human needs. Revolution rejects the corrupt and keeps the good. Revolution is the advance from barbarism to civilization. Revolution turns slaves into masters.[7]

This could hardly be a clearer statement of revolution as a key element of evolutionary civilization. Zou mobilized traditional ideas such as the belief that "revolution follows heaven" (*shun tian*) into a world of progressive history. In other words, heaven is governed not by cosmic principles but by the scientific laws of the universal principle (*gongli*).

While this pamphlet exemplified a pro-Western stance, it also laid the ground for pan-Asianism by being resolutely anti-imperialist. Indeed, the critique of the Manchus now became tantamount to an attack on imperialism. Zou explains that if a trespasser barged into someone's house, the inhabitants would be alarmed and drive the intruder away. But Zou complains that his fellow Chinese "put up with things as a country [*guo*] that they would not tolerate as individuals" and "tolerate things as a nation-lineage [*zu*] that they would not tolerate as a family."[8] This explains why the Chinese succumbed not only to rule by the Manchus but also to British rule in Hong Kong and Japanese rule in Taiwan. This emphasis on national independence and identifying with the nation reappears at various points in later pan-Asianism. Although anti-Manchu revolutionaries initially admired the West, their anti-Manchuism combined with resistance to Western imperialism eventually opened the way to pan-Asianism.

Zhang Taiyan, Zou Rong's revolutionary partner in crime and anti-Manchu propagandist, wrote a preface to *The Revolutionary Army* in which he reiterated many of Zou's ideas. However, his background was different from Zou's. Born in 1869, he was of the same generation as Kang Youwei and began his political activities with the reformers. Moreover, by 1903, he was already an established scholar of the classics, which he studied with the classicist Yu Yue (1821–1907). Thus, like Kang Youwei, he had one foot in the classical worlds of Confucianism, Buddhism, and Daoism and the other in modern science and Western political theory. He began to advocate the overthrow of the Manchus in 1900 and initially connected anti-Manchu revolution to evolution and progress.

Given that he and Zou advocated overthrowing the Manchu government, they were of course being watched by the Qing leaders. Moreover, Zhang wrote a preface to *The Revolutionary Army* that contained several direct attacks on the Qing government, and, in another essay during the same period, he called the Guangxu emperor (r. 1874/75–1908) a "clown."[9] The government arrested and imprisoned both Zou and Zhang in what became a highly publicized transnational case—the Subao case. The Manchu government wanted to execute Zou and Zhang for sedition, but both of them were in the British concession in Shanghai and protected by the extraterritorial rights of the British. Consequently, the Qing government had to show some restraint and sentenced Zou to two years and Zhang to three years in prison, respectively.

I have written about the importance of Zhang's prison experience elsewhere;[10] here I will just note that his hardships, suffering, and ideological encounters in jail made him increasingly critical of the West and encouraged his turn to pan-Asianism. For example, the fact that the prison was located in the foreign concessions in Shanghai meant that prison life was governed by Western norms. Inmates were primarily allowed to read only the Bible and books about Christianity. During this period, Zhang became critical of Western ideology in general, and when he was released from prison in 1906, he fled to Japan and began promoting pan-Asianism.

Japan and Global Pan-Asianism: Relations with Russia and Britain

While Zhang's prison experience was obviously a major factor in the development of his philosophy, which was critical of modernity and the institutions associated with it (including the state), his shift must be understood in a global context. When Zhang fled to Tokyo, people all around Asia were looking at Japan in a new light. Perhaps the most important reasons for this concerned Japan's resistance to Russia and its alliance with Britain, each of which pulled onlookers in different directions. As Yamamurō Shinichi notes, immediately after the Russo-Japanese War, people in Asian nations, including Arabic countries, began to believe that a new world was possible because an Asian nation had finally stood up to a Western power.[11] It is well known that this war was fought over Japan's and Russia's conflicting claims on Korea and

THE CRITIQUE OF LINEAR TIME

Manchuria, but what is less recognized is the impact Japan's victory had on other Asian nations. Unlike Japan's defeat of China in 1895, this time Japan overcame a Western nation, signaling that Asia could resist the West and at the same time be both modern and Asian.

The Russo-Japanese War influenced not only scholars such as Zhang Tai-yan in East Asia but also scholars in the Middle East. Indeed, the Chinese and even the Japanese response to the war must be understood in relation to how intellectuals around the global reacted. For example, the Ottoman intellectual Ahmad Rıza wrote in 1905:

> One cannot doubt the preeminence of the social and political institutions of Japan, a so-called inferior race by most of those People's upon whom the patent of superiority is conferred. The splendid victory of the Japanese has proved the Christian world arrogant; that it is not indispensable for a people to embrace Christianity in order to acquire morality, civilization, and aptitude for progress. . . . Likewise events of the Far East have put forth evidence of the uselessness of interventions, frequent if pernicious, of Europe reforming a people. On the contrary, the more isolated and preserved from contact with European invaders and plunderers a people is, the better is the measure of [its] evolution toward a rational renovation.[12]

Ahmad Rıza's remarks are important not because of their influence but because they show that the Chinese response to Japan's victory over Russia in 1904 was part of a larger global trend that reflected specific intellectual tendencies. These tendencies included a subversion of the categories of inferior or superior race. With this subversion, the ideology associated with the white race, namely Christianity, was also found wanting. To some extent, this attack on Christianity can be traced back to when missionaries first arrived in different parts of Asia; however, by the late nineteenth and early twentieth centuries, intellectuals connected Christianity to imperialism. For example, the civilizing mission was, in part, built on the conviction that the people of non-Western nations needed to learn from the culture of the West and Christianity before they could become free, and so "civilizing" became a rationale for imperialism. Rıza countered this discourse by claiming that Japan had shown that the people of the East had no need for European intervention and also that such intervention was often pernicious. Finally, his text points to the idea that Asia could have a logic of its own that leads to a "rational renovation."

While it would be wrong to say that the Russo-Japanese War caused the questioning of the relationship between Europe and Asia, Japan's victory clearly made pan-Asianism and the critique of Eurocentrism more salient.

58   CHAPTER TWO

Zhang Taiyan and other Chinese intellectuals who went to Japan in the years immediately following the Russo-Japanese War were influenced by the trend of criticizing the West and searching for alternatives in their own tradition.

However, the relationship between Japan, the West, and Asia was by no means simple. First there was the problem of Japanese imperialism, which already existed in its protean forms in the late nineteenth and early twentieth centuries. By the late nineteenth century Japan was already planning to annex Korea and had already seized Taiwan after the Sino-Japanese War. Its relations with China and Korea would only become worse as the twentieth century unfolded. But secondly, what is often overlooked are Japan's relations with Britain, which were extremely problematic from a pan-Asianist perspective. Partly because its relations with Russia were growing tense—both had designs on Manchuria and Korea—in 1902, Japan signed a treaty with Britain in which each would come to the other's aid in the event of an attack. Japan's original plan was to exchange influence in Korea, which it accepted as within Russia's sphere of influence, for a greater role in Manchuria. After the Russo-Japanese War, Japan signed another treaty with Britain stipulating that Japan would recognize Britain's right to rule India in return for Britain's recognition of Japan's territories in Asia. Given the importance of India in the pan-Asian imagination, it is no surprise that this latter treaty led Asian sympathizers to become critical of the Japanese government.

Zhang Taiyan's Pan-Asianism and Critique of Modernity: Rethinking Japan and India

When Zhang Taiyan was released from prison and fled to Tokyo, pan-Asianism was in the midst of a boom following the Russo-Japanese War. This was also a period in which Japanese intellectuals criticized Western modernity from various perspectives. As we have seen in the case of Okakura Tenshin described in chapter 1, by the turn of the twentieth century, Japanese intellectuals had become critical of the deleterious effects of capitalism and began searching for alternatives, both in Asian traditions and in Western socialism. Zhang thrived intellectually in this milieu. In Tokyo he became the editor in chief of the Chinese revolutionary journal *Minbao* (The people's journal). He also engaged with intellectuals from various parts of Asia, including Japan and India. His writings from 1906 to 1911 show that Zhang rethought nationalism in a way that ran counter to progressive temporality, and this merged with his pan-Asianism. During this period from 1906 to the Republican Revolution in 1911, he brought four ideas together: anti-imperialism, nationalism, pan-Asianism, and socialism (or anticapitalism). Zhang made

THE CRITIQUE OF LINEAR TIME

a distinction between radical and imperialist nationalisms, as Rebecca Karl and others have noted.[13] Pan-Asianists tended to connect anti-imperialist nationalism with a postcapitalist future, and the linking of anti-imperialism and socialism was a general characteristic of pan-Asianism until the 1980s, when faith in an alternative to capitalism began to wane.

This early phase of pan-Asianism is of particular interest because it represents a time before a clear idea of socialism was formulated and before the 1917 Russian Revolution, which suddenly made socialism look real and gave it an institutional form. Before this time, socialism was vague and encompassed disparate criticisms of capitalism. Shortly after Zhang came to Japan, he participated in the Socialist Study Group and the Asian Solidarity Society. Both of these were politically oriented meetings in Tokyo where intellectuals from various regions in Asia conglomerated to discuss socialism, imperialism, and the possible modes of resistance. The fact that he participated in both of these groups suggests that he saw a connection between socialism and pan-Asianism, insofar as the former opposed capitalist modernity and the latter, Western modernity. During Zhang's time, questions about capitalism were not posed with the same force as they were by later intellectuals; however, as we will see below, his project implicitly dealt with capitalism.

In *Minbao*, Zhang Taiyan spelled out his views on economic equality and anti-imperialism: "The ideology of this enterprise is as follows: Overthrow all evil governments, Establish a Republic, Maintain world peace, Nationalize land, Unite the Japanese and Chinese people, Ensure that the countries in the world support the Chinese Revolution."[14] Partly because this was written in Japan, it placed the Chinese Revolution in a global context. The first principle calls for the overthrow of unjust governments and the establishment of republics, thus situating China within a global movement, which relates to Zhang's final principle. According to Zhang, people will approve of the Chinese Revolution precisely because it is a movement for a republic. There is, of course, a temporality embedded in this movement from the past to the future, in which more modern republican governments replace the older, evil regimes. Nonetheless, it also makes a small gesture toward pan-Asianism in emphasizing the unity of Japan and China. This could be because the journal was published in Japan, but Zhang and others had previously spoken of the importance of friendship between China and Japan and wider concerns about world peace and recognition by other nations.[15] Finally, the idea of the nationalization of land gives us a sense of how Zhang and other revolutionaries hoped to overcome capitalism. To some extent, we see a resistance to the ordinary temporality of economic development, where feudalism was to be replaced by capitalism. This was a period when Adam Smith and others

60   CHAPTER TWO

were being translated into Chinese, and many Chinese intellectuals, especially pan-Asianists, embraced the idea that China could find a new path by drawing on earlier traditions. A critique of imperialism lies behind this claim because the imperialist powers were seen as mostly trying to re-create Asian nations in their own image. For this reason, the above principles were premised on gaining national independence.

Perhaps the most important political activity related to Zhang's pan-Asianism was his participation in the Asian Solidarity Society, also known as the Society for Asiatic Humanitarian Brotherhood. At meetings of this group at the India House (a collective in Tokyo established in 1907 by the Indian revolutionary students), Zhang exchanged ideas with radical intellectuals from China, Japan, Burma, the Philippines, and Vietnam. The society was established in 1907, the same year that Japan occupied Korea, which might be a reason Koreans refused to participate. The Japanese intellectuals who attended, however, were probably sympathetic to anti-imperialism, and many would eventually become radicals. Among the illustrious leftist Japanese who attended were the founder of Japan's first socialist party (in 1906), Sakai Toshihiko (1871–1933); the anarchist Ōsugi Sakae (1885–1923); and the future founder of the Japanese Communist Party, Yamakawa Hitoshi (1880–1958). It is more than likely that the radicals exposed Zhang to a mixture of anti-imperialist, antistatist, and anticapitalist thought.

Apart from Japan, and at least as important, is the symbolic value that India held. India House hosted a huge number of Indian freedom fighters exiled from India,[16] and it was a transnational institution. By 1910, there were India Houses in London and Vancouver in addition to the one in Tokyo, all of which drew independence movement exiles. The Tokyo India House was part of this larger conglomeration but perhaps operated differently from the collectives elsewhere because it was in Asia and could potentially be a meeting place for Asian radicals.

While they were in Tokyo, Zhang Taiyan and the anarchist Zhang Ji (1882–1947), the founder of *Minbao*, drafted a manifesto of the Asian Solidarity Society:

> Among the Asian countries, India has Buddhism and Hinduism; China has the philosophies of Confucius, Mencius, Lao Zi, Zhuang Zi and Yang Zi; then moving to Persia, it also has enlightened religions, such as Zoroastrianism. The races in this region had self-respect and did not invade one another. The islands in the south are influenced by Indian culture. The people from the Eastern seas are all influenced by Chinese culture. They rarely invaded one another and treated each other respectfully according to the Confucian virtue of humanity. About one hundred years ago, the Europeans moved east and Asia's power diminished day by day. Not only did the people of Asia totally

THE CRITIQUE OF LINEAR TIME   61

lack political and military power, but they also felt inferior. Their scholarship declined and they only strove after their material self-interest. India fell first and then China was lost to the Manchus. The Malaysian islands (including Malaya, Indonesia, and so on) were occupied by the whites. Vietnam and Burma were subsequently swallowed up. The Philippines were first ruled by Spain; it enjoyed independence for a while, but then America annexed it. Only Siam and Persia remain independent. However, they are also in the process of decline.[17]

Although Okakura Tenshin was not a member of the Asian Solidarity Society, he anticipated this style of pan-Asianist thought. Like Okakura, Zhang and his coauthor construct a counter-discourse that opposed the view of history as progress with Europe at the center by invoking the civilizational or cultural unity of Asia. Note that the manifesto identified Asia only in terms of culture, philosophies, and religions. It does not stress any sense of regional unity with respect to trade or other relations. It only states that, in the "Eastern seas," people treated each other with Confucian benevolence and rarely invaded one another. This point echoes Okakura's view that though boundaries separated the "states" (*guo*) of Asia, these states did not invade one another and were relatively peaceful until the arrival of the West. In the above discourse this original utopia became an important part of his temporal narrative of return. In other words, Zhang and his coauthor believe that rather than progression, nationalism was a return to a past before colonization. Thus colonialism appears as a rupture that makes pan-Asianism necessary.

The manifesto explains that about a hundred years earlier, Europeans moved eastward and changed the way Asians thought of themselves. The European invasion affected Asian nations objectively, from a military perspective, but also—perhaps more importantly—subjectively, in that Asians' view of themselves was now mediated by the West, causing Asians to feel inferior. This judgment or feeling is also present in Fukuzawa's and Kang's work. The manifesto describes feeling inferior (*zibei*), which might include feeling sorry for oneself. The source of this feeling is contained partially in the next sentence: "Their scholarship declined and they only strove after their material self-interest." Here we have Okakura's classic opposition between the East, connected with morality and scholarship, and the West as carrier of material and selfish interests. In other words, with the mediation of the West, Asian nations also began to take material wealth as a standard and from this perspective did not measure up to the imperialist countries.

The manifesto criticizes a culture that became dominant in capitalism, namely the pursuit of material interests. Scholars such as Hazama Naoki and Lin Shaoyang claim that Zhang's critique of imperialism did not include

62 CHAPTER TWO

criticism of capitalism,[18] but they reach this conclusion because they define capitalism too narrowly. It is true that Zhang, unlike later Japanese and Chinese intellectuals, did not explicitly use the term "capitalism," but they could not have understood the world of imperialism without taking capitalism into consideration. In fact, Zhang attacks the effects of capitalism without always explicitly identifying them as such.

The manifesto describes a transition from a world where scholarship dominates to one based on self-interest. The beginning of the manifesto in effect defines scholarship as the study of Confucianism, Buddhism, and other religions that were connected to morality and self-respect. But as Western imperialism encroached on Asia, this kind of scholarship declined and was replaced by self-interest. Or, as Marx would say, all holy shrines were washed in the cool waters of egoistic calculation.[19] Although Zhang did not separate capitalism from imperialism and then analyze them or their connections, he did nonetheless describe a shift that took place as capitalism became global through imperialism. His criticisms of capitalism are fewer, but he was conscious of the problems brought by capitalism as he tried to revive tradition. For example, in a speech to Chinese exchange students in Tokyo shortly after he arrived in 1906, Zhang made the following point about the Chinese imperial examination system:

> Because of such a system, even poor people had hopes of becoming officials. Had this not been the case, study to gain official positions would have to have been left exclusively to the rich. The poor would have sunk to the bottom of the sea, and the day when they participated in political power would not come for a long time.... Our present reverence for our own tradition is nothing less than a reverence for our own socialism.[20]

One could of course say that Zhang does not have any conception of capitalism because it is not mentioned here. However, such a conclusion would ignore the significance of Zhang's reevaluation of tradition. By using the term "socialism" (*shehuizhuyi*), Zhang engaged in an unusual type of translingual practice.[21] The term "socialism" takes on new valences when translated as "shehuizhuyi," but more important is the translation that occurs at another level. Zhang translates the Chinese historical experience of the examination system into the political project of socialism. From this perspective, given that socialism was and still is often regarded as a goal toward which one should strive, the Chinese past (traditions, the imperial examination system, and so on) became the future. This is similar to the "back-to-the-future" effect that we saw in Fukuzawa, except that the nature of the past and future have changed. The unsaid present in Zhang's discourse is capitalism, which

THE CRITIQUE OF LINEAR TIME   63

he associated with the West and marked as something to be overcome or avoided through a future that is socialism. He articulated this same point by discussing China and the West earlier in the same speech when dealing with the equitable-field system.

> What China has been particularly superb at, something the countries of the West can absolutely not approach, is the equitable-field [*juntian*] system. This institution conforms to socialism, to say nothing of the well-field [*jingtian*] system of the Three Dynasties of high antiquity. From the Wei and Jin eras through the Tang, the equitable field system was in effect.[22]

Zhang thus legitimates the Chinese nation by elevating the Chinese past. However, the way he does this again gestures toward socialism, and by contrasting the Chinese past with the West, he implies an opposition to capitalism. Part of the reason that the West will not be able to overcome its chronic inequalities is because it has become capitalist. In Zhang's argument, the opposition between China and the West is one between socialism and capitalism. He believed that the mediation of the West enables a reinterpretation of the Chinese past as something that points beyond the present, but that the discourse of imperialism and Eurocentrism blocks this movement to the future and asserts that a move back to an Asian past can only be of the past and never be the harbinger of a different future.

Pan-Asianists, and Zhang in particular, attempted to counter the feeling of inferiority mentioned in the manifesto by opening a space for Asian traditions to be used for the future. This approach aimed to extract Asia from the spatiotemporal matrix that placed it in the past and lay the groundwork for an alternative future. Zhang was concerned with liberating the Chinese past and by extension the Asian past. But such a liberation was inextricably connected to the actual liberation of Asian nations. After all, it was because of Western invasion that the Asian past became a problem in the first place, and if there was not sufficient resistance, Asian nations could disappear. In the second part of the manifesto, he and his coauthor recounted how the nations of Asia had either come under the yoke of colonialism or faced this threat.

The second part of the manifesto addresses a problem formulated by Lenin, namely, "What is to be done?" Part of the answer is that pan-Asianism needed to both stress cultural unity and strategically unite Asian nations to combat imperialism.

> In the past, the thirty-six kingdoms of the Tianshan were invaded by the Tujue and Huihe barbarians; as the result the races of Tianshan were destroyed. It appears that at a later time, China, India, Vietnam, Burma, the Philippines, and other Asian countries will suffer a fate similar to the thirty-six kingdoms

of the Tianshan. Learning from the experience of the Tianshan, we have established the Asian Solidarity Society in order to resist imperialism and protect our nation-states. In the future, we hope to drive away the foreign races and stand mighty. The groups of the Southeast will help each other and form a web of resistance. We must unite the clans and resuscitate old but broken friendships. We must revitalize our Hinduism, Buddhism, Confucianism, and Daoism and develop our compassion in order to squeeze out the evil Western superficial morality. We will lead the sages to avoid being conquered by the whites. We will not engage in separatism, and we shall not bow to form. All of our close friends of several different types have not completely united. First India and China must unite to form an alliance. These two old countries of the East are huge and if they can be fortunate and obtain independence, they will form a shield for the rest of Asia. The remaining dozen neighboring countries can therefore avoid being bullied. All the nations of Asia who support independence, if you want to take this precious step and take an oath to unity, pray that such unity will come to pass.[23]

Zhang draws from the history of China and then calls for India and China to be placed at the center of Asian resistance. He compares the international situation of his time to that of the Qin and Han dynasties and suggests that the Western invasion of Asia is similar to the barbarian invasion of the thirty-six kingdoms of the Tianshan. This parallel has important theoretical ramifications because it showed that what was happening in his contemporary world was not new. Rather, contemporary international relations were a strange repetition of Chinese history. Kang Youwei had already made a similar analogy between the Chinese past and the late Qing present. Like Kang, Zhang hoped to resist a full repetition, since the first time the barbarians invaded, they transformed society. However, while Kang aimed for unity, Zhang promoted diversity. Zhang lamented that after the barbarian invasion, the variety of races decreased, and the lands of Tianshan were unified. Zhang feared that this would happen again in contemporary Asian states, such as Burma, India, and China. The West would, in his view, annihilate the cultural plurality of Asia by force.

Zhang describes an Asia that was united because each of its individual states had become an object of invasion; however, as a way of resisting, he calls for the Asian states to become self-conscious of their cultural unity and push back against European expansionism. He affirmed the diverse races of Asia but aimed to unite the races at a higher level toward a common cause, namely mutual independence. Part of the strategy here, as noted earlier, is to return to earlier teachings and religions to combat egoism. The war for Asia must be fought simultaneously on the levels of culture and the military.

Moral ideology is of course imbricated in the military battle because it allows a type of transcendence that allows for justification of the battle. The manifesto states that one should not bow to form, which stresses the imperialists' craving for material goods. The teachings of Confucianism, Hinduism, and Buddhism, among others, emphasize the importance of transcending materialism, which can ensure that pan-Asianists are not seduced by the lure of the West, which was connected to the spread of capitalism.

In the process of articulating a plan for Asian resistance, Zhang placed India and China at its center. In the first section of the manifesto, Zhang emphasized that from a civilizational perspective, Chinese culture and Indian culture influenced the countries in the east and the south, respectively. He also provided a geographical reason for placing China and India at the center, namely that they were the largest countries in Asia and hence could protect the rest of the region.

Zhang's emphasis on a relationship between India and China represented a shift from a previous discourse on Asia that placed Japan at the center. After the Sino-Japanese War, a number of Chinese intellectuals, including Zhang Taiyan, called for China to adopt the Japanese model and unite with Japan, and in an essay written in 1897, Zhang explicitly advocates unity with Japan.[24] Late Qing intellectuals thought of Japan as an example of successful modernization and as an Asian nation that had become strong by following the Western path. But by invoking India in the manifesto, Zhang proposes an alternative civilizational discourse, which took the West not as a standard of progress but as an example of evil. In Zhang's thought, this ideological shift arose from his increasing interest in Buddhism and Daoism.[25]

Throughout the manifesto, Zhang uses Buddhist terms to point to differences between Asia and the West. For example, he uses the Buddhist term *zhantuoruo* (*cendala*), or evil, to describe Western morality. In his "Interpretation of the Equalization of Things," an essay published in 1910, Zhang discusses the relationship between what he called false morality and imperialism. He thus takes a transnational (and also transhuman) perspective first, then he advocates a form of Asian nationalism and emphasizes the importance of China uniting with India.

Strictly speaking, Zhang's theoretical presuppositions lead to the conclusion that there should be no nation-states and no distinction between the civilized and the barbarian.[26] However, as we have seen in the manifesto of the Asian Solidarity Society, he accepts striving for national independence as a primary goal and then reinscribes a distinction between civilizations. Instead of separating the civilized from the barbarian, he uses Buddhist terms to separate the culture of the sages from the culture of the evildoers. This is a compromise at work, since Zhang claims that though nation-states are insignificant and even illusory from a universal perspective, due to the realities of the international state system, China must strive to develop into an independent nation-state. Moreover, in order to achieve total independence, Asian states must unite. We might call this Zhang's strategic nationalism—a nationalism that aims to go beyond itself and institute a postnational world.

Zhang published several essays combining Buddhism, Daoism, and politics. In these essays he dealt with the contradiction between the transcendental perspective (in which the state should not exist) and his view of the importance of creating a strong state. In short, Zhang asserts the importance of the nation-state by separating historical from rational necessity: "The tools of modernity were made out of historical necessity not because of a rational necessity."[27] In some sense, Zhang stands directly opposed to Hegel, who believed that the state had religious significance and was ultimately rational—it was logically necessary. Zhang argues that although the nation has no absolute existence, given the historical circumstances of imperialism, the state is still important when it comes to defending against external threats. However, Zhang did not think that the state had eternal significance but rather saw it as being necessary at the current historical juncture.

Zhang's Geopolitical Vision of Nation and Unity with India

Zhang's discussion of Asia must be understood in the context of the relationship between the nation as history and the state as spatial boundaries and institutions for protecting territory. In his provocative essay "On the Five Negations" (1907), Zhang again notes the differences among different types of nationalism and the difference between nationalism and statism (*guojiazhuyi*): "These people hold on to something narrow, and only a narrow nationalism can achieve their ends. Their desire is for something broad and they do not separate in terms of races, but in terms of states. Nationalism follows feeling, but statism does not."[28] This Daoist perspective tends to transcend the nation-state; however, as we have seen, this ideal had to be compromised in a world of nation-states. In "On the Five Negations," Zhang laid out a path from a world of nation-states to a world without them. He began by identifying two types of nationalisms:

> As long as people establish nation-states, we must hold to nationalism. But there are more broad nationalisms. We uphold a nationalism that is not limited to the Han race. If we have enough power, we must also help other weak nations, nations that have been conquered by other nations, whose governments

have been stolen and made into slaves. Alas, India and Burma were destroyed by Britain. Vietnam was destroyed by France. The wise and benevolent races will be eliminated. Our nation must counter this trend. Except for our nation, which wise and ancient state allows its people to be enslaved? If we want a complete nationalism, we must extend our hearts to help people suffering from the same ailment, and make their land totally independent.[29]

Zhang goes on to explain that the imperialists used advanced technology to expand their borders and imposed harsh laws on their colonies. At the highest level of abstraction, he understands all regional boundaries as having no natural validity. However, given the reality of the nation-state system, he affirms that states must protect themselves. Within this system of states, Zhang separates imperialist from imperialized regions, with Asia representing a conglomeration of countries that confronted imperialism.

He emphasized the Asian/Western divide as he moved from a general theory of the state to a theory of the relationship between temporality and patriotism. In 1907, he wrote two important essays on Indian nationalism, both of which deal with temporality and nationalism. The first concerned the Indian "national essence" movement, and another dealt with Shivaji (1627–1680), a Maratha leader who revived Hindu traditions to resist the Moghul rulers. Inspired by these movements, Zhang and other revolutionaries embarked on building a national essence movement in China, which called for reviving the past to combat imperialism, which they saw as being embodied in the Manchus and the West, respectively.[30] The national essence movement was a classic back-to-the-future gesture, since proponents drew on past traditions (the national essence of China) to envision a future beyond imperialism. We can also understand Zhang's arguments about socialism described above as expressing the basic structure of national essence ideology, since he contends that the Chinese can achieve socialism by returning to their traditions.

In his essay "The National Essence Movement in India," Zhang transposes the above notion of a national essence from the Chinese to the Indian context. He emphasizes temporality and claims that "what separates humans from animals is that humans have the idea of the past."[31] Zhang argues that love and desire are strongest when focused on either the past or the future rather than the present. "This is because human consciousness moves in and out of existence like a long continuous flowing stream; it can recollect the past and long for the future. Since all things come into the realm of consciousness and conform to its rules, we express love not for what we have at present, but for that which is absent, in the past or future. In the same way, patriotism involves loving a country's history."[32] However, this love for the past leads to two

68 CHAPTER TWO

different types of action when linked to the future. In Zhang's view, although strong countries may use discourses to glorify their actions, patriotism and emphasis on national essence leads to imperialism. Hence he concludes that it is appropriate to criticize their patriotism. However, he argued that Asian countries were not like this. He asserts that countries such as China, India, and Korea "had only been trampled on by other countries and only want to get back what was originally theirs."[33]

Partly through the Asian Solidarity Society, Zhang came into contact with Indian freedom fighters in exile in Japan. One of the best testaments to Zhang's support for an India-China alliance during this time are his essays on Indian nationalism and on the Indian commemoration of Shivaji. In his essay on the Indian national essence movement, Zhang asserted that while a national essence movement may have negative consequences for Western countries, such movements were essential for countries such as China and India.[34] He noted that just as bullies will dominate a person who is not self-aware, some nations will bully other nations that are not self-aware.[35] In Zhang's view, a nation's self-awareness was intimately linked to recognizing its national essence and history; therefore, rejecting national essence would eventually weaken national self-awareness and invite invasion by other nations and races.

In Zhang's essay on Indian commemoration of Shivaji, Zhang begins by mentioning the two Indians who organized the event:

> Mr. Ben Luohan had come to Japan from the United States, and he visited me at the *Minbao* editorial offices. He said: "The treatment meted out to Indians by the British government was far worse than that of the Mogul dynasty of earlier times. Those who set their minds on learning have been unable to study politics and law, and, even if they go overseas to pursue their studies, they still feel under a strict prohibition in this area." . . . He granted this interview with the interpreting help of his friend Mr. Bao Shen, who speaks Japanese quite well.[36]

For a long time we were not sure who these two Indian freedom fighters were, but Lin Shaoyang has recently pointed out that one of them was Surendra Mohan Bose,[37] a founder of the Hindusthan Association of USA with his fellow freedom fighter Taraknath Das (1884–1948), who was a supporter of Japanese pan-Asianism.

Zhang's main reason for writing about the meeting was to argue that China should distance itself from Japan and ally with India. This was different from Taraknath Das's argument that India, Japan, and China must all unite. Zhang continued his earlier argument for China and India uniting

THE CRITIQUE OF LINEAR TIME   69

but explicitly argued against including Japan. In his essay "Indians in Japan" (1908), he provides another interpretation of the Russo-Japanese War:

> Since the Russo-Japanese War, the Japanese have become extremely proud and believe that they are the great dragons of the East! . . . They see India already gone, they defeated China in a war and they annexed Korea without a fight. They are extremely proud of this . . .
>
> All the Japanese who were previously ethical now believe this . . .
>
> Before Japan rose, although there were minor skirmishes in Asia, it was relatively peaceful. Now it is the opposite.[38]

Thus, although the Russo-Japanese War encouraged Asian intellectuals to promote pan-Asianism and create groups such as the Asian Solidarity Society, by 1907 Zhang was increasingly turning away from Japan. This was again a result of Japanese support for British imperialism. After narrating how the Japanese politician Ōkuma Shigenobu (1838–1922) praised the British rule of India, he notes the problems of imperialism and racism, which he connects to the development of civilization.

To counter Ōkuma, Zhang argued that evolution is two-sided. Using Buddhist concepts, he contended that as society evolves, good and bad increase in tandem, and consequently society becomes more brutal.[39] In his account of the commemoration for Shivaji, he writes: "We should know that the more civilization advances, the more it tramples humanity under foot. It has already taken our children and destroyed our homes. . . . Generally speaking, civilized countries clog up people's eyes and ears with false morality. The French treat the Vietnamese people like domesticated animals; the British treat the Indians like beggars."[40] With this criticism of the British, he attacked not only Ōkuma but also the larger trend toward evolutionary thinking, which we have seen in Fukuzawa and Kang Youwei. He also contested Ōkuma's comparison of India to colonies in the Global North, such as America and Australia. By pointing out the difference between India and these places, Zhang highlights the unevenness and also racial distinctions found in imperialism.

> Autonomy in Australia was given primarily to the British, not to the native population. Autonomy in Canada was given to Britons and other Caucasians, not to the native population. Even if the British government were to grant India independence, this blessing would be bestowed only on white men. . . . Take the American black man, who, although he possesses the franchise in name, is in fact not the equal of other citizens. He cannot escape being lynched and burned at the stake. . . . Do you think the Kingdom of Great Britain will make common cause with the Indian people?[41]

Zhang points here to a dimension of pan-Asianism that goes beyond the struggle against imperialism in Asia and moves toward advocating the universal liberation of oppressed peoples, including aboriginals and Native Americans. These are precisely the people who have been trampled on by capitalist imperialism and who are then forgotten.

Moreover, Zhang discusses the resistance of Indians and points in the direction of a critique of capitalism that will be continued by later thinkers:

> Indians have been thinking about Independence for almost four or five years. . . . Their strategies start from organizing strikes and boycotting products. Those who strike agree that they will not be employed by the British. . . . Those who boycott products agree not to buy British products. When the first village engaged in such a boycott, the British fined the villagers, but another village helped them pay the fine, so they suffered no loss.[42]

By invoking strikes and boycotts, Zhang clearly shows frustrating capitalist production and consumption to be part of the program of anti-imperialism. He notes that rather than waiting for the generosity of the British, the Indian people relied on themselves and resisted British imperialism by refusing to participate in its capitalist ventures. This is not yet a Marxist position that refuses both foreign and national capital, but Zhang would gesture toward such a position in other essays, where he stressed equality.

Li Dazhao's Theory of New Pan-Asianism

Zhang Taiyan was a propagandist of the 1911 Revolution, which aimed to transform China from an empire into a republic, and though this transition proved to be unattainable, it provided the backdrop for numerous struggles over ideology. In particular, by around 1915 and especially by 1919, intellectuals became critical of Chinese traditions and increasingly advocated learning from the West. This was a complicated era because the failure of the 1911 Revolution to achieve its goals suggested that political reform in itself was insufficient, and consequently intellectuals believed that the problem lay in Chinese culture, which was as yet unsuited for Western institutions such as democracy. But on the other hand, World War I revealed that Western civilization also had problems. In this new context, some of the early contradictions between East and West discussed earlier in this chapter and in the preceding chapter were reconstituted in a new discursive and political framework. To some extent, the antinomy between East and West can be seen in the two founders of the Chinese Communist Party: Chen Duxiu (1879–1942) and Li Dazhao.

In 1915, in the first issue of the progressive journal *New Youth*, Chen boldly claimed that all Chinese culture up to that point was a legacy of feudalism (*fengjian*):

> Our existing morality, law, scholarship, and customs are all remnants of the feudal system [*fengjian zhidu zhi yi*]. If we compare our race's conduct with that of people from other countries, we will find that our thought is far beneath them. If we just respect the thought of the four imperial courts and do not plan to improve, then what else can one say but that our people will be chased out of the twentieth century into the realm of slaves and animals.[43]

This sentiment echoes that of Fukuzawa described in the preceding chapter and shows a common concern about imperialism and a loss of faith in Asian unity or the power of Asian traditions to combat imperialism. This was of course due in part to the failure of the Republican Revolution and collapse of the dynastic system. Against this background, although Li Dazhao was more sympathetic to pan-Asianism, he was overly enamored with Chinese traditions. For the most part, his arguments for pan-Asianism revolved around geopolitics. In 1917, Li, like the early Zhang Taiyan, developed a theory of pan-Asianism with China at the center and Japan possibly playing a role.

In 1917, Asian intellectuals, like so many others, were closely watching the Russian Revolution. Occurring near the end of World War I, for some, the Russian Revolution represented an internal critique of the West and had the potential to push Russia back into Asia. We see here again that Asia was considered not simply a geographical entity but a normative concept. Thus, whereas Japan might lose its Asian status, Russia might regain it. Shortly after the February Revolution in Russia, Li wrote an essay introducing the revolution to Chinese readers. He urged readers to see the Russian Revolution not as an isolated phenomenon but as part of a series of revolutions—in Portugal and Mexico—and also in movements burgeoning in India and Turkey.[44] Clearly, Li connected revolution and independence movements, which already shows the seeds of a key component of pan-Asianism, namely the coupling of revolution and national independence. At this point Li was not quite thinking of socialism, but he did recognize the radical antiauthoritarian nature of the Russian Revolution. He also pointed to the revolution's economic origins, noting the plight of the peasants and the lack of bread that might push it in a socialist direction.

About a month later, Li published "Great Pan-Asianism," an essay on the theme of political alliance and resistance in East Asia. The essay was written after he read the article "What Is Great Pan-Asianism?" published by Wakamiya Unosuke (1872–1938) in the widely read Japanese journal *Chūō kōron*

(Central debates).[45] In this essay, Li argues from a cultural perspective that a "Great pan-Asianism" must be developed to counter Occidentalism. He follows Wakamiya's article in affirming that the spirit of Western civilization involves promoting capitalist oppression domestically and taking people's land through imperialism internationally.[46]

However, he also notes that Japan has been serving British imperialism, and he places China at the center of Asia:

> Our people believe that without China there can be no Asia; if the people of our country cannot be independent, Asia cannot establish itself in front of the world. Luckily there is a country that has boldly established itself as a leader of Asia. . . . Therefore, if we talk about Great pan-Asianism, we must take recreating the Chinese state and revitalizing the Chinese nation as key points.[47]

Li claimed that if the Japanese really wanted to create a pan-Asianism, they must first recognize that China is Asia's tower of strength. However, he argued that re-creating the Chinese nation was not merely a question of building its strength but rather that China must be re-created in order to find an Asia within. Here Li brings us back to Kang Youwei's vision of rethinking empire. In an earlier essay, "New Chinese Republican Nationalism," also published in 1917, Li writes:

> Our country has the longest of histories and has gathered numerous nationalities which have amalgamated into this Chinese nation. Paying no heed to borders, the bloodlines have long died out. This has created the lofty and extensive spirit of our nation. There are those who regret that in the early days of the establishment of the republic, there were proclaimed to be five nations. As far as I am concerned, the culture of the five nations has long since been molded into one under a free and equal republican system. In the past, what were known as Manchus, Han, Mongols, Hui, Tibetans, and even Miao and Yao, were names of fragments left over from history. Today the boundaries have long disappeared and all of these groups are native peoples of the Republic of China. They are all part of the new Chinese nation. Therefore, from this day the republic's political and education institutions should be aimed at establishing the spirit of the nation and the thinking of a unified nation. The ideology behind this is the new Chinese nationalism. There must be this new Chinese nationalism before carrying the movement on to East Asia. And only then can Great pan-Asianism find glory in the world. Otherwise, it is merely an illusion or some rambling in our dreams. Take note! Concerning the fate of the nation, we all have our responsibilities. As the Western wave crashes down upon us, the youth of the new Chinese nation must push on and leap forward, bearing this great responsibility.[48]

THE CRITIQUE OF LINEAR TIME   73

Li's argument cuts in two directions. He clearly implies the importance of moving toward an independent nation-state. However, one of the characteristics of the Chinese nation is precisely that it incorporates other nations and therefore represents something larger. In chapter 6, we shall see that the contemporary social critic Wang Hui has developed this theme in relation to his idea of empire. Li Dazhao notes that with the rise of nationalism, numerous pan-movements, such as pan-Germanism, pan-Slavism, and the Monroe doctrine, emerged.[49] In all of these cases, the nation was an alliance that reaches beyond the boundaries of the nation-state. China as a nation symbolized this overcoming of boundaries.

In Li's view, Chinese had to discover Asia in China. Moreover, he asserts that other Asian nations recognized that China is an essential component of Asia and claims that mainland China actually includes the Asian continent and that all the nationalities and civilizations in Asia have connections to China.[50] Such claims about identity are historical conditions and therefore, as discussed in the preceding chapter, refer to something akin to Hegel's idea of substantiality. This is the basic framework of Li's idea of Asia and also the Chinese nation, which he believed provided a way forward for political practice.

Part of Li's political strategy is not only to shift narratives of the Chinese nation away from race and consequently toward opposition to the revolutionary ideology of the late Qing but also to develop a cultural narrative that he thought could become the foundation for resistance to Western imperialism. He believed that what defines the Chinese spirit is the negation of national identities, such that when this new nation faces foreign powers, it can seamlessly unite with other nations in Asia and protect morality and peace, resulting in a "Great pan-Asianism" and the creation of a new civilization. Li refers to East Asia, but given that he also speaks of Mongols, Manchus, and Tibetans, Li shows that he is thinking of China in Asia more broadly. To some extent, he anticipates contemporary *tianxia* scholars, such as Zhao Tingyang (b. 1961), who envision a future world system of cooperation and harmony, free of hegemony. These scholars argue that one of the main characteristics of Chinese culture is that it tolerates and absorbs other cultures, thereby offering the potential for a new universalist world order.[51]

Li does not go as far as Zhao and contend that the future world order should be Confucian. Rather, he argues that the new Chinese nation might initiate transformations that could pave the way for a new world based on equality, liberation, and cooperation—a humanistic world.

> We hope our nation and state are not oppressed by others . . . and express our benevolent spirit to guide our neighboring brother countries so that they can

74   CHAPTER TWO

all become independent and self-governing countries, without being bullied
by others and escape from other's control. If this is the content of Great pan-
Asianism, then we want to work hard for it [knowing that] it causes no harm
to world humanism.[52]

As we have seen, Li was concerned about Japan's role in promoting pan-
Asianism and noted that pan-Asianist rhetoric could serve as a tool of imperialism. By 1919, the changes in global geopolitics probably contributed to
Li's concern about this as his evaluation of Japan became increasingly negative after World War I and the 1919 Treaty of Versailles, which granted Japan
the former German concession in Shandong. This slap to the face of China
caused outrage across the country, as the Chinese had joined the Allies and
declared war on Germany in 1917. A couple of months before the May Fourth
movement, where students protested the Japanese occupation of concessions
in Shandong, Li asserted that Japan's idea of pan-Asianism was really a front
for Great Japanism. This "pan-Asianism," Li declared, will "not only harm
Japan, but can harm all Asian nations and harm world peace."[53]

After he turned against Great Asianism, Li began to promote what he
termed "New Asianism" and in so doing presciently grasped a historical
trend. "If we look at the large historical trajectories, the American continent
must become the United States, and Europe also must become a union of
European states. We Asians should also become a similar type of organization. This will be the basis for a global alliance."[54] By this time Li already had
accepted elements of Marxist cosmopolitanism and hence argued that the
true goal of pan-Asianism is the liberation of all countries. In line with his
remarks above about nationalism, Li asserted that pan-Asianism must "take
national liberation as its foundation. . . . All Asian nations that have been occupied should be liberated and attain national self-determination and form
a three-part alliance with Europe and America in order to establish a federa-
tion to promote the prosperity of humanity."[55] When asked why he did not
immediately call for world unity, he explained that given the world situation,
it is necessary to begin with small associations in order to prepare for larger
ones. He also stated that "new Pan-Asianism is primarily to combat Japanese
Great Asianism and not because we are afraid that Euro-American forces will
oppress Asian nations. . . . The weaker countries of Asia must unite and de-
stroy Great Asianism."[56] Li hoped that someday all of Asia's peoples would
unite and enter a world organization, if such an organization ever came into
existence.[57] At this point, Li made little mention of the greatness of China and
Asian culture; in Li's view, Asia was defined geopolitically and connected to
the realization of universal principles. A couple of years after Li published

THE CRITIQUE OF LINEAR TIME   75

these essays, Sun Yat-sen, the first leader of the Chinese Republic, drew on classical philosophies to construct universal principles that would ground the idea of Asia.

Sun Yat-sen's Pan-Asianism

Sun Yat-sen, the leader of the first Chinese Republic and the Republican Revolution of 1911, brought together several different strands of pan-Asianism. Given Sun's position as a national leader, much has been written about his politics and pan-Asianism. In particular, scholars have pointed out that from the beginning Sun had been influenced by Japanese visions of Asia and indeed had many Japanese supporters. These included the prominent Japanese progressives and conservatives Miyazaki Tōten (1877–1922), Tōyama Mitsuru (1855–1944), and Inukai Tsuyoshi (1855–1932). All of them, despite their political differences, supported pan-Asianism and assisted Chinese revolutionaries.[58] I will focus on Sun's well-known statements about pan-Asianism here because they encapsulate major themes in the history of pan-Asianism and will pave the way for the chapters that follow.

About thirteen years after the Republican Revolution and amid the complex political situation both within and outside China, Sun went to Japan in 1924 and spoke on pan-Asianism at the Kobe Prefectural Girls School. Sun's brief lecture provided the basis for both left- and right-wing pan-Asianism and had a significant impact in Japan and some of its thinkers. In the next three chapters we will examine the work of Ōkawa Shūmei and Takeuchi Yoshimi, who pursued ideas related to Sun's pan-Asianism. Ōkawa directly connected pan-Asianism to World War II propaganda, while during the postwar period, Takeuchi drew on Sun to point to the Chinese alternative to imperialism.

In his lecture, Sun continued a basic theme seen in the manifesto of the Asian Solidarity Society, especially the drawing on Asian traditions for a normative framework and then briefly narrating history from that perspective. This brings us back to the problem of the grounds for community, with negativity or the power to change the world as a type of untheorized presupposition. Put simply, Sun's lecture was an attempt to argue from a quasi-Confucian perspective for an assertion of Asian ethics against imperialist power. Here again we see the notion of Asia as something more than mere geography; it points toward a new normativity loosely connected to Asian forms of thought and, in Sun's case, Chinese thought.

The lecture begins by reconceptualizing the world and history with Asia at the center:

The origins of the various civilizations of the modern world can be traced back to Asia's ancient civilizations. It is only during the last few centuries that the countries and races of Asia have gradually degenerated and become weak, while the European countries have gradually developed their resources and become powerful. After the latter had fully developed their strength, they turned their attention to, and penetrated into, East Asia, where they either destroyed or pressed hard upon every one of the Asiatic nations, so that thirty years ago there existed, so to speak, no independent country in the whole of Asia.[59]

With this Sun echoed Zhang's manifesto and traced the course of history after what Kenneth Pomeranz has called the "great divergence,"[60] the point where Europe alone industrialized and became increasingly imperialist. By asserting that the origins of the various civilizations can be traced to Asia, however, he imbues the Asian past with a certain moral legitimacy, a primitive normativity, or a normativity grounded in an ancient past that one cannot directly experience. Sun invokes this past to legitimate the struggles of Asian nations as they unfolded in the twentieth century.

Sun believed that Japan was crucial in the project of resisting Western domination, but the role of Russia in Sun's lecture is especially worth noting. While Sun wrote this lecture largely to urge the Japanese to protest against Japanese imperialism in Asia, he made Russia a symbol of the nongeographical nature of Asia. At first, his lecture follows the ideas of many intellectuals by pointing out how Japan's victory in the Russo-Japanese War brought hope to Asian intellectuals and uses this victory to argue that the legitimacy of the pan-Asian project lay in Confucian concepts. Finally, he shows how this new normative standard could make it possible for Russia to return to Asia. Sun begins his argument by affirming Japan's victory over Russia:

> Since the day of Japan's victory over Russia, the peoples of Asia have cherished the hope of shaking off the yoke of European oppression, a hope which has given rise to a series of independence movements—in Egypt, Persia, Turkey, Afghanistan, and finally in India. From the inception of this hope to the present day only 20 years have elapsed. The Egyptian, Turkish, Persian, Afghan, and Arabian independence movements have already materialized, and even the independence movement in India has, with the passage of time, been gaining ground. Such facts are concrete proofs of the progress of the nationalist idea in Asia. Until this idea reaches its full maturity, no unification or independence movement of the Asiatic peoples as a whole is possible.[61]

Echoing the remarks of Ahmad Rıza, Sun notes that Japan's victory in the Russo-Japanese War has inspired movements for national independence in

THE CRITIQUE OF LINEAR TIME   77

other parts of Asia. He develops his argument through a discussion of geopolitical regions, color/race, and ethical principles. Specifically, he emphasizes that responses to the Russo-Japanese War differed depending on whether one was white or Asian. In general, the whites, such as the British, were fearful that a larger anti-imperialist movement might emerge. Sun even declares that " 'Blood' after all 'is thicker than water.' "[62] But then he goes on to explain the normative ground of imperialism and describes Asian resistance in terms of ancient Chinese concepts of might and right: "Recently, this cult of force has been repeatedly employed by the Western peoples to oppress Asia, and as a consequence, there is no progress in Asia. To oppress others with the cult of force, in the language of the Ancients, is the way of hegemon or the rule of might. Therefore, European civilization is nothing but the way of hegemon." The way of the hegemon is rule by force, which is why some commentators translate the term as the "rule of might." Sun sees this as a characteristic of imperialism. The kingly way traditionally referred to rule by ritual, whereby rulers harmoniously governed the kingdom and observed rituals aimed at ensuring its peace and stability. The rule of might has always been looked down upon in Asia since "civilization makes people respect, not fear it. Such a civilization is, in the language of the Ancients, the kingly way."[63]

Like Okakura Tenshin, Sun described a world in which the West represented material civilization, while Asia represented ethical civilization. He reread global politics through Confucianism, thus provincializing Europe. From this perspective, modern Western politics, especially in the international arena, was analogous to the rule of right or the way of the hegemon (*badao*) in ancient China. It is as though the Western imperialist nations had re-created the situation in ancient China but now with the hegemon emerging victorious. Sun found a historical alternative to this way of the hegemon or the rule of might in the tribute system. His key point with respect to the tribute system is that it did not require submission to force; rather, tributary states "sent annual tribute to China of their own will."[64] The tribute system thus showed the ability of right to nonviolently change people's views and win their support. Sun noted that such conversion experiences were happening all around the world, including in the West, where people were turning to Asian philosophy.[65] They were turning to precisely the power of right over might—the supremacy of the kingly way over the way of the hegemon.

Sun then calls for a return to the ethical norms of Asian civilization and advocates pan-Asianism. "Only by unification of all peoples in Asia on the foundation of benevolence and virtue can they become strong and powerful."[66] Given that the survival of the kingly way is threatened by a world in

78 CHAPTER TWO

which the way of the hegemon prevails, Asian nations also must become powerful, but they must do so only to defend themselves.

Sun notes that Japan has already gone a long way toward contesting the military might of the West and now faces a choice.

> Japan today has become acquainted with the Western civilization of the way of the hegemon, but retains the characteristics of the Oriental civilization of the rule of the kingly way. Now the question remains whether Japan will be the hawk of the Western civilization of the way of the hegemon, or the tower of strength of the Orient. This is the choice which lies before the people of Japan.[67]

This passage is self-explanatory and follows naturally from Sun's argument. Unlike Li Dazhao, Sun holds out hope that Japan might change and abandon imperialism, opting instead for the fundamentally normative and moral Asian way.

Sun went on to connect pan-Asianism to socialism and, despite his comments about race, argued that moral principles could rewrite geography.

> At present, Russia is attempting to separate from the White peoples of Europe. Why? Because she insists on the kingly way and denounces the way of the hegemon. She advocates the principle of benevolence and justice, and refuses to accept the principles of utilitarianism and force. She maintains the kingly way and opposes the oppression of the majority by the minority. From this point of view, recent Russian civilization is similar to that of our ancient civilization. Therefore, she joins with the Orient and separates from the West. The new principles of Russia were considered as intolerable by Europeans.[68]

Just like the people in the imperialist nations who are turning to Asian principles of right, now a whole nation is turning. Given that Sun made these comments roughly seven years after the October Revolution, he can be interpreted as saying that being politically left embodies the kingly way. In other words, the contemporary instantiation of the kingly way appears most clearly in a socialist nation. This is a deeper expression of the anticapitalist ideas found in Zhang Taiyan's own formulation of pan-Asianism and its connections to Chinese culture.

Conclusion

The emergence of pan-Asianist thought in China paralleled that found in Japan and features some common themes. We see in both cases an interaction between the values found in community—or substantiality and subjectivity— and the human capacity to change the world. Early twentieth-century Chinese discourse featured some of the same themes that animated the work of Fukuzawa Yukichi, such as the idea that the West is a culture of motion while Asian or Eastern culture is static. Again, as in the Japanese case, Chinese pan-Asianists such as Zhang Taiyan constructed Asia as an alternative moral geography. Like Okakura Tenshin, Chinese pan-Asianists stressed communal values as a basis for creating a better world. This discourse was not so much about rejecting a Hegelian perspective as an attempt to rearticulate the relationship between substantiality and subjectivity from the perspective of downtrodden nations. Chinese pan-Asianists constantly faced both the possibility of social revolution and the threat of Japanese imperialism. And, as we have seen in the work of Sun Yat-sen, for some intellectuals pan-Asianism became intimately connected with socialism.

At the same time, Chinese writers from Zhang Taiyan to Sun Yat-sen constantly warned that Japan might use pan-Asianism to support imperialism. In the next chapter, we will return to Japan to examine how the Japanese pan-Asianist Ōkawa Shūmei took up some of these themes of pan-Asianism but rejected tradition, including Confucianism, in favor of Japanese militarism. He did so, however, by arguing against capitalism. Japan during Ōkawa's time represented Sun's nightmare because it became imperialist and used many tropes found in Sun's thought to legitimize aggression.

3

Asia as Anticapitalist Utopia:
Ōkawa Shūmei's Critique of Political Modernity

Pan-Asianism constituted a mixture of geographical and philosophical ideas seeking to become practice. Okakura Tenshin, Zhang Taiyan, and others developed plans for pan-Asianist resistance to imperialism, but none were ever institutionalized. They believed that one could be both radical and relevant, but despite their activism and involvement in revolutions, pan-Asianists such as Zhang Taiyan and even Sun Yat-sen could not put pan-Asianism into practice. They gave talks and published essays and tracts, and Zhang was part of an Asian solidarity society, but these remained removed from actual policy-making and also from the popular media. Ōkawa Shūmei was perhaps the only figure in this book who translated his political ideas directly into political practice, but he did so by supporting fascism and imperialism, the latter of which was explicitly what the pan-Asianism movement was supposed to resist. Ōkawa thus represents a dialectical tragedy, where anti-imperialism turns into its opposite. This would haunt the history of pan-Asianism from the postwar period to the present. We will see in chapter 5 how Takeuchi Yoshimi attempted to rescue the project of pan-Asianism after Japan's catastrophic experiences in World War II.

Ōkawa's work showed the danger of pan-Asian thinking and how it could be at once progressive and reactionary. The reactionary dimension of pan-Asianism emerged partly from the desire to be both radical and relevant. For this reason, we will return to the Russo-Japanese War, focusing this time on the Japanese context and outlining the various reactions of radicals to this crucial event. We have already pointed out how the Russo-Japanese War was heralded in Asia as a victory for the East, though some critics advocated a cosmopolitan alternative to the nationalism that the Japanese victory might spawn. Ōkawa chose a nationalist path, perhaps because anticolonialism appeared to entail nationalism. This chapter deals with both the cosmopolitan and nationalist responses because Ōkawa himself went from the former to the latter. This tension can also be found in the thinking of two intellectuals who visited Japan as Ōkawa was developing his ideas, namely the Russian anarchist Vasili Eroshenko (1890–1952) and the Indian pan-Asianist Rash Behari Bose (1886–1945). Both were given shelter in the Nakamuraya, a sweetshop in Tokyo, which, as discussed later in the chapter, became a hub of radical activities.

Ōkawa brought transnational and nationalist elements together to launch a critique of modernity from the standpoint of an organic vision of the Japanese state. Drawing on Harry Harootunian's felicitous phrase, this chapter shows how Ōkawa and his cohort were "overcome by modernity" as they attacked and attempted to transcend capitalist modernity while producing an oppressive variant of it.[1] Ōkawa, like Okakura Tenshin, emphasized substantial community against the abstract and hollow individuality of modern capitalist society, but his discourse ended up being incorporated by the state during a time of a global trend toward centralized capitalist development. During the 1930s and 1940s, many states turned toward state-centered capitalist development based on various ideological justifications, be they socialist, liberal welfare, or fascist. From this perspective, Ōkawa's being overcome by modernity is also a case of backing into a future that he did not completely understand.[2] His project to overcome capitalism and imperialism fed into new global configurations of capitalism, which would continue after World War II.

But merely stating that the road to imperialism was paved with good intentions fails to adequately account for the complexities of this story. Ōkawa's work points to a number of impasses in critical discourse that continue to haunt our world today. The first is the separation of the Marxist critique from a critique of modernity or European domination. In many Japanese and Asian Marxist formulations, Asian societies were depicted as backward. Consequently, the path forward ends up being one that stresses rejecting tradition. By the 1920s and 1930s, it was thus the right that both defended Asian traditions and vocally resisted imperialist and capitalist modernization. The rise of theories such as postcolonialism have responded to a similar problem in recent decades, which is why pan-Asianism anticipates postcolonial critiques of Eurocentrism. Ōkawa's thought serves as both an expression of the anti-Eurocentrism that continued throughout the twentieth century and a warning about the pitfalls of such a position. Either side of the antinomy between the affirmation and rejection of tradition provided space for the emergence of imperialism and fascism. Moreover, neither side was what it claimed

82   CHAPTER THREE

to be. If the modernizers advocated a fictitiously pristine break from the past, Ōkawa's celebration of tradition was always already mediated by the West and capitalist modernity.

This chapter outlines the genesis of Ōkawa's thought, showing how he moved from being a scholar of the classics to a politically engaged pan-Asianist, partly as a result of his cosmopolitan and anarchist background. The following narrative proceeds thematically rather than chronologically. Its purpose is to give the reader a sense of the political project of Ōkawa's pan-Asianism.

His interpretation of Confucianism, which he outlined in a lecture in 1928, reveals key elements of this thought.[3] In it, he provides a framework of community and substantiality that Ōkawa offered as a model for all of Asia, which later became part of his project of placing the emperor, the military, and the state in opposition to the capitalist market. Part of the impetus for this project emerged from Hegel and German idealism's own critique of liberalism as unable to sustain community. However, unlike Hegel, Ōkawa did not stress the moment of subjectivity.

Philosophical Origins of Ōkawa's Pan-Asianism

Ōkawa Shūmei was born in Yamagata prefecture in the port city of Sakata. During his years in junior high school, he studied French at a Catholic church and learned the Confucian classics with a private tutor. From an early age Ōkawa also studied Western philosophy. In his high school years, he immersed himself in German idealism, especially the philosophies of Kant and Hegel. He was also exposed to Indian philosophy, which he focused on at Tokyo Imperial University. He graduated in 1911 with a senior thesis on the Indian Buddhist philosopher Acharya Nāgārajuna. His thesis advisor was Anesaki Masaharu (1873–1949), who also greatly influenced many other intellectuals, including the famous revolutionary Zhang Taiyan. His knowledge of Indian Vedic philosophy provided a foundation for his later pan-Asianism, but his understanding of Indian philosophy was heavily mediated by Western philosophy.

In his mature years, Ōkawa's education in philosophy grounded his critical rethinking of his contemporary world, which was plagued with crisis.[4] He developed utopian theories that connected his initial contemplative stance to a practical perspective that confronted the global injustices of his times.

In the first decade of the twentieth century, he came into contact with some of the leftist groups with whom Chinese nationalists, such as Zhang Taiyan, were involved. He was an avid reader of *Heimin shinbun* (The people's newspaper), an anarchist newspaper founded by the anarchist Kotoku Shusui (1871–1911) and the socialist Sakai Toshihiko (1871–1933), which we will discuss below. Ōkawa attended lectures by people such as Kotoku, Sakai, and the Christian socialist Abe Isoo (1865–1949).[5]

Ōkawa's interest in Abe Isoo was part of Ōkawa's early engagement with Christianity, under the influence of his English teacher, Tōyama Saburō.[6] However, by the time Ōkawa entered college, he began to turn to nationalism and pan-Asianism. From 1910 to 1913, he was involved in the Dōkai (Association of the way), which was an indigenized Christian Church that offered a Confucian interpretation of Christianity.[7] The Dōkai affirmed a heroic vision that called for the "cultivation of the spirit."[8] This vision would be a part of his thought throughout the rest of his life and informed his conception of history as driven by elites and faith in military leaders. Moreover, Ōkawa's shift away from Christianity accompanied what may be considered an early case of *tenkō*, an ideological reversal from left to right.

We should refrain from evaluating this shift one-sidedly, however, because his move away from cosmopolitanism also was accompanied by a critique of Eurocentrism on many levels. Here Ōkawa anticipated a point made more recently by Timothy Brennan, namely that liberal cosmopolitanism usually serves to reproduce global inequality by downplaying the importance of national struggles.[9] Ōkawa eschewed abstractions such as cosmopolitanism; his thought aimed to make theory concrete. Indeed, in many ways he was applying his earlier philosophical training to the political sphere. In the preface to one of his major texts on pan-Asianism, "Problems Concerning Reviving Asia," published in 1922, he noted that he initially wanted to devote himself to pure scholarship separate from politics. He explained that he aspired to "work on his knowledge through becoming a monk and saw the Upanishads, which speak of a path being realized through Yoga, as a source for which he would always be thirsty."[10] And like Hegel, he aimed to overcome the duality between the pure inner life of the spirit and the outer world of politics. Kojima Tsuyoshi has pointed out that scholars during the Taishō (1912–1926) and Showa periods (1926–1989) attempted to synthesize German idealism and Wang Yangming's Confucianism; Ōkawa was part of this trend.[11] Indeed, his aim was to somehow overcome the perceived rift between what Confucians call the "inner sage" and the "outer king," and he can be seen grappling with this tension in all of his analyses of religion, including those on Islam. In a text published in 1980, Izutsu Toshikiko, Ōkawa's most famous student, contended that Islam had two faces, one that mystically turned inward and the other focused on law and keeping order.[12] Ōkawa's first essay on Islam, "Mystical Mohammedanism," published in 1910, dealt with precisely the first

84 CHAPTER THREE

part of this dichotomy.[13] These examples show that from an early age Ōkawa was trying to develop a synthesis of various Asian philosophies, including Wang Yangming Confucianism, Buddhism, Islam, and Hinduism.

Mobilizing the Inner Sage and the Outer King in an Uneven World

Much of Ōkawa's political involvement manifested itself in an attempt to overcome the rift between the inner sage and the outer king—that is, to create a world in which the outer world is in harmony with inner wisdom. The rift was not merely a Japanese problem but also a global one that characterized both imperialism and eventual Asian responses to it. Ōkawa's shift to politics was spurred by Sir Henry Cotton's book, *New India* (1885; revised edition 1907), which he happened to glance at in a bookstore in Tokyo in 1913.[14] Cotton, who has been called a "British Indian Service dissident," supported the Indian national movement during its early stages and became a member of the Indian National Congress.[15] The year 1913 was marked by a series of intense political events in Japan that are sometimes referred to as the "Taishō crises."[16] The third cabinet of Prime Minister Katsura Tarō was toppled, and the people and political parties were increasingly alienated from one another.[17] Among the events and movements leading up to this crisis were strikes against Tokyo street car prices in 1907, a rising socialist movement, and the assassination of the anarchist Kotoku Shusui in 1911. Part of the reason for this series of crises was that politicians such as Katsura failed to make sense of Japanese society, which politicians viewed as the cause of disorder but made no efforts to understand more deeply.[18]

The above domestic crisis, coupled with what he learned from Cotton's book, meant that Ōkawa could no longer look at Indian philosophy as mere abstraction. Up to this time, India, Islam, and Asia more generally might have represented for Ōkawa an abstract space of unity away from politics. For example, India signified for him philosophy and ancient history. In his view, India was a space defined by Brahminical practices, the birthplace of the Buddha, and deep thinking. From this Orientalist perspective, India did not exist in a contemporary geographical space but only as practices of interiority. Cotton presented India in a world of unevenness and colonialism, and his book praised the struggles of Indian anticolonial freedom fighters. The book, which is largely about the emergence of national consciousness in India, caused Ōkawa to consider how to interpret national consciousness from the perspective of larger anti-imperialist struggles. At one point, Cotton's text asks how Western colonialism would produce resistance:

The people of the country [India], enlightened and educated by ourselves, expanding with new ideas, and fired by an ambition to which English education has given birth, make demands which are continually more and more reasonable and more irresistible. The waves of the ocean of native progress are dashing against the breakwater of English prejudice. This growth of a national spirit marks the revolution to which India has been subjected in its political aspect. It proceeds hand in hand with the social and moral revolution to which I shall subsequently refer, and is due to the same initial cause viz. the spread of Western ideas and civilization.[19]

Cotton describes an India in transition, in which Indian national consciousness is fundamentally mediated by Western structures of organization, education, and ideas. This is precisely the problem of modern education (*Bildung*) of which Hegel spoke in his *Lectures on Fine Art*, which awakens people to such contradictions and conflicts as inner and outer. However, by the late nineteenth century, modern education had also begun to raise awareness of problems inherent in imperialism. As Western civilization moved beyond Europe, it created forms of resistance that imperialist nations could not quite control. Ōkawa focused on this uncontrollable resistance by reading Cotton's book against the grain.[20] The book was actually written as a wake-up call to the British, a warning that Indian national consciousness was changing, and the British colonial government would have to alter its policies if it were to continue ruling India. By highlighting the increasing organization of Indian society and politics through the mediation of British rule, Cotton adumbrates ideas of how "India" as a nation was created through the institutional structures of colonialism and global capitalism.[21] It is precisely this nation, produced by colonialism, that turned against it in an anticolonial movement.

Ōkawa interpreted the whole process of anticolonialism from a different position on the uneven globe, shifting perspectives from object to subject, from colonizer to colonized. He read many books on modern Asian history and colonialism and was moved by the way Asia had become a "stage for imperialist competition."[22] Ōkawa's understanding of the nature of the global system caused him to change his orientation from philosopher to anticolonial activist.

In a deposition after he was arrested for an attempted coup in 1932, he notes that earlier he could have been described as taking the Buddhist path of leaving the world, but now he realizes that he needs to enter it: "Ten years ago, I was completely immersed in a life of reclusion and devoted myself completely to being a student of the Way. But now at Takushoku University, I give lectures on colonial policy, colonial history, and news in East Asia.

86 CHAPTER THREE

Embracing the spirit of a knight-errant [*bukyō*] . . . I became a warrior for the revival of Asia."[23]

Cotton's book played a key role in Ōkawa's becoming politicized. The figure of the knight-errant, common to both China and Japan, conjures up a world of chivalry and sacrifice in struggle. The knight-errant combines both elite and military dimensions. However, the itinerant character of these figures indicates that they were not totally incorporated into the then-current organizational structures. From this perspective, they represented a moment of political action from outside official channels. This is one of the reasons late Qing Chinese revolutionaries and reformers such as Zhang Taiyan also drew on the figure of the knight-errant, and Ōkawa himself moved from a revolutionary elitism to an elitism embedded in the existing state. In both cases, although parallels with Marxism can be seen, they differ significantly in their visions of history. While Marxism and Maoism stress historical transformation from below, Ōkawa understood history as being created by heroes at varying degrees of distance from the state: heroes who could be understood as knights-errant.

In his thought, Ōkawa connected himself to the state through anticolonial nationalism. The anticolonialism here is different from the Indian or Chinese cases because Japan at this point was neither colonized nor semicolonized and was already beginning to annex colonies of its own. Ōkawa's anticolonialism identified with Asia and, paradoxically, underscored Japan's role in defending against colonialism. The nationalist dimension of his discourse can be seen in his description of Toyotomi Hideyoshi's rage when the Chinese emperor of the Ming dynasty treated him as a subordinate.[24] Ōkawa notes that it is with this same rage that he read modern Asian history, which led him to generalize the affective intensity of Japanese nationalism to Asia more broadly.[25] We will come back to this intersection between Japan and Asia later, but for now we should note how he conceived of nationalism, and the knight-errant, in relation to political action.

We can understand Ōkawa's trajectory from contemplative thought to heroic action in terms of what Lukács explains as the structures of consciousness in capitalism.[26] In short, because in capitalist society people confront a whole set of market processes, bureaucratic structures, and transnational developments over which they have no control, they feel helpless and become contemplative; they attempt to find freedom at the level of thought. This is where the inner sage feels confined to being merely inner and therefore helpless. As a result of reading Cotton, Ōkawa became critical of this contemplative perspective and indeed saw it as responsible for the downfall of Asia. For this reason, after 1913, he was involved in having the journal *Michi*, organized by the new religion Dōkai, publish the writings of well-known Indian intellectuals such as Anagarika Dharmapala (1864–1933) and Maulavi (Muhammad) Barakatullah (1870–1927). Dharmapala was a Buddhist revivalist and proponent of independence in Sri Lanka and India. Barakatullah wrote numerous articles about the anti-British movement in India.[27] At this time, numerous other journals also published articles on the Indian independence movement as well.

However, Ōkawa believed that the utopia he envisioned would be achieved by bringing the contemplative and the practical together. This is what allowed Ōkawa to imagine a world beyond modern separations. This shift in Ōkawa's thinking must be understood in the context of larger global crises taking place in the context of World War I, which precipitated a global questioning of modernity. In particular, although pan-Asianism had a geographical specificity, it was intimately connected to a global trend critical of Western civilization. This became especially prominent after World War I and affected Japanese intellectuals through various channels: for example, through contacts with French proponents of anti-Western thought such as Paul Richard (1874–1967), a figure to whom we shall turn in the section that follows. In short, while the particular configuration of Ōkawa's philosophy and activism must be understood in a Japanese context, his attack on Western culture was part of a broader discursive project that is examined in the next section.

India and the Problem of Competing Universalities after World War I: Vasili Eroshenko, Rash Behari Bose, and Paul Richard

Although Ōkawa himself identified the turning point of his life as when he read Cotton's text, we should understand his transformation in relation to larger global shifts in perceptions of modernity, capitalism, and East-West relations. We have already noted the rise in pan-Asian sentiment after the Russo-Japanese War, which was connected to anticolonial nationalism. But we must read this as a reaction to its dialectical opposite, namely a cosmopolitanism that was strangely pacifist. This cosmopolitanism was represented by the Russian Vasili Eroshenko and the Indian pan-Asianist nationalist Rash Behari Bose, both of whom took shelter at different times at the Nakamuraya, meaning that the Nakamuraya became a hub for both anarchist cosmopolitanism and pan-Asianist nationalism. A brief examination of the dichotomy between cosmopolitanism and pan-Asianist nationalism as it manifested in Eroshenko and Bose shows the context in which Ōkawa's shift toward pan-Asianist nationalism occurred.

Sho Konishi emphasizes the fact that after the Russo-Japanese War, a number of intellectuals and activists embraced an anarchism that simultaneously promoted anticolonialism, antinationalism, and cosmopolitanism, and Ōkawa's interest in this strand of thinking is evident in his early support for figures such as Kotoku Shusui. Konishi demonstrates that after the war many intellectuals turned to a "nonwar movement," a pacifistic anarchism associated with the constructed language Esperanto.[28] The attraction of Esperanto was that it was a language unconnected with a specific civilization or region. As noted earlier, Ōkawa avidly read the *Heimin shinbun*, which was coedited by Kotoku Shusui, an influential proponent of the nonwar movement. Kotoku used the term *heimin*, or "the people," as a way to promote direct links between movements from different nations beyond the strictures of the nation-state. The *hei* in *heimin* often means "flatness" and in one sense suggests a leveling out of differences based on class, nation, and other hierarchies. Anarchists believed it was necessary to be blind to such hierarchies if one was to reach beyond the nation-state, which they considered the root of war. This position ran contrary to pan-Asianism, however, because it made no distinction between East and West.

The blind Russian anarchist Vasili Eroshenko embodied this transcendence of national and hierarchical difference. In his early years, Eroshenko was a violinist in an orchestra for the blind. He studied Esperanto and English and in England met the famous anarchist Peter Kropotkin, who explained to Eroshenko his vision of anarchism. Eroshenko began to study Japanese, and through his contacts in Japan, he visited Japan around 1914 to study Japanese social practices related to the blind and also to promote Esperanto. He lived in the home of Sōma Kokko and Sōma Aizō, the owners of the Nakamuraya. Kokko treated Eroshenko like family and crossed racial and civilizational barriers in doing so. Around the time of World War I, the popularity of Esperanto had reached great heights in Japan,[29] and Eroshenko's popularity was such that he become an icon of Esperanto in Japan. The Japanese government, however, was nervous about Eroshenko's popularity and deported him. Eroshenko then went to China, where the Chinese Esperanto Association took care of him, and he eventually met the famous Chinese writer Lu Xun, who later became a key symbol of a pan-Asian alternative for Takeuchi Yoshimi, to whom we will turn in the next chapter.

At around this time the Indian pan-Asianist Rash Behari Bose, who was ideologically much closer to Ōkawa, also found shelter in the Nakamuraya and became part of the Nakamura family.[30] Unlike Eroshenko, Bose came from a country that was colonized, and he himself had been involved in revolutionary violence. Born in Burdwan, Bengal, Bose became a revolutionary at an early age. The highlight of his revolutionary career came on December 23, 1912, when he threw a grenade at the governor-general and the viceroy of India. The assassination attempt was unsuccessful, and Bose was forced to flee when the British government found out that he was behind the bombing. Bose moved from place to place until 1915, when he boarded a ship bound for Japan using an assumed name. Japan was a curious choice in some respects because, as noted in the preceding chapter, Japan and Britain were allies, but Bose was probably attracted by pan-Asian nationalist and pro-Indian sentiment there. In fact, Japan was one of the epicenters of the Indian independence struggle, harboring about a thousand Indian exiles by 1941.[31]

Bose quickly made the acquaintance of Japanese pan-Asianists, including the ultranationalist Tōyama Mitsuru (1885–1944) and Ōkawa. Before long, the British tracked Bose down, and the Japanese government, at the behest of the British, decided to extradite him. It was Tōyama who helped Bose find a hideout—the garden shed of the Nakamuraya.[32] In March 1916, due to conflicts between the Japanese and British government, the Japanese government rescinded the extradition order on Bose, which meant that he could stay in Japan. In contrast to the experience of Eroshenko, whom the Japanese government relentlessly pursued, Bose increased his personal and political ties in Japan. In July 1918, Bose married the Sōma's eldest daughter, Toshiko, and became a Japanese citizen in 1923.

All the while, Bose continued his adamant support for Indian independence. By the 1920s, he had become close to Ōkawa, and the two collaborated on projects related to both Indian independence and pan-Asianism. For example, with Ōkawa's help Bose smuggled arms to Indian revolutionaries, but he also organized numerous conferences that brought pan-Asian activists together. Ōkawa and Bose organized the first meeting of the Union of Asian Peoples in August 1926. The meeting held in Nagasaki drew representatives from Japan, China, India, Afghanistan, Vietnam, and the Philippines. Ōkawa and Bose saw in meetings such as this as an opportunity to promote an alternative world order. Bose remarked:

> We know some criticize today's meeting saying there is no need to establish another international union because we have one. But the two internationals are completely different in nature. The one is for the benefit of five hundred million of the whites and the other is for one hundred and a half a millions of Asian peoples. For thousands of years, the Easterners were a very superior people in civilization, spirituality and materially. . . . Its basis is on the pure faith and love for Asia. Let us unite and do our best to establish this union at all cost and let us make a big contribution to the happiness of all humanity in propagating our aims and objects all over the world.[33]

The background to this statement is Woodrow Wilson's famous support for self-determination and the establishment of the League of Nations. Erez Manela has shown how numerous Asian nationalists emerged after the so-called Wilsonian moment,[34] but as the above quote shows, the point of pan-Asianism was to create a new global order that more equitably and prominently incorporated Asian nations. This search for an alternative had already emerged earlier, as noted above, but it was given a boost following World War I.

Michael Adas has pointed out that immediately before World War I, intellectuals in both Europe and Asia attributed the success of Western nations to their putatively superior ideology and technology,[35] whereas critics of the civilizing mission of the West and Western hegemony were largely marginalized.

However, the huge number of casualties during the war that resulted from mechanized killing caused many to cast a more critical eye toward Western civilization. Even though in some ways the British and French empires emerged stronger after the war, with the absence of Germany, even "colonial apologists, such as Etienne Richet and Albert Bayet, employed new, less obviously hegemonic slogans that emphasized the need for 'mutual cooperation' between colonizers and colonized and programs for 'development' based on 'free exchanges of views' and 'mutual respect.'"[36] Ideas such as free exchange and mutual respect are entailed in capitalism; however, intellectuals also mobilized these concepts against colonialism.[37] Although these new terms were employed along with earlier ideas such as the civilizing mission of the West, after the war fewer people accepted the old discourse of the West's superiority.

Critiques of Western civilization appeared in Europe as well, including Oswald Spengler's famous *The Decline of the West* (*Untergang des Abendlandes*), which inspired Western scholars to rethink the significance of Asia, particularly India. Ōkawa's reading of Indian anticolonialism was intimately related to Western interpretations of India as a spiritual locus that offered an alternative to Western civilization.

In 1916, Ōkawa came into contact with Paul Richard, a critic of Western civilization and a devotee of Indian philosophy and theology, who had just come to Japan from Pondicherry. Richard studied theology and philosophy and was convinced that Asian philosophy offered a remedy for a decaying Western civilization. He, along with his famous wife, Mira Alfassa (1878–1973), was a follower of the philosopher, guru, and nationalist Aurobindo Ghose (1872–1950) and became one of his most important organizers.[38]

Ghose considered his ashram in Auroville, Pondicherry, where Richard and his wife stayed, a transnational utopia. But in fact, it alienated the people there. Despite advocating ideas that went beyond capitalism, it exploited the labor of the Tamils and therefore reproduced racial segregation and domination.[39] Although Richard was probably unaware of this, Auroville was a microcosm of contradictions similar to that of Japanese imperialist ideology, combining an ideology of unity with subtle (and sometimes not-so-subtle) practices of exclusion. In the end, he left Auroville for Japan in 1916 because of persecution by the French colonial government after being involved in the Indian liberation movement.

Richard urged the Japanese to reclaim their heritage but at the same time insisted that Japan respect the autonomy of neighboring Asian nations: "The Hero, the Leader of the East, Japan wishes to be. I agree with her in this grand aim. But, in return, she must also agree with me that the only way to fulfilling this aim is to be the first to find and follow the heroic path leading the nations of the East to a new civilization, a new wisdom."[40]

Richard extolled Japan as a leader of Asia and yet warned of the potential threat of Japanese imperialism. His writings strongly advocated Wilsonian self-determination and expressed what he thought should be the normative structure of international relations and used Western ideals to think about the mission of Asia:

> The days will come when all peoples shall be free. . . . For this war [WWI] while judging the peoples, settling old accounts, and preparing new destinies, offers the captives, if they are worthy of it, an occasion for breaking their chains . . . Russia has started, India will follow. . . . Colonization is indeed the mortal sin of Europe, who say "Equity" and commit iniquity; who say "Liberation," and keep in subjection entire races;—"Democracy" and submit multitudes to the autocracy of force,—"Rights of nationalities" and deny to the three hundred million people who inhabit India the right to be a nation.[41]

Just as the workings of capital lead to unfreedom and inequality in the domestic realm, the global relations of capital produce inequality and imperialism in the world system. Richard's discourse—replete with such terms as "sin," "action," and "resistance"—stresses the moral dimension of imperialism. Pan-Asianism as resistance is a response to the contradictions of this world system and its normative presuppositions, which Richard might have already begun to see in Japan. By mentioning Russia as the initiator of resistance to imperialism, Richard echoes Sun Yat-sen's point that the 1917 Revolution brought Russia into Asia. Likewise, as Tatiana Linkhoeva has recently shown, a great number of Japanese intellectuals were enamored with the Russian Revolution,[42] and Ōkawa was clearly one of them. More generally, Ōkawa freely drew on Richard's ideas as he constructed his own vision of Asia.

Ōkawa, Nonduality, and Anti-imperialistic Pan-Asianism

Ōkawa's experiences with Indian intellectuals and his encounter with Richard transformed his spiritual inclination into a passion for politics. A few years after his meeting with Indian freedom fighters, he narrated his own sentiments, in which he implicitly returns to the theme of the inner sage and the outer king: "I began to realize that the source of Asia's calamity lay in precisely the admiration of the life away from the world, which I had admired. Asia's efforts, and India's great efforts in particular, lay in obtaining inner spiritual freedom, and through this they grasp the great principle of the equality and non-duality."[43] Ōkawa did not deny the power of this inner spiritual freedom. In fact, he was committed to this idea throughout most of his life, though it later led him to advocate a heroic politics that sought to bring spirit and action together. He described this issue in a characteristically Hegelian manner, when he writes of realizing a spiritual principle:

> Asia lacked the lion-king type of effort required to realize this principle in society. The necessary result of this is that inner/individual life and social life became separated from each other and a Hinayana-style Asia emerged. On the one hand, this ossified the spiritual principle, and on the other hand it caused the social system to become loose and dysfunctional. As a consequence, Asians became subordinated to the white demons.[44]

Again, because Asia did not make the effort to realize its fundamental spiritual principles, not only did it lose these principles, but its political system also became stagnant and thus helpless in the face of the invading whites. However, for Ōkawa this structural separation required a messianic mission to realize a future utopia in which these contradictions could be overcome.

> For Asia to return to that high and noble realm, it must first leave this dual life and work toward the unique Mahayana-style Asia that seeks to realize the supreme dharma [myōhō] in real life. To do this, we must infuse the most concrete part of our social life, namely the life of our state, with institutions in harmony with our spiritual ideals.[45]

Using the language of Mahayana Buddhism, Ōkawa describes a messianic future, and attaining that future becomes his mission. From the perspective of Mahayana Buddhism, samsara (or "this life of suffering") and nirvana cannot be separate. In Mahayana, the bodhisattva does not leave the world but enters it to save all sentient beings. However, Ōkawa did not limit this messianic vision to Buddhism and often drew on the Islamic conception of jihad to convey this sense of mission, explicitly connecting it to a war in which Japan would take the lead. In a 1926 article called "The Japanese and Their Road," he writes:

If one looks at world history up to now and discusses the meeting of Eastern and Western civilizations, or the unity of Eastern and Western civilizations, almost without exception . . . it has only been realized through war. Mohammad said that heaven is under the shadow of the sword, but I believe that, to realize a new world, a war that risks the lives of the strong countries of the East and West as in the past would be difficult to avoid.[46]

Ōkawa's reading of Islam, like his reading of Buddhism and other Asian religions, calls for a kind of practice that involves a struggle against Western imperialism. Asia can no longer retreat and claim that although Asian nations are subordinate to the West materially, they are superior spiritually. Rather, elites in Asia must put philosophy into practice by engaging in state-building and anticolonialism with the ultimate goal of universal liberation.

Although Ōkawa continued to be heavily influenced by Islam throughout his life, geographically, he thought of Asia, or "East Asia," as primarily consisting of Japan, China, and India. Likewise, Cotton's book on India was crucial for Ōkawa's development, and that influence continued. Ōkawa's anticolonial writings combined the ethos of freedom fighters from India, such as Lala Lajpat Rai (1865–1928), with the pathos of Indian mystical and romantic thinkers, such as Aurobindo Ghose and Rabindranath Tagore (1861–1941). In an autobiographical essay written in 1953, Ōkawa notes that during World War I, the Japanese government was ambivalent about helping Indian freedom fighters, but he himself harbored two Indian nationalists in his house.[47] Ōkawa's own position on the Japanese state was certainly contradictory. He was clearly a nationalist, but he had a strained relationship with the Japanese government.

A few years after his encounter with Indian nationalists during World War I, in "Revolutionary Europe and the Revival of Asia," an essay published in 1922, Ōkawa explained what he meant by the liberation of Asia: "Slaves have only the will to follow their masters and they are only zombies who move for the interests of their masters. Therefore, the true meaning of the problem of Asia begins when Asia gains independence. Before anything else, Asia must break free from the realm of slavery."[48] Ōkawa applied the idea of freedom from slavery to the world stage, where imperialist powers act like slave owners and capitalists. He distinguished between European and Asian trajectories toward liberation. The French Revolution moved European society forward, but in Asia he saw a movement of return, which the term "revival" in the title of the essay was meant to convey. In both cases, one moves beyond slavery, but the temporal dynamics are different. Asia needs to return to the place where it was previously; at the time when Europeans were still living the lives of barbarians, Asians were already civilized. Moreover, Ōkawa argued that most of the culture, technology, morality, and religion in the premodern period emerged from Asia. Therefore, unlike Europe, the problem for Asians was one of revival, which involved rethinking the sweeping trajectories of history.

However, revival became necessary because of loss. For the preceding three hundred years Asia had been shamed, which accounts for the loss; however, the intellectual landscape changed after the Russo-Japanese War, and many people found hope in the idea of Asia. Ōkawa's essay on Asian liberation, noted above, which was written two years before Sun's famous lecture on pan-Asianism in 1924, also portrays the significance of Asia in terms of larger issues of decolonization, equality, and cultural unity. At Tokyo University, he heard Okakura Tenshin's lectures and was clearly influenced by Okakura's famous remark that "Asia is one," as seen in remarks published in 1922. In this essay, he presupposes the unity of Asian nations by writing of an "Asian nation,"[49] noting that after the Russo-Japanese War, "other Asians, who are the same as us [Japanese], also became awakened. However, it was not only Asian nations. There was an increase in the resistance of all those nations that were oppressed by the Western powers."[50]

In this way, he expanded the idea of Asia beyond mere geographical boundaries and began to confront the issue of oppression and resistance. Moreover, although he was influenced by Hindu nationalists, Ōkawa's own view was inclusive and embraced Arabs and Muslims as well. His conception of the Muslim world was part of his larger heroic vision of history. In *The Establishers of Asia*, a text published in 1941, which Ōkawa himself claimed was a continuation of "Problems Concerning Reviving Asia," he clearly articulates the idea of the hero in relation to the Middle East. In the preface he makes the following point about heroes and history: "Great tasks can obviously not be done by individuals. However, without the guidance of a valiant individual, one cannot hope for success in any task. As I studied the history of Asia, my heart was struck strongly by the great role played by heroes in this history."[51] In many ways, this continued his earlier emphasis on the hero, but here he further emphasizes the importance of Asian individuals and in particular Muslim elites, such as Kemal Atatürk and Ibn Saud. He contended that both of them were simultaneously great generals and great politicians.[52]

In discussing heroic leaders, Ōkawa brought together the military and political elite in one figure, but he also stood out among pan-Asianists in thinking of Asia beyond merely East Asia and encompassing the Islamic world and other dominated regions. However, anti-imperialism itself is not a politics, and Ōkawa's concrete vision is revealed in writings where he outlines his critique of political modernity.

Ōkawa's Ideal of Religious Unity:
From Sublating to Negating Political Modernity

Ōkawa argued that the Western powers did everything they could to ensure that Asian national subjects would not be formed.[53] His solution was to reject the existing liberal capitalist political structure in favor of a radical statist system. In a deposition he wrote after he was arrested for his involvement in an attempted coup on May 15, 1933,[54] Ōkawa noted that monumental global changes during and after World War I deeply affected Japan. First, Japanese capitalism developed at a breakneck pace, which suddenly made the Japanese people aware of social problems similar to those in advanced capitalist countries and, as in the West, sparked class struggle–like social movements and outrage over politicians sycophantically catering to the wealthy. Second, the deposition noted a worldwide rise in state socialism, communism, and social democracy, all targeting liberal capitalist regimes. Ōkawa mentions the Russian Revolution, the collapse of the German and the Austro-Hungarian empires, the Spanish Revolution, and rise of fascism in Italy—all part of a revolutionary movement of "national reconstruction." In Japan, the deposition continues, "reconstruction organizations" consisted of various "segments": anarchism, the Communist Party, social democracy, state socialism, and finally, a party that Ōkawa himself supported, the Yūzonsha. Although the political program of the Yūzonsha centered on state socialism, its "spiritual foundation was purely Japanese."[55] In short, Japan was part of a worldwide trend toward nation-state-centered development.

All of the movements that Ōkawa described, except for anarchism, emphasized centralization. Given the global trend toward state-centered capitalism, it is not surprising that anarchism was the one movement that had still to be realized, and many anarchists eventually supported Bolshevism. In his earlier text "Revolutionary Europe and the Revival of Asia," Ōkawa explains:

> From within World War I between the English and the Germans, the Russian Revolution emerged. However, the revolutionary Bolsheviks were warriors not only for Russia but also for revolutionary Europe. They negated the minority capitalists who monopolized the material profit of the people and through the ideology of workerism, which sought the welfare of all the people, they tried to unify economic life. Moreover, they discarded capitalist politics, namely democracy, like it was a pair of old shoes.[56]

In Ōkawa's view, the October Revolution attacked both capitalism and democracy, and in so doing was a political gesture against Taishō democracy[57] and fueled the emerging workers' movement in Japan. Japanese officials were also concerned about the influence of the October Revolution on the workers' movement in Japan. As Sheldon Garon notes, Bolshevism inspired student activists such as Asō Hisashi (1891–1940), who became the chair of the proletarian Japan Labor-Farmer Party in the late 1920s, and Nosaka Sanzō (1892–1993), who went on to become a founder of the Japanese Communist Party.[58] This was a period of global movements centered on the working class, and Japan was no exception; worker organizations in Japan increasingly began trying to unionize during precisely this period. By 1919, some capitalists, such as those associated with the Osaka Industrial Association, began to give in to workers' demands for unions.[59] In this context, Den Kenjirō (1855–1930), Japan's Minister of Communication, echoed Ōkawa's view when he wrote in his diary that "superficial democratic thought and radical communist ideology are little by little eating away at the brains of the lower classes."[60] Those on the right had to construct their own critique of capitalism. Ōkawa mobilized the Russian Revolution against democracy while looking to the organizational tendencies of the state, especially the Japanese state in the Showa period. In other words, he believed that state structures could provide a harmony that overcame the anarchy of the market. In this respect his ideology overlapped with conservative capitalists, such as those associated with the Japan Industrial Club, who were opposed to unions and stressed harmony.

From an international perspective, Ōkawa even saw the possibility of an alliance between the Soviet Union and Asia to promote shared political goals.[61] He argued that democracy was not an actual measure of the people's will but a curtain behind which the capitalists hide and that this curtain would eventually become a shield against the wrath of the masses. His critique of democracy identified the problem of atomization: "The characteristic of democratic politics is that it takes the majority as absolute. But is it not the case that the so-called majority in politics are mechanistically agglomerated in terms of their subjectivities? Truth is quality and not quantity."[62]

Ōkawa's critique clearly evidences an elitist mistrust of the majority, but it also expresses a concern about the way the majority implies merely following the will of the masses and how it can lead to homogenization. By mentioning the opposition between quantity and quality and pointing out the problem of homogeneity, Ōkawa invokes a Hegelian theme. In mass democratic societies, the individual becomes merely a number. The significance of this is made clear by Hegel's critique of mathematics:

> Its *purpose*, that is, its concept, is *magnitude* [*die Größe*]. It is precisely this relationship which is non-essential and devoid of the concept. For that reason, the movement of knowledge in mathematics takes place only on the surface; it

ASIA AS ANTICAPITALIST UTOPIA | 97

does not touch on the thing that really matters, does not touch on the essence, or the concept, and hence it does not constitute any kind of comprehension of what is at stake.[63]

Hegel contrasts number, or magnitude, and the concept that implies an organic relationship among its parts, which Ōkawa believed was lacking in democracy.[64] Number is devoid of all relationships, and this is precisely what happens to the masses: they are depoliticized and transformed into objects of political rule. They become atomized individuals alienated from the existing political institutions, which Ōkawa saw happening in early twentieth-century Japan.

This analysis has obvious political consequences for Hegel that are germane to Ōkawa's argument. In particular, social freedom in Hegel's view implies the integration of individuals into institutions such as the family and the state. Such freedom is impossible in the society that Ōkawa describes, where the masses become atomized and thereby diminished in magnitude as they stand against a nation-state that is alien to them.

In Ōkawa's view, the politics of democracy results in an alienation of the ruled from the rulers. While his basic logic resembles that of Hegel, his pan-Asianism pushes him partially in a left Hegelian direction, one in which the reconciliation of the individual with community happens in the future rather than in the present. Ōkawa's argument resembles that of Marx in "On the Jewish Question." Marx describes human beings as split between their everyday existence in civil society, where they buy and sell commodities, and their representation in the state. People interact in the market, which is protected by the state, but the state appears to relegate this realm to the private and apolitical. Far from being a space of reconciliation, in Marx's view capitalist civil society is a place of alienation and depoliticization.[65]

By late Meiji Japan, many conservatives vigorously criticized this split between citizen and state. The most influential of these critics for Ōkawa was perhaps Kita Ikki (1883–1947), often described as the foremost theoretician of Japanese fascism. We can get a sense of Ōkawa's own position by examining Kita's critique of civil society. In an essay about Kita written in the 1950s, Ōkawa recalls how Kita's *The Theory of the Body Politic and Pure Socialism* shook intellectual life in Japan when it appeared in 1907.[66] His analysis of the problems of civil society and how to overcome them was highly influential, and in the 1930s his texts were used as blueprints for militarist fascism.[67] He stressed the alienation of people from the state and especially underscored the continuation of economic oppression after the Meiji Restoration. He claimed that to overcome this oppression, another "restoration" (*isshin*) was needed. "Actually, to the extent that the *isshin* revolution is conscious of the goal of the state on the level of law and morality, it is socialist."[68] This implied the necessity of overcoming atomistic individuality and alienation at the level of civil society and continuing the revolution at the level of the state. As the historian and social critic Watanabe Kyōji explains:

> If we use Kita's terms, continuous revolution should be called a national revolution. The democratic revolution is the first stage of the national revolution, which realizes his ideals on a legal level. Social revolution is the second stage, which realizes his ideals on an economic level, namely at the level of the real life of the citizens. In other words, the democratic revolution is a potential social revolution and the social revolution complements the democratic revolution—social revolution completes the essence of the democratic revolution.[69]

This description reminds us not only of Marx's "On the Jewish Question" but more generally of Marx's idea that democracy was the truth of all constitutions and that this would be realized only after a radical social revolution. However, Kita's major difference with Marx lies in his attitude toward class. Rather than stressing class or labor, Kita emphasized the potential for Japanese society to go beyond civil society by means of Bushido ethics, which transcend the self-interested individualism that pervades capitalist society.

Watanabe points out that Kita's portrayal of samurai during the Edo-Meiji transition drew on a vision of the commune that goes back to Saigō Takamori, the so-called last samurai, whom history portrayed as resisting the Meiji modernization project. Watanabe provocatively explains:

> Japan's communism [*komyunshugi*] originates with Saigō Takamori. In 1872, Saigō was defeated. The reason for Saigō's defeat . . . was more than anything else because during the period when the modern Japanese state was being established, he held a vision of the commune that was diametrically opposed to the autocratic elites. In his ideal state, there would be a commune consisting of farmer-soldiers along with the farmers left in Satsuma, who communally owned their land. This would be a society which had low productivity, but was a moral country. On this point, Saigō's ideas resemble those of Mao Zedong.[70]

Watanabe's analysis highlights the problem of alienation that concerned Kita and why Kita found hope in Saigō's actions. Ōkawa clearly shared with Kita both a concern about alienation and a high opinion of Saigō. In his autobiography, Ōkawa claims that his two teachers were his mother and Saigō Takamori. "I admire him," he wrote, "because I want to become a human being like him and I think of him because I want to do the things that he did."[71] Although Ōkawa was no friend of democracy, he advocated a closer relationship between ruler and ruled, which he imagined existed in premodern religious societies. Moreover, both Kita's and Ōkawa's arguments reveal the ambivalent relationship between capitalism and the nation-state. Although the nation-state flourishes under capitalism, in a world where everything is reduced to exchange, the nation also yearns for community.[72] Kita, and later Ōkawa, sought to revive a different type of politics. Watanabe's reference to Mao Zedong echoes Wang Hui's recent analysis of the politics of depoliticization.[73] Wang describes a situation in which people are excluded from political practice because of the institutional separation of the market, which is usually thought to be apolitical, from the state. Ōkawa, however, was not concerned about mass participation. Rather, for both Kita and Ōkawa, repoliticization meant getting involved in the imperial politics of Japan, which to different degrees they both mistakenly took to be the solution to the problem of political alienation.

Repoliticization for Ōkawa implied fusing ideas of transcendence and religion with politics. At this point we glimpse Ōkawa's larger utopian vision, which he more fully articulated in the 1930s when he supported the Japanese occupation of Manchuria, which many Japanese intellectuals believed would be a place where utopian ideals were realized.

Like his allies who supported the Japanese state, Ōkawa had a conflicted relationship with the government. Ōkawa taught courses on Japanese culture and the history of colonialism at a school for future bureaucrats as part of his project to concretely repoliticize and transform Asia; however, he also believed that the government needed to be radically reformed or even overthrown. This led Ōkawa to launch the so-called Showa Restoration along with Kita Ikki and Mitsukawa Kametarō (1886–1936), with the goal of erasing any trace of liberal democracy and concentrating power in the hands of the emperor. He also participated in several coup attempts. In 1932, he cofounded the Jimmu Kai and the Kōchi Sha, both of which were organizations created with the goal of infusing the government with the spirituality of the emperor. He was arrested on May 15, 1933, for one of his coup attempts, and in his deposition, he explained his understanding of current political conditions and his utopian ideals at length as a way to justify his revolutionary or counter-revolutionary actions. The failure of these movements encouraged him to increase his cooperation with the state, but his fundamental political stance remained unchanged.

In his deposition, he outlined how politics had degenerated into a game in which the people are denied a stake. In particular, he pointed out the conflicts in party politics, such as the struggle between two foreign ministers and the political parties they represented, namely Shidehara Kijūrō (1872–1951; in office 1924–1927 and 1929–1931), who was a leader of the comparatively liberal Minseitō Party, and Tanaka Giichi (1874–1924; in office 1927–1929), who headed the more conservative Seiyūkai Party:

> Letting political parties and the *zaibatsu* run free everywhere, the majority of the citizens are increasingly impoverished. Consequently, who can guarantee that the people's loyalty to the ruler and love for the nation will not deteriorate? Not to mention, from the perspective of resources, our country certainly must create a greater economic circle in Manchuria and Mongolia and rationally control them. If we do not make these reforms quickly, it will be too late.[74]

Ōkawa's support for both the invasion of Manchuria and internal reform are good examples of his embrace of both imperialist and capitalist practices under the umbrella of anticapitalism and anti-imperialism. But it contained a populist element as well, since he claimed that the public was upset with Shidehara's failure to stand up to American imperialism. In particular, Ōkawa felt that Shidehara and the Minseitō were too lenient toward China and too eager to cooperate with the Western powers. Tanaka and the Seiyūkai also came in for criticism, however. Ōkawa condemned them for zealously cutting the military budget and for being in bed with big business.[75] Eventually, he said, people became fed up with party politics and claimed that the masses were united with the military against political parties and the zaibatsu/capitalists. Yet Ōkawa and the masses supporting the army both backed into a future they did not understand because by 1932, capitalists were also enthusiastic about the prospects of creating surplus value in Manchukuo through the use of force. In the end, using the militarist regime to overcome the alienation between civil society and the state only reproduced alienation.

In Ōkawa's view, however, militarism was a step toward utopia, which he saw as having seven goals: (1) to establish a restoration in Japan, (2) to establish the thought of citizens, (3) to realize freedom in the realm of intellectual life, (4) to realize equality in the realm of political life, (5) to realize fraternity in the realm of economics, (6) to liberate people of color, and (7) to unite the morality of the world.[76] To get a better understanding of what Ōkawa had in mind we will examine some of these goals more closely. First, we should note that all of them were built on a foundation of anticapitalism and anticolonialism. The first point, restoration, referred to completing the Meiji Restoration. In some respects, this ran counter to the position of the Lecture faction (*kōza ha*), a group advocating a Marxist theory popular in the 1920s and 1930s that suggested the Meiji Restoration was an incomplete bourgeois revolution. It argued that Japan must first become fully capitalist in order to reach the final goal of socialism. By contrast, Ōkawa and his cohort maintained that the goal was not to complete capitalism but to overcome it. He described the Meiji Restoration as consisting of two parts:

> The goal of the Meiji Restoration was to overthrow the Bakufu and revere the emperor and in this way they were to get rid of all of the power of the samurai, which the Bakufu represented. On the positive side, they were to establish reverence for the Emperor in the Japanese state . . .
>
> After the seven hundred years since the Kamakura period, Japanese citizens for the first time could look up at the sky. But in the years since the Meiji Restoration, the daimyo of money who replaced the daimyo of land hindered the realizing of a unity between the people and the ruler. They became an obstruction between the people and the ruler. Although the Meiji Restoration established sacred and unequaled respect for the ruler, the people have now begun to groan about the oppression of money.[77]

From this perspective, the first restoration toppled the oppression of the Bakufu, and the second will overcome capitalism or the power of money. The first was merely political emancipation, and the second would bring independence from imperialism. However, the revolution was not able to deal with the rule of money, which governed all of society. To overcome the problem of money, the state must be united with society. Indeed, the rule of money was premised on the separation between state and civil society (or market). In Ōkawa's view, this separation could be overcome through religion.

Religious transcendence can be related to politics in a number of ways. The Meiji period had already shown, in examples such as a Christian teacher refusing to bow to the imperial insignia,[78] how the transcendence of religion could work against the state. However, in Ōkawa's case, transcendence was harnessed in the name of nationalism, which became the basis for his critique of both capitalism and imperialism. In particular, he drew on state Shinto,[79] underscoring the idea of a cosmic emperor who would provide the foundation for a community beyond money.

He draws on the *Kojiki*, an eighth-century compilation of myths, legends, and semihistorical accounts of ancient Japan, to assert that the emperor is revered as "the Japanese emperor descendant from the sun and ruler of the cosmos," meaning that the Japanese emperor and the ancestors of the Japanese emerged from the heavens.[80] Ōkawa's fascist move lies in finding in this myth an alternative to both capitalism and communism in the modern world. He felt that in the contemporary world, the cosmic nature of the Japanese emperor meant that the emperor could carry out a messianic mission to save the rest of humanity. Ōkawa's goal was to offer an alternative to American imperialism, which ruled by the dollar, and the Soviets, who attempted to spread communism.[81] Simply put, Ōkawa's alternative was to revive the Japanese spirit. He contended that such a revival must not only be generally characterized by morality but also seek to liberate "colored people [*yūshoku minzoku*]."[82]

In Ōkawa's view, unifying morality and politics requires realizing the ideals of the French Revolution, and he offers his own interpretation of those ideals. He sees liberty as dealing with the life of the mind, equality with politics, and fraternity with economics.[83] However, though Ōkawa employs ideals associated with the French Revolution, he puts them in a Confucian framework. Confucianism allowed Ōkawa to move from seeing human beings as mere objects of beneficence to humans as subjects of action. But after making this shift from an ethical point of view, he must ask the Kantian question, "What should we do?" Kant realized that if one is to discuss rights meaningfully, the corresponding obligations must also be considered, and Ōkawa clearly endorses this point. Unlike Kant, however, Ōkawa bases the principles of correct action not on reason but in a natural order that goes beyond both the state and the individual. In this sense, his response is similar to Hegel's description of the Greek world, where morality was governed by a divine natural order that arises from his concept of substantiality as immediate unity with the absolute and with community. The difference, of course, is that Ōkawa emphasized a Confucian order connecting "heaven, earth, and human beings." This brings us back to the quest to unify the inner sage and the outer king, to which a cosmological dimension has now been added. In a work he wrote in 1927 on the Confucian text *The Doctrine of the Mean*, Ōkawa dealt with the issue of the underlying unity between self and cosmos:

> Confucianism aims to make clear "the Way." Moreover, because the Way is nothing other than the principle of a life with character, Confucianism investigates how people are supposed to live an upright and moral life. However, an upright and moral life implies finding a life that realizes correct relations between the "I" and that which is outside of us, the "not I." In Confucianism, this world of the "not I" involves heaven, earth, and human beings. Therefore, the Way of Confucianism is the Way of heaven, earth, and human beings. . . . Confucianism is a teaching that includes religion, morality, and politics. It does not divide life into religion, morality, and politics, but in the end grasps them as an amorphous whole. It attempts to clarify the Way that brings these three together and becomes a model for life as a whole.[84]

This passage describes a utopia that overcomes the political divisions that pervade the modern world. Ōkawa explains his utopian ideas more concretely in his deposition, where he notes that heaven is superior to human beings because it gives them life. But abiding by heaven requires other Confucian virtues such as filial piety, loyalty, and a web of relations that leads all the way out to the cosmos. Ōkawa's cosmological understanding of Confucianism is not that of the early dynasties but arises from the metaphysical philosophies of the Song (960–1279) and Ming (1368–1644) dynasties and is further influenced by German idealism. This synthetic philosophy is the root of what Ōkawa calls "Asian thought." He outlines his ideas about Asia clearly in his book *The New Spirit of Asia*, published toward the end of the war.

> The Orient does not recognize an essential opposition or difference between spiritual things and human things, between the life of the individual and the life of the cosmos, between reality and appearance, between past and the present or between the earthly realm and the heavenly realm. . . . Form is none other than emptiness and emptiness is none other than form. Westerners will say that this is illogical and irrational, but this emerges naturally from the feeling for life that flows from the Oriental monistic and pantheistic worldviews . . . in the deep origins of all existence, everything is tied together. Moreover, they [the people of the Orient] see things as united through the cosmos and the power that governs them all and gives them life. They see this not through a rational method, but through an internal grasp of experience. . . . The Orient respects the mutual harmonizing and equalizing of various powers. . . . The fruit that falls is connected to the whole cosmos. They connect the self to the cosmos so individual existence follows the cosmos. This synthetic intuition is a remarkable characteristic of the Oriental spirit that is completely different from [a European-style] separation.[85]

In this passage Ōkawa continues to develop certain Hegelian themes, especially the critique of abstract identity separate from a holistic context. However, he also seems to develop an Asian response to Hegel, who repeatedly criticized pantheism for not allowing for difference and believed that this was acutely expressed in the writings of Spinoza and in Oriental philosophies, especially Hinduism. Ōkawa asserts that Oriental philosophy allows for difference and posits a nondualistic form of transcendence.

In making this point, Ōkawa anticipates a distinction drawn in a recent work on pan-Asianism, namely Prasenjit Duara's *The Crisis of Global Modernity: Asian Traditions and a Sustainable Future*.[86] In this book, Duara distinguishes between dialogical and radical transcendence and in the process reveals the implications of Ōkawa's comments on the Orient. Moreover, Duara's perspective furthers our understanding of Ōkawa because it also provides a unique interpretation of the difference between Asian and Western modes of transcendence, one that is much more mediated by our contemporary values.

"I distinguish," Duara writes, "two traditions of transcendence in Eurasia: the radical transcendence, or strict dualism, and the more dialogical religious traditions, where transcendence is interwoven with immanent, polytheistic, pantheistic and plural religious practices."[87] Although Duara contends that we can find both types of transcendence in Asian and so-called Western religions, like Ōkawa he emphasizes the dominance of the dialogical approach in Asia, which allows certain political possibilities that radical transcendence forecloses.

Like Duara, Ōkawa claims that Western ontology leads to alienation and other problems of modernity. However, he stresses that the application of intuition can provide direct access to the transcendent, which is why it is not radically transcendent at all. Following the tradition of Wang Yangming, Ōkawa contends that through intuition, one can know the transcendent in itself. Having direct access to the transcendent through experience and practice implied a position of legitimacy vis-à-vis other nation-states. Eventually, Japan would emerge as the carrier of Asian culture, but Ōkawa was far from proposing simply Japanese exceptionalism: "Those who promote Japanism only vehemently proclaim admiration of one side of the Japanese spirit and cannot even convince the Japanese themselves. Moreover, aspects of their thinking are exclusionist with respect to foreigners. They cannot bear to listen to words of those with whom they do not agree and so attack them."[88] He goes on to explain that this cannot be the basis for pan-Asianist thought or the East Asian Co-prosperity Sphere[89] and offers a more expansive view that brings India and China into the picture. Here he echoes the sentiments of Zhang Taiyan and the Asia Solidarity Society but in a new context:

> The fundamental condition for reviving the Orient is that each of the nations in the Orient makes it such that in each person the purity of ancient culture comes back to life as a living thing. Moreover, we must now produce a new spirit of the Orient and for this the most important elements are the spirit of China and India. Therefore, we must first study Chinese and Indian ideas.[90]

Ōkawa repeatedly emphasizes a triangular unity of China, India, and Japan but also includes Islam in the picture. We have already seen that Ōkawa connected ideas that he associated with Islam, such as nonduality and dialogical transcendence, to the unity of religion and the state. On this point, Ōkawa affirms Hegel's point that the Orient makes no distinction between state and religion but contends that this is precisely what makes it superior to the West. Indeed, in Ōkawa's view, Asia, or the Orient, could overcome dualities such as subject and object precisely because it did not distinguish between religion and politics. However, he was disappointed with the developments

ASIA AS ANTICAPITALIST UTOPIA

in the contemporary Islamic world and especially with people such as Kemal Atatürk who were reforming Islam. By contrast, Ōkawa saw the Japanese and their unique emperor system as expressing the true unity of politics and religion that characterizes Asia. "The Japanese nation's loyalty to the ruler is different from the loyalty that China and the West show [to their rulers]. Through a specific history, there emerged in Japan a religious connection between the ruler and his subjects."[91] Other countries have this as well, but because the Japanese make this more explicit, they are best qualified to lead a pan-Asianist movement.

Ōkawa points out that although Japan occupies a privileged place, the institution of the Japanese emperor also represents a confluence of Asian ideals, ideals that overcome the alienations of modernity. In particular, this utopia of Asian traditions results from the breaking down of distinctions between religion, morality, and politics. The transcendent in religion that is relegated to the private realm along with one's daily exchange in the market now becomes the basis of public and private morality. In the following passage, which Ōkawa wrote immediately after the start of the war in the Pacific, he describes the varying traditions of Asia as featuring a connection between the cosmological and the political in order to drive home his key point:

> The trans-individual order of East Asia unites the cosmos as a whole. There is no gap in East Asia between the cosmical order of myriad things and the human societal order. In East Asia there is an intuitive and experiential lived unity between heaven, earth, and man that is God, nature, and human life. Therefore, there is no separation between religion, politics, and morality. Neither the Chinese "Way," the Indian "dharma," nor the Islamic law "sharia" separate religion, morality, and politics, and in the end grasp them as an amorphous unity. These principles [Dao, dharma, and sharia] become the model for life as a whole. On this point, they are the opposite of the Western trend that has provided the fodder for an ontological philosophy in which God and human beings are separate and nature is seen as something without life.[92]

Ōkawa included Judaism in his discussion of unity between religion, cosmology, and politics, which he again compared to the Japanese system.[93] Thus, Asia as he constructed it was part of an extremely broad geographical imaginary characterized by a symbiosis between the inner world—an intuitive, experiential unity—and the cosmos. Ōkawa hoped to achieve this symbiosis in both national and global politics.

We can again understand Ōkawa's argument as a response to both right and left Hegelians, and he differs from left Hegelians in terms of how he deals with the individual. In the section on the "Realization of Reason through

Itself" in the *Phänomenologie des Geistes*, Hegel discusses the importance of ethical life and how it is connected to reason and the individual; he also claims that the individual finds meaning in ethical life, a kind of life that existed in premodern societies. However, Hegel claims that with the emergence of modernity, one must move away from this community in ethical life. In the future, there must be a new reconciliation between the individual and community.[94] Hegel believed that this reconciliation takes place in the modern nation-state. Left Hegelians such as Marx claimed that this unification would take place later, in a communist society. In both the left and the right Hegelian case, the moment of modernity, that is, the emergence of the individual, and liberal ideas of equality and freedom are essential elements of the future utopia. Here sublation becomes important. The individual is sublated in that individuality remains an important moment of community in Hegel's vision. However, Ōkawa's sublation risks dwindling into an abstract negation where we do not see the individual return.

Ōkawa's response to political modernity was precisely to reject this mediation of the individual and assert that a superior alternative could be found in Japan and Asia. He argued that Japan could bypass the mediation of the individual because, unlike other societies' political systems, the emperor system ensures the unity of religion and politics. Of course, traces of the division between Japan as it is and Japan as an ideal still lives on. These traces not only were the basis of ideas of Japanese exceptionalism but also legitimated the use of force to realize them. Ōkawa believed that the subjective ideal of Asia could be made real in nation form. His was a movement to overcome capitalism in thought, but it was also a misguided attempt to accomplish this through existing institutions.

Rethinking China and the War

Ōkawa drew on China, India, and Islam both to promote an alternative Asian politics and to develop what he conceived as an anti-imperialist vision. However, he wrote his theoretical essays at a time when the Japanese army was invading China and other Asian nations and acquiring colonies of its own, which raises the question of how Ōkawa contended with this paradox. Speaking of the Chinese case in particular, he remarked:

> The China Incident preceded the European War and is a tragedy that emerged between China and Japan. To solve this, there is no question of a third country intervening. These two countries must directly negotiate to put an end to this situation. In addition, the Greater East Asia War has changed the nature of

the China Incident and caused internal chaos in East Asia. We must quickly suppress this civil strife and precisely this will enable us to bring the Greater East Asia War to a close.[95]

In this passage Ōkawa makes a distinction between the war with the United States and Europe on the one hand and the "China Incident" on the other. Ōkawa argues that war between China and Japan is a tragedy for the people of both countries. He asserts that if China and Japan cooperate and work toward Asian unity, they can both realize the ideals of the Greater East Asian Co-prosperity Sphere. In this case, India would also join the "Sphere."[96] The logic is similar to Zhang Taiyan's, but instead of India and China at the center, it is an anti-Western Japan and China, which would be joined by India. Zhang Taiyan had earlier turned to India because he believed that Japan had become subservient to Britain. By the 1930s and 1940s, despite Japan's clearly imperialist involvement in China, Ōkawa continued to hold out hope for peaceful cooperation between the two countries. His trenchant criticism of the West stood in stark contrast to his call for unity between China and Japan insofar as it turned a blind eye to Japan's own imperialist policies.

Conclusion

Ōkawa's pan-Asianism poses historical questions concerning not only how and why his utopia, and Japanese pan-Asianist utopias more generally, were complicit in fascism and imperialism but more broadly why critics of modernity and capitalism could end up being mobilized in support of fascism. The point here is not necessarily to criticize the right wing but rather, following Takeuchi Yoshimi, to understand the Janus-faced nature of Japanese fascism and imperialism. We should certainly acknowledge the sincerity of Ōkawa's sympathy for the Indian independence movement and also his attack on capitalism. Moreover, his use of remnants, especially of premodern religious imaginaries, had potential for both reactionary and progressive politics.

In analyzing the problem of a utopia based on remnants, we could follow the historian Harry Harootunian in arguing that Japanese antimodern thinkers did not completely understand what was possible given the conditions of the time and so unconsciously helped create nothing more than another kind of modernity. The arguments of Ōkawa unwittingly make fascism a prominent feature of modernity and give credence to a tradition beginning with Trotsky and carried on by the Belgian Marxist economist and activist Ernest Mandel and the Frankfurt school. Following Trotsky, Mandel stresses uneven development in his analysis of fascism. The "application of the theory of uneven and combined development to fascism," Mandel claimed, "made it possible for Trotsky to avoid two errors, two one-sided views of fascism: either as a relapse into pre-capitalist reaction and obscurantism, or as a late 'catching up' form of modernization."[97]

If one claims that Japan became fascist because Japanese society was filled with premodern remnants or that the Japanese failed to catch up with the modern world, one denies contemporaneity to Japan and more generally fails to acknowledge fascist thought as part of an unevenness constitutive of capitalist modernity. Fascism must be thought of as part of the "non-synchronism of economic and ideological forms."[98] In other words, elements of precapitalist society continue to exist in capitalism and serve both to resist and to reproduce various power and class structures.

However, the class character of Ōkawa's ideas is not easy to discern. Japan was clearly a site of class struggle during the early twentieth century. Industrial strikes, for example, grew from 107 in 1903 to 1,202 in 1927.[99] In this context, Mandel's description seems to fit Ōkawa's case: "In this mass movement [fascism] we find a combination of extreme nationalism and at least a verbal anti-capitalist demagogy, with an even greater hostility towards the organized labor movement."[100]

Ōkawa was clearly no friend of the labor movement, but he probably did not have the same hostility to it that fascists in Germany or Italy did, especially given his ambivalent evaluation of the communist movement in Russia. He characterized himself as a state socialist but stressed Japanese culture more than other socialists.[101] The class character of Ōkawa's thought became clearer as his support for the state and the elite grew. In other words, like many fascists, he advocated the use of organizations to fight capitalism.

However, the transnational character of Ōkawa's philosophy makes it necessary to consider the unevenness in the world system of nation-states. Ōkawa promoted an "imperialism of national liberation," perhaps similar to the "imperialism of democracy" that pervades our present world.[102] Moreover, his advocacy of imperialism and militarization explains not only Ōkawa's support for the existing bureaucracy but also his support for capitalism in the form of national capital. Since the nineteenth century, Asian countries had been facing the question of to what extent they could pursue the objectives of a wealthy state and strong military without embracing capitalism and imperialism. In the case of Japan at least, the ideals of liberation and prosperity became an ideological veneer used to cover practices of imperialism and capitalism. The similarity between Japanese and American imperialist ideology may account for the speed with which the United States rushed to exert influence over the former colonies of the Japanese empire, such as Taiwan and South Korea, after World War II.[103]

Regardless of what we think of Ōkawa's attack on capitalism and imperialism, both of the objects of his critique remain with us today and are still the targets of left-wing critiques. In other words, Ōkawa's discourse has a romantic and transcendental dimension that we should not reject out of hand even as we recognize its danger. We need to think about how the larger issues of remnants, unevenness, and religious and geographical imaginaries could serve to revive politics today. This is an important element in the thinking of many authors including Harry Harootunian, Michael Löwy, and Bill Martin. Martin advocates a postsecular society to counter the hypersecularization of neoliberal capitalism, and Löwy has shown how Marxism was often imbued with a romantic and religious sentiment that aided people in thinking beyond the shackles of the present.[104] We should keep this positive dimension of romanticism in mind even as we criticize Ōkawa for his obvious neglect of issues such as class, state, and capital. Ōkawa's romantic and utopian ideals make out the state to be a nonproblematic purveyor of a new society. In this way, Ōkawa in particular but pan-Asianists in general to some extent expected that the bureaucratic side of the state and its alienation would be remedied by the introduction of religion and mythological imaginaries, without fully realizing how these same imaginaries could reinforce the very structures against which they were struggling. The task of mobilizing religious and geographical imaginaries to achieve a future not characterized by social domination would continue through the postwar period and remains with us today. The next two chapters therefore offer an examination of Takeuchi Yoshimi's response to Ōkawa's legacy and pan-Asianism more generally.

4

Takeuchi Yoshimi, Part I:
Rethinking China as Political Subjectivity

As we have seen, pan-Asianism grew from a critique of Eurocentrism, a celebration of Asian values, and a call for a united front among weaker nations against an interimperialist struggle for world hegemony and the construction of a new world order. This movement was widespread throughout Asia, including the continent's largest countries, China, India, and Japan. In all these places, earlier forms of community were counterposed to the unembedded individuality of capitalism, which was associated with the West. Furthermore, the preceding chapter has shown that philosophers such as Ōkawa Shūmei mobilized pan-Asianism in support of Japan's imperialist expansion into Asia. Although Japan's defeat in World War II completely discredited any notion that Japan would be the center of Asian unity, it did not end pan-Asianism. The literary critic Takeuchi Yoshimi (1910–1977) is especially significant in the history of pan-Asianism because he vigorously carried on the project of pan-Asianism in the post–World War II era. Japan's defeat caused Takeuchi to reconsider his early sympathy for the Japanese project to resist the West and caused him to significantly change his thinking on pan-Asianism.

China and the Chinese Revolution became the key fulcrums of Takeuchi's reinvention of pan-Asianism in the postwar era. In the late 1960s, Takeuchi published a sympathetic essay on Ōkawa Shūmei that clearly set him apart from premodern pan-Asianists.[1] Among other things, in this essay, Takeuchi chided Ōkawa for ignoring contemporary China on an everyday level, something Takeuchi believed was essential for constructing Asian unity.[2]

Because of Takeuchi's central place in the history of postwar pan-Asianism, his work has begun to attract scholarly attention in various languages,[3] but most have not dealt adequately with the relationship between Takeuchi's pre- and postwar writings and have not explored the links between his theories on subjectivity, revolution, war memory, and pan-Asianism. However, an exploration of the way in which Takeuchi constructed a theory of subjectivity and then used it to rethink pan-Asianism during the postwar era is essential for fully understanding his thought.

This chapter outlines some of Takeuchi's basic ideas as they emerge in his seminal work on the preeminent modern Chinese author Lu Xun (1881–1936), *Rojin* (Lu Xun; 1944). In this early work, Takeuchi offered an entirely new way of understanding China, and Asia as a whole, by arguing that China rather than Japan was the center of resistance to the West, thus offering a very different vision of pan-Asianism.

Takeuchi's work reveals the intellectual transformations that occurred from pre- to postwar Japan because it straddles both periods. His work represents an important turning point in the development of pan-Asianist thought because he returned to a problem that had previously been dealt with primarily by the procivilization intellectual, Fukuzawa Yukichi, namely the subject, or subjectivity. For example, unlike Fukuzawa, Ōkawa stressed national subjectivity but rarely touched on individual subjectivity.

Takeuchi's *Rojin*, published during World War II, offers a cluster of concepts from his reading of Lu Xun on politics, literature, and subjectivity that serve as an alternative to the ideas of those who went before him. At this point, Takeuchi believed that the Japanese war against the West was on the way to putting such ideals into practice. But after the war, as we will see in the next chapter, he became critical of his earlier judgment but not of his overall framework. Consequently, Takeuchi helps us to see that despite the radical changes from the pre- to postwar periods, certain fundamental structures and dynamics had continued. In other words, the issues that prewar pan-Asianism identified—the problems of capitalist modernity—did not disappear after the war. Instead, as a result of rethinking community, negativity, and modernity, Takeuchi was able to formulate new responses to these issues.

In the prewar period and during the war, pan-Asianists put Japan at the center of substantiality and community. But in the postwar period Takeuchi mediated this stress on substantiality with the concept of subjectivity or negativity, which he found in China. For Takeuchi, rethinking Asia begins with reconceptualizing China, which in turn requires exploring subjectivity in the modern Chinese writer Lu Xun. We could say that Takeuchi turns Hegel's reading of China on its head since, more than substantiality, Takeuchi finds negativity in China and in Lu Xun in particular. From this perspective, he anticipates the work of scholars such as Michel-Rolph Trouillot and Susan Buck-Morss, who attempt to find freedom outside the West.[4] They argued that freedom emerged in Haiti before it emerged in the West, but Takeuchi's analysis stresses the difference between freedom in the capitalist world and freedom in twentieth-century China. In Takeuchi's intellectual world, subjectivity allowed him to reject or refute existing evaluative grids and evolutionary frameworks. Even before his romance with China, in his early years he expressed this type of sentiment by rejecting authority. His reading of Chinese thinkers as embodying subjectivity continued this tendency but added a spatial dimension. The symbolic geographical space of China represented for him an imaginary reconciliation between substantiality and subjectivity. Here Takeuchi connected subjectivity to an existential moment that goes beyond mere individuality and used this existential moment to challenge the reification of modernity.

The Genesis of Takeuchi's Early Ideas

Takeuchi Yoshimi's postwar conception of Asia developed out of his early experiences, described below, and his prewar thinking. Particularly important is his wrestling with the dialectic between subjectivity and transcendence. This dialectic emerged in his formative years and early in his career.

Takeuchi Yoshimi was born in 1910 in Nagano Prefecture. In the early Taishō period, his father was in the adult entertainment business. Takeuchi recalls that his early life was spent in poverty, and during his school days, he found the symbolic nature of poverty particularly vexing. What he dreaded most was not the actual material poverty but being called "poor."[5] For example, in his early years, he longed for new clothing and refused to go to the cafeteria during lunchtime because he could not afford a lunch box. These examples show that Takeuchi sought the status that commodities gave him in the eyes of others rather than the actual consumption of use-values. In other words, his conception of hierarchy was based on symbols that others attached value to. In his diary, Takeuchi wrote that his sense of inferiority was an important motivating factor during his early years, and Takeuchi's China itself appears similar to his childhood self. China was a failed student without recognition who, unlike the honor student Japan, learned from the West all too well. Since Takeuchi could not win recognition through wealth, he pursued integration and recognition through his achievements in school. However, he eventually rejected this as well and rebelled against the confines of the educational system. In his diary he explains that he originally aimed to be an honor student in primary school, and he felt proud when the teacher praised his poems. He kept all the poems with his teacher's comments on them. However, once he entered middle school, he changed his attitude about teachers and began to dislike being an honor student; he also burned all of the assignments on which his teachers had written positive comments.[6] In this way, shortly before high school, Takeuchi adumbrated his later concept of self-negation, which represented a refusal to occupy positions of institutional power and wealth. Jacques Bidet calls these positions "organization and market"—here represented by figures of authority and commodities.[7] The paradox is that in modern society, one's autonomy is necessarily circumscribed by these two. In Takeuchi's case, he initially wanted the recognition of his teachers but eventually realized that such recognition also undermined his autonomy.

In high school, around 1930, which was a high point in left-wing movements in Japan, Takeuchi participated in a student movement led by, among others, Yasuda Yojūrō (1910–1981), who would himself develop a romantic critique of modernity. During this time, Takeuchi began to study China, which became the locus of his romantic vision. As a result of Takeuchi rejecting the notion of trying to become an honor student, his grades fell, but he was nonetheless admitted to Tokyo Imperial University in 1931. He decided to major in contemporary Chinese literature because it appeared to be the easiest available subject. Not only was China studies an understudied field in Japan, but the modern period of Chinese literature, specifically the post–May Fourth literature that was Takeuchi's focus, was the most unpopular subfield of an unpopular field. Among the thirty-four students studying China in Tokyo Imperial University, Takeuchi was the only one studying modern Chinese literature. Later he would attack scholars of Chinese studies in Japan for neglecting recent developments in China. While he studied at Tokyo Imperial University, his worldview emerged as he rethought Japan's relation to China.

In 1932 Takeuchi traveled to China on a two-month study trip funded by a grant from the Japanese Foreign Ministry and began learning Chinese with a tutor. This study trip was transformative for him because China studies in Japan focused exclusively on the classics, and while in China, Takeuchi became enamored with contemporary Chinese literature and with China in general. As his Chinese improved, he began to read Chinese literature and saw in it the same quest he was pursuing, namely the search for an autonomy independent of outside power.[8] This search holds the key to understanding his idea of conversion when writing about Lu Xun.

Although autonomy is one aspect of Takeuchi's thought, his attitude toward China had another more visceral side that is clearly seen in his first impressions of the country. He went to Manchuria during his 1932 summer study trip and later wrote that "the moment I went, I felt that this was home. What mattered now was not whether doing Chinese literature would be interesting or not; I simply felt I could do nothing else."[9] We might say that this

114 CHAPTER FOUR

is a type of Orientalism, but we must remember that this is only the starting point in the development of his vision of China, which he would refine in his future work.

When Takeuchi returned to Japan, he formed a study group, the Association for the Study of Chinese Literature (Chūgoku bungaku kenkyūkai), in 1934, which among other things published essays on and translations of Chinese writing. Although Takeuchi was only twenty-four years old when he organized the society, he had a clear vision of China and an epistemological stance that served as the basis for his interpretation of Lu Xun. He developed his ideas about China and epistemology as he attempted to find a path between the old Japanese Sinology, *kangaku* (漢学), and the newer *shinagaku* (支那学). *Kangaku* referred to the traditional method of studying China, which was especially prevalent during the Tokugawa period and focused mainly on Confucian studies. As Margaret Mehl points out, during the Tokugawa period, Japanese intellectuals attempted to present themselves as the authentic inheritors of the Chinese tradition, a project that continued in a different guise during the Meiji era.[10] Shinagaku scholars, on the other hand, emphasized objectivity and deployed methodologies of the social sciences to study China. Takeuchi argued that neither of these schools understood subjectivity, and hence neither could see the significance of modern Chinese literature.

We can explain this blindness partly in reference to the shifts in Japanese visions of China. During the mid- and late Tokugawa periods, Japanese thinkers began to decenter China's position in the world. After the loss of the Chinese empire to the Manchus, many Japanese philosophers, especially those associated with the school of "national learning" (*kokugaku*), stopped seeing China as a bearer of universal values.[11] Like the Tokugawa rulers, the initiators of the Meiji Restoration saw themselves as the heirs to Chinese culture. However, by the Meiji period, Japanese thinking about China had changed considerably, as we have already seen in chapter 2 in the case of Fukuzawa Yukichi. Around the time of the Meiji Restoration, Japanese intellectuals witnessed China's defeat at the hands of the Western imperialist powers, beginning with the Opium War (1939–1942), and China soon came to represent a fate that Japan should avoid.[12] Japan's victory in the Sino-Japanese War further transformed how Japanese scholars approached the study of China. After that war, Japanese scholars typically viewed China as a nation-state separate from and inferior to Japan, which led to the spread of an epistemology that privileged Western learning.

This view of China as separate from Japan or as an object of knowledge in a scientific framework was also connected to some of the epistemological transformations resulting from the embrace of Western social sciences. Scholars began to think of China as an object of study rather than as the source of cultural authority. Even the way in which China was identified changed. Instead of calling China *Chūgoku* (which can be loosely translated as "central kingdom" and is still used by the Chinese today), Japanese began to use a newer term, *Shina* (支那), which attempted to approximate the pronunciation for "China" in Western languages.[13] With this linguistic gesture, the shinagaku scholars decentered China and situated it as merely one nation in a world of nation-states, with the notion of a world of nation-states implying that nations can be identical qua nation and yet different with respect to their particular characteristics. Shinagaku thus reconstituted China as an object of knowledge within a new theoretical world space in which China and Japan were separate.

However, within this new theoretical space, proponents of shinagaku constructed China in different ways. Scholars such as Naitō Konan (1866–1934) and Shiratori Kurakichi (1865–1942)—Japanese Sinologists and perhaps the most prominent historians of East Asia in the early twentieth century—conceived of China as part of (but no longer leader of) East Asia (*toyō*). Instead, as the inheritor of Chinese culture, Japan now stepped to the fore.[14] On the other hand, Shiratori's student Tsuda Sōkichi (1873–1961) was uneasy with the idea of East Asia, and using Western standards to evaluate China, he concluded that the legitimacy of Japanese culture no longer depended on China.[15]

To provide an alternative to the old guard of the kangaku tradition represented by Naitō, Tsuda, and others, and also introduce modern Chinese literature to a wider audience, Takeuchi participated in founding the journal *Chinese Literature Monthly* (*Chūgoku bungaku geppō*). The essays he wrote for this journal from 1932 to 1942 reveal how Takeuchi saw himself in relation to Japanese Sinology during this time; like the shinagaku scholars, he believed that most Japanese did not really understand China. After the China Incident in 1935, a key moment in Japan's imperialist adventure in Asia, concern about China sharply increased among the Japanese public. However, as well-known shinagaku scholar Yoshikawa Kōjirō (1904–1980) noted in an essay on translation published in Takeuchi's journal in 1941, "If one glances at our society, it appears there is a great interest in China. . . . However, sincere interest in China is extremely tepid. The China Problem has suddenly pressed upon the public, and people are forced to be interested, but actually, they dislike it."[16] Takeuchi completely agreed with Yoshikawa on this point and also supported his contention that the Japanese falsely believed that they and the Chinese had the same culture and language (*dōbun* 同文). For this reason, Takeuchi and

Yoshikawa agreed that more works about translation were needed. However, they disagreed about the nature of translation. Takeuchi wrote several essays on translation that were polemical, but they also presented some key ideas that he would develop further. These essays concerned what he considered the connection between politics and literature and showed that Takeuchi's pan-Asianism was based on an understanding of a separation between Japan and China that went beyond the translation or the use of particular words. For example, he stressed the importance of consciousness or attitude, which went beyond the question of whether one used *Chūgoku* or *Shina* to refer to China. He also argued that shinagaku scholars' attitude toward translation showed that their attempt to break free from the earlier kangaku world was not complete. In an essay published in the February 1941 issue of *Chinese Literature Monthly*, he highlighted the problems with traditional Japanese translations of Chinese that echoed the critique of the Tokugawa-period thinker Ogyū Sorai (1666–1728). Throughout much of pre-Meiji Japan, Japanese scholars read Chinese through a system known as *kundoku*, in which the order of the Chinese characters was rearranged, and Japanese grammatical particles were added. As a scholar of classical Confucian texts, Ogyū argued that this method obscured the alterity of the world in which the Chinese classics were written and resulted in texts that were not Chinese at all but essentially Japanese. He claimed that to grasp the meaning of classical Chinese texts, one had to learn the Chinese pronunciations of Chinese characters and then proceed to translate the texts into Japanese.[17] Moreover, he claimed that because *kundoku* simply made use of the existing Chinese characters, Japan was effectively still under China's sway:

> *Kundoku* and translation clearly differ. The point is not to mix the Japanese and Chinese languages [as *kundoku* does]. On the contrary, one should engage in independent translation, in which one explains Chinese through Japanese. . . . Because *kundoku* has not been abandoned, it reigns supreme. Therefore, generally speaking, today's translations are turgid. Those that are easy to read are often irresponsible. This is evidence that Japanese education is fragmented. On this point [*kundoku*], Japanese culture has still not freed itself from the domination of Chinese culture.[18]

Takeuchi goes on to argue that although they use virtually the same characters, Chinese and Japanese are two completely different languages. The comment about China ruling Japan underscores the importance he places on national independence even as he stresses pan-Asianism.[19] At another level, Takeuchi's goal is similar to Ogyū's in that they both made China into an Other to allow it to serve as a model. In Ogyū's case, he wanted to mobilize the ancient sage kings mentioned in the Chinese classics to criticize his contemporary society, something that would be impossible if one did not recognize the difference between China (especially classical China) and Japan. Takeuchi did the same while drawing on contemporary Chinese literature, and Lu Xun in particular, to create a critical standpoint from which to view both modernity and Japan.

In these early writings Takeuchi emphasizes consciousness and subjectivity, which for him were always mediated through the nation. In other words, while subjectivity is crucial and will constantly return, it is not unrooted but instead connected to communal history. He began to grasp this on his trips to China, one of which he describes in an essay on *Shina* and *Chūgoku*. He outlines an experience that goes beyond the distinction made by the use of those words and points to something transcendent.

> Often as the sun rose in Beijing, I lay on my bed watching sunlight move on the wall in front of me. . . . [M]y body was satisfied, but I felt the heaviness of human destiny, which I would not understand my whole life, encroaching upon me. When I went out on the streets, the rickshaws that I admired were moving. . . . Like many carefree exchange students, I made friends with those pulling the rickshaws and coveted a masochistic pleasure. On winter evenings, returning to a Japanese coffee shop, I would sit on a street corner on a mat elbow to elbow with the rickshaw drivers and slurp hot udon and burn my throat on sorghum wine. . . . If there is such a thing as a root of humanity, I felt here a vivid and endless obscure substance that goes beyond human life. In short, it is the feeling of the earth that expands in infinite space and time and gives birth to humanity. As I learned more, I could imagine the boundless environment that gave root to and nurtured the actions of Confucius, Mencius, Guan Yu, and Sun Wukong.[20]

This passage points beyond the linguistic distinction between *Shina* and *Chūgoku* and refers to an ontological ground eventually connected to both nationality and transnationality or even universality. This transcendence is found not in some supersensual realm but in everyday experiences of interacting with ordinary people. In the midst of eating udon and drinking sorghum wine, Takeuchi experienced the earth. He does not discuss the earth in detail, but we might conclude that it is akin to Heidegger's description of the earth: "Earth thus shatters every attempt to penetrate into it. It causes every merely calculating importunity upon it to turn to a destruction."[21] Takeuchi does not refer to the earth as something that one can grasp through rational explanation. Rather, in certain moments such as his time spent with the rickshaw drivers, the earth suddenly appears or, in Heidegger's terms, becomes unconcealed.[22]

In the above quote, the earth refers not just to something natural but also to something mediated by community—in this case, the Chinese nation. Through his experience of the earth, he gestures toward a substantial community that endures over generations. However, the nuances of Takeuchi's conception of substantiality differ somewhat from the substantiality that Hegel used to describe the static Oriental world. As noted earlier, Hegel contended that such a world was devoid of subjectivity. However, Takeuchi's interpretation invokes the heroic and in doing so emphasizes subjectivity. In his own way, Takeuchi hoped to integrate the substantiality of community and even nature into this subjectivity, and he does this by reinterpreting major figures in the Chinese tradition, including Confucius and Mencius, as heroes. As we will see, given the importance of revolution in Takeuchi's later work, the heroic subjectivity of Sun Wukong might come the closest to what he aimed to promote.[23]

The issue of subjectivity reappears in a debate between Takeuchi and the prolific shinagaku scholar Yoshikawa Kōjirō, who emphasized the importance of scientific scholarship and facts. We need not fully analyze these debates here, but Takeuchi's response to an article on translation sheds light on his reading of Lu Xun. In the December 1941 issue of *Chinese Literature Monthly*, Yoshikawa asserted that "a scientific system must be established based on hard evidence and intense reading."[24] In a series of responses, Takeuchi claimed that Yoshikawa had overlooked the important connection between literature and "self-negation." In the January 1942 issue, Takeuchi wrote, "If knowledge does not contain the juncture of self-negation (or this enthusiasm), it cannot survive as knowledge. Knowledge must be pursued as it negates itself. This is the attitude of literature. Unless I say otherwise, when I discuss Chinese literature, I refer to literature as an attitude."[25]

Takeuchi contends that this attitude of literature as self-negation was lacking in both kangaku and shinagaku. His concept of literature implicitly criticizes the epistemology of modernity for not allowing for subjectivity or negativity. In Takeuchi's view, the "attitude" of literature implies a critique of the epistemology of shinagaku and scientific epistemology in general. Shinagaku proponents urged researchers and translators to analyze language so that they could convey a reality represented by linguistic signs. Takeuchi attacked this epistemology by pointing out that shinagaku proponents did not adequately account for their own role in the construction of the objective world. But Takeuchi's critique does not merely point out the role of the subject; rather it alludes to both the insufficiency of language and the fundamentally problematic nature of the subject.[26] He felt that literature functions precisely to develop an alternative relationship between language, subject, and object because literature calls into question both language as a mere representation of the world and the subject who stands before that world.

After a series of debates with proponents of shinagaku, in 1943 Takeuchi decided to stop publishing *Chinese Literature Monthly*. This was in a sense a gesture of self-negation because he had created it. The decision to discontinue the journal struck contributors as abrupt, and Takeuchi responded by writing "The Abolition of *Chinese Literature* and Me," an essay in which he explained the relationship between his decision to end the journal and his general philosophical position. He notes that at first he did not want to dissolve the Association for the Study of Chinese Literature, but "something inside him" developed that pushed in that direction. This vague identification of "something inside" reflects a basic approach used by Takeuchi in his reading of Lu Xun and of literature in general, namely an attempt to counter the reification associated with modernity with a notion of feeling that resists rational explanation and at the same time represents a subversion or self-negation of the subject. Takeuchi eventually connects this type of emotive affectivity with politics.

Takeuchi points out that he suspended the publication of *Chinese Literature Monthly* because it had lost its sense of having a clear ideological position, or *tōhasei* (党派性). *Tōhasei* is often used to translate the German word *Parteilichkeit*, which originally referred to the class character of political ideas, but Takeuchi uses it in a positive sense to indicate that the ideals associated with the Association for the Study of Chinese Literature were specific to it. The *tōhasei* of the association was to oppose both kangaku and shinagaku and to do so from a position that opposed modernity and reification by drawing attention to a new type of literature. He notes that the association was unique not only in the way it studied Chinese literature but also because it was the only "party" (*tōha*) that attempted "to criticize contemporary culture from the inside."[27] This internal perspective recognizes that one is part of the problem that one is attacking.

Takeuchi saw contemporary culture as a culture of self-preservation and as intimately linked to bureaucracy;[28] he contends that bureaucratic culture implies abstraction and a retreat from history. Moreover, Takeuchi argues that this bureaucratic culture is leading to the marginalization of literature and the dominance of philosophy in academic practice: "Today's world is of philosophy rather than of literature."[29]

He associates the world of philosophy and bureaucracy with characteristics that reflect the exchange-value side of the commodity form, such as rationalization, abstraction, and development in stages, or evolutionary history. This world of philosophy is produced not only in academic circles but also in people's everyday lives: what Takeuchi calls the "secularization" or "making common" (*sezokuka*) of culture.[30] By secularization, Takeuchi means an overarching process that is at the root not only of the scientific practices of shinagaku but of scholarship and society more generally. He voices his concern that the association was slowly evolving toward an evolutionary vision of "development in stages,"[31] suggesting that Takeuchi probably also had in mind some of the intellectual movements in Japan that he explicitly mentions slightly later in the essay: the schools of East Asian history, the leftist literature movement, and the perspective of materialist history. He contends that the association derived its meaning from being different than all these because using China as the basis for study negated the usual framework for studying foreign literature.[32]

Through this negation, he hoped to construct a different type of culture:

> When the Association for the Study of Chinese Literature was disbanded, if the space where this association used to exist remains, as I expected, it would express itself with a strange elemental groan. I want to hear this groan. I want to wait for the day when the original movement of life emerges from the depths of nothing from nowhere. I really believed that the association was like this and I would like to seek the place where the fabric of our life until today can be reborn in the formless root of the world of nothingness.[33]

Takeuchi juxtaposed this "elemental groan" with the world of nothingness to the reified sphere of the bureaucratic culture of autonomy. The elemental groan arises from the visceral experiences that he had with rickshaw drivers while sitting on a mat slurping udon noodles. Takeuchi now connects this prereflective experience to nothingness, and the political dimension comes to view. The structure of his argument resembles that of Heidegger's description of the feeling of angst, which breaks through the they-self (*das Man*). Philosophy, like bureaucracy, represents the reified culture of modernity, which does not allow room for subjectivity. The various fields that Takeuchi criticizes, including East Asian history and foreign literature, all participate in this loss of self. What he calls "literature," on the other hand, opens one to the abyss and to life. Takeuchi's project was precisely to make his journal and study group a catalyst for the experience of life and the elemental groan emerging from nothingness. He later develops tropes that flesh out the idea of a concrete transcendental in his book on Lu Xun, to which we will turn shortly. At this point, we should note that he contends that the new culture resulting from his project would refrain from "supporting oneself through taking the freedom of others," and "subsume [*hosetsu*] the other through self-negation."[34] In Takeuchi's view, literature was required to develop this new culture; however, the various forms of existing literature and literary criticism in Japan were insufficient for the task because they merely reproduced the reified structures of modernity. The study of another nation's literature was therefore necessary in order to develop an alternative culture, and Chinese literature gave Takeuchi the vehicle he needed to do that.

However, after ten years he realized that the association began to reproduce the structures already prevalent in the study of foreign literature in Japan, which were basically the same as those of shinagaku. Takeuchi asserts that the Asia-Pacific War (which in imperialist Japan was dubbed the "Greater East Asian War") made him aware of the "meaninglessness of the general studies of foreign literature."[35] In an essay written in the same period, "The Greater East Asia War and Our Resolution (A Manifesto)," he supports the war and puts forth his ideas about modernity:

> The Greater East Asia War may be called the rewriting of the history of the world. I deeply believe this. It means the denial of modernity, of modern culture, and out of this denial, to build for oneself a new world and new culture. . . . Modern culture must be denied because it is the projection of Europe onto ourselves. Thus, we must in a sense deny ourselves. For the creation of history, the world must be produced from within.[36]

This essay was controversial, and after the war he acknowledged that he was mistaken. However, we should understand the reasons behind his support for the Asia-Pacific War, which for him was retroactively transformed by the attack on Pearl Harbor and more generally the confrontation with the United States. In his diary, he explains that when Japan invaded China, he felt unhappy and guilty. However, he contended that the war against the United States retroactively legitimated the war against China.[37] At the time, Takeuchi saw the war with the United States as being about national liberation. Although Takeuchi had not fully developed a theory of a pan-Asianism at this point, he was already interested in uniting with China and was concerned about the national liberation of weak nations. He later came to believe that his judgment about Japan's role in the war was misguided, but he never changed his basic philosophical position. As late as 1972 he wrote:

> If I simply speak about it now, that manifesto was wrong at the level of political judgment and wrong in every other way. But with respect to the thought that is expressed through the essay, I do not believe I was mistaken. Regardless of what other people think, I can only take that thought to hell with me.[38]

Following Takeuchi's own remarks, we must ask what this fundamental thought was that he expressed in the essay. Takeuchi's view of the Asia-Pacific

War must be understood as part of his project to resist the abstraction related to reification associated with Western capitalism and his interpretation of subjectivity as an act of negation, which he saw as intimately connected to the creation of history. He further anticipated postcolonial theorists by criticizing the projection of European values onto the colonized. From this perspective, the postcolonial critique points to a lack of subjectivity. Asia and Japan accepted the imperialist West's standpoint as universal and forfeited their own subjectivity as a result. To counter this required initiating a negative movement and making or remaking history. Takeuchi believed that the Asia-Pacific War was in the process of making history, but his Association for the Study of Chinese Literature was not living up to this historical event. It is precisely at this time, during the early 1940s, that Takeuchi began to write his work on Lu Xun, in which he would show that Lu Xun embodied many of the tenets of real literature and thus expressed the possibility of the denial of modernity and negation.

Takeuchi's Lu Xun

Takeuchi published his book on Lu Xun in 1944, after Japan had invaded China in 1937 and after the attack on Pearl Harbor in 1941. He had already been to China, and like a number of Japanese Sinologists, he had mixed feelings about Japan's involvement in the war. He had a great sentimental attachment to China, but he had perhaps an even stronger resentment of the United States and Americanism. His writings about Lu Xun are thus constantly mediated by ideas about resistance and the nature of China, Japan, and Asia.

On the eve of the 1911 Revolution, a few years before World War I, Europe was the center of imperialist power; however, by the time of World War II, this power was shifting toward the United States. For many Japanese intellectuals, Americanism represented a continuation of the domination of Europe and so was criticized by a number of scholars, including the philosophers of the Kyoto school and romantics such as Yasuda Yojūrō. Like Takeuchi, these romantics envisioned literature as separate from politics, but as we shall see below, Takeuchi inflected the romantics' vision in such a way as to produce a new form of politics that he associated with China.

Yasuda is mentioned here not only because he was a high school classmate of Takeuchi and one of the leaders of the Japanese romantic school but also because he was extremely active during the 1930s and 1940s when Takeuchi published his book on Lu Xun. At first glance it may seem that Takeuchi's work is derivative of Yasuda's, and in fact they do have some clear similarities.[39] Like Takeuchi, Yasuda was an outspoken critic of European modernity and Americanism. But perhaps more importantly, Yasuda also argued that literature was separate from politics. He berated proletarian literature in a manner that Takeuchi echoed in his work on Lu Xun:

> The danger of nationalism without feeling or emotion is that it is no different from the totalitarianism of Marxism. In the early years of the Showa period, when anarchism disappeared and Marxism entered into its best days, the Marxist group claimed to respect culture . . . but there is neither any atmosphere of the arts nor emotion and sentiment there.[40]

Yasuda rejected politicized literature, regardless of the political stance of the author. He criticized ideology from both the left and the right. He believed that Marxists were not truly revolutionary since true revolution required aesthetics and feeling.[41] Scholars such as Kobayashi Hideo (1902–1983), one of Japan's most influential cultural critics, had previously tried to separate literature from politics by arguing that literature could exist in a space of its own,[42] and both Yasuda and Takeuchi responded to this separation in different ways. Marxism made aesthetics subordinate to politics; Yasuda hoped to reverse this relationship. However, Yasuda's aestheticism eventually led him to support Japan's ultranationalism, including the invasion of China.

Takeuchi's book on Lu Xun rethought the Chinese experience in a way that responded to the crisis of conscience about the war and the impasse between discourses such as those of Yasuda on the one hand and advocates of proletarian literature on the other. In the book, Takeuchi followed Kobayashi Hideo in separating literature from politics but then moved in the opposite direction by recombining the two. Here as before, literature represents fundamental subjectivity beyond reification, but in Takeuchi's view, literature goes beyond itself to encompass religion, politics, and revolution. He then proceeds to explore the productive tensions between these three elements of culture to rethink China.

LU XUN'S CONVERSION: RELIGION AND SUBJECTIVITY

Takeuchi repeatedly returns to the problem of "conversion" in his *Rojin* (Lu Xun). He does so to carry out two major agendas: first, to think of conversion in relation to religion and, second, to destabilize earlier narratives about Lu Xun's decision to be a writer and publish his first collection of short stories, *Na Han*. Usually translated as "a call to arms," the title could also mean "screaming," which seems to anticipate the groan that Takeuchi spoke of. Takeuchi asks how the advent of this scream can be explained. To start with the conclusion first, Takeuchi explains: "The 'scream' that proceeds from the pain associated with the 'inability to forget' is a 'call' and not 'a detailed clearing away.' This is just as repentance comes after sinning."[43] By using the concept of sin, Takeuchi moves into the realm of religion and its notions of conversion. According to the dominant narrative that scholars of Chinese literature continue to reproduce even today, Lu Xun went to Japan to study medicine in 1904 and then, after a biology class, saw a slideshow in which a Chinese was being decapitated for spying during the Russo-Japanese War, an event at which the many Chinese onlookers at the execution did nothing. Lu Xun was disturbed by seeing the lack of sympathy of the Chinese for their fellow national. He concluded from this that it was not the bodies of the Chinese that needed to be cured but their minds; so he switched from medicine to literature.

Takeuchi contends that Lu Xun's turn to writing is more complex than this story suggests. He draws attention to another incident that Lu Xun narrates in an essay called "Mr. Fujino" (1926), in which Lu is accused of cheating. This incident happened before the slideshow incident and again involved shame. Takeuchi quotes Lu Xun's own description of the incident:

> China is a weak country. Thus Chinese children are naturally of low ability. If I scored more than 60 points, it was not because of my ability. It is not surprising that they had such suspicions. After this, I had the fate of seeing a Chinese person being executed [on a slide]. In my second year, I switched to taking bacteriology, and one always used slides to show the form of bacteria.[44]

Takeuchi contends that reading the slideshow incident and being accused of cheating together reveal that Lu Xun's turn to literature was the result of a more fundamental conversion experience. The above passage in Lu Xun is crucial for understanding Takeuchi's own position because it connects Lu Xun's experience and the problem of global unevenness and Asia's place in it, which Takeuchi would become increasingly concerned with during the postwar period. We can understand his reading of Lu Xun as again echoing Takeuchi's early childhood experience of being looked down upon. In Takeuchi's view, the experience of shame for being a Chinese, a person from an oppressed country, is similar to Lu's feeling of shame at seeing the slideshow. We can continue Takeuchi's logic by noting that Lu Xun then mentions the use of slides to show forms of bacteria. It points to a type of mediation that is common to both Chinese and the bacteria, which is to say that there is something dehumanizing about the gaze of the Japanese on a country that is the victim of imperialism. But now the problem is not about seeing other people, whom he must change, but about himself. Takeuchi writes: "More than anything else this was a shame directed at himself. Rather than pitying his fellow citizens, he pitied himself who had no choice but to pity his compatriots. He did not think of literature alongside pitying his compatriots. His pitying his compatriots was a signpost of his own loneliness."[45] This loneliness was the key to Lu Xun's conversion. In Takeuchi's view, these experiences made Lu Xun turn inward and eventually attain a type of transcendence—the ability to look at himself as another. This transcendent perspective provided him a critical distance from which to analyze the present. We could call this a quasi-religious perspective, since Takeuchi speaks of transcendence and conversion (*kaishin*), a change that happens after one realizes one has sinned. However, he eventually connects this experience to the "Eastern people."

> The term "religious" is vague and the form of Lu Xun's ethos was unreligious and even anti-religious, but his manner of holding on to his position was religious. Or, if we can say that the Russians were religious, we can also say that Lu Xun was religious in this sense. . . . I wonder whether there was not something that Lu Xun sought to atone for. Lu Xun himself was probably not clear about what this something was. . . . Perhaps the Chinese word *gui* [demon] comes close. Zhou Zuoren's [Lu Xun's brother, who was also a writer] statement about "the sadness of Eastern people" could perhaps work only as a note.[46]

We see here the problem of the internal other, which is connected to the Easterners and also the Russians, which, given that he was writing after the October Revolution, suggests both global unevenness and revolution. Perhaps more importantly for the issue of conversion and subjectivity something emerges from inside Lu Xun and that something strengthens his integrity.

Takeuchi explains Lu Xun's conversion in this way:

> He stayed in a room of the institute where "the soul emerges" and buried himself in old books. He did not have any contact with the outside world. His "scream" had not yet burst forth as a "scream." He only felt the call fermenting in a painful silence. I imagine that in this silence, he grasped the decisive event of his life, namely what is called his conversion [*kaishin*].[47]

Out of the silence a scream bursts forth, but it was preceded by an incubation period during which Lu Xun did not write anything. The key here again is the loneliness that Lu Xun himself expressed in his preface to *Na Han* (Screaming). He withdrew totally from the world, at which point something akin to a primal scream, perhaps related to Takeuchi's groan, emerges. In Takeuchi's view, when the scream appeared in silence, although Lu Xun had no contact with the outside world, he experienced something like an internal "other." Between the silence and the scream, this "other" emerges and provides atonement. Takeuchi describes Lu Xun's other in the following manner.

When one reads his work, one feels like one is under a constant shadow. This shadow is always in the same place. The shadow itself does not exist, but light emerges from there and vanishes into it. Through this movement, there is a point of darkness that seems to hint at existence. If one carelessly reads him, one will not notice this darkness, but if one pays attention to it, one will never forget it. As if a skull is dancing in a bright dance hall, in the end it appears that the skull is the one with substance. Lu Xun lived with such a shadow on his back throughout his life. It is in this sense that I call his literature a literature of atonement [*shokuzai*].[48]

This internal other resembles what Jean Laplanche calls "the permanence of the unconscious, the primacy of the address of the other,"[49] but we should understand this in a religious context. The term that Takeuchi uses to refer to "atonement," *shokuzai*, consists of two characters, *shoku*, meaning "redemption," and *zai*, or "sin." We here have a concrete way in which the idea of shadow or nothingness—the shadow that does not exist—entails a debt to the "other." We can compare Takeuchi's idea of shadow and atonement to Heidegger's concepts of guilt (*Schuld*) and conscience, which he associated with being pulled away from the reified world of the everyday. Heidegger's work is usually thought of as being individualistic, and his idea of being-toward-death is thought of as pulling away from community toward an isolated self, or Dasein. Scholars often interpret Heidegger as arguing that death is something that only an individual can experience and that people cannot experience the death of another. However, in order to understand Takeuchi it is helpful to keep in mind another reading of Heidegger. Christopher Fynsk contends that in Heidegger, contrary to first appearances, the call of conscience is about the death of the "other."[50] The key insight here is that precisely when one appears to be most alone, there is an uncanny call from the other. This is the sense in which Takeuchi's Lu Xun understood sin, which represents a debt that is owed to the past and to those who died in the resistance or revolution. It is also an acknowledgment of their role in the reproduction of the present system.

AN ALTERNATIVE CHINESE POLITICAL PRACTICE

Through recounting these experiences of loneliness, shame, and sin, Takeuchi formulated a different type of politics. He developed his politics throughout his work, but here we will focus on the fourth chapter of his book *Rojin*, in which he expresses these ideas most clearly.

The link that mediates between literature and politics is religious consciousness, which in Takeuchi's formulation countered secularization. Religiosity constitutes another dimension of the concept of nothingness and can be connected to the negation of the self and also gesture in the direction of substantiality. In other words, the "nothing" referred to here is not simply empty but at times appears to have a mysterious content. In the third chapter, "The Formation of Thought," Takeuchi defines Lu Xun's stance toward literature by deploying the concept of nothingness described above. While he concedes that Lu Xun was committed to certain political ideals, he emphasizes that Lu did not conceive of literature as a means toward political ends: "Lu Xun lived sincerely, was an enthusiastic nationalist and a patriot. However, he never supported his literature through these things. Rather, he established his literature by sweeping these things aside. The source of Lu Xun's literature is something that we can call 'nothing.' "[51] Takeuchi argues against what already in the 1940s had become the prevalent reading of Lu Xun's literature: it was primarily politically motivated. In Japan, this reading was promoted by influential figures such as Oda Takeo (1900–1979), the first Japanese to write an in-depth analysis of Lu Xun, and Masuda Wataru (1903–1977), a member of Takeuchi's literature study society who had met Lu Xun in China. In addition, Kaji Wataru (1903–1982), an often overlooked but vocal critic of Takeuchi, went to China in 1936, met Lu Xun, became convinced that Takeuchi had overemphasized concepts such as nothingness and religion, and turned Lu Xun into a sort of "monk" rather than a revolutionary. I note his criticism of Takeuchi in the postwar period because it was probably shared by a number of scholars who promoted proletarian literature, and it clarifies a fundamental aspect of Takeuchi's thought. "Of course, for this Buddhist monk," Kaji wrote, "each entanglement with reality, even if he acted externally as an enlightener or in politics, is just a superficial secondary phenomena. . . . However, it goes without saying, Takeuchi's Lu Xun has nothing to do with [the real] Lu Xun."[52] Although these lines were written during the postwar period, this was a critique that Takeuchi must have faced throughout his career. In Kaji's view, Takeuchi turned Lu Xun into a Buddhist monk who was more concerned about nothingness than about politics. After Lu Xun was canonized as a revolutionary writer who continued the legacy of May Fourth, Takeuchi's reading was naturally subject to this kind of criticism. This is not the place to go into which author correctly grasped Lu Xun's writings, and Takeuchi never responded to Kaji's criticism. Yet Kaji's comments help us to understand a key issue that we will revisit in the next chapter: namely the relationship between nothingness and a politics of Asia. We already have the beginnings of a response to this question in the idea of the "other," but one can further unpack the significance of nothingness by briefly considering Hegel's comment about the dialectic between the religious and political

128   CHAPTER FOUR

readings of nothingness in his critique of Hinduism. In the *Elements of the Philosophy of Right*, Hegel explains:

> The human being is pure thinking of himself, and only in thinking is he this power to give himself universality, that is, extinguish all particularity, all determinacy. . . . This form of freedom occurs frequently in history. The Hindus, for example, place the highest value on mere persistence in the knowledge of one's simple identity with oneself, on remaining within this empty space of one's inwardness like colourless light in pure intuition, and on renouncing every activity of life, every end and every representation [*Vorstellung*]. In this way, the human being becomes *Brahman*. . . . This form [of freedom] appears more concretely in the active fanaticism of both political and religious life. An example of this was the Reign of Terror and the French Revolution, during which all differences of talents and authority were supposed to be cancelled out. . . . For fanaticism wills only what is abstract, not what is articulated, so that where differences emerge, it finds them incompatible with its own indeterminacy and cancels them out. This is why the people, during the French Revolution, destroyed once more the institutions they had themselves created, because all institutions are incompatible with the abstract self-consciousness of equality.[53]

Hegel here brings together two seemingly contradictory tendencies, the absolute rejection of the mundane world by the Hindu ascetic and the radicals of the French Revolution. It also suggests that the flip side of absolute substance is absolute negativity, a type of hypersubjectivity. Both the "Hindu" and the revolutionary stances are connected to pure subjectivity, which Hegel characterizes as light; it enables everything to be seen but stays separate. Takeuchi mobilizes this category of nothingness in politics. Nothingness as radical subjectivity enables the constant negation and critique of the institutions that people have constructed. In the next chapter we will see Takeuchi interpret Mao's China and potentially Asia in this manner.

This dialectic is also at work in Takeuchi's portrayal of Lu Xun, but we should remember that his conception of nothingness is vague. Takeuchi's earlier comments about nothingness and the other suggest that for his Lu Xun, simple self-identity is constantly mediated by both elemental force and a debt to the other. Immediately after his abovementioned comment on nothingness, he writes: "Because this fundamental awareness turned him into a writer, without this, the nationalist Lu Xun and the patriotic Lu Xun are ultimately [only] words. By claiming that Lu Xun wrote a literature of atonement, I express my resistance."[54] The term "atonement" suggests that the idea of nothingness entails a debt to the other. This is precisely the sense in which both Lu Xun and Takeuchi understood sin, as a debt that they owe to the past and to those who died in the resistance or revolution. In this case, negativity is conditioned by that which goes beyond it; in this way, subjectivity and its movement of negation are not blind and have a certain direction. But, as in the example from Hegel, the path is endless, and negation continues. In a sense, Takeuchi is playing with a paradox here: he wants an abstract perspective that enables constant critique of everything that exists or will exist, but at the same time his standpoint of critique is not merely an abstract self but is connected to both life and the other.

Takeuchi explains his unique conception of the self as he outlines the relationship of religion to literature.

> That which makes a writer possible is probably some type of awareness. Just as a religious person is made possible by an awareness of sin, for the writer as well some type of awareness is probably necessary. Through this awareness the religious person sees God and in the same way the writer sets words free. This person is not controlled by words, but rather stands at the place where language is controlled. In short, he creates his own God. All such awareness is not limited ultimately to individual experience and perhaps it is impossible to attain. . . . The path is endless. He was just a traveler on this unending path. However, at some time this traveler transformed the unlimited into a small point on his self and through this he became unlimited. He emerged out of the foundation of incessant self-construction, but the self that emerged was always himself. In short, this was his fundamental self. I call this literature.[55]

Here Takeuchi continues themes from his earlier essay where he described the elemental groan and life that would resist reified bureaucracy. But we now see that Takeuchi conceived of such ideas of life or a specific type of awareness as possibilities for freedom. Although one might usually connect religion to a transcendent goodness, Takeuchi claims that it is rather the awareness of sin, an evil act that has always already taken place, that forms the foundation of religion. Moreover, the religious person's vision of God or the good is always mediated by his or her own temporal awareness. Consequently, one cannot experience any eternal good by holding this view, and everything is haunted by the destruction of time. But attempts to bring the infinite within the finite lie within this—attempts to transform the infinite into a point. This then becomes the root of infinite self-construction in which the same-self always emerges. This presupposes that a self exists that is both identical to and different from its various concrete instantiations. This implies a strange type of transcendence that Takeuchi identifies as religious.

A recent debate over Jacques Derrida's concept of religion can help illuminate Takeuchi's position.[56] Martin Hägglund counters John D. Caputo's religious reading of Derrida by outlining a position that Takeuchi anticipates. Hägglund explains, "If I seek to prolong my life or the life of another, I seek to transcend the limits of a particular time—to live on—but I do not seek to transcend the conditions of time altogether. Far from fulfilling the desire to live on, a timeless state of eternity would eliminate the temporal life I want to maintain."[57]

The concepts that Takeuchi often uses, such as "life," the "everyday," and the "elemental," refer to processes in the world that are precarious and that one should seek to transcend. He believed that one should affirm the desire to transcend but also both the impossibility of eternity and the undesirability of it. If one attained eternity, it would be a kind of reification, an elimination of temporal life; the aim of achieving the eternality of temporal life presents an unresolvable paradox.

As the writer confronts reification, he or she stands in relation to language and occupies a space from which one can control language. From this amorphous space, the writer creates his or her own gods, which are not eternal. Takeuchi in some sense implies that Lu Xun's characters, such as Ah Q and others, are gods who are the epitome of finitude and imperfection. As characters, they are abstract personae, which allows them to be identified with and by various people. However, such figures do not stand opposed to life; they exemplify the tribulations of life and attempts to overcome them. Moreover, through such constructions, the writer insists on the continuation of temporal life, which turns into an unending dialectic that Takeuchi will eventually connect to endless revolution that is the plight of China/Asia.

In Takeuchi's view, Lu Xun was on this kind of unending path of self-renewal, but this constant renewal arose from a source that Takeuchi identifies as both nothing and literature. He simultaneously problematizes and asserts subjectivity. In this way, a type of consciousness or awareness that emerges before the subject as writer serves as a moment of prereflective transcendence. However, this conscious moment is still temporal. The writer does not stop at this prereflective moment but controls words—and uses words to give shape to experiences that seem to escape conceptualization. In this way, transcendence points inward and is shaped by language. Because transcendence points inward, it is in fact unlimited, that is, not limited by any concrete object and not everlasting. Drawing on such a mediated transcendence, the writer sees something beyond the contemporary reified ways of using language and creates the possibilities of a new world by reorganizing conventional signs. This process never ends because new conventions can be reified, and the process of destruction and reconstruction must be constantly repeated. The writer constantly returns to the unlimited point within themselves, the source of negativity and transcendence, to create a new world out of language.

As suggested above, creativity and language break from reified politics, but by delinking literature from one type of politics, Takeuchi hopes to relink it to politics in a new way. In Lu Xun in particular, Takeuchi sees the possibility of a noninstrumental relationship between literature and politics. Although Lu Xun is often revered as someone who turned to literature because of political motivations, Lu himself made a distinction between literature and politics: "I have often felt that literature and politics are often in mutual conflict. . . . The purpose of politics is to maintain the status quo, and naturally it points in a direction different from literature, which is not satisfied with the status quo. Politics seeks to maintain the status quo to consolidate it, whereas literature prompts society to progress and gradually detaches it [from politics]."[58] Takeuchi also attempts to use literature to attack the status quo and specifically thinks of the relationship between literature and action. He quotes the following comment by Lu Xun about revolution and literature: "For a revolution to appear, one needs 'revolutionaries'; 'revolutionary literature' is not urgent. The product of revolutionaries is revolutionary literature."[59] He then asserts the following:

> This is a point that Lu advocates throughout his life. Revolution needs revolutionaries; actors, not spectators. "Revolutionary literature" created by spectators is not real revolutionary literature. This is because real revolutionary literature must naturally emerge as the result of action. On this point, it makes no difference if one replaces the term "revolution" with "patriotism" or some other term.[60]

Action here again goes beyond abstractions. Because literature is action, it can bear on politics and revolution, but Takeuchi qualifies the way in which literature is action. He calls attention to two points that Lu Xun makes when discussing revolutionary literature: that it is powerless with respect to revolution and that it is a type of excess. He seeks to reconcile literature as activity and its impotence in politics.

> This does not mean that literature has no relation to politics. . . . Literature is powerless with respect to politics because it alienates [sogai] politics and does this through its confrontation with politics. That which leaves politics is not literature. By means of politics, literature sees its shadow and through repelling this shadow, in other words, through becoming aware of its powerlessness, literature becomes literature. Literature is action, not a concept. However, its action is action that establishes itself through alienating action. Literature is not outside of action; amid action, like the axis of a rotating ball, it has the form of a sublime stillness that has gathered the motion of a whole body.[61]

In Takeuchi's description of the dialectic between literature and politics—a dialectic that implies self-externalization and a "contradictory unity"[62]—we hear echoes of the Kyoto school philosopher Nishida Kitarō and also Hegel.[63] If action takes place in time, literature is movement in time and yet alienates such movement. Similar to Hegel's discussion of Hinduism and the French Revolution, it is precisely because of literature's distance from politics that it can constantly return to haunt and critique politics, pushing it in new directions. In Takeuchi's view, because the unity between politics and literature is contradictory, it opens new vistas to theorize action, and this theorization is done through language.

Literature can create a new politics precisely because of its relation to language dereification and the creation of a possible new world, meaning that language is the precursor of the possibility of both literature and politics. But each of these practices needs to retain its autonomy. Literature should not become a servant of politics, but the worlds constructed by literature can be used to critique politics, which in turn can point the way to a new type of politics. Literature embodies what might be called the "power of powerlessness." It has no direct power over people in high positions, but writers can construct worlds that depict the failures of those in power. The audience for this literature is not those who govern but the governed themselves, leading Takeuchi to see literature as having the potential to spark mass movements. His final allusion to stillness and motion echoes the earlier point about the infinity of subjectivity. Such an infinity entails a certain type of motion, but this motion appears motionless from the perspective of the empirical world and acts to gather the movement of the world to represent it in a new way. By bringing literature and politics together this way, Takeuchi shows that for all their independence, literature and politics mediate each other. Politics must fix language and the world in a particular way, but literature serves constantly to destabilize already reified conceptions of the world.

Lu Xun and Revolution

Because the dialectic between literature and politics never ends, Takeuchi's ideas amount to a philosophy of endless revolution. Takeuchi claims that the 1911 Revolution in China clearly showed the relationship between literature and revolution. Takeuchi read Lu Xun on the 1911 Revolution and investigated the relationship between Lu Xun and Sun Yat-sen, who represented literature and politics, respectively. He cites the following passage from Lu Xun to show that for both Sun and Lu, even revolution should not reify subjectivity:

Schopenhauer makes the following statement. "Your estimation of a man's size will be affected by the distance at which you stand from him, but in two entirely opposite ways according as it is his physical or his mental stature that you are considering. The one will seem smaller the farther off you move; the other, greater. In the former case, a great distance appears small, while the latter case, the opposite is true. In the case of the body, from a distance it appears small."[64] In the case of the spirit, on the contrary, distance makes it appear larger. Not only does the greatness of the spirit appear small when one approaches it, but the wounds and weak points strike the eye. In this way, the people with a great spirit are the same as us. They are not gods, demons, or strange beasts. They are human beings. They are only this and because of this, they are great people.

When a warrior dies in battle, the flies first find the weak points and wounds. They whizz and buzz and are satisfied as if they are braver than the warrior. But because the warrior is already dead in battle, he cannot wave them away. Here the flies also buzz and believe that they have an eternal voice. This is because they are more complete than the warrior. But in the end, the warrior with weak points is still a warrior and the flies are nothing but flies. Shoo flies. Even though you have wings and fly about, you can never surpass the warrior.[65]

Takeuchi notes that this text was written in 1925, shortly after Sun Yat-sen's death. The warrior in the above passage was Sun Yat-sen. Sun represented eternal revolution, which Takeuchi will eventually read as emblematic of China/Asia. The flies represent those who do not understand the meaning of revolution. When one comes close to a great warrior, one realizes the warrior's finitude and humanity. The warrior is finite: failings, problems, and incompleteness are part of human existence. The warrior, like the revolutionary, is someone who attempts to complete this incompleteness despite the impossibility of this task. Indeed, revolutionaries are complete only insofar as they understand their inherent incompleteness and incessantly struggle against this. Takeuchi quotes Lu Xun who says:

Whatever anyone says, Sun Yat-sen lived his whole life seriously. Sun Yat-sen was a revolutionary from the time that he was born, and was a revolutionary even in failure. He was not satisfied even when the Republic of China was established. He did not revel in idleness. He still worked continuously to realize his goal of a complete revolution. Even when the revolution was close to completion, he claimed that the revolution was not successful and told his fellow revolutionaries to persevere. He was a complete person and an eternal revolutionary. Each of his actions were revolutionary. No matter how later people count his shortcomings and criticize him, in the end, he was a complete revolutionary.[66]

From the above passages, Takeuchi infers that Lu Xun respected Sun or that which he represented, that revolution is never complete and always fails but that it is important precisely because of its failure. He says, "The 1911 Revolution was no revolution. The second and third revolutions are not revolutions. This is because 'revolution has no end.' True revolution is eternal revolution,"[67] which points to the dialectic between literature and politics mentioned above. Moreover, in Takeuchi's view, those who say that the revolution has succeeded are like the flies that gather around the corpse of the warrior. The 1911 Revolution was part of a larger process, the beginning of a series of political transformations from the anti-Manchu revolution to national revolution to the proletarian revolution, all of which Lu Xun supported.

Takeuchi suggests that revolution has a more abstract wholeness that encompasses concrete instantiations such as the anti-Manchu revolution and proletarian revolution. He believed that Lu Xun had recognized in Sun and the 1911 Revolution an abstract principle of politics, the principle of eternal revolution. He saw this as corresponding to China's historical praxis and contended that the relationship between literature and politics is actually embodied in the relationship between Lu Xun and Sun Yat-sen. Lu Xun, he believed, saw in Sun "the eternal revolutionary" and saw this eternal revolutionary in himself as well.[68]

In Takeuchi's view, Lu Xun thus brought himself into a dialectical relationship with Sun:

> Lu Xun sees the "eternal revolutionary" in Sun Wen [i.e., Sun Yat-sen]. Lu probably stood in a relationship of contradictory unity [*mujun teki dōitsu*] to Sun through the mediation of the "eternal revolutionary." Was he not fighting for his life with a certain of image of himself reflected through Sun Wen? Perhaps one could put it this way, through his resolve to death, he constantly repeated the creation of his self and he took this contradiction in the form of crisis with him to his natural death.[69]

Takeuchi interprets Lu Xun's writings about national character (*guominxing*) as advocating perpetual revolution and notes how in Sun's revolution the object keeps changing, from anti-Manchu revolution to constituting a republic to national revolution or proletarian revolution.[70]

In Takeuchi's reading of Lu Xun, perpetual revolution results in the constant reconstitution of the subject. It constantly externalizes itself and must repel its shadow, but at the same time it "chooses itself from amidst politics."[71] According to Takeuchi's dialectic, history is not evolutionary, and novelty can emerge from the dialectic. The new emerges through the subject negating itself and constantly facing death. Takeuchi asserts that Lu Xun held fast to the attitude of literature throughout most of his life: "In other words, he continued to live while confronting death. Through this at times he transcended death and became the hero of the people."[72] Here again Takeuchi gestures toward his novel understanding of eternality as not separate from the temporal world.

Through literature, Lu Xun confronted death, enabling him to enter the world of action in a novel manner and connect with the people, which in turn created a link to politics. Thus, in an essay written in 1948, Takeuchi calls Lu Xun the "poet of the people," which he contrasts to "the idol of bureaucratic culture."[73] Unlike the Japanese writers who reproduced the bureaucratization and reification characteristic of Western modernity, Lu Xun represents the possibility of people controlling their history and constantly remaking themselves anew.[74] This came to be a type of history from the bottom that Takeuchi later saw as characteristic not only of Lu Xun but also of the Chinese Revolution and Mao Zedong.

Takeuchi's interpretation deals with reification and alienation, the two interdependent problems that characterized the social form of capitalism. In Takeuchi's view, bureaucratic culture conceals the true power of the people, and the people are alienated from a bureaucracy that reifies them. Takeuchi's critique of reification therefore makes possible a return to an experience of the self—a dealienation that makes possible dereification. Takeuchi then proceeded to develop a dialectic that reconnects the moment of experience with the moment of conceptualization to create the possibility of novel action.

Conclusion

Takeuchi's early work and his reading of Lu Xun laid the foundation for his pan-Asian thought that came to fruition in the postwar era. During the interwar period, the politics Takeuchi supported were similar to that of Ōkawa Shūmei, at least on a superficial level. They both supported Japan's Asia-Pacific War. In fact, after the war, Takeuchi was instrumental in rehabilitating Ōkawa's thought. However, an important difference between the two was their differing interpretations of the role of China and subjectivity, two themes that are further explored in the next chapter. In the prewar era, Takeuchi had already begun identifying with China, a region that Japan was itself colonizing, and he also wanted to explore subjectivity, which he found in Lu Xun. Paradoxically, it was after the war, when pan-Asianism appeared to be a total failure, that Takeuchi began seriously promoting Asian unity. We will now turn to this important juncture in both Takeuchi's work and pan-Asian thought.

5

Takeuchi Yoshimi, Part II:
Pan-Asianism, Revolutionary Nationalism, and War Memory

After the Japanese surrender in 1945, Takeuchi rethought his earlier ideas about Lu Xun and revolution. By constructing China as an ideal, Takeuchi supplemented his views on subjectivity with a vision of the world and hints of an idea of community. The inspiration for much of his work was revolutionary China, which he linked to the larger context of Asian revolutions and resistance. Although Takeuchi's most influential work, *Rojin* (Lu Xun), was published during the Asia-Pacific War, it was in the postwar period that Takeuchi became a prominent pan-Asianist. This resulted from his rethinking the significance of the Chinese Revolutions of 1911 and 1949 and Asia within a theory of modernity. The problem of subjectivity was again central to this theory of modernity, and he used the idea of subjectivity to question linear representations of history as a way to liberate Asia from existing teleologies.

Scholarship on Takeuchi's postwar writings is relatively scarce, and even authors who have done scholarly work in this area have failed to analyze the problems of subjectivity and revolution that Takeuchi raises because they have failed to recognize the importance of Marxism in his work. Takeuchi's critique of teleology was directed at Marxists and modernists, but it also drew on both the Chinese Revolution and an ideal of Third World unity associated with the Bandung Conference of 1955, where Asian and African nations discussed following a path beyond the Cold War stalemate between the United States and the Soviet Union. His support for both the Chinese Revolution and Third World unity confirms that he supported aspects of the socialist project. Takeuchi envisioned Third World nationalism as involving subjectivity and liberation from imperialism. By reading pan-Asianism and Third Worldism together, Takeuchi denaturalized Asia and delinked it from any simple geographical connection. In his scheme, "Asia" refers to the subjective and national process of resistance to imperialism, which would occur through revolution and lead to the creation of new domestic and international orders. He believed bringing Japan back into Asia would not be possible without confronting the controversial issue of war memory, a problem he grappled with during the last decades of his life and one that continues to haunt international relations in Asia today.

Takeuchi felt that the Japanese Communist Party (JCP) did not live up to this ideal, whereas China under the communists appeared to be implementing Takeuchi's project. But for Takeuchi, that ended with the death of Mao Zedong in 1976, one year before Takeuchi himself died. This marked the start of a new era in the discourse of pan-Asianism.

Situating China and Asia in the Postwar World

After the Asia-Pacific War and especially after 1949, the image of China in Japan shifted radically. As early as 1946, the stage was set for Japan's reconceptualizing of China, when hundreds of Japanese communists, including a founding member of the party, Nosaka Sanzō (1892–1993), returned from China and wrote about the communist movement there. Nosaka had traveled to China in 1940 to convince Japanese soldiers to support the Chinese resistance and met Mao Zedong and Zhou Enlai while he was there. When he returned in 1946, he wrote enthusiastically about the success of the Chinese Communist Party (CCP) and the real possibility of a Chinese communist revolution.

Takeuchi and other Japanese intellectuals were deeply influenced by such writings, and China began to symbolize for them resistance to the global capitalist system. Takeuchi had been sent to China in a railway guard unit in 1943 and remained in China as an interpreter until 1946.[1] He was in Hankou when the Japanese emperor issued his famous statement surrendering to the United States. Many have noted that the emperor spoke in literary Japanese and consequently was not easily comprehensible by the common people. However, Takeuchi experienced an added layer of complexity by virtue of being resident in a land against which Japan was at war. When he read the Potsdam Declaration of July 26, 1945, he felt that it came from a distant world.[2] When he later heard the broadcast of the emperor's imperial rescript on surrender, he was neither happy about continuing to live nor angry about anything.[3] His emotions began to change once he returned home and began to experience the reality of the war. During this time, he was out of a job and recounts using streetlights to read and not having much to spend on books and journals.[4] At the center of his process of reestablishing his position as a writer and critic was a rethinking of Japan's significance in the context of China, Asia, and global modernity.

138 CHAPTER FIVE

Takeuchi's works in the postwar period cannot be understood without recognizing the impact of numerous world-historical events, such as the American occupation of Japan, the Korean War, the liberation of the old colonies, and the move toward the Fordist mode of capitalism that underpinned state-centered development in Japan. While this development spread across the globe, it did so following three distinct models: Western advanced capitalist welfare states, communist states, and newly liberated colonies. Communist states offered a socialist alternative to capitalism, while many of the newly liberated colonies combined anti-imperialism with socialism as a potential alternative to both the US and Soviet models.

The liberation of old colonies was a two-sided problem for the Japanese. In Asia, a number of the colonies were liberated from Japan after World War II. At the same time, and perhaps more importantly, the postwar period was accompanied by the American occupation, which was eventually perceived as another form of colonialism, as Takeuchi suggested in an entry in his "Diary of Repatriation" ("Fukin nikki"), which he wrote in 1946 to describe his experience of returning to Japan after World War II. He notes that one of the problems facing writers and critics at that time was the heavy censorship of Douglas MacArthur, the supreme commander of the United States military and of the American occupation. He noted that "one could of course not criticize America, but there was also extreme sensitivity toward communism. They [the Americans] continue to support the emperor."[5] In 1953, the popular intellectual Shimuzu Ikutarō (1907–1988) claimed that many Asian nations were beginning to discard their long and stained histories and walk the "path of beautiful independence" but that the Japanese had been drawn into "a new type of colonization."[6] This marked the beginning of a new era of imperialism that did not entail direct colonization. To some extent, Japan had already practiced this type of rule in Manchukuo, where the Japanese state claimed that it was not colonizing Manchuria but "liberating" it.[7] The American occupation also spoke of liberating the Japanese and bringing democracy to them in the same way, and initially, Japanese intellectuals on the left also saw the US forces as liberators freeing them from a repressive regime. However, after the first few years, and especially with the "red purges" in which the United States occupation along with the Japanese government persecuted radicals and communists, it became clear that the United States was practicing a new form of imperialism. In this new imperialism, Japan would play a role in the American empire, which had as its goal making the world receptive to global capitalism and antagonistic toward Soviet-style communism.[8] From this perspective, Japan went from being colonizer to colonized in a new framework of imperialism, leaving the way open for Japanese intellectuals to paradoxically and controversially identify with the colonized in the postwar era.

In the postwar context of anticolonial nationalism and new forms of imperialism, a split opened between the official policy of the Japanese government and how Asia was represented by leftist intellectuals, but both involved a continuation of pan-Asianism. With respect to official policy, as is well known, the position of the United States was fundamentally defined by the Cold War division between so-called free nations, communist nations, and nonaligned nations. To support the free nations and make the world receptive to global capitalism, the United States hoped to influence Asia through Japan and promoted regionalism in the service of its economic goals. Again, the issue was not just how Asia would be acted upon but what kind of Asia would result and what purpose it would serve. The leaders of Japan, and especially Kishi Nobusuke, who was prime minister from 1957 to 1960, actively implemented a policy of regionalism that would benefit Japan. But this was largely limited or governed by the United States as it pursued its own agenda in Asia.[9]

Although the Japanese government was pro-American, the Japanese media and many Japanese intellectuals took a different view and largely supported the nonaligned movement and the Third World. In the first years of the postwar era, Japanese writers churned out a plethora of articles and essays on the new China, most of which had a positive slant.[10] In this context, Takeuchi expanded his consideration of China to include an analysis of Chinese historical events in the context of global modernity, and this became the foundation of his new pan-Asian worldview.

Rethinking China in the Context of Global Modernity

Takeuchi attempted to understand new China in relation to modernity in his essay "What Is Modernity?" written in 1948. The full title of the essay is "What Is Modernity? (The Cases of Japan and China)," which indicates that his understanding of China was mediated by his view of Japan.

This essay was written only three years after Japan's defeat in the war and one year before 1949, and the context is thus different from that of his book on Lu Xun, published four years earlier. One of his most widely read essays, "What Is Modernity?" describes the possibility of an alternative Asia or Orient that might be based on a subjectivity arising from a distinction between Chinese and Japanese responses to modernity. To contextualize this difference and to construct his larger vision of Asia, Takeuchi outlined a theory of modernity and revolution. By presupposing eternal revolution, he connected the past, the 1911 Revolution, with the specter of political upheaval in late 1940s China, its most recent two manifestations of resistance to imperialism. He treated the 1911 Revolution as a case of resistance to Western modernity, which was represented by both Europe and America. The essay begins with a discussion of how Oriental modernity was created out of its confrontation with Western imperialism, which led to self-consciousness on the part of China. This self-consciousness in turn led to, among other things, a sense of national continuity, as scholars developed narratives of how modernity can be found in China's indigenous history and culture. Takeuchi argued that this can be seen in several contemporary studies that pointed to evidence of modernity in the Chinese Song dynasty, for example. However, Takeuchi asserted that "the direct moment that produced this self-consciousness was the invasion by Europe."[11]

Although Europe and the Orient presented themselves as reified categories, Takeuchi suggested that there was a deeper process at work that made these static categories inadequate. We see this in his discussion of European modernity:

> Modernity is the self-recognition of Europe as seen within history, that regarding of itself as distinct from the feudalistic. . . . Therefore, it can be said that Europe is first possible only in this history, and that history itself is possible only in this Europe. History is not an empty form of time. It includes infinite instants [*mugen no shunkan*] in which one struggles against obstacles so that the self may be itself, without which both the self and history would be lost.[12]

This passage first asserts that modernity involves the recognition of the self or a type of self-consciousness. Takeuchi saw this as crucial for understanding resistance, which he will ground in subjectivity and self-consciousness. Europe was born out of this consciousness of the separation between feudalism and what came after, and this separation of the past from the present contains the root of modern ideas of freedom. In other words, freedom implies being free from the shackles of the past—being able to create history anew.

The statements that "history itself is possible only in this Europe" and that "Europe is first possible only in this history" suggest that Takeuchi is identifying a rupture in time. There was, so to speak, no history before modernity, or at least history before and after modernity were radically different. To a degree, Takeuchi's position is echoed in Moishe Postone's more recent attempt to connect history to capitalism.[13] Postone argues that with the emergence of capitalism, capital itself became the subject of history, and never before had such a unitary but also contradictory subject ever existed. Postone contends that capital strives to greater levels of productivity, which becomes the fulcrum of various global shifts, including the shift from liberal to neoliberal capitalism.

Although Takeuchi also emphasized a break from the premodern or feudal world, he did not treat it as a complete break from prior history and society. Rather, his perspective is akin to a turn in Marxism over the last decade, which stresses that capital's process of subsumption is incomplete.[14] From this perspective, the subject of history is not capital but life, self-consciousness, and other agentive elements that capital cannot fully subsume. Based on a different reading of capitalist modernity, Takeuchi separated those who embody subjectivity and those who do not (a distinction between *kaishin* and *tenkō*). Capitalist modernity might present itself as complete and totalizing and in doing so would seem to leave no room for human action. However, capital's self-representation is not achieved in actuality. Thus the self-recognition of Europe in history is not really history, and the self-recognition of capital in history cannot subsume all of history. For this reason, after the assertion about Europe's self-recognition in history, Takeuchi makes a Benjaminian point about time. Although history might present itself as an empty form of time, it contains infinite instants, which are opportunities for action and making history. Note here that Takeuchi speaks of "infinite instants," rather than an infinite series of homogenous instants. This suggests that each of these instants is heterogeneous and unlimited in its own way. Takeuchi's infinite instant is somewhat akin to the fullness of time connected to the moment when a student learns about God from a teacher described by Kierkegaard:

> Such a moment has a peculiar character. It is brief and temporal indeed, live every moment; it is transient as all moments are; it is past, like every moment in the next moment. And yet it is decisive, and filled with the Eternal. Such a moment ought to have a distinctive name; let us call it is the fullness of time.[15]

Using Kierkegaard to think about Takeuchi is particularly appropriate because they both emphasized the problem of guilt, which Takeuchi connected to a concept of conscience and being pulled away from ordinary temporality, as described in the previous chapter. Moreover, they both refer to the type of transcendence that we encountered in Takeuchi's reading of Lu Xun, in which he argues that transcendence does not really exist outside of time. However, unlike Kierkegaard, Takeuchi was concerned with the implications of transcendence for political action and making history. The difference between those who cling to their subjectivity and those who give up on it could be described as the difference between those who make and those who are made by history. In addition, Takeuchi was interested in epochal shifts and the way they imply structures and obstacles that could undermine, or at least make difficult, the efforts of individuals to realize agency or make history.

Freedom, or making history, means being free from the shackles of the past—being able to create history anew. This means that freedom requires the past, which one must refuse or negate, and the sovereign subject has a history but is also free from that history.[16] One can make history by struggling to be oneself and breaking free from the past, and this constant struggle happening at the personal level manifests on the national level as endless revolution.

In "What Is Modernity?" Takeuchi applied his analysis of Lu Xun and Sun Yat-sen as eternal revolutionaries to the case of Europe. He never adequately analyzes the causes of the processes of self-generation and temporality, but the logic of capitalism forms a penumbra around his discourse about modernity. We see this in passages such as the following: "Once liberated, people cannot return to their originally closed shells; they can only preserve themselves through activity. This is precisely what is called the spirit of capitalism. It grasps itself in the course of its expansion through time and space."[17] Takeuchi's discussion of the spirit of capitalism is surprisingly similar to his description of Lu Xun's and Sun Yat-sen's revolutionary spirit. Capitalism is a movement that constantly renews itself and expresses a type of history in which the self is constantly reborn, and discussion of the spirit of capitalism as constantly expanding recalls Hegel's concept of spirit, which continually reconstitutes itself at different levels of self-consciousness.

Takeuchi's narrative of the development of Oriental capitalism is like the expansion of Hegel's spirit in another way, in that he sees it transforming economic, political, and cultural aspects of life: "Europe's invasion of the Orient resulted in the phenomenon of Oriental capitalism, and this signified the equivalence between European self-preservation and self-expansion."[18] Takeuchi saw capitalism in the Orient as resulting from European invasion, which itself was a capitalist act. Echoing Marx, who claimed that capitalism constantly needs to expand in order to resolve crises such as overproduction, Takeuchi contends that Europe needed to expand to preserve itself, and this has cultural consequences:

> The form of invasion was first conquest, followed by demands for the opening of markets, and the transition to such things as guarantees of human rights and freedom of religious belief, loans or economic assistance, and support for educational and liberation movements. These changes symbolized the progress of the spirit of rationalism. From within this movement was born the distinctive characteristics of modernity: a spirit of advancement that aims at the infinite approach toward greater perfection; the positivism, empiricism, and idealism that supports this spirit; and quantitative science that regards everything as homogenous.[19]

Many of the elements in this passage, such as the progress of the spirit of rationalism, are traits of capitalist modernity and, specifically, reification. György Lukács, for example, clearly connected reification to the abstraction emerging from the commodity form and modern bureaucracy and then further contended that within capitalist society, human subjectivity is conditioned by this gaze.[20] However, Takeuchi pondered how reification is mediated by global inequalities embodied in distinctions such as the West and the Orient and concluded that conquest is crucial to epistemological transformation. Conquest of this kind is an act of direct coercion, and capitalist markets follow. Here Takeuchi perhaps recalls the experience of Japan and the Black Ships or the violent expressions of British imperialism in India. Imperialism therefore is the direct coercion of one nation-state by another to promote capitalism. In Takeuchi's view, the reification that results is due to both capitalism and Western imperialism, but they are all legitimized by a narrative that contends that reification/rationalization and capitalism symbolize the victory of rationalism. Consequently, resistance to reification, to the narrative of rationalism, and to imperialism must go hand in hand.

However, because of the homogenous worldview offered by quantitative science, imperialism does not appear as such, and capitalist imperialism presents itself as eradicating all difference.

> If we suppose the existence of a third eye that was neither European nor Oriental, Europe's step forward and the Orient's step backward (this relation is essentially one of heads and tails) would be seen as a single phenomenon. It would be seen as a natural phenomenon equivalent to that of mixing together liquids A and B. This is precisely the concept of the fusion of eastern and western culture (and the varieties thereof). This concept is abstract in its abstraction of values. But even apart from this, our very supposition of a third vantage point represents a European form of thought.[21]

In Takeuchi's view, capitalist imperialism works on two levels. At the first level, as the passage has adumbrated, all things are equalized; however, at another level, subjectivity and another movement in history emerges and breaks through such homogenization. In elucidating the first level, Takeuchi explains how the abstraction that takes place in both the commodity form and modern bureaucracies spreads to encompass virtually all of life. Just as Marx notes that in capitalism, the exchange value of two commodities is calculated by abstracting from their concrete qualities and measuring them based on socially necessary labor time, Takeuchi describes a scenario in which specific cultural forms or values are abstracted from the Orient so that it loses all its autonomy. It is as if only one type of liquid permeates the world. From

144 CHAPTER FIVE

this perspective, rather than a history characterized by qualitative difference and different trajectories, one has the quantitatively measurable categories of "advanced" and "backward." Add to this the characteristic of speed, and the world ends up being evaluated using metrics of quantity and speed employed by the reifying gaze of a spectator, a circumstance that Takeuchi had already criticized in his book on Lu Xun:

> Japanese literature does not enter history in this way; it looks from outside at racehorses running the course of history. Refusing to enter history, it loses sight of the resistance that brings history to completion [*rekishi wo jūjitsu saseru*]. Instead it clearly sees which horse will win. The Chinese horse is lagging behind while the Japanese horse quickly pulls ahead. Such is how things appear, and this view is an accurate one. It is accurate because one is not running.[22]

Takeuchi refers here to the relationship between action and time. Because one does not enter history, one merely reifies time and looks at nations as if they are racehorses running toward a common goal. This objective outsider stance presupposes an abstract conception of time as a series of "now points" separate from the viewer and from the movement or action occurring. It is this abstraction that allows one to make distinctions such as fast or slow[23] and makes it possible to describe history as that which moves forward at different speeds.

However, Takeuchi sought to understand movements of history that occurred at levels beyond the abstract time of the spectator: he saw history as the advent of something new that redefines the relationship between the past and future. Massimiliano Tomba explains this point effectively when discussing Benjamin's conception of the past. He writes, "It is a past that represents itself as an arsenal of futures that have been blocked and are allowed to re-emerge by the subjects actually acting the field of history and not by the spectator or the historian."[24] It is precisely when one ceases to look at the past from the spectator's perspective that one begins to see that Asian pasts and presents may not all lead to Western or capitalist futures. Takeuchi goes further, adding a geographical context to this argument by highlighting the role of imperialism, global unevenness, and resistance to this process. In this theoretical and geographical context, Takeuchi returned to the subject of the 1911 Revolution. We will see this below in our analysis of Takeuchi's understanding of the distinction between *tenkō* and conversion (*kaishin*) and his reading of Lu Xun's parable "The Wise Man, the Fool, and the Slave." But in "What Is Modernity?" Takeuchi also emphasized this negative moment because from the perspective of immediacy, without reflection or mediation, liberation is also defined by the forces of rationalization associated with the West. The possibility of creating something new requires a moment in which mediation goes beyond its particular context. This is the form of revolution that Lu Xun and Sun Yat-sen together symbolized.

This is a state in which the mediation that results from negation exceeds a particular historical context, and revolution is never reified. This idea arises from a rich background. In the context of intellectual history, it has clear similarities with the Kyoto school philosophers, who in the 1920s and 1930s constantly underscored the importance of entering and making history.[25] Like these philosophers, Takeuchi distinguished between seeing and acting. However, he changed the terrain of this discourse on action by bringing the geopolitics of the Chinese Revolution and its relation to Japan and the West into play. He equated the Japanese with the Western world of seeing and objectivity, while he saw in the Chinese the possibility of action. A similar opposition appears in Lukács's writing, where he argues that the proletariat can potentially play the role of an agent who breaks through the reified world of the bourgeoisie.[26]

Takeuchi thus created a framework that made it possible to distinguish those who can break out from those who cannot and mapped it geographically onto the West/Japan and China/Asia. At another level, he used the concept of *tenkō* (turning), observed in Japanese Marxists who turned to the right around the time of the Asia-Pacific War, to describe those without subjectivity. Here Takeuchi was not merely endorsing the left over the right but drawing on his earlier discussion of *kaishin*, or conversion, to distinguish now between those who hold on to a position—following their own development and transformation—and those who jump from ideology to ideology. The term *tenkō* implies a shift in ideology without any change in subjectivity. There is a paradox here, since a person who is described as experiencing *kaishin*, or conversion, changes precisely because he or she holds fast to a position. The person who *tenkōs* does not experience a fundamental change and merely seeks to get ahead within the existing framework or continues to be constrained by the existing moral and political grid. This can be described as a kind of oblivious alienated subjectivity in which choosing worldviews or ideologies is not very different from choosing between different commodities in a market or shopping mall. Takeuchi highlights the element of will involved in *tenkō*.

> *Tenkō* is a phenomenon that necessarily occurs when honor students act following their conscience. . . . Conscientious behavior consists in abandoning communism for totalitarianism when the latter appears newer. If democracy

comes, the progressive attitude most befitting the honor student is to follow democracy. *Tenkō* comes about through progress, and so is not shameful. Rather, it is the refusal to commit *tenkō* that is conservative, and thus (as all the evidence suggests) reactionary.[27]

By mentioning the conscience (*ryōshin*), Takeuchi is pointing a type of reflection that emerges as a person confronts the world. The Japanese word for conscience, *ryōshin*, and the word for conversion, *kaishin*, are related in that they share the character for heart-and-mind (*shin* or *kokoro*), but the conscience expressed by *tenkō* signals a type of conventional morality and represents a situation in which turning inward is continuously displaced by a progressive vision of history. At the precise moment where subjectivity might enter, it is blocked and twists from position to position. Returning to the ideas of Heidegger discussed in chapter 4, we could say that *tenkō* expresses what Heidegger described as curiosity, or *Neugier* (literally, a desire for the new).[28] This is a situation where Dasein constantly searches for new forms of excitement while being oblivious to a deeper existential dimension of subjectivity. The ideology of progress covers this deeper dimension with the result that expressions of *tenkō* are not conservative but progressive.[29]

In postwar Japan this is an important point because after the war, the people *tenkō*ing during the 1930s and 1940s appear reactionary because the position they shifted to had been discredited. However, Takeuchi's main purpose here is to go beyond the mere phenomenon of turning from left to right and to uncover a deeper structure of subjectivity (or lack of it) behind *tenkō*. Indeed, Takeuchi mentions people *tenkō*ing from both right to left and left to right. For this reason, in his view, the turn from right to left in the postwar era implied not an overcoming of *tenkō* but a continuation of it. In other words, the Japanese had been *tenkō*ing from the point at which they entered global capitalist modernity, the Meiji era, and continued to do so after the Pacific War. In fact, Takeuchi later connected the failure of both the JCP and Japanese democracy to *tenkō* and the lack of subjectivity. Moreover, for Takeuchi, even pan-Asianism is rendered meaningless if one comes to it through *tenkō*. In an essay written in the 1960s about Japanese pan-Asianism, he specifically gives the example of Hirano Gitarō as showing a lack of subjectivity and total "regression":

> In the past, he was a competent scholar in the Lecture Faction Marxist camp. He was a thinker. Then he diligently followed the legacy of Yoshino Sakuzō and worked on the history of the Meiji Restoration, especially the Movement for Freedom and People's Rights. . . . He honored Ōi Kentarō, but at this time his scholarship had still not deteriorated too much. From the time when

he got into geopolitics and participated in planning the colonization of the Southern Region, his scholarship had already become dubious. He personally described a caricature of the Greater East Asia Prosperity Sphere. Moreover, during the war he attacked the Chongqing government, but with Japan's defeat he completely turned around and praised the Nationalist government. He also vigorously supported the Japanese translation of Chiang Kai-shek's *China's Fate*. When the Nationalist government was ruined, he turned once again and became a major proponent of the Chinese Communist Party. So he repainted previous pan-Asianism as pacifism and the unity of Asian and African unity.[30]

If one looks at the surface and focuses on the positions Hirano supported, some of them are obviously ones that Takeuchi also endorsed. For example, clearly pan-Asianism as the unity of Asia and Africa along with support of the CCP are political positions that Takeuchi probably held. However, Takeuchi points out that more than the actual position of a given thinker or politician, we should focus on the subjectivity behind adopting any given political stance. Hirano's case fits perfectly what Takeuchi describes as the Japanese style of *tenkō*, or turning from position to position without really experiencing despair. Rather, the motivation behind this kind of *tenkō* appears to be nothing more than to be on the winning side.

Takeuchi eventually used the terms *tenkō* and "resistance" or "conversion" to represent national character, specifically those of Japan and China, respectively. He explained the difference between Japan and China in his essay "What Is Modernity?" by comparing the Meiji Restoration to the Chinese 1911 Revolution. In China, the failure to succeed in a reified vision of modernity opened a space for radical change. He contended that both the Meiji and the late Qing governments attempted to succeed within the norms of the time by implementing reforms from above. However, the Meiji reforms succeeded while those of the Qing repeatedly failed. The Meiji reforms and the Japanese experience represent, for Takeuchi, a "Prussian model" in which the colonized attempt to asymptotically approach the colonizers or advanced nations: "There is no nation in the Orient in which revolution succeeded so easily as Japan. Japan displayed scarcely any resistance against Europe. While Russia incorporated capitalism only through the most barbaric resistance, Japan's encounter with capitalism produced less resistance than did the industrial revolution in Europe."[31] Japan did not resist because it could not transcend the ideology and reality of development. The Japanese never even pondered whether something else was possible. Japan made no attempt to transcend capitalism; it had no force of negativity or subjectivity. Therefore, all the Japanese could do was *tenkō* from position to position:

When in Japan a concept becomes discordant with reality (this is not movement, and so not a contradiction), one abandons former principles and begins searching for others. Concepts are deserted and principles are abandoned. Writers abandon some words and search for others. The more faithful these writers are to scholarship and literature, the more fervently they abandon the old and incorporate the new. Thus, in Japan the failure of liberalism leads to totalitarianism, and the failure of totalitarianism to communism. Or again, the failure of Stalin leads to Mao Zedong, and the failure of Mao Zedong to De Gaulle. The failure of the materialist dialectic leads to the self-identity of absolute contradiction, and the failure of absolute contradiction leads to existentialism. Hence the following sentiment: "Where Tōjō Hideki failed, another may succeed—perhaps *me*." Such things constantly fail, yet these failures themselves never fail.[32]

This was possible in Japan precisely because it could easily modernize. In China, hopes for modernization were constantly thwarted; as a result, like Lu Xun's literary experience, China was forced back upon itself and continually had to create itself out of nothing. This distinction offers a good example of the difference between conversion (*kaishin*) and *tenkō*. As we have seen, conversion represents the painful moment when one realizes that one's worldview is no longer sustainable, and when that happens, failure itself fails, which is what happened in China but not in Japan.

When failure itself fails, one's paradigm breaks down and one must not only seek new answers but rethink the very questions one poses and the spaces in which one poses them. In other words, one must return to the framework that conditions how one looks for answers. In the earlier paradigm, one shifted from one object of desire to the next without ever questioning the conditions that produced one's desire. In that case, even if one admires revolutionaries, one cannot become revolutionary. In China, failure itself failed, and the question of reform gave way to revolution. "After China's defeat [in the Sino-Japanese War of 1894], various reform movements were initiated . . . but these were all crushed by the reactionaries. Kang Youwei's attempt to imitate the Meiji Restoration in China did not succeed. . . . In China, reactionism was so strong that it prevented all reform from above, but this caused a revolution to rise up from below."[33] The conditions that gave rise to this revolutionary action were numerous, but Takeuchi singled out two: the uneven temporality of the global capitalist world and the overlapping of conservative and progressive forces in China. We have already touched on the first point; in Takeuchi's view, uneven temporality is implied in the distinction between advanced countries and late-developing countries. He argued that China and Japan each made different use of their lateness in entering or being forced into the global capitalist system.

The perception of lateness, of course, implies a narrative of progress and teleology, which became pervasive in both late Qing China and Meiji Japan. Once one accepts this narrative, the initial question is how does one catch up? This is where conservative reaction enters the scene. In China, however, "reactionism was so strong that it prevented all reform from above. . . . This caused revolution to arise from below."[34] Takeuchi refers to the successive failures of China's attempts at economic and political modernization, including the Self-Strengthening movement, the Hundred Days Reform, and the 1911 Revolution. Each of these moments represented an effort to catch up within the framework of progressive time. Takeuchi claimed that because all of these movements failed, China was reduced to nothing. This view was influential in postwar Japanese Sinology and is perhaps most clearly expressed by Nishi Junzō (1914–1984), a scholar of Chinese philosophy whose ideas overlapped with Takeuchi. In the well-known essay "Confucianism and Chinese Thought from Now On," published in 1958, Nishi wrote, "When the West invaded, as China retreated, the Chinese substance discarded its skin, flesh, and even bones. China preserved itself only as marrow."[35] From this marrow, or nothingness—a space of resistance—China then developed the power to create a different future for itself.

The idea that the failure and nothingness lay behind the root of self-transformation and a novel political practice is clear in Takeuchi's reading of Lu Xun's parable "The Wise Man, the Fool, and the Slave." The parable is worth recounting in full because it encapsulates many of Takeuchi's ideas and his reading of China.

> The slave's work is hard and he constantly complains. The wise man consoles him, "Your luck will surely improve before long." But the slave's life is hard, and he next complains to the fool, "The room given me doesn't even have a window." "Tell your master to have a window made," says the fool. "What an absurd idea!" answers the slave. With this the fool goes to the slave's house and begins tearing down a wall. "What are you doing, sir?" "I am making a window for you." The slave tries to stop him but the fool does not listen. The slave then shouts for help, and other slaves appear and drive the fool off. Finally, the master appears and the slave informs him what has happened, "A bandit began destroying the walls of my house. I was the first to discover this and together we drove him off." "Well done," says the master. The wise man visits the master after this incident and the slave thanks him: "Indeed, sir, you are very prescient. My master praised me, so my luck has improved." The wise man seems pleased. "That's right!" he replies.[36]

In the figure of the slave, both Lu Xun and Takeuchi invoke the complexity of the paradigm of liberation. The wise man represents the prevailing ideology—what Takeuchi called "honor student" culture. This is where one accepts the paradigm of those who dominate oneself and delights in their praise. In Takeuchi's view, Japan was constantly doing this, which is why it eventually entered the imperialist game and attempted to gain recognition from those in power. In this situation, there is no subjective transformation, and one has even forgotten that one is a slave.

The key to the position of the Chinese is that they realized they were slaves and that they could not take a simple path toward succeeding within the existing paradigm. The fool and the wise man represent two attempts to reform within the existing paradigm but without really changing the framework of imperialism or the fundamental subjectivity that reproduces it. Takeuchi's point here anticipates that of postcolonial theorists: he contends that anticolonial movements often took over the paradigm of the colonizers and consequently were engaged in what Lydia Liu and others have called "self-colonization,"[37] all the while believing that they were striving for freedom. The wise man expresses this when he says that the slave's luck will improve, and the slave takes this vision as his own toward the end of the parable. The fool appears more radical in that he attempts to make a window but does not question the fundamental condition and subjectivity of the slave. In Takeuchi's view, the path to liberation is much more difficult and involves facing emptiness and despair, which he had already adumbrated in his prewar writings. Takeuchi explains the state of liberation for the slave:

> This is the state in which one must follow a path even though there is no path to follow; or rather, one must follow a path precisely because there is no path to follow. Such a slave rejects being himself at the same time that he rejects being anything else. This is the meaning of despair found in Lu Xun; it is what makes Lu Xun possible. Despair emerges in the resistance of following a path when there is no path, while resistance emerges as the activation of despair. As a state this can be seen as despair, whereas as a movement it is resistance. There is here no room for humanism to enter.[38]

This passage accurately describes the state of the Chinese after a series of failures. They had to follow a path when there was no existing path to follow. All existing paths were blocked or rejected, which meant that they had to create a new path and perhaps even redefine what a path is. Takeuchi's point might bring to mind Zhuangzi's thoughtful words in the "Discussion of the Equalization of Things" ("Qi wu lun"): "A path is made by walking, a thing is made by naming."[39] In other words, one can constantly create new emergent properties and methods through action. But in Takeuchi's view, such creation of the new is connected to despair because it emerges out of a combination of an attachment to the past and an attempt to create something new.

Takeuchi contrasts despair with humanism, which represents ideologies of Western modernity, which determine what it means to be human—the human being of the Enlightenment. We could place Takeuchi's ideas as part of a global movement against humanism,[40] which we have already seen him express in his reading of Lu Xun. Paradoxically, he asserts that one cannot become free without negating the human subject and existing ideas of being free. This is the moment of the negative about which Hegel and others have written. Hegel distinguishes between "doubt" (*Zweifel*) and "despair" (*Verzweiflung*) in a manner that helps us understand Takeuchi's point:

> This path can accordingly be regarded as the path of doubt, or, more properly, as the path of despair, for what transpires on that path is not what is usually understood as doubt, namely, as an undermining of this or that supposed truth, followed by the disappearance again of the doubt, and then a return to the former truth so that in the end the thing at issue is taken as it was before.[41]

Hegel distinguishes between a doubt in which the subject stays intact and despair, which transforms the root of the subject. On this path there is a self-transformation, and one does not return to what one was before. One faces the "untruth of knowing as it appears,"[42] which suggests that a whole world disintegrates. As we have seen, this is close to how Takeuchi characterizes the Chinese *kaishin*. However, unlike the Hegelian solution, for Takeuchi there is no progression of shapes of consciousness; one must constantly return to the abyss and actively transform the self and the world. This is why China repeatedly returns to revolution.

In Takeuchi's view, China went from failure to despair to resistance, which entailed a resistance against oneself as much as the other. The ideas of failure and revolution were especially important in postwar Japan because Japan had itself just encountered failure in 1945, and now Japanese intellectuals felt that the people must re-create themselves. Takeuchi's question was whether the defeat Japan suffered in 1945 could create the conditions for a new literary and political consciousness, similar to that of Lu Xun, Sun Yat-sen, and Mao Zedong. He eventually became pessimistic about such a possibility.

However, Takeuchi was of the opinion that the significance of the Chinese experience and the type of subjectivity it entailed did not stop at China's borders; Chinese subjectivity connected to the fate of Asia. He believed that Asia could potentially overcome the reified structures of imperialism, and he saw Lu Xun and Sun Yat-sen as ideal types for connecting China and Asia. This

152   CHAPTER FIVE

is consistent with Takeuchi's earlier essay in which he supported the Greater East Asian War; in both cases resistance to the West lay at the heart of the problem. In "What Is Modernity?" he developed this spatial logic a bit further:

> Europe's invasion of the Orient extends across time and space, and so the cutting of this extension at spatiotemporal points results in European and Oriental becoming determined, actual things. Thus while resistance at this point may also be understood as something individual, can such individual differences be explained as homogeneous? Indeed, various types of people emerge from this individual resistance. These types would include, roughly speaking, Lenin and Gorky, Sun Yat-sen and Lu Xun, Gandhi and Tagore, Kemal Atatürk and Ibn Saud.[43]

Europe's invasion of the Orient extends space and time. Europe is required to make parts of the region into things. The above passage presents Takeuchi's ideas about a dialectic between reification and action. Without reification there would be no states. Through this dialectic between imperialism, reification, and resistance, Asia emerges as a transnational movement, and intellectuals such as Lu Xun, who Takeuchi considered an archetype, emerge across the Asian world. China and Lu Xun are again the fulcrum, but Takeuchi now places them in a global context.

These various places are united in a common cause against imperialism, and among the persons Takeuchi includes here are not only Gandhi and Tagore but also Kemal Atatürk and Ibn Saud. The inclusion of the latter two reflects Takeuchi's continued interest in Islam. In Japan, this interest developed from the 1920s, as seen in the work of Ōkawa Shūmei and others. However, by beginning with Lenin, Takeuchi stresses the importance of socialism and its connection to anti-imperialist nationalisms. His conception of Asia is more an idea than a geographical space. Resistance to the West and the attempt to create a different future are crucial to the concept of Asia, which is why Sun asserted that Lenin brought Russia into Asia. Building on such insights, Takeuchi constructs a more capacious concept of Asia in the 1950s and 1960s, which begins with a critique of the JCP.

Takeuchi in the 1950s: Ideology, Revolution, and Asian Nationalism

The 1950s witnessed important shifts in Japanese thinking about the world. In 1949, the Chinese Revolution went from being a possibility to a reality, and this had a major impact on Takeuchi and others. Indeed, by the 1950s, Takeuchi's earlier writings could be read as almost prophetic. The Japanese government followed the United States and continued to play the role of the honor student or the wise man, and not surprisingly, this led the government to be relatively anti-China. Indeed, the Japanese government did not have diplomatic relations with China after the war. By contrast, the Japanese media painted a relatively positive picture of the Chinese Revolution and the regime that emerged afterward, and in 1950, when China entered the Korean War, Japanese intellectuals characterized China as a weak country attempting to resist American imperialism.

The Korean War is especially significant for one of the main arguments in this book, namely that pan-Asianism must be understood in the context of global capitalism and its correlate, imperialism. In the early 1950s, Takeuchi himself alluded briefly to this in a discussion of independence in literature.

> Among the Japanese citizens there are clearly those who reap benefits through being subordinate and delight in it. Looking at it from the standpoint of class, these are the capitalists who subcontracted to the US military, the finance capitalists connected to them, and the politicians who represented them. It would be a mistake to call them slavish traitors. From their perspective, rather than subcontracting, they are thinking much more about their immediate profit. Going from internal to external conditions, they could also be patriots.[44]

Here Takeuchi highlights how the Japanese economy could flourish under global capitalist imperialism. Japan was a pseudo-colony while at the same time enjoying a degree of economic prosperity. But the problem was not just with the Japanese government or capitalists, since even leftist organizations, including the JCP, contributed to this type of self-colonization. In contrast to the course Japan followed, Takeuchi believed that the Chinese Revolution provided a possible path to autonomy. In the early 1950s, Takeuchi wrote several essays aimed at drawing out the significance of the Chinese Revolution using some of the concepts he had introduced in his earlier writings. Many of these essays targeted the JCP, which he thought could be part of the solution to Japan's lack of subjectivity but had ended up being part of the problem. He was asked by Tōma Seita (1913–2018), a well-known Marxist historian, to join the JCP in January 1949, but he refused and later began to vehemently criticize the party.[45] A turning point with respect to Takeuchi's views on the JCP occurred in October 1949, when the Chinese communists seized control of the mainland. This was of course a major event for Takeuchi and other Japanese Sinologists. Some months later, in January 1950, the Communist Information Bureau (Cominform) in the Soviet Union pointed out that the JCP was wrong to label the US occupation army as a liberation army and to take the path of peaceful revolution. A split subsequently appeared in the JCP between the Impression faction (*shokan ha*), which rejected the Cominform's judgment, and the International faction (*kokusai ha*), which accepted it. Takeuchi agreed with the Cominform's criticism but not with the responses of the JCP.[46] The problem had partly to do with the Cold War structure. "Sitting in the low world," Takeuchi wrote, "the JCP should not take lightly the disorder of the high world of America and the Soviet Union. It should stop naively believing in its exaggerated delusions and using the words of a slave. [These delusions include] mobilizing this opposition between the United States and the Soviet Union to protect the JCPs own legitimacy."[47]

To counter actions and positions of the JCP, Takeuchi wrote a number of essays between the years 1950 and 1952 and eventually published them in a volume entitled *Japanese Ideology* (*Nihon ideorogi*). The title of this book echoes that of a well-known work by the Marxist intellectual Tosaka Jun (1900–1945). Tosaka analyzed Japanese fascist ideology and in the 1930s published *On Japanese Ideology* (*Nihon ideorogi ron*). Tosaka also became a well-known martyr in postwar Japan who died in prison without budging from his beliefs, unlike many other leftists at the time. In other words, to use Takeuchi's term, he is an example of someone who did not *tenkō*, or turn from left to right, under pressure. To this extent, he exemplified the tenacity that Takeuchi admired and saw lacking in much of Japanese political culture.

In the preface of his *Japanese Ideology*, Takeuchi explicitly noted that his work was inspired by Tosaka but added that if Tosaka were still alive, he would probably view Takeuchi himself as representative of another branch of Japanese ideology.[48] This is crucial because it contains a recognition of the different contexts of the interwar and postwar periods. Takeuchi himself in fact adhered to one of the branches of what Tosaka called "Japanese ideology," since he supported the war, promoted pan-Asianism, and criticized modernity. In this way, he had much in common with Ōkawa Shūmei. In this preface, Takeuchi adds that he wanted to break free from Japanese ideology but was not sure how to do so, which also points to the different contexts of the pre- and postwar periods. In Tosaka's time, it might have been safe to say that a major problem in Japan was imperialism masquerading as pan-Asianism and the atavistic rejection of modernity. However, during the postwar period, the new configuration of power fed on the simple negation of critics of modernity and pan-Asianism. Indeed, American imperialism promoted a modernization theory that sought to purge the questioning of modernity as harmful or dangerous, meaning that accounting for both the fascist and modernist faces of Japanese ideology required a new critique. Takeuchi saw both fascism and modernization theory as resulting from the larger complex he identified as modernity. Although modernity might also be seen as offering the possibility of subjectivity, as we have seen, one of the key symptoms of modernity was in fact the lack of subjectivity.

Takeuchi used the Chinese experience in his analysis of the shortcomings of the JCP based on this concept of subjectivity. By focusing on subjectivity, he rethought the role of intellectuals in political practice. Takeuchi was struck by the role of the masses in China and their transformation through everyday life, which harkens back to how Takeuchi distinguished the 1911 Revolution from the Meiji Restoration. During the postwar period, however, the contrast was even starker because China had a socialist revolution, while Japan turned into a democracy that was built and maintained from outside. According to Takeuchi, the Chinese and Japanese communist parties, respectively, also embodied this difference.

Takeuchi believed that Japanese ideology was the cause of Japan's inability to create revolution and take control of its own destiny. This ideology that promoted a lack of subjectivity was at the root of both Japanese imperialism and Japan's becoming subordinate to the United States. He contended that the JCP, although ostensibly critical of the United States, lacked autonomy and was inconsistent in its position on the Soviet-dominated Cominform. He criticized the JCP for moving toward the Soviet Union because of its lack of subjectivity and felt that this lack of subjectivity meant that it could not respond to the people. All of this led Takeuchi to seek a position beyond the opposition between the Soviet Union and the United States.

> Most importantly, from the subjective perspective of the JCP, it does not think it is turning its back on the people. It does not even see the people. Moreover, [as far as the JCP is concerned] those who it does not see do not exist. For the JCP, which is not beyond Japanese-style hedonism, the category of the people only exists as this or that particular being, A or B.[49]

The JCP had difficulty seeing the people because of the epistemological structure of its subjectivity. "Japanese-style hedonism" refers to the situation Takeuchi described earlier in his "What Is Modernity?," in which the Japanese change from position to position depending on their mood or on intellectual fashion. One cannot help but note the similarity between this and the way individuals move from commodity to commodity in the marketplace. Perhaps more importantly, Takeuchi attacked the JCP as being controlled by the Cominform and the Soviet Union, which themselves were unable to grasp the significance of the people:

> The Cominform only calls on fabricated [kakū] sleeping people. The JCP represents this, and the Japanese people who apologize for the Cominform are

not real people. They are people under the grip of the JCP. They are children of slaves and consequently are themselves slaves. Slaves are not people. People have their own morals. They are free people who have the potential to make revolution.[50]

What Takeuchi describes here is the creation of a phantom public, to borrow a phrase from Walter Lippmann.[51] Although Takeuchi probably never read Lippmann, he was concerned with the problem of a public lacking self-consciousness or subjectivity and lamented that the JCP, which should have promoted oppositional politics, instead contributed to the lack of subjectivity. Lippmann suggested in 1925 that the phantom public could be manipulated to support fascism. By 1950, Takeuchi had already witnessed how this had happened in Japan, not to mention in Germany and Italy. Lippmann did not believe that a real public was possible in the United States and advocated that government primarily perform administration. The pragmatist philosopher John Dewey countered in 1927 with *The Public and Its Problems*, arguing for the possibility of a real public that could bring about a true democracy. Takeuchi came to share Dewey's faith in democracy and even some of his views on China.

Takeuchi wrote a well-known essay about Dewey that praised his understanding of China and Japan. He even contended that the Chinese May Fourth movement had made an impact on Dewey when he visited China in 1919. Although Takeuchi did not mention Dewey's theory of democracy, it is perhaps not surprising that he had a similar goal and operated from similar assumptions: namely, the goal of realizing democracy and the assumption that a real public existed behind the phantom. This belief in the existence of a real public returns us to the problem of breaking free from slavery and taking one's subjectivity back. In Takeuchi's case, writing in the 1950s, the goal of awakening the public or seeking the true public and its morals is a recipe for both democracy and revolution. The emphasis on revolution is crucial and represents a difference between his own position and Dewey's. Takeuchi explains that according to Dewey,

> Christian nations are mistaken in their superior belief that they must give to China, and should on the contrary attempt to learn from it. Japan appears to be a much more modern nation, yet it is essentially one in which feudalistic elements remain in force. Because of its old culture, China is more conservative than Japan, and thus its attempts at modernization have lagged behind. Precisely because of this, however, its reform has been all the more thorough and sound because it began with the groundwork of revolutionizing the people's way of thinking. Henceforth only an industrial revolution remains necessary.[52]

Much of this description is in line with Takeuchi's own position. Like Dewey, Takeuchi contended that China was conservative but that this dialectically led to sweeping change in thinking and reform. Dewey, nonetheless, claimed that China still needed to implement an industrial revolution.

From a contemporary perspective, this position seems to make sense, and we could even say that Mao's China in fact completed the industrialization of which Dewey, in Takeuchi's interpretation, spoke. Dewey's actual views on China both overlap and contrast with Takeuchi's own position. Dewey did contend that China's problems were "economic at root due to the struggle for existence, and that a new industrial development will in time crowd them out."[53] However, he also lamented that the Chinese would "take on many Western vices, and lose many of their old virtues, by carrying love of money, intrigue, mutual suspicion, and calumny into the new situation."[54] Takeuchi, by contrast, believed that the Chinese had found a way to avoid many of these problems of modernity through Mao's socialism. For Takeuchi, the key was that the Chinese Revolution was not merely industrial but created a transnational socialist movement in an Asian country. In Takeuchi's view, Dewey could not completely understand the Chinese case precisely because he began from a position rooted in the advanced capitalism of the United States. Consequently, he failed to see the alternative possibilities that emerged in the Chinese Revolution, and in Takeuchi's eyes, Dewey's shortcomings overlapped with those of the JCP.

Takeuchi devoted considerable space in *Japanese Ideology* to outlining the characteristics of revolutionary China and the reasons why the revolution succeeded there. The key points he makes return to the problem of the masses and subjectivity. To a certain extent, Takeuchi believed that Mao and the Chinese communists realized the power of the masses to create history even when, according to Marxist theory, so-called objective conditions were not ripe: "The Chinese Communist Party does not have illusory power like the JCP. This is not because the Chinese Communist Party stands on a relativistic vision of values, but because all values are connected to the will of the people, an absolute. In front of the people, the CCP often is ready to sacrifice itself."[55] Takeuchi underscores that the CCP is based on the people and consequently is not empty. On this point, Takeuchi represents a populist tendency that ran counter to the positions of Japanese Marxists who stressed class. His position drew on the experience of the Chinese Revolution, a revolt that did not rely on the working class. It also dovetailed with his argument against those who believed that China needed to have an industrial revolution that would release the power of the proletariat. In the scenario that Takeuchi imagined, the

Chinese people and the Communist Party expressed a subjectivity that could transform reality and stage a revolution against the odds:

> One must resist. No matter how much the outer world violently moves, in the depths of phenomena there is something eternal that one cannot overlook. To the extent that there is human history, we cannot deny that people live. Even if humanity is heading toward extinction, it is our will that buries it step by step. Even those who believe in the deterministic theory that humanity will definitely become extinct have responsibility with respect to whether this happens sooner or later. It is not meaningless to say that one must save the world from extinction. "Knowing that one cannot do something and still doing it," this is the Confucian spirit, but at the same time, it is a teaching of communism and all philosophies of life.[56]

Takeuchi ends with a passage from Confucius's *Analects*: "Although one knows that something is impossible, one still does it."[57] He claims that this statement underpins Chinese revolutionary thinking. He connects this to a negative moment that he finds in Marx, Mao, and Lenin.

> Before a great power, in the face of one's helplessness, one is struck with despair. When one despairs, one might commit suicide, but sometimes it gives one courage. When Marx wrote a "Critique of Hegel's *Philosophy of Right*," he was working in the latter mode. Because one is nothing, one decides to have everything. In their respective conditions, Mao and Lenin followed this attitude of Marx and constructed a unique revolutionary theory.[58]

Here we return to the problem of despair that Takeuchi mentioned in "What Is Modernity?" However, now he connects this more explicitly to the Chinese Revolution, finding other examples to make negativity concrete. Takeuchi used a similar idea to discuss revolutionary practice. Negativity and despair here refer to the possibility of subjectivity and the angst that this can cause. They underscore the potential we have to change the world and the despair we might feel when we realize the enormous task of producing a socialist or communist world. Takeuchi sees this negativity as being at the root of communist practice but also present in Asia. He mentions Mao, and one might recall here Mao's parable "The Foolish Old Man Who Removed the Mountains," delivered in a speech in 1945. The parable tells of an old man whose house was obstructed by two great peaks. The old man "called his sons, and hoe in hand they began to dig up these mountains with great determination." Another graybeard, the Wise Old Man, derided them for trying to do the impossible. The Foolish Old Man retorted,

> "When I die, my sons will carry on; when they die, there will be my grandsons, and then their sons and grandsons, and so on to infinity. High as they are, the

mountains cannot grow any higher and with every bit we dig, they will be that much lower. Why can't we clear them away?" Having refuted the Wise Old Man's wrong view, he went on digging every day, unshaken in his conviction. God was moved by this, and he sent down two angels, who carried the mountains away on their backs.[59]

The parable is originally from the fifth-century BCE Daoist text *Liezi*, but Mao reinterpreted the story symbolically to relate it to the tasks of the Chinese Revolution. He explains, "Today, two big mountains lie like a dead weight on the Chinese people. One is imperialism, the other is feudalism. The Chinese Communist Party has long made up its mind to dig them up. We must persevere and work unceasingly, and we, too, will touch God's heart. Our God is none other than the masses of the Chinese people. If they stand up and dig together with us, why can't these two mountains be cleared away?"[60]

This is a messianic moment, which is perhaps implicit in the quote from the *Analects*. As the Foolish Old Man works while imagining an infinite series of children and grandchildren, a divine force completes the task. In this parable, Mao replaces God with the masses, a step akin to Takeuchi's approach as well. However, in Takeuchi's version, standing before the grand mountain or the power of imperialism gives rise to despair. From Takeuchi's perspective, the whole parable may be considered a struggle within subjectivity, where the Wise Old Man represents the moment of doubt and despair, which reduces one to nothing. However, out of this nothingness a new determination arises.

We have already seen that Takeuchi believed that even when China was reduced to nothing, it still had the potential to create revolution. By the 1950s, it appeared to Takeuchi that China had even defeated American imperialism in World War II. This pure negativity also lay at the heart of an infinite revolution. Takeuchi goes on to contrast the Chinese experience with the Japanese, with the Chinese Revolution on the one hand, and Japanese democracy on the other.

> The Japanese Communists start from a condition in which two worlds are opposed. On the one hand, the world is quickly expanding. On the other, it is moving toward extinction. It is close to dawn. Even tomorrow, the revolution could happen in Japan, but only at that time will people's lofty courageous actions be recounted with praise. This is a way of appealing to martyrs. I aver that the Communist Party's "patriots" are a fake currency [*kara tegata*]. The revolution will definitely not emerge from the outside. It is illusory to speak about being saved from the outside apart from thinking and acting in the field of everyday life. Revolution is not something that happens once; it is something that continues eternally. Anyone who believes in the illusion of a one-time revolution and tries to accomplish everything at once is foolish. Making

160   CHAPTER FIVE

a revolution is not like gambling. If we do not make efforts on our own, even if a revolution comes from outside, it will pass us by [*sudōri shite shimau*]. This is the lesson we have learned in the first five years after the war.[61]

Takeuchi ends this passage by pointing out the lack of the negative in Japanese democracy. Like the JCP following the Cominform, the Japanese government did not express subjectivity. The paradox here is that in postwar Japan, democracy, which is fundamentally about self-determination, was associated with passivity. The Japanese government was handed democracy from the outside and as a result was merely passive. In Takeuchi's view, the Japanese needed to negate the democracy that was given to them and make it their own.

This point is crucial since it shows that Takeuchi's idea of nationalism does not view the nation as a self-same identity but necessarily involves self-negation. In other words, Takeuchi contended not that democracy is bad merely because it comes from outside Asia but rather that the Japanese needed to internalize this potentially liberating ideology. Takeuchi's stance toward the Japanese constitution explains his position. In an essay also included in *Japanese Ideology* entitled "Letter to a Young Friend," Takeuchi included a section on the Japanese constitution and briefly described the process by which he made the constitution his own: "One day, I took the old constitution out and read it. [When I read] '1. The Japanese empire will be ruled by the emperor whose lineage continues for a thousand generations,' I became frightened. From that point, I resolved to make the new constitution my own and protect it."[62]

As we shall see, Takeuchi will return to the new constitution, promulgated in 1946, when he decided to resign from his position as professor at Tokyo Metropolitan University in protest of the government's failure to follow the constitution. When he did return to it, Takeuchi made the new constitution his own by placing it within Japanese history. Although the constitution was given to Japan by the United States, by appropriating it, this constitution could be turned into a weapon against both the United States and Japanese conservatism. In addition to looking at the past, another crucial moment in Takeuchi's turn toward supporting the new constitution was the constant threat from officials who might trample on its tenets.[63] Takeuchi stressed the subjective moment in upholding the constitution, which brought him back to the theme of endless revolution in the everyday. When turning to the problem of morality and the constitution, he wrote, "Morality is not something that is given. It is not something that stays forever once it is in one's hands. One must continuously work to create it. It is like the basic rights of the constitution."[64] Takeuchi cites the part of the Japanese constitution explicitly stating that Japanese citizens must constantly protect freedoms and rights provided for in the constitution, which gives credence to his interpretation. In this way, he presented the constitution as a continuous process; in line with his earlier quote from Confucius, he saw it as something that can never quite be complete. Here again, Takeuchi comes down on the side of the temporal, or life, against the forces that corrode it. The constitution is vulnerable to subversion, and so it must be constantly defended. Moreover, by underscoring subjectivity, Takeuchi suggests that the constitution is not an end in itself but part of the larger pan-Asian struggle for liberation that he saw happening in China.

However, in Takeuchi's view, Japan was caught between a government dominated by the United States and the JCP, which attempted to resist but could not break free from the shadow of the Soviet Union. He believed that the JCP's passivity was connected to its approach to revolution and suggested that the JCP and its followers separate themselves from the revolution in a temporality of waiting. The problem was that they were committed to the idea that the revolution is a one-time event after which things will be different and so chose to wait for a subject to bring this about. This stance of waiting, like that of the spectator, is separate from action and the everyday, which led Takeuchi to believe that the JCP viewed revolution as something distinct from the everyday. Takeuchi himself, on the other hand, considered revolution as fundamentally about the everyday: "The meaning of practice does not refer narrowly to political movements; rather, it is often the case that it refers to everyday events taking place in the midst of the sphere of life."[65] By focusing on the everyday, Takeuchi echoes Tosaka Jun, who he had earlier mentioned in the preface of his *Japanese Ideology*. In the 1930s, Tosaka addressed the principle of everydayness: "The principle of everydayness is the principle of presentness. It is the principle of reality, the principle of factualness. Accordingly, it is the principle of practice."[66] Everydayness refers to the practice of daily life and how that must change to create revolution. Takeuchi, following Tosaka, criticized an overly intellectualized version of Marxism that failed to see the beginning of revolution in mundane practices. In this light, he discussed the transformation of intellectuals in revolutionary China, which in turn led him to touch briefly on the issue of class, his purpose being to emphasize that the "everyday" of an intellectual and that of a worker or peasant could be radically different.

Today it has become commonplace to criticize intellectuals for inhabiting a so-called ivory tower or for developing theories without connecting them to the everyday practice of direct producers. Indeed, commodity fetishism makes it such that we buy ready-made objects without thinking about the people who make them, which contributes to the gap between mental and manual labor. Takeuchi, however, praised the Chinese Revolution for connecting intellectuals to the experience of peasants and also found figures in Japanese history who similarly criticized the separation of mental and manual labor. From this perspective, the everyday is a space of transformation; one does not just take the everyday as a given—it is also what needs to be transformed and remade. In an essay on the Edo-period thinker Andō Shōeki (1703–1762), which Takeuchi also included in his *Japanese Ideology*, he explains how the everyday of intellectuals was transformed in revolutionary China. He contends that the Chinese

> combined the so-called "elevation and generalization" of culture. This experience can be a point of reference for Japanese literature. I plan to study this more carefully. However, if we look at the leader of this movement [in China], Mao Zedong, the basic spirit that flows out from him is similar to that of Andō Shōeki. This is both obvious and surprising. During the Second Sino-Japanese War, officials in the Chinese Communist Party had to spend time cultivating the land. When the military was stationed in the countryside during the harvest season, they also had to do agricultural labor without pay. Although this may have augmented agricultural productivity a little, the spirit behind this movement involved the concept of making a social contribution by connecting with production.[67]

The key here was to reconnect the intellectual with the everyday practices of production. Andō had attacked the class distinctions in the Edo period, and Takeuchi sees Mao doing the same in a radically different context. Takeuchi stresses the importance of reviving the spirit of Andō through experiencing the life of peasants and grasping their knowledge.

Takeuchi described numerous scenarios in which intellectuals initially resisted going to the countryside but were eventually transformed by the experience. Here he returned to his concept of religious conversion, discussed in his book on Lu Xun and his essay "What Is Modernity?" He describes intellectuals who resist change as follows:

> For example, there is scholar A. He is relatively old and has some scholarly accomplishments. He has been a professor at a national university for a long time. In the past, his positive feelings for the Nationalists were exhausted. In general, he believes that politics is bad and therefore shuns the sphere of politics. He believes that concentrating on scholarship itself is a mission on behalf of the people and that scholarship transcends class. In Beijing, after the Liberation Army entered and established a new government, even if he

had been taken into a university, he would not change his attitude toward scholarship. His loneliness caused him to immerse himself increasingly in his scholarship.[68]

This is a case of an intellectual who withdraws from politics and concentrates on scholarship in the abstract and pretends to transcend class. However, the hope is that in the new society and through new policies, a time will come when loneliness breaks through the defensive mechanisms against a larger consciousness. This will be the starting point for conversion. "Some intellectuals will feel that this state of conversion [*kaishin*] is like a religious person's feeling of sin. It is propelled by the drive to confess."[69]

These themes return us to Takeuchi's book on Lu Xun. The feeling of sin that Takeuchi attributed to Lu Xun connects the intellectual to the working people at large. Recall that in Takeuchi's view, this religious feeling went beyond the nation or nationalism. In this case, repentance and sin are linked to the lives of the people. This is the subjectivity that can connect intellectuals to the direct producers of goods. Takeuchi argued that "intellectuals are a necessary evil. They are an unavoidable surplus in society. Moreover, they should be neutral with respect to class, but in Japan at present, they are mostly connected to state power and have become tools for exploitation and invasion."[70] Here Takeuchi echoes Mao in asserting that through practice and involvement in political movements of the masses, intellectuals can overcome their egoism; he goes on to trace the contours of Maoist-style education in which intellectuals and the masses learn from each other.

This view of intellectual labor goes against the Marxist emphasis on the development of capitalism and technology, which aims to make manual labor increasingly obsolete for the production of wealth. Consequently, intellectual labor, or what Michael Hardt and Antonio Negri call "immaterial" labor, becomes dominant—and one's vision of labor's role in social transformation must change.[71] In particular, some thinkers tended to look at subjects other than the working class as revolutionary subjects. However, as the economic historian Kaoru Sugihara has noted, development in Europe differed from that in Asian countries, such as Japan, China, and Korea, in an important respect. In these large agricultural regions, rather than an industrial revolution, he claims that an "industrious revolution" took place.[72] This is especially relevant for our purposes because it means that in these places, labor-intensive practices continued rather than being displaced by technology. If we add to this the unremitting reliance on manual labor in the service sector, Takeuchi's somewhat Maoist point about the enduring importance of labor politics might continue to be relevant today. He hoped to bring intellectual labor back

164 CHAPTER FIVE

to a different "everyday" and thereby create the conditions for revolutionary consciousness.

Asian Nationalism

Takeuchi's belief that intellectuals would come to recognize their connection to workers through a transformation of consciousness might be described as Marxist, but this did not lead Takeuchi to support a global movement of the working class like that found in the Marxist narrative. On the contrary, he affirmed a type of nationalism, which is an essential component of his pan-Asianism. During the early 1950s, the same period in which he wrote *Japanese Ideology*, he explained the connections between Asian nationalism, revolution, and the everyday in a series of essays published in popular intellectual journals, such as *Chūō kōron* (Central debates). These essays echo the work of people such as Zhang Taiyan in how they separate anticolonial nationalism from imperialist nationalism. In 1951, in one essay titled "On Asian Nationalism" ("Ajia no nashonarizumu"), he engaged scholars such as Maruyama Masao (1914–1996) who had distinguished between Asian and Western nationalism. In this essay, he responds to Maruyama's argument in "Nationalism in Japan: Its Theoretical Background and Prospects," published earlier in 1951 in *Chūō kōron*. Maruyama contended that unlike in other nations in Asia, nationalism had lost its virginity in Japan. This loss refers both to Japan's involvement in imperialism and to the absence of social revolution.

> Among the nations of the East, Japan is the only one to have lost her virginity so far as nationalism is concerned. In contrast to the other Far Eastern areas, where nationalism brims with youthful energy and is charged with adolescent exuberance, Japan alone has completed one full cycle of nationalism: birth, maturity and decay.[73]

Maruyama uses the metaphor of virginity to characterize both Japan's launching into imperialism and its inability to combine revolution and nationalism. Like Takeuchi, Maruyama contrasted China with Japan. He contended that "a consistent union of nationalism with revolution, though classically apparent in China, is in point of fact common to nationalism throughout Asia."[74] With this move, Maruyama, like Takeuchi, used the Chinese case as a stand-in for all of Asia. Maruyama contended that the ruling class in China and other Asian nations needed to collaborate with imperialists in order to survive, and therefore anti-imperialism had to combine with social revolution:

In reacting against imperialism, Chinese nationalism ironically enough came under an obligation to transform, not preserve, the old socio-political order. Having more or less joined hands with imperialism in order to survive, the ruling class had been forced to "compradorize." An extensive anti-imperialist, national independence effort could therefore not emerge from that quarter. The adhesion to the old order to imperialism inevitably inspired the fusion of social revolution with nationalism.[75]

This line of thought is similar to Takeuchi's argument about the 1911 Revolution, which he claimed succeeded because, unlike the earlier reforms from above, it was a movement from below. However, Maruyama noted that most of the Asian elite ended up aligning with imperialism, so that driving out the foreigners implied overthrowing the old leaders and the old regime as well. In Japan, the elite were more independent, and nationalism became independent of social revolution as a result. Thus for Maruyama, as for Takeuchi, Japan's success ended up being its failure, and for China, failure led to revolutionary success.

Like Maruyama, Takeuchi attempted to explain the difference between Japanese nationalism and politics in relation to nationalism in other Asian nations. In an essay devoted to national literature (*kokumin bungaku*) entitled "Modernism and the Problem of Nationalism," Takeuchi argued that one of the reasons the Japanese had not been able to follow other Asian nations was not only because Japan lost its virginity by invading other nations but also because it had not been able to deal adequately either with its past or with nationalism. We will touch on the problem of the past and memory in the next section, but here let us briefly examine how Takeuchi deals with nationalism:

> With the loss of the war, the idea that nationalism was evil became dominant. People thought that the path to salvation was to break free from nationalism (or national consciousness). The people who resisted fascist nationalism in some way during the war continued to express the same posture of resistance after the war. Moreover, this type of expression brought a feeling of liberation. We must conclude that such reactions were a natural course of events.[76]

Takeuchi points out the importance of taking history into consideration when theorizing Asia. Otherwise, one will mistake the feeling of liberation for actual liberation, even though the content behind such a feeling might reinforce a new oppression. The ideology he felt was responsible for creating this false sense of freedom is what he refers to as "modernism" (*kindaishugi*), which we would probably today call "modernization theory." He includes Japanese Marxists in this category.

Modernists, including Marxist modernists, avoided the problem of a nationalism soaked in blood. They positioned themselves as victims, and believed that they were free from responsibility for nationalism becoming ultra-fied. They contended that it was correct to ignore the "Japanese romantic school." But they were not the people who toppled the "Japanese romantics"; rather, a force from the outside toppled the Japanese romantics. Did not the modernists overestimate their own power by claiming the agency for toppling a group that an outside force actually toppled? In this way, they perhaps forgot a bad dream, but probably could not cleanse themselves of blood.[77]

Takeuchi describes a position similar to the loss of self associated with *tenkō*, or switching from one position to the next. Here without acting, one (the victim) takes on the (non)action of another (the United States occupation) and moves to criticize ultranationalism and in so doing ceases to see one's own implication in the earlier ultranationalism. Some of those who may have actually supported ultranationalism during the war have now conveniently forgotten this past. Consequently, as we will see in the next section, Takeuchi stresses the importance of memory. However, we should note here his belief that responsibility is not limited to those who participated in ultranationalism. Rather, he shows how modernization theory and romantic nationalists are conceptually connected in a dialectical love-hate relationship.

> The resurrection of modernism during the postwar recognized "Japanese romantics" as its anthesis, but we cannot forget the historical fact that originally "the Japanese romantics" themselves were seen as an antithesis of modernism. They first took the nation as one element. Then, if we think [about this] without being concerned about the problem of power, the reason that the nation later became not just one factor but all powerful was related to the force of the times [*toki no ikioi*]. That is, the modernists did not recognize that their position was an antithesis. Modernism evaded a confrontation with nationalism, and consequently made nationalism rigid and uncontrollable.[78]

In Takeuchi's view, conservatism was reacting to a real problem in modernization theory and with modernity more generally, and neither side of the nationalism-modernization theory dichotomy could address the problems of modernity by tackling them one-sidedly or by not realizing their connection to the opposite side. He describes the one-sided character of modernization theory by targeting Marxist cosmopolitanism:

> At a certain point it was necessary to fix human beings abstractly as free humans or as class-humans, but like all the schools of Japanese literature, the proletarian literature group were rash in their self-assertion as they severed the link between the above conceptions and concrete, complete human

beings, and took only the above abstract conceptions as complete human beings. They forgot the original role of literature to grasp everything and covered the whole with a part. One must say that it is natural that the painful cry of a search for a complete humanity emerges from a dark deserted corner.[79]

Nationalism thus expresses something elemental with respect to the complete human being. Concepts such as literature and the everyday point toward this wholeness that is eventually split up by modernity. With the loss experienced in modernity, human beings search for narratives of community. And given the global context of an international system of nation-states, people often find the nation occupying a "dark corner":

> The nation takes root in this dark corner. The problem of the nation has a nature such that it becomes a problem when it is ignored. National consciousness emerges out of oppression. Even if one needs other forces for it to develop into nationalism, its emergence is always related to the demand for the return of humanity. It will not emerge to the surface if there is no oppression, but the nation exists dormant as a possibility. One cannot evade the effort to bring back a lost humanity, and with one-sided force make a dormant nationalism lie dormant forever.[80]

Here Takeuchi tells Japanese intellectuals that the nation becomes a problem when it is ignored. In his formulation, the nation plays a role similar to Marx's working class: the role of bringing back an alienated humanity. In an essay written around the same time, Takeuchi goes even further: "If one cannot grasp nationalism while avoiding the danger of falling into ultra-nationalism, then the only path is, on the contrary, to extract real nationalism out of ultra-nationalism. This is extracting revolution out of counterrevolution."[81] This was the situation of Japanese nationalism. As we will see in the next section, this dialectic between counterrevolution and revolution, or conservatism and radicalism, will play a crucial role in Takeuchi's thinking about war memory. At the same time, Takeuchi continued to emphasize the contrast between the nationalisms of Japan and China.

Asian Nationalism versus Western Nationalism

Around the time of the Asian-African Bandung Conference of 1955, Takeuchi wrote a series of essays on the problem of Asian nationalism and the key issue of colonialism. For Takeuchi, Asia was more an idea than a mere geographical region, and it was an idea that emerged from a particular geopolitical framework. Takeuchi echoed Maruyama Masao's theory of the unity between socialism and anticolonial revolution, but he added that the global goal of

168   CHAPTER FIVE

pan-Asian nationalism should be to transform the capitalist and imperialist world. This added a new dimension to his earlier points about the difference between China and Japan. It also continued his earlier theme of social revolution but now extended the goal to that of creating a new world. Takeuchi describes the difference between Western and Asian nationalisms in the following manner:

> People call the uniting of various Asian countries nationalism [*minzokushugi*]. This Asian nationalism is qualitatively different from Western nationalism. The latter is inseparable from the development of capitalism and is built on the principle of free competition. Just as in the case of the individual, states recognize the principle of the survival of the fittest and believe that this is the only principle of human progress.[82]

Takeuchi distinguishes between Asian and Western nationalism in a manner that follows Sun Yat-sen's distinction between Western and Asian politics. As we saw in chapter 2, in 1924 Sun connected Asian politics with socialism by suggesting that Russia, after the October Revolution, separated itself from the West and became similar to Asian civilization. Here Takeuchi continues this train of thought and associates Western nationalism with a Darwinist worldview and the promotion of capitalist imperialism.

He describes Asian nationalism as fundamentally overcoming a world in which people merely struggle against one another for survival:

> To get rid of the force of imperialism that weighs heavily on it [nationalism], there are only two paths: either to become an imperialist oneself or to rid the world of the roots of imperialism. Among the countries of Asia, Japan chose the former strategy and China and all the other countries chose the latter. In place of an exclusive nationalism, they promote a nationalism that is an alliance of the weak.[83]

Asian nationalism involved an attempt to break free from the force of imperialism. In Takeuchi's view, Asian nations were created through the invasion of the West and thus were born under attack. They were compelled to choose a path of resistance. In this situation, two paths were blazed, one by China and one by Japan, the former resisting and the latter following the pattern of Western imperialism. By making this distinction, Takeuchi tries to atone for his former support for Japanese imperialism as a form of pan-Asianism. He tacitly admits he was not able to recognize politics in wartime Japan as imperialism in pan-Asianist clothing. Now he proclaims that pan-Asianism is about not just the unity of the nations of Asia but a unity of weak nations by which he voices support for the Third World. A natural corollary of this position is support for Mao Zedong, who in many ways exemplified Third Worldism *avant la lettre*. The point of stressing late-developing countries turns on their marginal space within the global capitalist system. Here again the idea of an outside of Western capitalist development becomes a fulcrum of resistance. Takeuchi specifically alludes to aspects of Mao's thought in the Yan'an period (1935–1947), when the CCP headquarters were in poverty-stricken northwest China:

> The center of Mao Zedong Thought is perhaps the "revolutionary base area." This is a type of ancient utopianism. It is a unity that represents a lived, self-sufficient community. The earlier liberated areas were like this. Now, when the liberated area has spread to the whole country, it has become a revolutionary base area for world peace. Here one can see a masterly combination of Marxism and Asian nationalism. Just as Marx derived a principle of progress from class conflict and Lenin derived such a principle from the opposition between advanced countries and late-developing countries, Mao Zedong discovered the principle of eradicating colonialism from the opposition between the imperialist and the colonized.[84]

Mao's idea of revolutionary base areas (*genjudi*) were local strongholds outside the control of the Nationalist government and spaces that combined resistance to the state along with experimentation with a revolutionary form of life. By creatively interpreting these bases, Takeuchi brings together notions of the local and the global. Despite the common interpretation of Mao as a modernizer, Takeuchi finds the idea of ancient community in his work and in the Yan'an revolutionary base. Yan'an was a lived community as opposed to one dominated by representation. Such communities' self-sufficiency indicated to Takeuchi that China could delink from the capitalist system of the West and launch a different future for the world. From this perspective, Asian nationalism is not just about the past but also about the future.

"Cuba Is Part of Asia": Takeuchi Yoshimi and Umesao Tadao

By generalizing based on the Chinese case and constructing an Asian model of nationalism, Takeuchi created the conditions for the delinking of Asia from geography. He argued that Asia is formed by a movement and subjectivity of resistance. In this way, what started out as an analysis of the Chinese and Asian response to imperialism now became a way to define Asia. Takeuchi's position emerged clearly in the 1961 dialogue that he had with the prominent anthropologist Umesao Tadao (1920–2010), published in the journal *Science of Thought* (*Shisō no kagaku*),[85] in which both Umesao and Takeuchi argued for pluralism against authors such as Takeyama Michio (1903–1984). To introduce the dialogue between Takeuchi and Umesao, the editors of the journal noted how Takeyama had advanced Fukuzawa Yukichi's position and his own by following a universal standard, setting up Takeyama as a foil for modernization theory against which both Umesao and Takeuchi positioned themselves.

In an essay written in 1958, Takeuchi agrees that Takeyama was heir to the idea of leaving Asia but notes that the contexts were different. Fukuzawa was writing during the Meiji period, when Japan was struggling to become a nation-state, and so his work is filled with tension. Takeyama, on the other hand, wrote in postwar Japan, when Japan had already become a modernized nation-state. According to Takeuchi, in Fukuzawa's view, Japan had to modernize and leave Asia, while for Takeyama, Japan was from the beginning not part of Asia.[86] Takeuchi explains the difference between Takeyama and Fukuzawa in a way that brings out the logic of capitalism and imperialism:

> His [Takeyama's] "leaving Asia" is different from Fukuzawa's because the former is not a result of an internal tension. Takeyama emphasizes that Japan is not in Asia, but originally was part of the West. This is not a result of his investigations of Asia, but merely because he knows nothing about Asia, does not want to know, and from a subjective perspective collected a number of materials that could make Japan and Europe appear similar. . . . Comparing Fukuzawa's Japan to today's, the population has tripled, and citizens' energy and purchasing power has multiplied many times. Moreover, transportation, production, and education have greatly progressed. As Umesao points out, Japan has a degree of wealth to which other Asian countries cannot compare. . . . Japan cannot make diplomatic decisions on its own. Recently, Japan is not able to have foreign relations with Korea or China. The situation has become the opposite of Fukuzawa's time. "The temperament of the people's independence," which Fukuzawa thought would be the foundation for an independent nation, has disappeared.[87]

Takeuchi here repeats his caution about the consequences of a loss of subjectivity in the raptures of economic development, which entailed subordinating political autonomy to the United States. He points to a type of blind capital accumulation that has increased the consumer power and the wealth of Japan but notes that the Japanese nation has no control over this. He makes the claim that people justify this "progress" and the imperial relations that accompany it by invoking a universal standard that judges all development, a claim that is reminiscent of the racehorse metaphor that he used in his earlier essay "What Is Modernity?"

Takeuchi continues by saying that because of this blind wish to leave Asia, the Japanese people have been unable to grasp the mode of subjectivity through which Gandhi resisted British capital with his spinning wheel or heed the warnings that both Tagore and Sun Yat-sen gave to Japan about becoming imperialist.[88]

Unlike Takeuchi, Umesao did not tie his analysis of Asia and Japan directly to politics, although he had constructed a pluralist position that still ended up privileging the West. Indeed, he contended that because Japan is like the West, other countries should not try to follow the Japanese model since their conditions are different.[89] In this manner, Umesao is perhaps one of the earliest deconstructors of Asia. In 1956 he wrote, "If one perceives Asia or the Orient as a monolithic whole, one is embracing an Occidental bias. . . . Each Asian country has its own unique characteristics, none more so than Japan. Thus the problems we face are different from those faced by other Asian nations."[90] From this perspective, although his position is diametrically opposed to Takeuchi's in some respects, he agrees that Asia is strongly subject to Western projections and that one must not simply accept the Western image of Asia. He agrees that one must create pathways to mutual understanding among Asian nations but warns against a Takeuchi-style pan-Asianism:

> But as we do so [promote understanding] it would be a mistake to rely on a simplistic, vague sense of unity or Asian solidarity. If out of a misguided sense of identity, we thrill to the heroic struggle of Asian nationalism versus Western colonialism, it is no more than the enthusiasm of a spectator at a sumo match. It is only when we engage in our own sumo match that we truly face the substance and subtleties of our problems.[91]

Again, Umesao voices concerns that overlap with Takeuchi's, but he takes these in a different direction. Like Takeuchi, he warns against being a mere spectator and calls for a return of the everyday practice and the concrete life-worlds of people in Asia. However, his vision of these life-worlds is different from that of pan-Asianists, doubtless because he was one of the few Japanese intellectuals in the 1950s who visited numerous regions in Asia. In 1955, he went on an expedition to Western and South Asia that greatly influenced his understanding of Japan's relation to Asia. On his return, he wrote essays stressing the difference between Japan and other Asian countries, stating for example that "India is India; Japan is Japan. The conditions of these nations differ greatly."[92]

The bulk of Umesao's work is devoted to using a theory of ecological zones to analyze the conditions that divided the Asian countries, leading him to account for the differences in culture in terms that do not map onto existing continents. Umesao divides Asia into two ecological zones: Zone One includes Japan and the countries of Western Europe, including Britain, Germany, France, and Italy; Zone Two comprises Asian countries and regions, including China, India, and Western Asian nations, such as Iraq.[93] The key difference he saw between Zone One and Zone Two countries is that capitalism and the bourgeoisie emerged in Zone One but not in Zone Two. Umesao conceives of the world as an ellipse and places Zone One on the eastern and western edges. Zone Two occupies the center. Western Europe found itself on the edge of the Roman empire, and Japan was on the periphery of the Chinese empire.

Umesao offered numerous reasons for why the bourgeoisie developed on the periphery of empires. Echoing Fukuzawa, he contended that Japan and Western Europe developed in a similar manner because they had feudal systems:

> With the concept of parallel feudalism as our starting point, we can identify further parallel phenomena in the social evolution of Zone One countries during or near the time of the feudal age. One example is religious change. During the Middle Ages, popular religious movements flourished, and something we can call a citizenry emerged. Guilds were established, autonomous cities developed, overseas trade began, and peasant rebellions occurred. All these events took place in both Japan and Europe.[94]

Recall that Fukuzawa Yukichi also contended that feudalism allowed a certain amount of religious freedom. Fukuzawa argued that most of Asia, and China in particular, ended up with a regime in which the spaces of religious and military authority were united. Umesao similarly labeled the regimes in Zone Two as "despotic empires"[95] that could evolve into bourgeois systems only with great difficulty.

At this point we should note that although Umesao's theory labels the West and Japan advanced civilizations,[96] unlike Fukuzawa, he does not endorse a linear model of development.

> The old evolutionary view of history posits that there is only one path, and that everything will, sooner or later, follow it to the same destination. Any seeming divergences are explained as some other developmental stage that will eventually lead to the same place. In reality, biological change certainly does not work this way. From the ecological viewpoint, there are naturally many paths of change.[97]

Umesao asserted that development is not uniform. He noted that people in Zone One were at one point behind those of Zone Two, but because of their different structures, the people in Zone One eventually modernized and became more advanced.[98] This suggests that Umesao saw modernity as the goal all Asian nations must pursue:

> The fact remains that, regardless of Japan's suitability as a model, Asian nations must modernize. They are, in fact, making steady efforts at modernization. Even if our country cannot be a model, we ought to offer help for their efforts in the form of technical and other aid. But we must not forget that Japan's position relative to those nations is one of singularity, not one of the *primus inter pares* in a group of similar nations.[99]

Asian nations must modernize, but they cannot take Japan as a model because Japan is exceptional. Although Umesao often described Asian nations such as India in disparaging terms, focusing on poverty and other problems, he underscored the possibility of a different socialist modernity emerging in Asian nations, or in Zone Two. He also noted that Zone Two countries did not pass through a bourgeois phase but often moved directly to socialism. In a comment that echoes the Frankfurt school of Marxists, he wrote: "One could say that the communist and socialist governments are trying to play the role that capitalism plays in Zone One."[100] But this does not mean that Zone Two would necessarily become capitalist. He cautions:

> Recent phenomena such as China's human wave[101] lead me to suspect that something unique will develop in Zone Two, beyond the imagination of Zone One. I sense that there may be enduring differences between the consciousness and behavior of people in societies which have passed through a feudal stage and those which have not. One possible difference is that individuals in a society that has experienced feudalism have a relatively strong sense of self. In contrast, individuals of a society which has not experienced feudalism are more collective in their orientation.[102]

Umesao, like Takeuchi, suggested that Asia could produce something different but, contra Takeuchi, appeared to say that Zones One and Two have such different conditions that neither can be a model for the other. Given the impact and popularity of Umesao's work, Takeuchi knew that he had to reconstruct Asia and its significance for world history in his dialogue with Umesao. Takeuchi's side of this dialogue also touches on his conception of Asia not as simply a geographical region but as an idea involving the politics of imagining a region in relation to a possible future that also acknowledged the constraints of the Cold War on national sovereignty.

> Today apart from the two major powers, it is impossible for a nation-state to be sovereign. This corresponds to the fact that through the broad development of the economy, the world has become smaller. . . . From this perspective,

a situation has emerged in which one cannot even think the nation without committing to one of the two camps or if one does not feel this urgency, one still cannot conceive of the nation without unconsciously depending on one of these camps. I am dissatisfied with this commonplace view and viscerally resist it. Through criticizing this conception of civilization and thinking about the movements concerning Asia, Africa, and Japan, which gained momentum during the postwar, I have concerns that are different from those of Umesao when it comes to the question of what Japan is.[103]

Takeuchi points out that during the postwar period, the situation was in some sense worse than during the Meiji period because of the dominance of the two global superpowers. In this context, a discourse such as Takeyama's has the peculiar effect of legitimating the dominant forces of history. In another essay written in 1958, Takeuchi argues that "Takeyama's method is the opposite of that of Umesao. Rather than making history zero, he makes it almighty. Here history is a heavy 'thing.' Takeyama lives from head to toe in a world of values. Umesao believes that we can return everything to parallel elements, but according to Takeyama, there are only hierarchically arranged values."[104] In the 1950s and 1960s, the weight of history was inextricably connected to the Cold War and created a bipolar scenario in which the only alternatives were the United States or the Soviet Union. By focusing on spatial determination and geography, Umesao turned history into nothing. Imperialism and the Cold War played no role in his argument. However, in Takeyama's narrative, history is about values, which in turn act by universalizing a hierarchy based on the West and the Japanese elite.[105] Unlike both Umesao and Takeyama, Takeuchi hoped to find a way to break free from the US-Soviet binary opposition and in doing so anticipated what the Taiwanese critic Kuan-hsing Chen calls "de-cold war."[106] At the heart of the Bandung Conference was precisely the idea of presenting another alternative to a world in which there were only two choices, either the Soviet Union or the United States. This nonaligned movement implied a new political imagination, where geography sublates itself and becomes an ideal part of a process toward liberation.

Umesao was not thinking of such movements when he argued that the category of Asia is meaningless owing to the great differences in culture, skin color, language, religion, and other aspects across Asia.[107] Takeuchi responded to this in a classically dialectical fashion by first agreeing that Asia in effect does not exist as a simple unity but was produced through modernity. Continuing a line of argument that he began in "What Is Modernity?" thirteen years before this dialogue, he writes:

The power of Western Europe came in [to non-Western nations] and many ancient and medieval practices collapsed from the inside. This power was perhaps that of the mode of production, perhaps spirit, but in any case, this movement began with modernity or the establishment of capitalism. If we follow Arnold Toynbee and others, we can say that this was a response to a challenge. The specifics change based on the nature of the challenge, also based on the particular elements connected to the conditions in various countries. However, I wonder whether we can stipulate the meaning of Asia based on the form of response. Speaking generally, perhaps we can call Asia the form in which there is an internal movement in the countries colonized by Western Europe or imperialism to become independent and form a nation-state. Even if a country is in Asia geographically . . . , if this movement is not present, we should perhaps not call such a country Asian. . . . If one takes a recent example, a country such as Israel might be geographically in Asia, but is not Asian. But a country like Cuba is in the Americas, yet in terms of form it is nearly Asian.[108]

It is not just that Western imperialism and capitalism caused traditional practices to collapse but that such invasions triggered an internal movement that led to resistance. Takeuchi here draws on the work of Arnold Toynbee, who had visited Japan in the 1950s. Toynbee famously argued that cultural evolution is the result of stimulus and response to challenge. However, Takeuchi's key point is that the response could break free of the paradigm that produced the stimulus. It is this process of resistance, he argued, rather than regional identity, that defined Asia. For this reason, a place like Cuba, which even bad geography students would not identify as part of Asia, could be considered part of the idea of Asia as resistance to imperialism. From this perspective, Takeuchi's Asia, similar to Vijay Prashad's Third World, is not so much a place as a project implying transnational unity in the face of imperial domination.[109]

In an essay written almost ten years after the Bandung Conference, Takeuchi clearly describes how liberation from imperialism is a fundamental aspect of how we perceive Asia:

There are many countries in Asia. Even grammar school children can rattle off the names of ten countries in East Asia alone. However, this is after World War II. Before the war, the map of Asia was much simpler. Apart from Japan, China, and Thailand, the others were not independent countries, but were called by such names as Dutch Indonesia and French Indochina. Burma was part of British East India and the Philippines was part of the United States.[110]

Takeuchi uses the geopolitical dimension of Asia to show that from the very beginning, Asian identity involved struggling against colonialism, and that this struggle was a condition for Asian nationalism. Asians' own identity involved the subjectivity mentioned above as resistance to an Other, and only through this struggle could Asian nations come to life. In this project, "first the People's Republic of China emerged. Apart from this, other countries became independent. Africa then also rode this wave of independence. They aimed to have a neutral or nonaligned foreign policy."[111] This reference to the nonaligned movement refers to the Bandung Conference, which Takeuchi deploys in his effort to expand the meaning of Asia. Moreover, just as he brought Latin America into Asia by mentioning Cuba, the above comment makes a similar gesture toward Africa.

Umesao did not accept this nongeographical conception of Asia and, reminiscent of Fukuzawa, contended that the real problem with Asian nation-states stemmed not from imperialism but from the failure to modernize from within. In a nutshell, he argued that "perhaps the idea of Asia in the Bandung Conference has had the effect of suppressing internal contradiction and turning one's eyes outward."[112] To some extent, this presages the thinking of contemporary theorists who argue that the problems in the Middle East are caused not by American imperialism but by the failure of the Arab states to modernize. Moreover, in Umesao's view, a nonaligned policy under the banner of Asia would fail because the larger countries of Asia, which might be able to modernize, will eventually impose their concept of civilization on the others. Given that Asia does not exist, it will be created by others—either the Western nations or the powerful nations of Asia.

Takeuchi countered by claiming that what is at issue is how one understands history and its possibilities. He drew on his earlier point about history not being a series of abstract self-identical moments passing into infinity, and just as we should not see all moments as equal, we should not see the world as a congeries of nation-states all moving toward the same destination. The point is that the modernity of countries on the periphery of global capitalism is determined not just from the inside but rather, as Takeuchi had already argued, by the dynamic of imperialism. Moreover, the effect of imperialism becomes invisible because "we at present passively receive the values created on the basis of the spirit of Western European modernity."[113] Takeuchi felt that the Asian nations accepted as reality the Western vision of the world as being an even field of nation-states. However, Takeuchi contended that this vision covers up the struggle for decolonization, a struggle that produced Asia as a provisional unity that points beyond itself. In other words, Asia is not a fixed or eternal entity. Rather, it is constructed through the specific history of capitalist imperialism and points beyond this history toward the dissolution of both Asia and the history that makes it necessary.

By underscoring the history of colonization, Takeuchi avoided essentializing Asia, meaning that his interpretation offered an important counterpoint to theories of Asia that stress inherent Asian values or the specificity of any particular culture. Toward the end of "Asia as Method," a lecture Takeuchi presented in 1960, someone in the audience suggested that one should resist the West by stressing a particular Asian culture. Takeuchi responded by situating Asia in a broader trajectory of humanity and history:

> I do not make distinctions on the basis of human or individual types, for I would like to believe that men are everywhere the same. While such things as skin color and facial features are different, I would like to think that men are substantively the same, even in their historicity. Modern societies are thus the same around the world, and we must recognize that these societies produce the same types of people. Likewise, cultural values are everywhere the same. But these values do not float in the air; rather they become real by permeating man's life and ideas. In the process by which such cultural values as freedom and equality spread from the West, however, they were sustained by colonial invasion—or accompanied by military force (Tagore) or by imperialism (Marxism). The problem is that these values themselves thus came to be weakened as a result.[114]

Because Takeuchi is often read as a particularist pan-Asianist, this passage might strike readers as strange. In fact, what Takeuchi tries to do here is mobilize pan-Asianism as part of a larger project of realizing the goals of modernity beyond the contemporary distorted forms that are pervasive around the world. Cultural values become real through practice, and the practices governing such realizations today are dictated by capitalist imperialism. In the face of this, Takeuchi believed that Asia's goal should be to radicalize the Enlightenment and core Western values. From this perspective his goal overlapped significantly with the goals of socialism, which was committed to the ideals of the Enlightenment, values that also undergirded capitalism but could not be realized within a capitalist world. Takeuchi proceeds in his speech to express a sentiment that envisions a reality beyond a simple East-West binary:

> The Orient must re-embrace the West, it must change the West itself in order to realize the latter's outstanding cultural values on a greater scale. Such a rollback [*maki kaeshi*] of culture or values would create universality. The Orient must change the West in order to further elevate those universal values that the West itself produced. This is the main problem facing East-West relations today, and is at once a political and cultural issue.[115]

In other words, the goal is to take the ideals of the West to a higher level and create a new type of universality, at which point the Orient, or Asia, will cease to exist. The Orient cannot simply act on itself but must transform the other, the West, and thus create a new world. A key term in the above passage is "rollback" (*maki kaesu*), which has two basic meanings, each with a different temporal valence. Richard Calichman uses the term "rollback" to refer to a temporality of return—to return things to their original state, in this case, before Western imperialism. But the Japanese term *maki kaesu* can also signify to "rally from behind" when things do not appear to be going well. The idea of rollback is implicit in this second meaning as well because the idea is to stage a counterattack from a weak position and through this regain the upper hand, as in the common phrase in Japanese, *dotanba de maki kaesu*, which means "to successfully counterattack at the last moment." Takeuchi's use of this term suggests that time is running out and that Asia must counter from an inferior position, transforming this inequality into something positive. To some extent, this idea was part and parcel of his concept of nothingness. In particular, he earlier described how China was pushed to the limit and reduced to nothing, but out of this inferior position, China resisted and created something new.

Takeuchi uses the nominative form *maki kaeshi*, which is also the term used to translate the Cold War American foreign policy referred to as "Operation Rollback," which implied what we would now call "regime change." This policy originated in the Truman administration but became prominent during Eisenhower's presidency (1953–1961). The US involvement in Korea was part of this policy, as was the attempt to overthrow the Castro regime in Cuba. Given that "Asia as Method" was published in 1961, Takeuchi's readers must have understood his use of the term as an oblique reference to the US attempt to "roll back" communism.[116]

The cultural regime change advocated by Takeuchi is not merely a change from the outside but entails a cultural dialectic that stresses subjectivity and a Hegelian *Aufhebung*, or sublation/retention; it aims to neutralize Western values while at the same time realizing them at a higher level. This echoes the way in which socialists at the time spoke of socialism as realizing many of the values inherent in capitalism, such as freedom and equality.

Because the Orient, or Asia, is the subject that initiates this radical transformation, Takeuchi had to deal with the legacy of the Asia-Pacific War. He gave an explanation for Japan's role in this war, namely that Japan followed the West. But his project required that he speak not just about the future but also about how to heal the wounds of the past. If pan-Asianism is about mutual support and building transnational bonds, clearly the concerns of people in formerly colonized countries in Asia who felt betrayed by the Japanese needed to be addressed.

In postwar Japan, Takeuchi contended that the sins of Japan are both obvious and not being dealt with seriously because of a constellation of forces in the postwar era, especially the influence of the United States. This postwar geopolitical situation made collaboration with other Asian nations difficult and reproduced a lack of knowledge about Asian nations in Japan. In "Asia as Method" Takeuchi laments:

> There must thus be collaboration. But such collaborative research has not really gotten off the ground, as Asian Studies continues to be neglected both deliberately and institutionally.
>
> Let me provide just one example of such an institutional difficulty. There are currently hundreds of colleges and universities in Japan, among which a few teach Chinese. I am at Tokyo Metropolitan University and even there, we teach Chinese. However, there are no universities here that teach Korean. (Tenri University, where Korean is required for missionary work, is the sole exception.) Korean used to be taught in the prewar period at Tokyo University, but that has changed since the war. We Japanese really don't know anything about Korea, despite the fact that it is geographically closest to us.[117]

Takeuchi speaks of the contrast between postwar Japan, when Asian studies was not supported, and the prewar period, when the Japanese imperial project led the state to support the study of other Asian countries. At that time, this interest in Asia arose from the contradictory imperialist/anti-imperialist ideology of the Japanese state. During the postwar period, once this ideology was discredited, there was little interest in places like Korea.

Once again, Takeuchi contrasted Japan with China and asserted that in China, the communist government actively promoted the study of Asian languages.[118] This contrast between wartime Japan, postwar Japan, and post-1949 China reveals Takeuchi's contradictory stance on Japanese imperialism. After all, the study of Asian languages in wartime Japan was intimately connected to Japan's imperialist venture. Takeuchi goes on to point out that in some ways, Japan's wartime imperialist ideology agenda has features in common with the ideology of communist China, especially in its critique of Western imperialism. This brings us to Takeuchi's controversial statement about "imperialism against imperialism."

Imperialism against Imperialism, the Everyday, and War Memory

At the same time that he outlined a new nongeographical vision of Asia, Takeuchi wrote essays that treated the legacy of the war in Asia, which he saw as undermining any hope of Asian unity. Part of the difficulty of outlining a subjectivity adequate to pan-Asianism in Japan is that such a subjectivity must take responsibility for the horrors associated with pan-Asianism. Takeuchi dealt with this problem in the context of Japanese imperialism and war memory explicitly in the late 1950s and early 1960s. Scholars have recently pointed out that after the Asia-Pacific War, Japanese leftist intellectuals often forgot or ignored Japanese wartime imperialism and sided with the colonized.[119] This was especially problematic because many of the countries with which Japan was attempting to unite in the 1950s were precisely those that Japan had colonized. Before leaping into solidarity with the colonized, a first step of reconciliation and repentance was necessary. This is important because, as chapter 3 shows, before 1945 the Japanese government used the rhetoric of anticolonialism and pan-Asianism to promote its imperial project. Because of this, any pan-Asianist project must critically come to grips with the history of Japanese imperialism and acknowledge it frankly when discussing the countries that Japan colonized.

Takeuchi's responses to this problem were varied. We have already seen the first of these in his "What Is Modernity?" In that essay, in comparing Japan and China, he notes that Japan was an honor student of the West, which points to the fact that like the West, Japan became imperialist. Japan's imperialism emerged from the West, and countering it required countering Eurocentrism and finding alternatives in Asia. Takeuchi offered pan-Asianism as the remedy for imperialism of all kinds, both Western and Japanese.

However, this does not tackle the question of the role of pan-Asianism in Japan's imperialism. Here Takeuchi offered two answers. The first is his controversial claim that Japanese involvement in the war had a doubled structure. The second concerns the transmission of the wartime experience to those who were infants during the war or born during the postwar period.

With respect to Japan's role in the war, Takeuchi contended that Japan's involvement was two-pronged: the war of invasion against its neighbors and its attack on the United States. The latter, he argued, was a case of imperialism resisting imperialism. Treating these two acts separately makes it possible to argue that Japan must take responsibility for the war of invasion but that the war against the United States is another matter, and in fact Takeuchi had difficulty making a judgment on the latter.[120] Yet the problem is even more complex because, as the following quote indicates, at times Takeuchi recognized that although the two aspects of the war must be logically separated, they are in fact all of a piece:

> The Greater East Asian War was at once a war of colonial invasion and a war against imperialism. Although these two aspects were united in fact, they

must be separated logically. Japan had no intention of invading the United States and England, and while it usurped control of the Dutch colonies, it never attempted to take over Holland itself.[121]

In Takeuchi's reading, Japan's invasion of Asian countries was inextricably connected to a confrontation with Western imperialism.

We see this most clearly when he considers pan-Asianism in Japan. Here again he distinguishes two types of pan-Asianism, that of association and that of invasion, but claims that it is not always easy to distinguish the two.[122] For example, he notes that some Japanese pan-Asianists in the late nineteenth and early twentieth centuries supported invading Korea, but one could argue they did so at least partly in the belief that this would ward off the Qing empire and Russia. Of course, Takeuchi did not want to affirm the position of people such as the novelist and literary critic Hayashi Fusao (1903–1975), who unconditionally supported Japan's imperialist project in the Asia-Pacific War, but he did want to make it clear that the two parts, the invasion of Asian nations and the development of associations of those nations in the interest of pan-Asianism, were not clearly separable. In another essay, he asked, "If one hates invasion so much that one also negates the association that appeared in the form of invasion, is this not throwing the baby out with the bathwater?"[123] Takeuchi hoped to rescue the idea of Asia from the depths of the war and imperialism in Japan, an effort confounded by the fact that Japan's imperialism was the one place that pan-Asianism was practiced. Moreover, the problem of the imperialist domination of Asia did not disappear after the war. If anything, the danger of Asian nations becoming part of an American empire increased.

Consequently, according to Takeuchi, one could easily criticize Japanese imperialism from an abstract ethical perspective, but from the standpoint of politics and history, one had to formulate a critique of Japan on the one hand and the world in which it became imperialist on the other. Takeuchi's analysis here is connected to his earlier analysis of Japan's imperialism in "What Is Modernity?" where he argued that Japan followed the West in invading other countries. From this perspective, the problem of imperialism stemmed not from pan-Asianist nationalism but from the opposite, namely leaving Asia and following the West. In a 1964 essay Takeuchi noted: "I wrote that the Greater East Asian War mixed the ideas of 'raising Asia' and 'leaving Asia,' but to put this more precisely, one should perhaps say that the idea of leaving Asia absorbed that of raising Asia and that the idea of raising Asia became devoid of content and was just used."[124]

In Takeuchi's view, criticizing Japanese imperialism required coming to grips with the global imperialized world rather than using one imperialism to criticize another. For this reason, in 1958 he remarked that "while imperialism cannot be overthrown by imperialism, it is nevertheless also true that imperialism cannot be judged by imperialism."[125] Takeuchi follows here the position of Radhabinod Pal (1886–1967), a judge in the Tokyo war crimes trials in 1947 who contended that the defendants accused of war crimes should not be declared guilty.

Pal's judgment and the Tokyo Tribunal are worth examining briefly here because during the postwar period it was difficult for both Indians and Japanese to critically assess the war crimes trials. In Japan, leftists shied away from criticizing the trials because doing so would have been considered a right-wing gesture. Some on the right voiced criticisms of the trial, but leftists tended to ignore them. Rama Rao, the Indian ambassador to Japan, warned Pal not to damage India's relations with the Western powers by being vocal about his views during the trials,[126] especially since the trials occurred in 1947, the same year that India won its independence.

However, Pal did not refrain from voicing his criticisms, and his doing so may be seen as part of the project that Takeuchi called a "rollback," since he criticized Western values using Western values. Pal argued that imperialists cannot not judge imperialists and stated that the United States' firebombing of Japan, and especially the dropping of the atom bombs, should be considered war crimes, since they took numerous civilian lives.[127] In other words, Pal drew attention to the global imperialist structure within which the Tokyo war crimes trials were taking place. The postcolonial theorist and critic Ashis Nandy has argued the following:

> Pal points out the larger political and economic forces released by the nation-state system, by modern warfare, by the dominant philosophy of international diplomacy, and by the West's racist attitude to Japan, all of which helped produce the political response of the Japanese. The West had to acknowledge that wartime Japan wanted to beat the West at its own game, that a significant part of Japanese imperialism was only a reflection of the West's disowned self. . . . If the accused were guilty, so were the plaintiffs.[128]

Takeuchi probably welcomed such an emphasis on the global system that made both Western and Japanese imperialism possible, though he never commented on it. While there is no doubt that Japanese war criminals should have been tried, the problem is that there was no entity in the international realm with the moral authority to do this. Moreover, if the Japanese should have been tried, one might immediately ask whether the British, French, and the Americans also should have been put on trial for their imperialisms. The irony of the Tokyo war crimes trials is that they helped consolidate a new regime of American imperialism in which Japan was to play a major role.

However, in Takeuchi's view, none of this is to say that war memory is not an issue. On the contrary, his second point about the role of pan-Asianism in Japan's imperialism was that the war experience must be transmitted across generations and that Japan's atrocities in the war could be recognized without succumbing to the Western imperialist worldview. In was only in this way that the Japanese people could regain their subjectivity. The problem was that the generation born after the war did not live in conditions conducive to reflecting on the experience of the war. In his "The Generalization of War Experience" published in 1961, he lamented that the younger generation had forgotten about the war:

A part of the younger generation or even the majority [of it] looks down on the older generation's experience with the war and rejects it. This happens to the extent that the experience of the war is blocked or frozen. However, even if they think that they can reject this experience from a subjective point of view and separate themselves from those who have wartime experience, this act itself will not liberate them from the wounds of the war. It only proves that they are victims of the particularization of war experience. The act of negating the legacy itself makes one a slave to this legacy. I am not against actively breaking oneself off from history, but one needs a method to do this. I do not think that one can do this without consciousness of the war.[129]

Takeuchi here uses a narrative of repression when he notes that the younger generation blocks or freezes the experience of the war and consequently becomes a slave to its legacy. In doing so he highlights a question that is still raised today: Should the people of Japan continue to be held responsible for the war even though they were not direct participants? This brings us back to the issue of subjectivity. Takeuchi's goal was to create a subjectivity that was not shackled to the past but could only emerge through actively dealing with history. One might see here a distinction between a simple negation and the labor of negativity in a Hegelian sense. In Hegel's *Phenomenology*, one continues to be dominated by past shapes of consciousness to the extent that one has not understood nor come to terms with them.[130] For Takeuchi, coming to terms means more than achieving an abstract understanding and implies something more visceral, a moment that will compel one to understand the fundamental cause of the war. Takeuchi see this in the consciousness that he thought should connect the pre- and postwar generations even though the postwar generation did not directly experience the war. In other words, he highlights that the fundamental epistemological and affective conditions for the possibility of the war continue long after the war itself. To explain this point, Takeuchi once again invokes the everyday: "War is a state of exception, but at the same time it is an extension or a congealing of the everyday. . . . The Japanese people's method of knowing and aesthetic consciousness changed during the war, but on the other hand they also remained constant."[131] Everyday consciousness made the war possible. While much had changed in the transition from before and after the Asia-Pacific War, some of the fundamental dispositions of the everyday that continued were connected to the problems of modernity. The issue of reification returns in "The Generalization of War Experience" in what Takeuchi calls "naturalism," referring specifically to literary movements in postwar Japan. He connects naturalism to the formation of the state and contends that

> according to the theory of the national body [kokutairon], the state is not something that is created; rather there is a tendency to take the state as something given and natural. This tendency has basically not changed after the war. If it changed at all, during the experience of 1960 there were minute signs of movement. But what was the source of this movement? We can probably not find the source outside the experience of the war.[132]

In this passage Takeuchi connects the problem of subjectivity and reification to war memory. If revolution and anti-imperialism are never-ending projects, Japanese imperialism and the Asia-Pacific War are also events that continue long after they have formally ended. To some extent this position anticipates the recent book by political theorist Shirai Satoshi, *A Theory of Perpetual Defeat* (*Eizoku haisenron*),[133] which contends that Japan continues to lose the war to the extent that the same structures of subjectivity and politics abide throughout the postwar era. The relevant context both now and in Takeuchi's time is the way Japan continues to promote war through the United States. In contemporary Japan, we might think of the controversies around Article 9 of the Japanese constitution, which forbids Japan to engage in warfare or have a military. However, Takeuchi published his essay on the generalization of war memory in 1961, which was one year after widespread protests against the renewal of the Treaty of Mutual Cooperation and Security between the United States and Japan, which was first ratified in 1951. The so-called Anpo movement ("Anpo" being an abbreviation of the name of the treaty), which took place during May and June of 1960, was one of the largest protest movements in twentieth-century Japan. Without getting into the details of this treaty and the debates surrounding it, we can see that Takeuchi saw opposition to the treaty in relation to Japan's own experience in the Asia-Pacific War and represented the type of generalization of the war experience that he advocated. His generalization of the experience of war was a call to rethink temporality and the everyday in relation to the war.

By connecting the Anpo protests to the Asia-Pacific War, Takeuchi linked his ideas about revolution to his ideas about war memory. Takeuchi contended that the revolutionary everyday has to be part of the response to the problem of war memory. Just like revolution, war is not a one-time event and must be grounded in larger structures of consciousness and overarching practices. Like Maruyama, Takeuchi believed that Japan's entry into the war was intimately connected to its lack of social revolution. But he also believed that the Anpo movement perhaps offered the hope of a more active citizenry that would resist both the Japanese government and Western imperialism. If this scenario ever came to pass, it would launch Japan on an Asian trajectory.

However, Takeuchi was frustrated by both the failure of the Japanese public to generalize the experience of the war and the government's suppression of the Anpo antisecurity treaty movement. In 1960, he resigned from his post as professor at Tokyo Metropolitan University in protest. He made the following statement to friends at the time of his resignation, which anticipates contemporary debates about the Japanese constitution:

> When I began my employment as a professor I took an oath to the effect that I would respect and protect the constitution as a public official. Since May 20, I believe that parliamentary government, which was one of the objectives of the constitution, has been lost. Those responsible for the loss of the function of the Diet, the highest organ of state power, are none other than the speaker of the House and the prime minister, the most senior public officials. In view of their disregard for the constitution, for me to continue in my post as a professor would be to break my oath of office. It is also against my conscience as an educator. Therefore, I have decided to resign. . . . I have the ability to support myself by writing, and I choose this step as my way of protest, after full consideration.[134]

Takeuchi's declaration made a huge impact, and many people sent him letters: two-thirds supported him and about a third condemned him.[135] There are two parts to Takeuchi's action here. First, there is subjectivity, comparable to Gandhi's. Above we have seen that Takeuchi took a Maoist perspective by attempting to do the impossible by supporting revolution. However, he also took a Gandhian perspective, especially in his emphasis on self-negation. As Gandhi notes in his 1909 book, *Hind Swaraj* (Indian home rule), "If I do not obey the law, and accept the penalty for its breach, I use soul-force. It involves sacrifice of the self."[136] When Takeuchi invokes self-negation, he invokes this type of Gandhian practice, since he suffers the consequences of resigning from the university.

Second, Takeuchi tried to transform the constitution into something of his own. He sought to protect the constitution while officials and the prime minister violated it. In so doing, he practiced what he urged the Japanese to do: take the democracy that the Americans handed to them and modify it according to their own needs. Here we see him accepting the constitution that was forced on the Japanese by the Americans but using it against the pro-American officials. However, he came to feel that his efforts had no impact on society, and as a result his thought underwent subtle changes in the 1960s and 1970s, and his view of China evolved as well. This happened at the time of the outbreak of the Cultural Revolution in China in 1966, when numerous intellectuals had begun to follow Takeuchi's lead in seeing great hope in China.

The Cultural Revolution: Japanese Sinologists and Takeuchi

The 1960s marked the beginning of a transition to new forms of pan-Asianism. China's Cultural Revolution, which began in 1966, was the high point of the global 1960s. It served as the center of a vortex of student and mass revolt around the world while at the same time marking a turning point away from revolution. In view of Takeuchi's early expression of support for endless revolution, one would expect him to have been a major supporter of the Cultural Revolution. However, his comments on the Cultural Revolution were circumspect, especially when compared to the way his contemporary Sinologists celebrated it.

As noted earlier, the Japanese media initially reported positively on the Chinese Revolution of 1949. However, at the time of the Cultural Revolution, negative reports of events in China began to appear. For example, the reporter Ōya Sōichi went to China in 1966 and on his return wrote a number of essays contending that the Cultural Revolution, which he called a "revolution of brats," had plunged China into chaos. He also published photos of the violence associated with the movement, presenting readers with a strikingly negative image of China.

Moreover, the celebrated writers Kawabata Yasunari, Ishikawa Jun, Abe Kōbō, and Mishima Yukio issued a joint statement protesting against the destruction of art during the Cultural Revolution. In 1967 in the *Mainichi shinbun* (The Japan daily news), they wrote that "the Chinese Cultural Revolution is fundamentally a political revolution. At times, the revolution uses power to infringe on the autonomy of scholarship and art, and against this the artists in a neighboring country protest, regardless of whether they are politically left or right."[137] This negative view of the Cultural Revolution is similar to viewpoints commonly heard in advanced capitalist nations, perhaps not surprising given that during the 1950s and 1960s, Japan was already on its way to becoming a major player in the global capitalist world. On the other hand, Japanese Sinologists, often echoing Takeuchi's earlier arguments about China, generally resisted this interpretation of the Cultural Revolution and painted a more positive portrait of China in the late 1960s.

Some of Japan's pro-Mao Sinologists visited China and came back to write positive reports about the Cultural Revolution. They often interpreted the Cultural Revolution as creating a "commune," which they described as harmonious and democratic. This represented an embodiment of the subjective resistance that Takeuchi associated with China. He had already identified the substantiality of community with the base areas during the Yan'an period, and in the 1960s leftist Sinologists such as Yamada Keiji and Niijima Atsuyoshi claimed that such communes were being realized in China as a result of the Cultural Revolution.

Yamada assessed the significance of Chinese politics in terms of a larger Asian and Third World problematic:

> Highly industrialized societies are based on a highly compartmentalized system of division of labor, which tears human existence asunder. The goal of human life itself is lost. Late-developing countries in Asia, Africa, and Latin America have been left behind by the economic development of the early-developing countries and the relative gap between them grows. These countries agonize because they are not able to overcome poverty, sickness, and ignorance. The path of the Chinese working class perhaps shows the way to overcome both of the above problems. Perhaps the secret to overcoming modernity lies here.[138]

Yamada criticizes the division of labor from a global perspective. In his view, the problems of the advanced capitalist countries are different from Third World problems. In the former, the alienation that resulted from modern capitalism and the division of labor shattered any sense of community and the goals of life. In the Third World, by contrast, economic development lagged. Yamada does not go as far as Takeuchi in connecting the prosperity in industrialized societies and the poverty in the late-developing countries: unlike Takeuchi, he does not reckon with imperialism. Nonetheless, like Takeuchi, he placed his hope in China, believing that it would someday create a new world beyond inequality, a world in which the substantiality of the late developers combines with the prosperity of the advanced capitalist nations. As we have seen in chapter 3, Ōkawa Shūmei dreamed that Japan would combine substantial community and individuality, and in the 1960s, Japanese Sinologists began to anticipate the realization of this ideal in China. Their optimistic outlook echoes the term "overcoming modernity," used by the Kyoto school of philosophers to legitimize the Asia-Pacific War. Of course, Yamada's highlighting of the Chinese working class in the above passage serves to change the above discourse and push it in a Marxist direction.

However, Yamada does not stress the working class in his analysis of the Cultural Revolution. Rather, he reads it more as a gesture toward traditional China, aiming at a reconciliation between individuality and community, or negativity and substantiality, and references the universalization of the idea of the sage. Describing the Mao period, he wrote: "Any human being can through effort, through internal transformation, infinitely approach an ideal human being. The ideal human being is what one calls a sage. . . . The sage is not someone absolute but is the most complete human being."[139]

Yamada contended that Mao offered the promise of the universalization of the earlier discourse of the sage. In Mao's China, everyone could become a sage, meaning that they could help construct a different society. The political effect of this was that the whole of China was turned into a commune. According to Yamada, in such a commune the people

> are not atomized individuals who move mechanistically within a totality. . . . They live as a totality, and as a totality, they are liberated from alienation. In order to create a "kingdom of freedom" they incessantly attempt to transform themselves. There is no place for individual freedom to enter here.[140]

The last sentence negates individual freedom, which might raise fears of a Hegelian lack of negativity, but Yamada conceived of the commune not as a strong state but rather as an anarchic community: "China is now advancing step by step to becoming a large, organized commune. Clearly, China has taken the first step toward abolishing the state. The new 'state' is a state without a state. It should be called a 'commune state.'"[141] In a commune state, people are able to assert both their individual and collective freedoms.

In moving beyond the opposition between individual and community, Japanese intellectuals saw China as being on the road to becoming a commune state. In his 1968 essay "China Commune," Niijima Atsuyoshi further developed Yamada's argument, beginning with the claim that people were not able to see what was going on in China at the time. He wrote that the situation was a bit like the fable about the palace nobleman who loved dragons. The nobleman put figurines of dragons throughout the palace, and when the dragons heard about this, they descended upon him. When the real dragons came, the nobleman ran away in fear. Similarly, in Niijima's view, Marxists and others were failing to recognize that the Cultural Revolution was realizing many of the ideals of Marxism and offered a comparison between the Paris Commune and the Shanghai Commune[142] of the Cultural Revolution to show the continuity between the two.[143]

Unlike Yamada, who described the negation of the individual as the result of being absorbed into a communal totality without a state, Niijima underscored the democratic nature of the Shanghai Commune. He pointed out that Chinese officials and Mao himself took the Paris Commune as a model for their political projects, leading them to try to practice democracy. As in the Paris Commune, in the Shanghai Commune all representatives had short-term appointments and were accountable to the working class.[144] He also made points that echo Takeuchi's earlier work on elite politics and educational reform. Overall, Niijima read the Cultural Revolution as a radical overcoming of organizational hierarchy in society as a whole. He pointed out, for example, that when the Chinese military was reformed in June 1965, all military ranks were abolished, and generals were lowered to the status of common soldiers.[145]

With such positive interpretations of the Cultural Revolution from Yamada, Niijima, and other leftists, one might have expected that Takeuchi would join the chorus. Takeuchi did praise the Cultural Revolution at times, finding in it his concepts of the everyday and endless revolution, but for the most part he repeatedly said that he did not have enough information to judge the effectiveness of the revolution and claimed that the situation was complex. Some of his comments about the Cultural Revolution were seen in his critiques of Japanese perceptions of China and the suppression of news about the Chinese Revolution, which he again explained in terms of the everyday:

> Such suppression did not disappear after the war. I believe that it remains a Japanese habit of thinking. It is difficult to get rid of laziness. For Chinese people, revolution is a purifying of the everyday. We cannot overlook that the image of revolution that floats in our minds is one that is an anti-everyday to an extreme. We see this even when we see the reports on the Great Cultural Revolution. There is a psychological overreaction that makes one conclude that revolutions happen all of a sudden and are chaotic. The Chinese view is completely different.[146]

The Japanese were not able to see the Chinese Cultural Revolution as an event that happened in the everyday because they were still wedded to the notion that revolution is a one-time occurrence. In another essay written around the same time, Takeuchi expands on this point:

> From the perspective of the Chinese people, revolution is attached to their everyday. They believe that everyday life directly connects to revolution. Moreover, the revolution does not end. It is an everyday activity and is simultaneously semipermanent. These are two points that form a set, in a truly long-term vision of revolution. They see the Cultural Revolution as one step in this extremely long process.[147]

190 CHAPTER FIVE

He also gestures toward a different temporality among the Chinese, a temporality containing an eschatology that had no goal outside the everyday.[148] In other words, the root of revolution was in present everyday practices. To some extent this position is implicit in his remarks about history in "What Is Modernity?," but the final sentence about a "long process" indicates that we do not know yet how this process will turn out. By 1967, Takeuchi began to see that the Chinese were trapped in a movement that itself was caught in the contradictions between domestic and global politics. In a discussion with the popular intellectual Yoshimoto Takaaki in 1968, Takeuchi is recorded as making the following remark:

> In short, I believe that there are exterior and interior motivations for the Cultural Revolution. The external motivation for this movement, namely the international motivation, is preparation for war. This motivation concerns the problem of how to protect oneself from an attack by the United States. The internal motivation concerns resistance to the bureaucratism, or the existing structure of the party, governmental institutions, and the military. They aimed to restructure these institutions.... The result will be determined by a struggle over whether one should protect the state or dismantle the state and fight for world revolution.[149]

Here Takeuchi perceptively underscores the contradiction between the withering away of the state that is a goal of socialism and the geopolitical reality that forced the Chinese to establish a state. He reads Mao as wanting to overcome the party and bureaucracy but as failing to do so because of the threat of war with the United States. In other words, the Cultural Revolution was caught in a web of international ideals about socialism that among other things led to Maoist support for Third World countries and also for liberation movements around the world. However, China also had to prepare itself militarily for an attack by the United States. This led to China's acquisition of nuclear weapons in the 1960s, a subject that sparked debate in Japan at the time. Takeuchi's position was based on hope for revolution in Asia and the Third World. But at the same time, he believed that such a possibility was not unlimited. As this hope dwindled in the 1970s and 1980s, visions of China and Asia changed as well, bringing us closer to the present moment.

Conclusion

Takeuchi mobilized China to defend his version of pan-Asianism and revolution. Unlike earlier pan-Asianists from Okakura Tenshin and Zhang Taiyan to Ōkawa Shūmei, Takeuchi clearly focused on subjectivity and revolution more than Chinese or Asian traditions. Moreover, he struggled with complex issues associated with war memory while attempting to graft the dreams of Asia onto the Chinese Revolution of 1949. While he did refer to Confucianism and a Chinese worldview from time to time, the major thrust of his argument lies in how China expressed a subjectivity that could be a model for other Asian nations (and weak nations anywhere). For this reason, he connected his ideas not to traditional philosophies but to the Chinese experience of revolution and the everyday.

While the concept of the everyday was prevalent in certain circles in postwar Japan, it was not common among Japanese Sinologists. Both Yamada Keiji and Niijima Atsushi agreed with Takeuchi in many respects, but unlike Takeuchi, they typically drew on ideas from classical Chinese thought. Connecting the Chinese Revolution to Chinese philosophy and then making that the basis for resistance throughout Asia was popular in the postwar period but changed in character by the 1970s and 1980s when intellectuals around the world began to doubt the possibility of an alternative to global capitalism. Takeuchi himself anticipated an age of leftist melancholy, where faith in socialism was no longer firm. Anyone attempting to combine pan-Asianism, Third Worldism, and socialism after the 1980s faced an issue similar to what Takeuchi faced during the postwar period: namely, how to revive an ideal that appears to have been discredited. By the 1990s, it was not just pan-Asianism that appeared discredited but socialism and revolution as well. In the next chapter, we will examine how the Chinese critical intellectual Wang Hui revived elements of Takeuchi's vision of Chinese revolution in a postsocialist world.

6

Wang Hui: Contemporary Pan-Asianist in China?

By the 1980s and especially the 1990s, popular and academic works alike began to speak of the "rise" of Asia and China. This sparked increasing interest in pan-Asianism but left open the question of what happened to the pan-Asianism of Takeuchi Yoshimi and other thinkers of an earlier age. Wang Hui provides us with a window into contemporary pan-Asianism and the legacy of the Chinese Revolution. Like Takeuchi, Wang invokes the Chinese Revolution but in a different context and with different consequences. While Takeuchi drew on the Chinese Revolution to criticize pro-West narratives of Japan, Wang returns to the Chinese Revolution, when the Chinese state itself gained legitimacy from this same revolution.

As we shall see, the basic impulses of pan-Asianism, especially with respect to the revolutionary tradition, did not die out entirely. Chinese critical intellectuals, who have often been described as members of China's New Left, have proposed a politics of revolution in the postrevolutionary, postsocialist world of the twenty-first century. A leading figure in the New Left (and the subject of this chapter), Wang Hui, a professor of contemporary Chinese literature and intellectual history, can be described as a nonrevolutionary revolutionary. That is, he is a revolutionary who does not favor immediate revolution but believes that one must rethink the contemporary Chinese state from the standpoint of the revolution and thus try to influence its policies. However, Wang leaves open the question of how to reconcile his support of mass action in the Maoist period with his support of contemporary Chinese policies such as the Belt-Road Initiative (BRI).

The point of examining Wang's work is not to endorse his views but to highlight their significance. In particular, his recent work represents an incomplete attempt to rescue the legacy of the Chinese Revolution in a postrevolutionary world. In his critique of Chinese neoliberals, Wang shows that the Chinese state is intimately connected to global capitalism and market reforms, meaning that support for expansion of capitalist markets actually amounts to support for the state. This insight haunts Wang's own attempt to read policies like the BRI as a socialist project. In actuality, such policies might in fact support global capitalism while also doing the important work of resisting Euro-American hegemony.

Wang Hui's Critique of Chinese Neoliberals and the West

Wang Hui was born in 1959, meaning that he was nineteen years old when Deng Xiaoping launched China on the path to market reforms. I have given the historical context of Wang's early works elsewhere;[1] here I focus on his recent writings, which bear some similarities to Takeuchi's work. I also highlight some of the essays in which he engages in self-contextualization, especially in relation to the transition from the 1980s to the 1990s and the 2000s. Similar to Takeuchi's point about postwar Japan, Wang contends that after the 1980s and 1990s, the Chinese people and their leaders uncritically took the West as a model.

Wang's major contribution to tracing the genealogy of our present moment is his radical rethinking of the 1989 social movement in China and its suppression on June 4. Most discussions of this movement portray its supporters as liberal democrats attacking an autocratic communist state, especially since activists rallied around concepts such as freedom and democracy. However, Wang Hui tells a different story, which paves the way to understanding his own intellectual development. According to Wang,

> the issue we must squarely face is that, while the 1989 social mobilization clearly criticized the traditional system, what was before it was no longer the old state but rather the reform-minded state, or that state that was gradually moving toward the market and social transformation, and thus the consequences of those policies. I do not make this distinction—between the old state and the reform-minded state—in order to deny the continuities between the two types of state, but rather to point out the transformations in state functions and their social conditions. For, in reality, the very state that was promoting markets and social transformation was utterly dependent upon the political legacy of the old state and its method of ideological rule.[2]

This passage suggests that the 1989 movement, in which Wang participated, was not able to grasp its own conditions of possibility. Specifically, in addition to seeking democracy, the movement targeted issues of corruption and inequality that went hand in hand with the reforms. Consequently, those who attacked the state and the Communist Party of the Mao period failed to understand that the object of their critique had changed. During the 1990s, China's problems were no longer that of the communist period but rather emerged from the manner in which the communist state had been reconstituted in a new age of market reforms. Moreover, reformers drew on the legacy of the state constructed during the Mao period to implement market reforms, which makes problematic any simple opposition between the market and the communist state. Promarket officials needed the autocratic dimensions of the communist state created under Mao to promote the market and continued to use these mechanisms to crush opposition to marketization.

Chinese neoliberals have advocated that China rid itself of the remnants of the communist state and that things would be better if only China could further reform and promote freedom and democracy through further opening of markets. Such arguments show that despite the official narrative about Mao, which is partially supportive of his legacy, Chinese intellectuals suffer from a complex of fear and amnesia when it comes to Maoist China, which has led to attempts to compare Mao's China to Hitler's Germany and other autocratic states. Behind this model is the old idea of a backward Asia, somewhat reminiscent of Fukuzawa Yukichi's interpretation but perhaps even more like the postwar Japanese intellectual Takeyama Michiyo's writings, discussed in chapter 5. In short, the argument asserts that Asian regimes are backward because they do not allow the realization of freedom and that China inherited this problem from the Mao period, which itself could not break free from Asiatic modes of production and subjectivity.

Wang criticizes this position in a manner that paves the way for his defense of the legacy of the Chinese Revolution. He laments that

> beginning with the generation that grew up after the Cultural Revolution, the only worthwhile knowledge comes from the West, particularly from the United States (and, as before, this too is a sort of bias). Asia, Africa, and Latin America, not to mention Eastern and Southern Europe—those places that used to be the sources of such vital knowledge and culture—have now basically fallen out of the purview of popular knowledge. In the literary production and reassessments of the Vietnam War in the 1980s, what dominates is not a consideration of the relationship between foreign relations and the war, but rather considerations of the Cultural Revolution, as if repudiating the Cultural Revolution could lend these reassessments all the rational support they needed. This is a perfect example of how repudiating the Cultural Revolution has turned into a defense of [the] ruling ideology and state policy.[3]

Just as Takeuchi complained that the Japanese students who were born after the war did not reflect on Japan's experience in the Asia-Pacific War, Wang Hui is concerned about a type of forgetting in China. This forgetting concerns not just the memory of war but also the loss of a revolutionary consciousness that connected China to other Asian and Third World countries and served to contextualize war. Indeed, Takeuchi also held the Chinese model up to the Japanese to encourage identification with Asia. The irony of this history is that by the 1990s, China dialectically turned into the opposite of what Takeuchi had imagined. Rather than Japan following China's earlier Third Worldism, with the death of Mao and China's opening and reforms, China followed Japan in making the West, especially the United States, a standard. Wang picks up where Takeuchi left off by using the Cultural Revolution as a discursive mechanism to legitimate capitalist ideology, with the Cold War and US imperialism again visible in the background. Wang explains how the transformation of the Cold War might legitimate American politics:

> Because the socialist system has ended and has overlapped with a Cold War structure that has not yet ended, the West and the countries in the Western camp, such as Japan and Korea, have become the victors of the Cold War. The so-called end of the Cold War implies only that a part of it has disintegrated. Moreover, the disintegration of this part became the condition of the globalization of the other part of the Cold War. The ideological effects of this configuration are the complete legitimation of anti-communism and anti-socialism, along with the "naturalization" and "making harmless" of American hegemony. When the Cold War ended, America was the largest hegemon and the only one to use nuclear weapons and to have close to nine hundred military bases around the world. The United States also made nuclear weapons enter North East Asia and numerous times there was a risk of using them. However, in the so-called "post–Cold War" environment, for societies within this hegemonic structure, American hegemony has already become "natural" and "harmless."[4]

Like Takeuchi, Wang understands the importance of going beyond the Cold War. However, he calls attention not only to hegemony but also to the centrality of anticommunism and antisocialism, which became much more prevalent by the 1990s. Moreover, he explains that American hegemony is connected to the universalization of the American empire, which is the part of the Cold War that continues without resistance. Wang here makes a dialectical maneuver that he does not fully explicate. The Cold War was a dual structure, and if the Soviet Union had not completely disintegrated, American empire and hegemony would not have become what it did. American hegemony is naturalized; however, the other side of the Cold War, namely the socialist state, has not completely vanished. If communism and socialism were in fact completely absent from the world, antisocialism would be unnecessary. Wang identifies two possible reasons for the continued conjuring of the specter of communism. First, the naturalized American ideology requires this negative image of communism/socialism because it represents one of the Others that American ideology must have to legitimize its empire. In short, communism survives as an object of negation. We see this in the contemporary discourse on Asia in the constructed images of North Korea and to some extent China. Wang explains that "North Korea is generally described as the most dangerous and completely irrational country" and China is also sometimes described as the "axis of evil."[5] The position of North Korea, a relatively small country with limited military capacity, must be exaggerated in order to accomplish the ideological work of justifying the presence of many American bases in Asia.

The other reason for invoking the continuing specter of socialism is that capitalism is a crisis-ridden system that constantly delegitimizes itself by systematically undermining its core values, such as freedom. For this reason, even people in capitalist societies continue to imagine a future beyond the profit motive. Wang's point is that the left has an opening that it could use to reappropriate the legacy of socialism to rethink both the Third World and Asia. This prompts him to take on the complex task of both imagining the relationship between the Chinese tradition and modernity and reinterpreting the Chinese Revolution.

Wang has to show that the Chinese Revolution can serve as a critique of the present but at the same time cannot be so distant from the present that it loses relevance. Hence, Wang and other Chinese New Leftists are caught in the difficult situation of both affirming the revolutionary past as different while positing a connection between the revolutionary past and the post-Mao present. Takeuchi made a similar move by contending that Japan and China were both Asian nations that struggled against capitalist imperialism, and this situational analogy made it possible for Japan to correct itself by looking at the Chinese mirror. Using China's revolutionary past, Wang constructs a politics of revolutionary remnants that now lie hidden beneath the world of commodified power and the Chinese state that is increasingly complicit in the logic of global capital. His hope is to rethink these remnants and use them to contest the complete privatization that is engulfing China. China's revolutionary past thus becomes a template for criticizing the present.

Although it is said that the past is another country, this statement overlooks the difference between time and space, especially when dealing with the politics of remnants. When a theorist conjures Chinese revolutionary remnants that both exist and are suppressed by the present government, he or she both criticizes and legitimates the current Chinese government. The distance between the past and the present may make possible criticism of the present government. However, the continuity between the past and present can also be used to argue against revolution in the present moment. For this reason, Wang is a nonrevolutionary revolutionary, a revolutionary who believes that the revolution has already happened, and one must perfect or realize the ideals embodied in the 1949 Revolution. From this perspective, his position on the Chinese Revolution is similar to that of Hegel on the French Revolution. Hegel was a major supporter of the French Revolution, but he believed that in the nineteenth century one did not need another revolution; rather, what was needed was the realization of the ideals of the French Revolution, which would be accomplished by embedding liberal rights in a social context.[6]

Part of the problem can be seen in how people argued for revolution after the 1990s. After the collapse of the Soviet Union, many in China and around the world believed that China should follow the path of the Soviet Union and overthrow the Chinese Communist Party (CCP). This implied a different kind of revolution, one that opposed the communist regime and worked to establish liberalism. However, for some scholars of the Chinese New Left, Russia served as a cautionary tale for the CCP.[7] In particular, they pointed to the numerous events surrounding Boris Yeltsin's presidency, especially the constitutional crisis of 1993 in which Yeltsin attempted to dissolve the legislature. The legislature responded by trying to impeach Yeltsin and declared that the vice president should take over. In October 1993 Yeltsin countered by using the military to regain power, sacrificing numerous lives in the process.

Wang Hui was among the first intellectuals to point out that the Russian method of radical regime change was not the best policy for China, and his analysis of it enables us to situate his later writings. "The import of Russia's October Incident," Wang explained, "was profoundly felt, especially by idealists possessing a rosy view of the West, those who believed that history had already come to an end, and those who saw the Cold War as already over."[8] Wang thought that this would eventually cause Chinese intellectuals to turn away from the West and toward their own traditions. From the 1990s, other intellectuals and activists also began criticizing the United States and advocated that China not follow their lead.

Between 1993 and 1997, the Chinese economy grew at a prodigious rate, and China was also able to avoid the Asian economic crisis of 1997. In addition, as the Chinese economy developed, both the government and intellectuals began to envision a world in which China would play a greater role, as

198   CHAPTER SIX

we see in China's BRI. Wang Hui defends the BRI by placing it in the history
of Asian revolutions, starting with Lenin's October Revolution and the Chinese Revolution.

Lenin, Russia, and the Chinese Revolution

Early twentieth-century pan-Asianists, as discussed in chapter 2, were divided into two camps over the issue of Russia's place in Asia. While Sun Yat-
sen claimed that Russia became part of Asia after the October Revolution,
numerous radical intellectuals turned their gaze toward Asia after Japan defeated Russia in the Russo-Japanese War. For them, Russia represented the
West that was defeated by an Asian nation. However, Wang Hui follows Lenin
in showing that one could rethink the effects of the Russo-Japanese War from
the Russian side and construct a different picture of Asia, one akin to Takeuchi's view of Asia as the possible birthplace of an anti-imperialist movement.
Lenin makes the following comment about the 1905 Revolution:

> In Eastern Europe and Asia the period of bourgeois-democratic revolutions
> did not begin until 1905. The revolutions in Russia, Persia, Turkey and China,
> the Balkan wars—such is the chain of world events of *our* period in our "Ori-
> ent." And only a blind man could fail to see in this chain of events the awak-
> ening of a *whole series* of bourgeois-democratic national movements which
> strive to create nationally independent and nationally uniform states. It is pre-
> cisely and solely because Russia and the neighbouring countries are passing
> through this period that we must have a clause in our programme on the right
> of nations to self-determination.[9]

Lenin affirmed the importance of the right of self-determination and began by describing it as the product of a bourgeois revolution. Eventually, this
became the basis for his recognition of the connection between socialism
and anti-imperialist nationalism. The various places that he mentioned as
the Orient—China, Russia, Persia, and Turkey—were all considered backward. Following the interpretation of history offered by Georgi Plekhanov,
the Russian theorist of the second international, these places would first need
to experience capitalism before they became socialist. Lenin at times seemed
to agree with Plekhanov, but Wang uncovers another side to Lenin's theory,
a side that recognizes the potential for revolution in backward land-based
societies. From this perspective, he looks at the land-ocean relationship from
a position opposite that of Mackinder, who he explicitly draws on.[10] Wang
follows the thinking of Okakura and other figures in this book, but he does
so at a different time, when it appears that China is both emerging as a power

and yet losing its revolutionary credentials. We can grasp the significance of Wang's work when we consider it in relation to Alfred McCoy's recent analysis of the rise of China, which also draws on Mackinder's work. McCoy argues that despite today's technological advances such as the rise of air power, Mackinder's point about controlling the large landmass of Eurasia presages the trajectory of American imperialism, which has long tried to control Asian land through the seas.[11] This project worked for a while, but things have changed. McCoy writes:

> Mackinder was a bit premature in his prediction. The Russian Revolution of 1917, the Chinese revolution of 1949, and the subsequent forty years of the Cold War slowed much actual development for decades. In this way, the Euro-Asian heartland was denied economic growth and integration, thanks in part to artificial ideological barriers—the Iron Curtain and then the Sino-Soviet split—that stalled infrastructure construction across it. No longer.[12]

McCoy, like Wang, follows Mackinder in theorizing the rise of China as fundamentally characterized by the construction of a land-based project. In other words, despite its development of air and naval power, China today is expanding its power through control of neighboring regions and also by developing its huge landmass. However, he views the Russian and Chinese revolutions as hindrances to such development and suggests that the Chinese are now following a path that runs counter to its earlier socialist project. Wang also sees such a difference, but his reperiodization of the Chinese Revolution in the twentieth century carries with it the possibility that contemporary Chinese can still draw upon remnants of the socialist period. From this perspective, when a technologically advanced China stops relying on its land, it does not merely gain a strategic advantage; rather, Wang sees ideological elements of the Chinese Revolution that might still guide China's future.

Wang's periodization of the Chinese Revolution offers a modified version of Eric Hobsbawm's idea of the short twentieth century.[13] He contends that the short twentieth century began around 1905–1911 and ended with the death of Mao Zedong in 1976, meaning that China's short twentieth century is fundamentally defined by the beginning and end of the Chinese revolutions but also that these revolutions define Asia as a whole. The key to the opening moment is the beginning of the period after the First Sino-Japanese War and the Russo-Japanese War. Wang believes that these wars triggered a series of revolutions, including the 1905 Revolution in Russia, the 1911 Revolution in China, and Mao's revolution in 1949. He comments: "It was not a matter of imperialist war; but rather, the 'awakening of Asia' that was prompted by these wars, and which was distinguished by the revolutions listed above.

These new forces comprise the multifaceted point of departure for the 'short twentieth century.'"[14] Lenin saw the awakening of Asia as a movement from the weakest part of the imperialist system that could create an alternative world. This is Lenin's theory of the weakest link, which mobilizes the terrestrial (agriculture) against the oceanic (capitalist imperialism).

Wang has argued that the Russian and Chinese revolutions (both the Republican Revolution of 1911 and the Communist Revolution of 1949) can only be understood in relation to continental and maritime forces.

> The revolutions in China and Russia, representative incidents of the twentieth century, may also be understood as revolutions on the land opposing capitalism on the sea. These two terrestrial revolutions were wholly derived from the impetus of new maritime powers. Not only were they revolutions to resist foreign invasions or colonial governance, but they also transformed the continental order. At a fundamental level, the continuation, profundity, and fortification of these revolutions inevitably depended on the resources and powers of the land, including a huge number of peasants, the vast countryside, and a dense network of geopolitical relations. If the main topic of twentieth century politics was "countries want independence, nations want liberation, and the people want revolution," then the quest for an independent state and national emancipation within the era of colonialism and imperialism was perforce bound to undergo people's revolution, forging a new kind of political form. For this reason, the most important political achievement of this era was indeed the birth of China as a modern political subject.[15]

Here the resistance of land-based people is connected to the mediation of the ocean as a form of subjectivity. This is the moment of self-negation to which Takeuchi alluded. Again, like Takeuchi, Wang repeatedly highlights the combination of nationalism and revolution in Asia. However, he brings a sensibility to the idea of land that is different from Takeuchi's. Takeuchi gestured toward labor in his treatment of the Edo-period philosopher Andō Shōeki and Mao Zedong, but his discussion did not make much of peasant labor or the connection of revolutionary movements to land. In fact, his arguments about Asia in the 1960s tended to despatialize it and highlight the fluidity of the concept of Asia depending on where resistance to imperialism was occurring.[16] Wang, on the other hand, depicts the opposition between the early twentieth-century modernizers and the conservatives as an opposition between the ocean and the land. He mentions that during the Russian Revolution, Russian politics were split between Narodniks and the pan-Slavics on the one hand and the Westernizers on the other. He underscored that such an opposition had parallels in China and elsewhere in Asia.

However, Wang next makes a Hegelian gesture by claiming that the Chinese Revolution overcame this distinction. Wang combines the abstract subjectivity associated with the maritime world and the so-called conservative forces of the land. He contends that continental China utilized the power of the maritime world and its ideas to attack and renew its traditions. In this way, the land-based region participated in its own defeat, leading to a new synthesis with subjectivity that was influenced by the maritime world and offered an alternative to older models. In this alternative construction, the distinction between land and ocean would be rendered meaningless. After the synthesis, subjectivity is no longer merely individual but has a fundamentally communal dimension from which social movements may arise. This suggests the potential of a pan-Asianism that is embedded in a radically new subjectivity. Wang finds this subjectivity exemplified in the concept of the People's War in China's short twentieth century.

The Twentieth Century and People's War

By proposing revolutionary action originating from land, Wang offers a revolutionary alternative to an alliance between the peasants and the urban proletariat, an alternative that had the potential to influence the character of both subjectivity and the state. He argues that Chinese revolutionaries made the people's state a telos that incorporates and goes beyond the visions of the nineteenth century. Drawing on Lu Xun, Wang writes:

> Lu Xun declared that the creative power of the "nineteenth century" had already fallen into decline by the century's end, with freedom and equality having already degenerated into new despotic forms evoking autocratic forms of old. For this reason, China's goal for the newly arrived twentieth century should be to overcome Europe's two revolutions and their consequences, establishing a "people's state" in which each person can freely develop.[17]

The twentieth century represented a new synthetic vision that was present in the revolutions of Asia, namely in China and Russia. Takeuchi never wrote about Lu Xun's distinction between the nineteenth and twentieth centuries, but his interpretation of Lu in "Asia as Method" anticipated Wang Hui's reading of Lu Xun's vision for the twentieth century. As we have seen in chapter 5, Takeuchi called on Asia to transform the values of the West to create a new universality. He also judged Western values to be in decline and saw the job of the Orient as saving the West from itself. Wang sees the Chinese Revolution as a means to achieve a global postcapitalist world, and he envisions Asian revolutionary nationalisms as playing a major part in realizing this goal. A key part of this vision entails achieving the ideals of equality and freedom beyond the limited forms that resulted from earlier European revolutions. In this sense, Wang's appropriation of modern Chinese revolutionary history from Lu Xun to Mao and beyond is fundamentally different from conservatives such as Liu Xiaofeng (1956–) who have recently turned to Mao as a symbol of anti-Enlightenment culture.[18]

In Wang's reading of Lu Xun, he understands the nineteenth century to have been primarily Western, while noting that the French Revolution and the industrial revolution failed to live up to their ideals. Here again we see the specter of Hegel, who in *The Philosophy of History* contends that the contradictions and the ideals of the French Revolution are something with which history "is now occupied and whose solution it has to work out in the future."[19] He also argued that when ideals such as freedom and equality become embodied in capitalism, they lead to overproduction, which in turn encourages overseas trade and imperialist expansion.[20] Once the ideals of the French Revolution turned toward imperialism, they expanded spatially and transformed into something beyond themselves. The freedom and equality of the Enlightenment became unfreedom and inequality. Both the Russian and Chinese revolutions by contrast aimed to transform political institutions by making them constantly accountable to the people, thus realizing the ideals of the French Revolution at a higher level. As Wang Hui puts it, "The twentieth century was an epoch of internalizing the other's history into oneself, of positioning one's own history within a global scope"[21] that made possible the overcoming of the nineteenth century:

> The nineteenth century European socialist movement was powerless to break the internal contradictions of capitalism, such that the completion of China's undertaking demanded passing through a so-called "pre-capitalist" and "agrarian" revolution; and yet, the state in which this revolution burst forth also confronted economic, political, and cultural forms of the nineteenth century. As such, China's revolution was invested with a dual task, from Sun Yat-sen's "political and social revolution [which] must be achieved in a single stroke" to Mao Zedong's concept of "New Democracy."[22]

Because the twentieth-century revolutions occurred in places that were backward, land based, or agrarian, they had to complete both a political and social transformation in one stroke. A political revolution encompasses the struggle for national independence, but a transformation in one stroke also requires a social revolution that must be carried out in a way that avoids the inequalities associated with capitalism. Moreover, in the process of this synthesis, the liberal separations of the nineteenth century were both extirpated and taken to a new level, even though these separations had not completely taken root in Asian societies. In this way, the Chinese revolutions of the twentieth century aimed to complete and transform the ideals of the nineteenth century.

The development of revolutionary ideals in Asia revealed that many of the prerequisites of socialism spelled out in Marxist theory did not exist. In particular, the material conditions such as industrialization and increasing mechanization, to which we will return in the epilogue, existed only in protean form during the Russian and Chinese revolutions. Consequently, as Lu Xun pointed out, the spirit of the twentieth century had to rely "on the power of the will in order to carve out a new path for one's life."[23] In other words, the importance of subjectivity extended beyond material conditions. In a manner that again turns Hegel on his head, Asia became a space of subjectivity and the future.

Wang gestures in the direction of the Marxist philosopher Ernst Bloch and his concept of the "not yet" in the process of constructing a quasi-Hegelian theory of practice in which subjectivity and material conditions are both crucial. Wang paraphrases Bloch as follows:

> If the future expresses the emergence of a "not yet" object or world, then we may follow Ernst Bloch's distinction: there exist two conditions of "not yet," of which one is a kind of material condition of Not-Yet-Become and the other is a subjective condition, one of the consciousness which is Not-Yet-Conscious. "Not yet" is latent under our feet, repressed within our designs, consciousness, and desires. Twentieth-century politics simultaneously contained both senses of "not yet."[24]

Bloch argued that human beings must activate the potentiality within objective matters to create socialism. In this view, human agency is the "active form educed in matter."[25] His point is in keeping with interpretations of Marx that attempt to reconcile the force of human structure with the creativity embodied in human agency. Most Marxists thought that the material conditions for socialism were already in place in nations where capitalism had developed and all that was needed was to transform the subjective conditions. One could even go further and say that the repressed possibilities latent under our feet are precisely the contradictions in historical conditions, contradictions that have both subjective and objective dimensions. In other words, becoming subjectively conscious requires discovering substantial contradictions in history, which form the context for revolutionary action. Much of the above discussion overlaps with Wang's approach, but he contends that the Chinese situation is different because its revolutionaries saw a future defined by the struggle against an enemy.

Wang Hui argues that the Chinese Revolution was different from Bloch's utopianism because revolutionaries presaged the future not only temporally but also through "the logic of action, of politics, and of military strategy."[26] Concepts of action, politics, strategy, and so on had to develop through the category of a "'temporal tendency' [*shishi*], always indicating movement of contradiction or relations between ourselves and the enemy within a defined situation."[27]

The characters Wang translates as "temporal tendency," *shishi* (*jisei* [Japanese]) 时势, make up the same compound that Fukuzawa used to distinguish between Asia and the West. Fukuzawa used this term in his description of the "ethos of the nation" and the spirit of civilization that represented a unified logic and represented a single global standard. Wang sees this term as lacking a simple teleology and as indicating forces in conflict. In the modern capitalist world, temporal tendency involves a conflict between friend and enemy, a struggle between imperialism and oppositional movements. People's War, then, is an example of radical mobilization and participation that transcends self-interest and works to resist enemies. By rethinking time in terms of mobilization, Wang appears to splinter any idea of a grand narrative and suggests what might be called a type of "postmodern moment." Action, politics, and military strategy have different logics, and all must be developed through the "temporal tendency," which is able to reflect the contradictions inherent in a particular situation. If Wang stopped here, it would be difficult to see his socialism as having a universal dimension, but he goes on to recognize the category of the people as being crucial in reuniversalizing political practice. In this way the temporal tendency represents a movement in which a particular contradiction, namely the contradiction of imperialism and resistance, points toward a new universality, which is intimated in the political activity of the people. Wang contends that the Chinese Revolution, the Chinese Civil War, and China's entry into the Korean War were all forms of People's War. He explains the category of the people in the following manner.

> The birth of "the people" [*renmin*] as a new political subject, with the peasants as its essential component and the alliance between the peasants and the working class as its foundation, facilitated the generation or transformation of all politics (for example, border area governments, the Party, peasant associations, labor unions and so on).[28]

Wang articulates how this category emerged in the context of the struggle between the Nationalist Party (KMT) and the CCP by explaining how the latter eventually inherited and radicalized the KMT's attempt to mobilize peasants and workers. In his formulation, People's War brings together the institutions of war, such as the army, political institutions, such as the party, and the amorphous category of "the people," which consists of primarily peasants and workers. This amalgam returns us to the problem of the ocean and land, since the peasants, a category clearly associated with the land, constantly serve to disrupt and dereify the institutions of the military and the party and make them accountable to those below. The idea of People's War implies a dialectic between organization in the form of the military/party and the mass participation by peasants/workers.[29] This dialectic not only was present in institutions but pervaded the everyday lives of people. In this sense, Wang echoes Takeuchi's emphasis on the everyday.[30]

We see evidence of this emphasis on the everyday in Mao's idea of the "mass line," which asserted that the party had to consult with the masses as they developed political projects. The prevalence and success of the mass line in China returns us to some issues raised in chapter 5. Maruyama Masao argued that in colonized countries, anti-imperialism could combine with socialism because in such countries the bourgeoisie became a comprador class. Wang makes a similar argument by pointing to Mao's "mass line" but notes the uniqueness of the Chinese case, since China was not completely colonized. Approximately a decade after the 1911 Revolution, China was divided up by warlords who had to rely on imperialist support, but they did not control all of China, meaning that the CCP had spaces in which it could establish base areas. In Wang's view, this type of resistance to imperialism from base areas continued after 1949, and a prime example is China's role in the Korean War.

People's War and the Korean War

The idea of People's War was taken to a higher level during the Korean War, where China's involvement represented an Asian-style resistance to the Cold War structure of the 1950s. By the time of the Korean War, the CCP had already seized power and formed a nation-state that had a national defense army, and conducting a People's War was part of state-building and national defense. However, the Korean War was connected to pan-Asianism because the war took place outside China's borders, with the Chinese uniting to fight for the liberation of another people. Moreover, the result of this struggle lay not in building base areas as had been done in China but in allowing the Korean people to govern themselves. Wang explains this in a way that shows how Chinese participation was part of a pan-Asian project:

Just after the Korean War broke out, Mao made a statement that the affairs of the nations of the world should be left to their peoples and the affairs of Asia to the Asian people. This principle, which would later characterize the theme of the Bandung Conference, formed the underlying basis for the War to Resist U.S. Aggression and Aid Korea as a necessary and just war.[31]

Wang, quoting Mao, invokes the principle of self-determination and the Bandung Conference as an integral part of Chinese socialism. He further explains that by participating in the Korean War, Mao aimed to criticize the world order defined by both the Potsdam Conference and the Yalta Conference, which asserted that stronger countries could incorporate weaker nations into their spheres of influence.[32] He goes on to explain how the Korean War was intimately connected to both nationalism and internationalism.

> Under the conditions of war, the people's democracies (including the Soviet Union) formed a united front with the national liberation movements in Asia, Africa and Latin America. When we explore the significance to the East and the world of China's entering the war, the profoundly political nature of the war manifested itself exactly in its close connection to the continuation of the revolution in a new world order.[33]

Using Takeuchi's words, we could say that Wang underscores that China was undergoing a type of self-negation by entering the Korean War, in that it was not seeking its own interests but sincerely working to promote a world-historical goal. It was about lending aid to another.[34] This is precisely the perspective that other scholars, such as Shen Zhihua, believe is impossible.[35] Shen is skeptical of Mao's ideological motivations and argues that one cannot explain Chinese foreign policy during the Mao period without considering geopolitical pressures and national interests. He believes that China was mainly concerned about keeping its northeastern borders safe and solidifying the new Chinese regime through a Sino-Soviet alliance[36] and pays little attention to Mao's commitment to the larger principles of socialist internationalism. Wang's work argues that China's entry into the Korean War shows how self-negation and a type of internationalism were possible in the past and perhaps will be feasible again in the future; Wang also suggests an alternative to the idea that Mao's China engaged with other nations merely to protect its own interests. Wang believes that the interests of a revolutionary socialist nation overlap with those of other oppressed nations because the ultimate goal is to create a socialist world. From this perspective, he might agree with Shen Zhihua's point that Mao joined the Korean War "to assume personal responsibility as the leader of the Asian revolution."[37] However, their visions of the Asian revolution differ. While Shen sees Mao's foreign policy as based on national interest and at times strategic miscalculations, Wang aims to rescue the legacy of the Maoist revolution and revive its influence in Asia.

However, Wang notes that China retreated from this revolutionary position after the Cultural Revolution, the end of which marked the end of the short twentieth century. As Eric Hobsbawm suggested, the short twentieth century ended in a series of failures. The Soviet Union ended up becoming bureaucratic, and the Chinese Revolution lapsed into permanent revolution, which eventually led to political exhaustion. This led to a type of leftist melancholy both in China and elsewhere in the world.[38] But Wang holds out more hope for China's future and the possibility that the revolution might inspire new kinds of political practice in the coming years. In Wang's view, although the revolution continues to be trapped in the contemporary structures of the Communist Party, the continuity of the CCP in fact implies hope for the revolution. He asks, "If China's economic development attests to liberalism's hitherto unfulfilled success and China's push to globalize potentially leads to the completion of neoliberal globalization, then what finally is the relationship between China's reality, its future, and the continuous revolution of the twentieth century?"[39] In short, Wang ponders the meaning of the rise of China. Should we consider the rise of China as a failure or a success? Wang connects failure and success in a manner reminiscent of Takeuchi to the extent that he suggests that for Mao and his philosophy of victory, constant failure was the key to or condition of eventual success. We do not need to go into Mao's philosophy of victory in detail since the more pressing question with respect to an Asian alternative is how we should interpret the recent rise of China and the BRI, which Wang Hui has also supported in numerous recent essays. The BRI is perhaps one of the most concrete instances of Wang's idea that there is still a progressive dimension to the contemporary Chinese government.

Land, Water, and the Belt-Road Initiative

In his discussion of the Belt-Road Initiative (BRI), Wang connects the legacy of the revolution to the twenty-first century. He analyzes the relationship between the short twentieth century and the beginning of the twenty-first century and concludes that revolutionary practices continue today. However, the continuities between the revolutionary century and the BRI are not obvious. Xi Jinping has constantly engaged in a discourse of mutual winning, and the BRI has been seen as important mainly because of its proposals to develop infrastructure in poorer regions. Without a doubt, the BRI is part of China's attempt to get resources and find places to invest its surplus capital,[40] but in doing so the BRI faces challenges with respect to both international relations and the environment, as Prasenjit Duara has pointed out.[41]

Wang's discussion of the BRI, on the other hand, suggests what such an initiative could and should be and offers a standard by which to evaluate and reform the BRI. He returns to the idea of the ocean and the inlands. In "The Legacy of the Twentieth Century and the Belt-Road Initiative," an essay published in 2015, he points out that "using the ocean to play down the significance of the inlands is an important characteristic of the period of capitalism."[42] This strategy of using capitalism as a standard also appears in other modernization theories, whether they explicitly used the trope of the ocean or not.

One might think of this initiative as China's way of responding to overproduction and searching for new raw materials, labor, and markets. But Wang suggests that the BRI ought to resist capitalism and argues that the BRI should go beyond the opposition between the ocean and the inlands seen in the development of capitalism and imperialism:

> "One Belt One Road" is bound to be a long process of reforming the capitalist economic model, and it is necessarily a process of connecting historical civilizations and socialism. The reason for talking about historical civilization is that the four key concepts of this new plan, namely roads, belts, corridors, and bridges, are the bonds of the trans-systemic social systems or historical civilizations of Asia. I say that this project must have socialist characteristics because if it cannot overcome the logic of capitalism's control of this broad and complicated network, this plan will inevitably lead to failure and retaliation.[43]

From its inception, proponents of the BRI have connected it to a transnational Asian imaginary associated with the Silk Road. But Wang attempts to draw a historical connection to socialism as a way of linking the BRI to the twentieth century. In this way he finds the radical subjectivity of Mao, Lu Xun, and Sun Yat-sen in a present political movement. His reference to socialism is not completely without a basis in contemporary Chinese ideology, as Xi Jinping himself stated in a speech to the United Nations a couple of months after Wang published this essay.

> We should promote open, innovative and inclusive development that benefits all. The 2008 international financial crisis has taught us that allowing capital to blindly pursue profit can only create a crisis and that global prosperity cannot be built on the shaky foundation of a market without moral constraints. The growing gap between rich and poor is both unsustainable and unfair. It is important for us to use both the invisible hand and the visible hand to form

synergy between market forces and government function and strive to achieve both efficiency and fairness.[44]

Although this is not socialism, Xi raises concerns about income inequality, global prosperity, and the control of capital. Xi here claims that China's goal is mutual flourishing, which was a key principle of socialism, and his tone suggests a global version of social democratic desires to tame capitalism. Wang hopes to radicalize such ambitions.

The goal of mutual flourishing involves conceiving of a political structure that incorporates both unity and difference. Wang attempts to do this by advocating a trans-systemic society and in doing so extends his earlier work on the Chinese empire. He understands China to be a society made up of many different cultures, religions, and other forms of organization. In Wang's view, the Chinese empire, particularly the Qing, was also a multicultural system. By invoking empire in an analysis of pan-Asianism, rather than emphasizing unity, he highlights the harmonization of dissimilarity. We have seen this gesture in Zhang Taiyan's description of Asia as consisting of numerous religions and cultures that coexisted peacefully. In his promotion of the BRI, Wang uses this concept of empire as difference to explain how Asia and Europe involve different structures. In a recent interview about the BRI, Wang explains:

> Europe's [the European Union's] politics has a unified democratic system as a base. Their market economy has a common cultural source, which they do not want to acknowledge, namely, Christianity. In other words, the commonalities among the countries in Europe makes it possible for them to create a transnational nation. But Asian nations do not have such a foundation.[45]

In this reading of Europe and Asia, the key characteristic of Asia is that its people do not have a clear political and cultural foundation. This means that no transnational nation will come to be in Asia, but another form of political organization akin to the Chinese empire will arise. Wang believes that the proponents of the BRI can learn lessons from the Chinese empire and address problems of identity politics, including issues raised by China's handling of Xinjiang and Tibet.

> Once the Soviet Union disintegrated, China became the only country that had been a traditional country with agriculture as a base before the twentieth century. It is a country with many nationalities, many cultures, many religions. How can it continue to maintain its unity of land and population in the world?[46]

Wang sees the BRI as having the potential to combine the legacy of Chinese revolution based on agriculture and the porous identity politics of imperial

China. Let us examine these two points a bit further, beginning with the latter. Wang shows how issues internal and external to China are relevant to the BRI project. Domestically, Tibet and Xinjiang have always haunted Chinese identity, and Wang hopes that the BRI might help Chinese officialdom to rethink Chinese identity along the lines that he suggested in his 2004 *Rise of Modern Chinese Thought*. In short, Wang stresses that China is not merely East Asian but has South and Central Asia as part of its identity. Tibet and Xinjiang, which are connected to South and Central Asia respectively, have been essential parts of China since the Qing dynasty. However, the Qing could integrate these regions into its empire precisely because it was a multiethnic empire. Once China became a nation-state, it was bound to experience conflicts in these regions. On the other hand, Wang believes that China never actually became a nation-state, and therein lies its potential. He would likely agree with the American political scientist Lucian Pye, who once said, "China is a civilization pretending to be a nation-state."[47] It embodies two contradictory tendencies: a tendency toward homogenization, partially driven by the global system of nation-states, and the legacy of the earlier multiethnic empire, which incorporated the inland regions such as inner Mongolia.

Note that in the quote above, Wang contrasts the Soviet Union to China, thereby drawing attention to the links between communist movements and a legacy of land and uneven development. The opposition between the ocean and land produces a conflict between two types of empires: the empires of capitalist imperialism used the oceans to colonize older land-based empires such as China. But Wang shows how China as a continent actually could and did make use of its underdeveloped inland regions to confront imperialism. He paraphrases Mao, stating that if the war with Japan had happened in Europe, and Japan had occupied a few central cities such as London, Madrid, or Paris, the Japanese would have won the war. In China, however, although the Japanese occupied Shanghai, the communist forces had a great deal of land in the northwest and southwest to which they could escape and then counterattack.[48] From this perspective, China benefited from its uneven development, which made possible the communist base areas that were undeveloped and separate from those penetrated by capital and the state.

Since the 1949 Revolution, China has constantly attempted to overcome these inequalities. Wang points out that this has been possible because of the state, which continues to have important effects. For example, during the economic crisis of 2008, the Chinese state actively aimed to overcome the inequalities that resulted from it.[49] This represents a different version of the tension that Takeuchi had already alluded to when discussing the Cultural Revolution: on the one hand, decentralization is essential to a multiethnic empire, but on the other, a unified state is essential when responding to economic crises and confronting Western imperialism.

Applying this logic to the international arena, we can conclude that a global system is needed that is capable of regulating the world economy in a manner different from the contemporary neoliberal system. This poses the difficult question of what a socialist world would look like: How might global governance be conducted in practice? The BRI does not directly answer this question, but it does suggest how new connections might remake the world. The BRI reconnects the world, starting in Asia and running through other parts of the world. We can understand this movement using two historical metaphors: the Silk Road and the tribute system. Both of these point to historical connections within Asia and imply a different world order. About a hundred years after Kang Youwei's Great Unity, a world order initiated by China in the form of the BRI appears possible even if its links with socialism are not clear. To explain the nature of the BRI, Wang focuses on the metaphors used to describe it:

> What we call road, belt, corridor, and bridge includes railroads and of course mutual networks. This implies that the transportation infrastructure that led to industrial capitalism's absolute domination, hegemonic control, and mastery over the inner lands is disappearing. From this perspective, if One Belt One Road succeeds, it will be an earth-shattering change, not just something that China brings but a global change. This is because the whole oceanic discourse from the sixteenth to the nineteenth centuries in which Europe and then the United States were at the center must necessarily end.[50]

This passage brings us to the present moment, in which scholars such as Radhika Desai contend that the age of American hegemony is over, and it is for this reason that the United States is struggling to rally allies against China in what some call a new Cold War.[51] Seen in this way, China is the main actor in bringing about a great change, and Wang's narrative about the BRI can be read as a counterargument to those who contend that China must follow the West, control the seas, and become another hegemon. This is in line with Takeuchi's early concern: that anti-imperialist nationalism does not itself become hegemonic in its expansion. In Wang's view, in order to avoid becoming a hegemon, China must go beyond the logic of the ocean. Indeed, the rise of China and its development of the BRI seem to be bringing about a world in which the oceanic discourse will come to an end, and even the distinction between ocean and land will be overcome. However, the question to which we must return is whether this really implies a movement toward liberation and the realization of a new universality.

One point that seems to raise questions about Wang's support for the BRI is the issue of subjectivity, which was a critical element of his support for the revolution. In his interview about the BRI, he gestures toward the formation of a transnational subjectivity:

> We barely understand Africa or Latin America and know little about the countries that surround us. Consequently, it is almost impossible to find internationally influential scholars who work on these areas. This is a problem with the whole period. Therefore, "One Belt One Road" also presents us with an enormous intellectual challenge. Many parents of people in our generation were fluent in Russian, but few scholars of this generation can speak Russian. However, the problems of Russia and India are all issues we must directly face and deal with. The whole Central Asian region is extremely unstable, so we need real experts in the Turkic-speaking countries. A true expert must understand not only their language but also their history, culture, politics, and economics.[52]

This point echoes Takeuchi's remarks in "Asia as Method," where he lamented that Japanese scholars were more interested in European languages and cultures than they were in their Asian counterparts. Wang goes further and makes it clear that the Chinese need to understand politics, history, and economics in addition to studying languages to get a complete understanding of these regions, though he leaves open how such knowledge will create a new world. China certainly needs experts in the cultures of various Asian regions, but such experts must combine development with a revolutionary ethos and subjectivity, which could be the beginning of a movement against a crisis-ridden neoliberal capitalism.

Conclusion

If Wang is correct, today we are seeing an unraveling of the imperialist oceanic discourse and modernization theory. He stresses that we need to focus on nations such as Russia and other regions in Asia, which at least originally were all land based. However, the role of the revolution is crucial here. The remnants of that past revolution may be the seeds for a possible future revolution, one that requires remembering one's land-based past even as the land/ocean distinction fades away. Wang himself writes of a short twentieth century and yet speaks of residues of the revolution that might continue to be effective, which suggests that although the century was short, it continues to affect the work of the current Chinese state.

Assuming that the CCP today in the early twenty-first century can prepare the way for a new world order beyond global capitalism by drawing on the legacy of the Chinese Revolution, we are left with the question of how it might do so. Answering this question requires a narrative that is different from Wang Hui's. His analysis primarily looks to the past and focuses on concepts such as People's War and land-based revolution but does not use these concepts to inform discussions of the present. Indeed, Wang's work produces an antinomy between radical subjectivity/People's War and visions that do not really have revolutionary subjectivity, such as empire and the opposition of land versus the ocean. Empire and land are perhaps the conditions for the possibility of revolutionary subjectivity, but their role has changed in the past few decades. I suggest that we take a consideration of the importance of capitalism a bit further than Wang, as I explain briefly in the epilogue.

EPILOGUE

Pan-Asianism, the Chinese Revolution, and Global Moments

I would like to conclude this study with some remarks about the possibility of China continuing the legacy of a socialist or anticapitalist pan-Asianism and placing this in the context of the recent trend to affirm globalization. I do so by briefly examining two films dealing with Chinese labor: *Youth Is Like Fire* (*Qingchun sihuo*), which was released in 1976, the year that Mao died; and *American Factory* (*Meiguo gongchang*), made in 2019.[1] These two films, when read together, not only shed light on the logic of automation but also pose questions about the recent global and transnational trend in Asian studies and in area studies more generally. The first film, *Youth Is Like Fire*, shot in 1975–1976, expresses many of the key ideas from the Cultural Revolution and the Chinese Revolution, especially the conviction that workers rather than administrators should govern the factory.[2] It clearly conveys ideas that Wang Hui sees as important, such as People's War and putting politics in charge. However, looking at the film from the standpoint of the twenty-first century, equally striking is the goal of such worker governance, namely increased productivity and automation. Throughout the film both the protagonist, a female worker, and the administrator/intellectual villain struggle to find a way to mechanize production, and the film is mainly taken up with showing how the workers, and especially the protagonist, struggle to achieve this goal. This underlines a continuity with the post-Mao period, which we must theorize without eliminating the differences between these two epochs. A major difference lies in the mode of production, which is in turn connected to the form in which people participate in production and politics.

The emphasis on automation, the replacement of labor by machines, suggests a dynamic in which the project of resistance to capitalism follows a trajectory spanning the nineteenth, twentieth, and twenty-first centuries, which

PAN-ASIANISM, CHINESE REVOLUTION, GLOBAL MOMENTS 215

is also the past, present, and future of pan-Asianism. We began our discussion with Okakura Tenshin's critique of the West. In an implicit criticism of capitalism, Okakura counterposed the substantiality of community against the rabid individualism of the West. He anticipated Wang Hui's opposition of the land and ocean. The search for an Asian/Third World alternative to capitalism culminated in Chinese Maoism. And, as we have seen, both Takeuchi and Wang Hui see in Maoism a vision of a future beyond capitalism.

However, viewed from today, one cannot help but consider the continuities between the socialist and postsocialist periods from another perspective. After all, didn't Mao's China eventually give rise to contemporary China, which is increasingly integrated into the capitalist world? Here we must proceed slowly. Despite the similarity between the ideologies of socialist and postsocialist China in emphasizing productivity and technological development, I would not call Mao's China capitalist.[3] This is an important point to keep in mind today because there is a recent trend in China studies to make China contemporaneous with the West by placing it in the context of a truly global process, and this often implies erasing, overlooking, or belittling the difference between revolutionary China and the capitalist world that it confronted. We see this gesture in extremely different spheres, from pop culture to economic history to intellectual history.[4] For example, in his recent book, Andrew Jones makes the provocative statement that despite their differences, "somehow" the Chinese revolutionary song "The East Is Red" ("Dongfang hong") and the Beatles hit "All You Need Is Love" "are unmistakably and emblematically products of the 1960s and emerge from a shared historical moment."[5] Jones's analysis returns us to the theme of *Youth Is Like Fire* because, in his view, the "somehow" or the condition for the possibility of such a global moment lies in a specific technology, namely transistorized electronics.[6] This may be sufficient to explain certain underlying similarities between the two songs; however, the above locution appears to suggest that technology, even when embedded in different social and political contexts, can serve to constitute one "moment," where the term "moment" refers to more than an abstract temporal signifier but the advent of a shared structure within a larger historical process. In arguing for such a moment, Jones and others assert a specific type of synchronicity. Others, such as Michel-Rolph Trouillot caution us against this. Trouillot explains that "changes in the spatialization of markets—the market for capital (both financial and industrial), the market for labor, and the market for consumer goods—create overlapping spatialities that are not synchronized but together help to give the world economy its current shape."[7] For Trouillot, describing the global capitalist economy does not require asserting that social, spatial, or temporal dynamics are shared across the world.

How we interpret a film like *Youth Is Like Fire* is significant in this context because a reading following Moishe Postone's interpretation of Marx could support Jones's argument by arguing that despite differences in ideology, the drive for increasing productivity is grounded in deeper structural similarities beyond the socialist-capitalist divide.[8] This would concretize the "shared historical moment." I employed a similar argument in my book on Zhang Taiyan when I argued that the late Qing must be understood in relation to a "global capitalist world."[9] This strong version of the thesis about a global moment entails that the globality is not merely based on technology in the abstract but encompasses deeper logics such as the commodity form and the logic of relative surplus value (increasing mechanization). The Postonian reading implies that China, even during the Mao period, was capitalist, and this entails that "anticapitalist" pan-Asianist and Third Worldist movements rest on misrecognized difference. As we have seen, pan-Asianism and Third Worldism highlight multiple temporalities and possible trajectories.

Frederic Jameson anticipates some of Postone's arguments about the globality of capitalism in his 1984 essay "Periodizing the 60s," in which he distinguishes between the nineteenth- and twentieth-century expansion of capitalism. "In the 19th and early 20th centur[ies], capitalist penetration of the Third World did not necessarily mean a capitalist transformation of the latter's traditional modes of production. Rather, they were for most part left intact, 'merely' exploited by a more political and military structure."[10] This passage describes what Marx calls the formal subsumption of labor under capitalism, where capital leaves earlier modes of production intact and capitalists merely extract surplus value from existing structures. However, Jameson contends that by the mid-twentieth century, things change. After the green revolution, he contends that "the older village structures and precapitalist forms of agriculture are now systematically destroyed, to be replaced by an industrial agriculture whose effects are fully as disastrous as, and analogous to, the moment of enclosure in the emergence of capital in what was to become the first world. The 'organic' social relations of village societies are now shattered, an enormous landless preproletariat 'produced,' which migrates to the urban areas."[11] At this point, Jameson shifts to describe something akin to the real subsumption of labor under capitalism, where the form of labor undergoes a transformation. We seem to be dealing with the complete proletarianization of labor. Reading the two passages together, it seems that Jameson is describing a movement from formal to real subsumption throughout the 1960s, which would include imperialist countries, developing nations, and the socialist bloc.

PAN-ASIANISM, CHINESE REVOLUTION, GLOBAL MOMENTS   217

I say almost because his essay also points in other directions. One of the keys lies in the following passage: "The older village structures and precapitalist forms of agriculture are now systematically destroyed, to be replaced by an industrial agriculture." The preceding sentence appears to describe the past, something that has already taken place, but drawing on Massimiliano Tomba and Harry Harootunian, one could argue that formal subsumption never completely recedes, and consequently unevenness continues to persist in society. In other words, the process entailed in the phrase "to be replaced" is forever deferred to the future—there are always remnants that are essential to capitalism, yet which could serve to destabilize the system. Moreover, such remnants are mediated differently throughout the globe. Indeed, Takeuchi and Wang Hui each argue that the Chinese Revolution was intimately connected to such older village structures and precapitalist forms of life. Perhaps more importantly, one has to highlight the difference between the post-1949 mode of production and the capitalist world. In the Chinese case, we then have neither formal nor real subsumption of labor under capital but a different form of production, one that is not based on the production of surplus value. In this way, despite its failures, one conceives the Maoist project as genuinely non- or anticapitalist, which fundamentally ruptures global moments.

Jameson's essay might allow for this reading because he does not explicitly subsume China within this global moment, and he speaks of a Chinese Thermidor,[12] which highlights the significance of the Chinese Revolution. This would also be in keeping with Jameson's well-known essay about Third World literature as national allegory, which suggests that the abstract global "moment" is fractured by different modes of production, especially during the 1960s. In this contradictory globe, simultaneity is overdetermined by radically different social and political trajectories.

But how do such revolutionary political trajectories look today? Although the socialist period, which spanned the short twentieth century, pointed to a different future, it also formed the basis for the post-twentieth century, or the postsocialist period. Understanding China in the contemporary period is complex, but the recent documentary *American Factory* provides some clues.[13] The documentary shows a Chinese capitalist who comes to the United States to start a branch of his factory, Fuyao, in Moraine, Ohio. The film was shot from 2015 to 2017 in the midst of severe unemployment in that community. Initially, workers saw the coming of Fuyao as a boon. However, as the documentary progresses, the central conflict in the film becomes clear: a struggle over unionization. The Chinese capitalist is used to conditions in China, where independent unions are not allowed, and, the Chinese capitalist claims, workers sacrifice themselves for the factory. He notes that Chinese workers strive for greater productivity as part of a larger narrative of creating a stronger country. This shows some continuity with the socialist period, since *Youth Is Like Fire* also depicts workers as striving for greater productivity, which raises the question of how to interpret the drive for greater productivity within the context of socialism.

A critique of capitalism must go beyond merely affirming a revolutionary past and show how another world is possible. Following Postone, one might contend that the transformative potential of automation makes a postcapitalist world possible by making labor obsolete. Such a theory follows Marx's idea of the changing composition of capital and the thesis that fixed capital (machines) would come to replace variable capital (human labor). Toward the end of *American Factory*, the question of unionization is severely undermined when the Chinese capitalist decides to replace workers with machines. *American Factory* shows how accomplishing this productivity actually undermines the role of the worker and even the strength of traditional unions.

Capitalism forces firms to produce with increasing speed. Postone terms this a "treadmill dynamic" because, in capitalist society, firms must continually increase their rates of production just to survive—one must run faster to stay in the same place. As *American Factory* shows, this increase in productivity makes labor increasingly superfluous and even anachronistic. This logic is global, and capitalists in various capitalist nations respond to it accordingly. However, in this reading of Marx, this dynamic has a silver lining, namely that increasing technological innovation makes it possible to envision a world in which proletarian labor is no longer the fulcrum of society. From this perspective, the dynamic of productivity and technological innovation creates the conditions for the sublation of the proletariat and the overcoming of capitalism. In postcapitalist society, people would bring machines under collective control, and society would cease to be organized around wage labor. This is Marx's projection of an ideal society, where people have an increasing amount of free time. But this future does not spring from capitalism like a deus ex machina; it requires workers to engage in struggle.

The above reading of Marx is persuasive and is a good antidote to much of the pessimism that pervades leftist circles today. However, similar to Marx's theory that the rate of profit will fall, we must understand the process of increasing automation as one movement in a complex temporal tendency—a conjuncture of forces. Consequently, the outcomes of technological change are not given in advance. Indeed, the situation in 2022 looks quite different from how it did in 2017. People expected unemployment to increase radically over the course of the pandemic. However, the opposite happened.[14] Japan provides a poignant example of this opposite problem of an insufficient workforce amid an aging population.[15]

Moreover, it is not just that the connection between technology and jobs is not linear; rather, from their inception, computers and mechanization were intimately connected with another aspect of capitalist development, namely surveillance at the factory, state, and global levels.[16] Such methods of undermining the formation of a worker subjectivity at both domestic and international levels return us to the rise of China along with the problem of imperialism, both of which relate to the narrative of the documentary.

The scenario that plays out in Moraine shows the changes that have occurred in the spatial and power dynamics of China-US relations. Narratives of the rise of Chinese socialism often involve stories of China being exploited by American and other foreign capital. Indeed, one could film innumerable documentaries about American capitalists attempting to establish the conditions for the extraction of surplus value in China and other parts of the world. However, the idea of Chinese capital moving to the United States is new. One might suggest that this makes the thinking of the figures discussed in this book obsolete and calls into question the possibility of a politics of anti-imperialism. However, such a conclusion may be premature. American economic power is waning, and China appears as if it could become a new hegemon. At the same time, the United States still has military bases around the world and does not intend to relinquish its hegemony. This is the root of the new Cold War emerging today. Moreover, as Sam Gindin and Leo Panitch argue, the goal of American imperialism is to secure the conditions for global capitalism.[17] This suggests that capitalism forms a deeper foundation for American empire than the mere pursuit of specific American interests and that capitalism might thrive even if American hegemony were replaced by the hegemony of another state, such as China. Given the continued existence of American imperialism, resistance to the expansion of American hegemony is still a desideratum for any socialist project, but movements would need to transform capitalism's basic logic.

American Factory articulates the general logic of capital. On the one hand, in capitalism, the drive to productivity creates crises of overproduction that encourage capitalist nations to find new markets, cheaper labor, and resources overseas; on the other hand, in certain contexts, it also leads to increasing unemployment. Consequently, future anti-imperialist movements, be they pan-Asianist or not, must develop more expansive strategies that involve the taking over of machines and technology by workers and common people. This ideal of putting people in control goes beyond issues of technology replacing labor. For example, the goals of technological innovation in *Youth Is Like Fire* are "independence and self-reliance" (*dulizizhu* and *ziligengsheng*), which suggest a socialist delinking from the imperialist world of global capitalism.

In *American Factory*, the idea of socialism and worker participation do not take center stage; the film highlights the importance of worker autonomy through showing its absence. It suggests that beyond the goal of seeking productivity and development, one has to return to the subjective activity of the people, which both Takeuchi and Wang Hui invoked.

The "people" continues to be a major ideological trope of the Xi regime, and we see this in his speech at the Twentieth Annual Party Congress.[18] The present Chinese regime does not usually affirm, even at the ideological level, the activity of the people as, for example, was the case during the Cultural Revolution. Rather, at their best, Xi's speeches focus on the party representing the people or a better distribution of resources. Both of these points are important, but they do not get to the problem of mass activity, which is highlighted by radical pan-Asianists and the Cultural Revolution.[19]

Given that labor is at the core of capitalism, the subjective activity of labor will be a key to future anticapitalist movements. However, the goal will be to find ways in which workers can participate in a politics that leads to the negation of their own present conditions of possibility by taking hold of new technology. This is a politics in which the proletariat organizes to transform its own role in the reproduction of capitalism. This could be the basis for a new interpretation of Takeuchi's politics of self-negation. The future of socialism lies in the search for such a politics.

Acknowledgments

One of the joys of completing a project after many years is the opportunity to express gratitude to the friends and colleagues whose support helped make the work possible. Sun Ge first introduced me to Takeuchi Yoshimi and pan-Asianism in Beijing in 2002. At the time, I did not know who Takeuchi was and was immersed in a project on Zhang Taiyan. However, the next year, when I was conducting research in Tokyo, I realized the importance of Takeu-chi's work for understanding not only Japanese Sinology but the study of mo-dernity more generally. I knew at that point that someday I would make pan-Asianism a subject of research. For the past twenty years, Sun Ge has been an ideal interlocutor, both generous with her time and patient in explaining the intricacies of Japanese intellectual history. While I cite Sun's work in specific places, her influence on this project goes beyond such references.

This project emerged out of my previous work on Zhang Taiyan, and I must acknowledge my continued debt to Wang Hui, both intellectually and institutionally. He invited me to come to Tsinghua University numerous times while I was working on the project. The intellectual community at the Tsinghua Institute of Advanced Studies in the Humanities provided an ideal environ-ment for me to develop my ideas.

This project continues an impulse that began with my book on Zhang Taiyan, namely that Chinese and Japanese intellectual history mediate one another. This book largely examines China through the lens of Japanese intel-lectuals, and consequently much of the research for this project was done in Japan. At Tokyo University, Murata Yūjirō and Nakajima Takahiro were both extremely hospitable, and they each enlightened me about Japanese pan-Asianism from both Sinological and philosophical perspectives. Umemori Naoyuki and Nojiri Eichi from Waseda University and Osaka University, respectively, opened me to new ways of combining social theory, Hegel, and Japanese intellectual history.

Prasenjit Duara has always been an inspiration and has discussed aspects of this project with me from its inception and even in its prehistory in my previous project. He invited me to speak about Takeuchi and Asian Modernity at the National University of Singapore in the summer of 2015, and I received helpful feedback during the discussion.

In the summer of 2016, Anne Cheng invited me to speak about pan-Asianism at the Collège de France in Paris, and I learned a great deal from my interactions with various participants at that venue. I would especially like to thank my friends, Jacques and Annie Bidet, who both came to my talk and discussed my project with me when I visited Paris.

Axel Schneider invited me to Göttingen University in 2016 to present about Takeuchi Yoshimi and pan-Asianism. He and others at the workshop were generous in providing helpful feedback.

In the summer of 2018, I gave a series of lectures on pan-Asianism at the Social Research and Cultural Studies Center at Chiao T'ung University in Taiwan. I am grateful to my hosts, Joyce C. Liu and Kuan-hsing Chen. I presented some early versions of my chapters at their center and received valuable feedback.

In fall 2022, when I was in the midst of putting the final touches on the manuscript for this book, Loren Goldman invited me to present a chapter of my work at the Political Theory Workshop at the University of Pennsylvania. I thank Loren and all of those who attended the workshop for providing invaluable feedback on my project. Thomas Henry "Hank" Owings was my discussant and alerted me to some conceptual issues related to imperialism and international relations.

Harry Harootunian had deeply informed my thinking even before I met him in 2005. Since then, he has offered helpful advice and pointed me in the direction of various writings about pan-Asianism and its critique. His long-standing interest in deprovincializing Marxism informs my approach in this book. Needless to say, had I not met him, this would have been a very different project.

Much of this book was developed after I moved to the University of Wisconsin–Madison, and I have benefited greatly from conversations with various colleagues within and beyond Asian studies. In particular, Charles Kim, Joe Dennis, Suzanne Desan, Judd Kinzley, Tony Michels, Sarah Thal, and Louise Young have all helped me work through specific issues related to Chinese, Japanese, and global history throughout the years. I would also like to thank my graduate students for participating in courses related to this

ACKNOWLEDGMENTS

project and commenting on aspects of this project. These include Yaowen Dong, Jonathan Hackett, Michael Hayata, Lin Li, Lin Ye, Shatrunjay Mall, Hamni Hyemin Park, Zhijun Ren, Yuji Xu, and Nick Zeller.

Apart from the above scholars, I would like to thank Cemil Aydin, Richard Calichman, Chen Chunyan, Chad Goldberg, Richard Gunde, Jiang Tao, Kurashige Taku, Katarzyna Lecky, Lin Shaoyang, William Londo, Ethan Mark, Gregory Novack, Qiao Zhihang, Suzuki Sen, Jensen Suther, Saul Thomas, Christian Uhl, Robert Wallace, and Susanne Weigelin-Schwiedrzik for reading, editing, or discussing aspects of the project with me.

Three anonymous reviewers gave me insightful comments on the complete manuscript, which helped me think about how to make the whole project more coherent.

The staff at the University of Chicago Press has been extremely supportive of this project from its early stages. I must thank the late Moishe Postone for showing a summary of my book to David Brent and Priya Nelson, both of whom are no longer with the Press but encouraged me to work on the project in the early stages. Mary Al-Sayed took over during the final stages of editing the manuscript and guided me through the review process and production. She showed just the right combination of encouragement with respect to my own ideas and suggestions to make my arguments appeal to a larger audience.

I revised this book while I received a grant from the University of Wisconsin–Madison Institute for Research in the Humanities for the fall of 2021. I am grateful to the Institute for their support. I would also like to thank the Berggruen Institute for Philosophy and Culture, where I was a fellow from 2016 to 2018, and the Institute for Advanced Studies at Nantes for providing me a fellowship during the spring of 2016. The University of Wisconsin–Madison, Office of the Vice Chancellor of Research and Graduate Education, and the Wisconsin Alumni Research Foundation provided support during the fellowships at Nantes and at the Berggruen Institute for Philosophy and Culture. The University of Wisconsin–Madison, Office of the Vice Chancellor of Research and Graduate Education, also generously provided me a subvention fund to assist in publishing this book.

I would finally like to thank my late mother, Prema Murthy; my father, M. P. Murthy; his partner, Lynn Narasimhan; and my wife, Yuhang Li, for providing love and support as I thought through the logics of pan-Asianism.

My parents-in-law, Li Zhou and Han Min, have encouraged me to work on East Asian history and have offered a special vantage point from which to view some of the topics in the book because they have lived through radical changes in East Asian history, including the second Sino-Japanese war, the Chinese Revolution, the Cultural Revolution, and China's turn toward the open market. I dedicate this book to them. Li Zhou (my father-in-law) passed away shortly after I submitted my manuscript for review. I am certain that he along with my late mother would have been happy to see this book in print.

Parts of this book have appeared in different publications. Certain sections of chapter 1 appear in "The Politics of Time in China and Japan," which was published in Leigh Jenco, Murad Idris, and Megan C. Thomas, eds., *The Oxford Handbook of Comparative Political Theory* (Oxford: Oxford University Press, 2019), 191–217. Parts of chapter 2 appear in Tansen Sen and Brian Tsui, eds., *Beyond Pan-Asianism: Connecting China and India, 1840s–1960s* (Oxford: Oxford University Press, 2020), 94–128.

Chapter 4 draws on the following essays: "The 1911 Revolution and the Politics of Failure: Takeuchi Yoshimi and Global Capitalist Modernity," in *Frontiers of Literary Studies in China* 6, no. 1 (2012): 19–38; and "Resistance to Modernity and the Logic of Self-Negation as Politics: Takeuchi Yoshimi and Wang Hui on Lu Xun," in *Positions: Asia Culture Critique* 24, no. 2 (2016): 513–54.

Chapter 5 draws on the following essays: "Takeuchi and the Problem of *Tenkō*," in *Tenkō: Cultures of Political Conversion in Transwar Japan*, ed. Irena Hayter, George T. Sipos, and Mark Williams (London: Routledge, 2021), 65–85; and "Takeuchi Yoshimi and Deweyan Democracy in Postwar Japan," in *Confucianism and Deweyan Pragmatism: Resources for a New Geopolitics of Interdependence*, ed. Roger T. Ames, Chen Yajun, and Peter D. Hershock (Honolulu: University of Hawai'i Press), 157–89.

The above materials have been reworked and reorganized to support arguments specific to this book.

The transcription of Chinese and Japanese personal names follows the East Asian practice of placing the surname first, followed by the given name. Exceptions to this convention are limited to Chinese and Japanese authors of publications in European languages who have put their names in Western order. The book transliterates Chinese-language terms according to the Hanyu pinyin system. Exceptions include the name of individuals well known by other transliterations (e.g., Sun Yat-sen). Japanese-language terms are transliterated according to the modified Hepburn system, with the exception of widely known names such as Showa, Osaka, and Tokyo.

All translations from Chinese and Japanese are mine except when noted otherwise.

Notes

Introduction

1. There is now a considerable body of literature on pan-Asianism. See, for example, Thorsten Weber, *Embracing Asia in China and Japan: Asianism Discourse and the Contest for Hegemony, 1912–1933* (Cham, Switzerland: Palgrave Macmillan, 2018); Chen Kuan-hsing, *Asia as Method: Towards De-imperialism* (Durham, NC: Duke University Press, 2010); Prasenjit Duara, *The Crisis of Global Modernity: Asian Traditions and a Sustainable Future* (Cambridge, UK: Cambridge University Press, 2015); Pankaj Mishra, *From the Ruins of Empire: The Intellectuals Who Remade Asia* (New York: Farrar, Straus and Giroux, 2012); and Eri Hotta, *Pan-Asianism and Japan's War 1931–1945* (New York: Palgrave Macmillan, 2007). The respective works of Chen, Duara, and Mishra combine intellectual analysis with an explicitly programmatic vision for pan-Asianism in the present. My exploration of pan-Asianism has benefited from their work. However, I take the socialist project to be a central part of pan-Asianism, and this allows me to see different aspects of pre- and postwar pan-Asianism.

2. Takeuchi Yoshimi, "Ajiashugi no tenbō" [The vision of pan-Asianism], in *Ajiashugi* [Pan-Asianism], ed. Takeuchi Yoshimi (Tokyo: Chikuma shobō, 1963), 12.

3. The pan-Asian critique of modernity overlaps with that of postcolonial theory. I have dealt with the latter in relation to Marxism in Viren Murthy, "Looking for Resistance in All the Wrong Places: Chibber, Chakrabarty and a Tale of Two Histories," *Critical Historical Studies* 2 (2015): 113–53.

4. G. W. F. Hegel, *The Science of Logic*, trans. George Di Giovanni (Cambridge, UK: Cambridge University Press, 2010), 81–82.

5. I use the term "moment" here in the Hegelian sense of being elements of a process that are logically linked. They are like parts, but the moment-process relation is more dynamic than the part-whole relation.

6. Hotta, *Pan-Asianism and Japan's War.*

7. Cemil Aydin, *The Politics of Anti-Westernism in Asia: Visions of World Order in Pan-Islamic and Pan-Asian Thought* (New York: Columbia University Press, 2007).

8. Weber's *Embracing Asia in China and Japan* is another example of a new trend to place Japanese pan-Asianism in a larger comparative context and in some ways anticipates Smith's work.

9. Craig A. Smith, *Chinese Asianism, 1894–1945* (Cambridge, MA: Harvard University Press, 2021).

NOTES TO PAGES 4–16

10. C. Smith, *Chinese Asianism*, 12. Note that Smith uses the term "Asianism" rather than "pan-Asianism" perhaps to be closer to the Chinese terms *yaxiyazhuyi* or *yazhouzhuyi*. However, I will primarily use the term "pan-Asianism" because doing so allows for comparisons with other pan-movements such as pan-Africanism and stresses a unity extending beyond a particular nation. Japanese and Chinese sometimes use two different terms to denote pan-Asianism, *Ajiashugi* or *yazhouzhuyi*, literally "Asianism," and *han ajiashugi* or *fan yazhouzhuyi*. I translate them all as "pan-Asianism" to avoid confusion.

11. Prasenjit Duara, "The Discourse of Civilization and Pan-Asianism," *Journal of World History* 12, no. 1 (2001): 126.

12. For more on this problematic, see Viren Murthy, *The Politics of Time in China and Japan: Back to the Future* (London: Routledge, 2022).

13. Duara, *The Crisis of Global Modernity*, 10.

14. Rebecca Karl brings this aspect of nationalism out in her book *Staging the World: Chinese Nationalism at the Turn of the Twentieth Century* (Durham, NC: Duke University Press, 2002).

15. Kelly A. Hammond, *China's Muslims and Japan's Empire: Centering Islam in World War II* (Chapel Hill: University of North Carolina Press, 2020), 222.

16. Takeuchi, "Ajiashugi no tenbō," 14; Weber, *Embracing Asia in China and Japan*, 32.

17. Arif Dirlik points out that in the late Qing dynasty, conservative thinkers were often the ones who were more critical of imperialism. Arif Dirlik, *Anarchism in the Chinese Revolution* (Berkeley: University of California Press, 1991).

18. Kishore Mahbubani, *Can Asians Think?* (London: Marshal Cavendish, 2009), 42.

19. Frederic Jameson, "Future City," *New Left Review* 21 (May–June 2003): 76.

20. Eric Hobsbawm, *The Age of Extremes: A History of the Word, 1914–1991* (New York: Vintage, 1996); Wang Hui, *China's Twentieth Century*, ed. Saul Thomas (London: Verso, 2016).

21. Wang, *China's Twentieth Century*.

22. Wang Hui, "Twentieth-Century China as an Object of Thought: An Introduction, Part 1: The Birth of the Century: The Chinese Revolution and the Logic of Politics," *Modern China* 46, no. 1 (2020): 5.

23. Theodor Shanin, *Late Marx and the Russian Road: Marx and the Peripheries of Capitalism* (New York: Monthly Review Press, 1983); Kevin Anderson, *Marx at the Margins: On Nationalism, Ethnicity, and Non-Western Societies* (Chicago: University of Chicago Press, 2016). For a discussion of this line of argument in relation to postcolonialism and Marxism, see Murthy, "Looking for Resistance."

24. The Bandung Conference of 1955 refers to the first Asian-African conference, where leaders from nations in Asia and Africa met to discuss a future delinked from the two nuclear superpowers, the United States and the Soviet Union. Although I do not discuss this movement in this book, its goals clearly overlapped with that of pan-Asianists.

Chapter One

1. I borrow the term "pharmakon" from Jacques Derrida's reading of Plato. Jacques Derrida, *Dissemination*, trans. Barbara Johnson (Chicago: University of Chicago Press, 2017), 95–117.

2. Harry Harootunian, "Tracking the Dinosaur: Area Studies in a Time of Globalism," in *History's Disquiet: Modernity, Cultural Practice and the Question of Everyday Life* (New York: Columbia University Press, 2000), 25–59. Recently, numerous attempts have been made to deconstruct the West; we shall deal with this problem historically when we deal with Takeuchi

NOTES TO PAGES 18-21

Yoshimi's debate with Umesao Tadao in chapter 5. For contemporary discussions, see Ian Buruma and Avishai Margalit, *Occidentalism: The West in the Eyes of Its Enemies* (New York: Penguin, 2004), and Naoki Sakai, "The West—A Dialogic Prescription or Proscription?," *Social Identities* 11, no. 3 (2005): 177–95.

3. Prasenjit Duara, *Rescuing History from the Nation: Questioning Narratives of Modern China* (Chicago: University of Chicago Press, 1995).

4. Mark Driscoll, *The Whites Are Enemies of Heaven: Climate Caucasianism and Asian Ecological Protection* (Durham, NC: Duke University Press, 2021), 24–25. Driscoll contends that "for Hegel, firm connections to local ecologies and cosmologies doomed East Asians philosophically, politically, and racially." Both Duara and Driscoll share with pan-Asianists the desire to rescue local ecologies and cosmologies from Western imperialism and capitalism. I contend that Hegel contains resources that can assist in implementing such a project since, as we shall see, "local ecologies" and moral frameworks are what Hegel calls "substantiality."

5. Driscoll, *The Whites Are Enemies of Heaven*, 28.

6. G W. F. Hegel, *The Phenomenology of Spirit*, trans. Terry Pinkard (Cambridge, UK: Cambridge University Press, 2018), 21. I will deal with Hegel's idea of negation in more detail in my discussion of Takeuchi Yoshimi in chapter 4. For a recent positive interpretation of Hegel's theory of history, see Gilles Marmasse, *L'histoire hégélienne: Entre malheur et réconciliation* (Paris: Vrin, 2015).

7. Aakash Singh Rathore and Rimina Mohapatra, *Hegel's India: A Reinterpretation, with Texts* (New Delhi: Oxford University Press India, 2017).

8. G. W. F. Hegel, *The Encyclopaedia Logic*, trans. T. F. Geraets, W. A. Suchting, and H. S. Harris (Indianapolis: Hackett, 1991), 226.

9. On this point, see Nicholas Adams, "Hegel's China: On God and Beauty" (unpublished manuscript), 2, accessed August 9, 2020, https://www.academia.edu/16888871/Hegels_China _on_God_and_beauty. This text has appeared in Chinese in *Meimei yu gong: renlei wenming jiaoliu yu hujian* [Beauty and commonality: The interaction and mutual examination of human civilizations] (Beijing: Religious Cultures Press, 2016).

10. Susan Marchand, *German Orientalism in the Age of Empire: Religion, Race, and Scholarship* (Cambridge, UK: Cambridge University Press, 2009), 58–66. See also Oliver Crawford, "Hegel and the Orient" (unpublished manuscript), 2, accessed August 9, 2020, https://www.aca demia.edu/4985405/Hegel_and_the_Orient.

11. G. W. F. Hegel, *The Philosophy of History*, trans. J. Sibree (Kitchener, ON: Batoche Books, 2001), 128; *Vorlesung über die Philosophie der Geschichte* (Frankfurt am Main: Suhrkamp, 1986), 142 (translation amended).

12. See Partha Chatterjee, "Response to Charles Taylor's Modes of Civil Society," *Public Culture* 3, no. 1 (1990): 119–32.

13. Andrew Buchwalter stresses that Hegel's view of freedom actually overlaps with Asian visions because of his emphasis on social roles and obligations. See Andrew Buchwalter, "Is Hegel's Philosophy of History Eurocentric?," in *Hegel and History*, ed. William Dudley (Albany: State University of New York Press, 2010), 94.

14. Hegel, *The Philosophy of History*, 129; *Vorlesung über die Philosophie der Geschichte*, 142–43 (translation amended).

15. G. W. F. Hegel, *Gesammelte Werke* (Hamburg: Meiner, 1968), 15:10–11, quoted in Brady Bowman, *Hegel and the Metaphysics of Absolute Negativity* (Cambridge, UK: Cambridge University Press, 2013), 56–57.

16. Hegel, *The Philosophy of History*, 412; *Vorlesung über die Philosophie der Geschichte*, 472.

228   NOTES TO PAGES 22–29

17. There is some debate as to whether Hegel believed that the Prussian state had achieved such a reconciliation. Terry Pinkard suggests a more open interpretation. See, for example, Terry Pinkard, *Hegel's Naturalism: Mind, Nature and the Final Ends of Life* (Oxford: Oxford University Press, 2013).

18. G. W. F. Hegel, *Aesthetics: Lectures on Fine Art*, trans. T. M. Knox (Oxford: Oxford University Press, 1988), 1:53–54; *Vorlesung über die Ästhetik* (Frankfurt am Main: Suhrkamp, 1986), 80–81 (translation amended). Cf. Pinkard, *Hegel's Naturalism*, 197, note 11.

19. G. W. F. Hegel, *The Philosophy of World History*, trans. J. Sibree (New York: Dover, 1956), 90.

20. Robert Pippin, *After the Beautiful: Hegel and the Philosophy of Pictorial Modernism* (Chicago: University of Chicago Press, 2013), 74–77. Pippin here draws on T. J. Clark, *The Painting of Modern Life: Paris in the Art of Manet and His Followers*, rev. ed. (Princeton, NJ: Princeton University Press, 1999).

21. Georg Lukács, *History and Class Consciousness: Studies in Marxist Dialectics*, trans. Rodney Livingston (Cambridge, MA: MIT Press, 1971), 90.

22. Karl Marx, *Capital: Volume One*, trans. Ben Fowkes (New York: Penguin, 1990), 477.

23. Jacques Bidet, *État monde: Libéralisme, socialisme et communisme à l'échelle globale* (Paris: PUF, 2010), 52.

24. Louis Althusser, *Lenin and Philosophy and Other Essays* (New York: Monthly Review Press, 1971), 127–89.

25. Pinkard, *Hegel's Naturalism*, 176.

26. For a discussion of how the Meiji Restoration represents the beginning of Japanese capitalism, see Jamie C. Allinson and Alexander Anievas, "The Uneven and Combined Development of the Meiji Restoration: A Passive Revolutionary Road to Capitalist Modernity," *Capital and Class* 34, no. 3 (2010): 469–90.

27. The concept of "enlightenment" during the Meiji period is complex because, on the one hand, Meiji thinkers were influenced by the eighteenth-century Enlightenment, and on the other hand, "enlightenment" also is part of the slogan "civilization and enlightenment," which was a call to modernize and accept the standards of a universal civilization.

28. Mark Ravina, *The Last Samurai: The Life and Battles of Saigō Takamori* (New York: Wiley, 2003). Readers might also recall the film *The Last Samurai* (Los Angeles: Radar Pictures, 2003). The film does not contain a character named Saigō but is loosely based on Saigō's life.

29. On Saigō's significance for pan-Asianism, see chapter 3. In his recent book, Mark Driscoll also reads Saigō as a critic of capitalist modernity and imperialism. See Driscoll, *The Whites Are Enemies of Heaven*, chap. 3.

30. Li Zehou, *Zhongguo xiandai sixiangshi lun* [On modern Chinese intellectual history] (Anhui: Anhui chubanshe, 1991), 11–53.

31. Fukuzawa Yukichi, *An Outline of a Theory of Civilization*, trans. David A. Dilworth and G. Cameron Hurst III (New York: Columbia University Press, 2008); Japanese text in *Bunmeiron no gairyaku* (Tokyo: Iwanami bunko, 2004).

32. Fukuzawa, *Outline*, 22; *Bunmeiron*, 31 (translation amended).

33. Fukuzawa, *Outline*, 22; *Bunmeiron*, 31.

34. Fukuzawa, *Outline*, 18; *Bunmeiron*, 26.

35. Fukuzawa, *Outline*, 18; *Bunmeiron*, 27.

36. Confucius, *Lunyu yizhu, Yang Bojun yizhu* [*Analects* with notes and translation by Yang Bojun] (Beijing: Zhonghua shuju, 2002), 128.

37. Fukuzawa, *Outline*, 18–19; *Bunmeiron*, 27 (translation amended).

NOTES TO PAGES 30-39

38. Fukuzawa, *Outline*, 29; *Bunmeiron*, 40.

39. Fukuzawa, *Outline*, 29; *Bunmeiron*, 40.

40. Fukuzawa Yukichi, *The Autobiography of Yukichi Fukuzawa*, trans. Eiichi Kiyooka (New York: Columbia University Press, 1966 [1899]), 216.

41. The term would be developed further during the 1930s and 1940s. For a discussion, see Satofumi Kawamura, "The National Polity and the Formation of the Modern National Subject in Japan," *Japan Forum* 26, no. 1 (2014): 25–45.

42. Benjamin Schwartz, *In Search of Wealth and Power: Yen Fu and the West* (Cambridge, MA: Belknap of Harvard University Press, 1964).

43. Marx, *Capital*, 178.

44. Lionel Babicz, "Fukuzawa Yukichi to Yono-sama: The Nostalgic Image of Korea in Modern and Contemporary Japan" (unpublished manuscript, 2006), 6–7.

45. Tsukiashi Tatsuhiko, *Fukuzawa Yukichi to Chōsen mondai—"Chōsen kaizō ron" no tenkai to satetsu* [Fukuzawa Yukichi and Korean problem: The development and failure of the "Discourse on the Reconstitution of Korea"] (Tokyo: University of Tokyo Press, 2014).

46. Fukuzawa Yukichi, "Datsu-a ron" [On leaving Asia], in vol. 10 of *Fukuzawa Yukichi zenshū* (Tokyo: Iwanami shoten, 1952), 240. Quoted in Nakajima Takahiro, "The Progress of Civilization and Confucianism in Modern East Asia: Fukuzawa Yukichi and Different Forms of Enlightenment," in *Chinese Visions of Progress, 1895-1949*, ed. Thomas Fröhlich and Axel Schneider (Leiden: Brill, 2020), 92–93.

47. Fukuzawa Yukichi, "Leaving Asia," quoted in Uemura Kunihiko, "Fukuzawa Yukichi and Eurocentrism in Modern Japan," *Kansai University Review of Economics* 14 (2012): 12.

48. Urs Mathias Zachman, "Blowing Up a Double Portrait in Black and White: The Concept of Asia in the Writings of Fukuzawa Yukichi and Okakura Tenshin," *Positions: Asia Critique* 15, no. 2 (2007): 345–68.

49. The following outline of Okakura's early life draws on F. G. Notehelfer, "On Idealism and Realism in the Thought of Okakura Tenshin," *Journal of Japanese Studies* 16, no. 2 (1990): 309–55.

50. G. W. F. Hegel, *Elements of the Philosophy of Right*, trans. H. B. Nisbet, ed. Allen W. Wood (Cambridge, UK: Cambridge University Press, 1991), 199.

51. Notehelfer, "On Idealism and Realism," 316.

52. Notehelfer, "On Idealism and Realism," 321.

53. Notehelfer, "On Idealism and Realism," 322.

54. Andrew Gordon, *Modern Japanese History* (Oxford: Oxford University Press, 2003), 123.

55. Inaga Shigemi, "Okakura Kakuzō's Nostalgic Journey to India and the Invention of Asia," in *Nostalgic Journeys: Literary Pilgrimages between Japan and the West*, ed. Susan Fisher (Vancouver: Institute of Asian Research, University of British Columbia, 2001), 119–32.

56. Okakura Kakuzo (Tenshin), *Ideals of the East: With Special Reference to the Art of Japan* (London: John Murray, 1903), 1.

57. Okakura Tenshin, "The Awakening of the East," in *Okakura Tenshin Collected English Writings* (Tokyo: Heibonsha, 1984), 136; cf. Nakajima Takeshi, *Ajiashugi: sono saki no kindai e* (Tokyo: Ushio shuppansha, 2014), 213.

58. Halford Mackinder, "The Geographical Pivot of History," *Geographical Journal* 23, no. 4 (1904): 433.

59. Alfred W. McCoy, *In the Shadows of the American Century: The Rise and Decline of US Global Power* (Chicago: Haymarket Books, 2017), 32.

60. Halford Mackinder, *Democratic Ideals and Reality* (New York: Holt, 1919), 67.

61. Okakura, "Awakening of the East," 131.

62. Okakura, "Awakening of the East," 136.

63. G. W. F. Hegel, *The Science of Logic*, trans. George Di Giovanni (Cambridge, UK: Cambridge University Press, 2010), 113.

64. Marx, *Capital*, 125–78.

65. Hegel, *Science of Logic*, 119. Hegel believed this type of infinity to be present only in Christianity, but we see it in Chinese philosophies, including Daoism, Buddhism, and Confucianism, which posit an infinite process that encompasses the finite.

66. Okakura, "Awakening of the East," 151–52. Rustom Bharucha points out that "The Awakening of the East" might have been cowritten by Sister Nivedita (Margaret Elizabeth Noble [1867–1911]), an Irish devotee of Swami Vivekananda (Rustom Bharucha, *Another Asia: Rabindranath Tagore and Okakura Tenshin* [Oxford: Oxford University Press, 2006], 34–35). For my purposes, the author of the text is less important than the critique of modernity that we find in it.

67. Mark Anderson, *Japan and the Specter of Imperialism* (New York: Palgrave Macmillan, 2009), 95.

68. Max Weber, *Economy and Society*, trans. and ed. G. Roth and C. Wittich (New York: Bedminster Press, 1968 [1921]), iv.

69. Okakura, "Awakening of the East," 136.

70. Okakura, "Awakening of the East," 137.

71. Karl Marx, "The Manifesto of the Communist Party," in *The Marx-Engels Reader*, ed. Robert C. Tucker (New York: W. W. Norton, 1978), 475.

72. On this point, Okakura anticipates Eugene McCarraher, *The Enchantments of Mammon: How Capitalism Became the Religion of Modernity* (Cambridge, MA: Belknap of Harvard University Press, 2019).

73. Okakura Tenshin, "The Awakening of Japan," in *Okakura Tenshin Collected English Writings* (Tokyo: Heibonsha, 1984), 215.

74. One might also call this the pathological freedom of capitalism. Hidden within this desire is still some version of self-determination, but in capitalist society, it undermines itself, even in cases where narrow (individualist) desires can be realized. I am grateful to Jensen Suther for this formulation.

75. Cf. Marx, *Capital*, 229; McCarraher, *The Enchantments of Mammon*, 61.

76. Okakura, "Awakening of Japan," 215–16.

77. Okakura, "Awakening of Japan," 217.

78. Okakura, "Awakening of Japan," 217.

79. Marx, *Capital*, 439–55.

80. Moishe Postone, *Time, Labor and Social Domination: A Reinterpretation of Marx's Critical Theory* (Cambridge, UK: Cambridge University Press, 1993).

81. Okakura, "Awakening of Japan," 217.

82. Okakura, "Awakening of the East," 150.

83. Okakura, *Ideals of the East*, 4.

84. Friedrich Schelling, quoted in *German Aesthetic and Literary Criticism: Kant, Fichte, Schelling, Schopenhauer, Hegel*, ed. David Simpson (Cambridge, UK: Cambridge University Press, 1984), 130.

85. Okakura, "Awakening of the East," 162.

86. Okakura, "Awakening of the East," 159–60.

87. Okakura, *Ideals of the East*, 2.

NOTES TO PAGES 48–62

88. Okakura, *Ideals of the East*, 3.

89. Okakura, "Awakening of the East," 164–65.

90. Vijay Prasad, *Darker Nations: A People's History of the Third World* (New York: New Press, 2007).

Chapter Two

1. Kang Youwei, *Kang Youwei zhenglunji* [A collection of Kang Youwei's political writings] (Beijing: Zhonghua shuju, 1981), 1:301. Quoted in Wang Hui, *Zhongguo xiandai sixiangshi de xingqi* [The rise of modern Chinese thought] (Beijing: Sanlian shudian, 2004), 2:741.

2. Cited from Liu Xi, "Kang Youwei's Journey to India: Chinese Discourse on India during the Late Qing and Republican Periods," *China Report* 48 (2012): 174–75.

3. Liu, "Kang Youwei's Journey to India," 177.

4. Liu, "Kang Youwei's Journey to India," 176.

5. Jung Tsou (Zou Rong), *The Revolutionary Army: A Chinese Nationalist Tract of 1903*, trans. John Lust (Paris: Mouton, 1968), 56; Chinese text in Zou Rong, *Geming jun* [The revolutionary army] (Beijing: Huaxia chubanshe, 2002), 5.

6. Jung, *The Revolutionary Army*, 58; Zou, *Geming jun*, 7.

7. Jung, *The Revolutionary Army*, 58; Zou, *Geming jun*, 8.

8. Jung, *The Revolutionary Army*, 109; Zou, *Geming jun*, 44 (translation amended).

9. Zhang Taiyan, "Bo Kang Youwei geming shu" [Refuting Kang Youwei's theory of revolution], in *Zhang Taiyan xuanji—zhushiben* [Zhang Taiyan: Selected works, with notes], ed. Zhu Weizheng and Jiang Yihua (Shanghai: Shanghai renmin chubanshe, 1981), 155–86, 168.

10. Viren Murthy, *The Political Philosophy of Zhang Taiyan: The Resistance of Consciousness* (Leiden: Brill, 2011).

11. Yamamurō Shinichi, *Nichiro sensō no seiki: rensashiten kara miru nihon to sekai* [The century of the Russo-Japanese War: Looking at Japan and the world through the perspective of interconnected points] (Tokyo: Iwanami shinsho, 2005).

12. Quoted in Cemil Aydin, *The Politics of Anti-Westernism in Asia: Visions of World Order in Pan-Islamic and Pan-Asian Thought* (New York: Columbia University Press, 2007), 76.

13. Rebecca Karl, *Staging the World: Chinese Nationalism at the Turn of the Twentieth Century* (Durham, NC: Duke University Press, 2002).

14. This was printed in all issues of the *People's Journal* from 1905 to 1908. See Lin Shaoyang, "Zhang Taiyan 'zizhu' de lianya sixiang" [Zhang Taiyan's ideas of independence and Asian unity], *Quyu* 1, no. 3 (2014): 201–27.

15. On friendship between China and Japan, see Zhang Taiyan, "Lun Yazhou yi zi wei chunchi," *Shiwubao* 18, no. 22 (1897): 5–8; reproduced in *Zhang Taiyan zhenglun xuanji*, vol. 1 (Beijing: Zhonghua shuju, 1977).

16. Herald Fischer-Tiné, "Indian Nationalism and the 'World Forces': Transnational and Diasporic Dimensions of the Indian Freedom Movement on the Eve of the First World War," *Journal of Global History* 3 (2007): 325–44.

17. Zhang, *Zhang Taiyan xuanji*, 428. Although Zhang wrote this text with Zhang Ji, given the language and the use of Buddhist terms, especially in the second section, I believe that the manifesto expresses Zhang's ideas.

18. Hazama Naoki and Matsumoto Kennichi, "Shō heirin to meiji no 'ajiashugi'" [Zhang Binglin and Meiji pan-Asianism], *Chishiki* (August 1990): 249; Lin, "Zhang Taiyan," 208.

232   NOTES TO PAGES 62–71

19. The metaphor comes from Karl Marx, "The Manifesto of the Communist Party," in *The Marx-Engels Reader*, ed. Robert C. Tucker (New York: W. W. Norton, 1978) , 469–501.

20. Zhang Binglin [Taiyan], Speech in Tokyo, July 15, 1906, cited in Shimada Kenji, *Pioneer of the Chinese Revolution*, trans. Joshua Fogel (Stanford, CA: Stanford University Press, 1990), 41.

21. Lydia H. Liu, *Translingual Practice: Literature, National Culture and Translated Modernity—China, 1900–1937* (Berkeley: University of California Press, 1995).

22. Liu, *Translingual Practice*, 40.

23. Zhang, *Zhang Taiyan xuanji*, 429.

24. Zhang, "Lun Yazhou."

25. When Zhang was in jail, he avidly read Buddhist texts, which he claimed helped him get through the experience. For a discussion, see Murthy, *The Political Philosophy of Zhang Taiyan*.

26. For a discussion, see Murthy, *The Political Philosophy of Zhang Taiyan*, chap. 5.

27. Zhang Taiyan, *Zhang Taiyan zhenglun xuanji* (Beijing: Zhonghua shuju, 1977), 368.

28. Zhang Taiyan, *Gegudingxin de zheli: Zhang Taiyan wenxuan* [The philosophy of reform and improvement] (Shanghai: Shanghai yuandong chubanshe, 1996), 254.

29. Zhang, *Gegudingxin de zheli*, 255.

30. The term "national essence" (*guocui* [Chinese], *kokusui* [Japanese]) originated in Japan and then was picked up by Chinese revolutionaries who imbued it with new meaning, specifically connecting it to socialism and anarchism.

31. Zhang Taiyan, *Zhang Taiyan quanji* [The complete works of Zhang Taiyan] (Shanghai: Shanghai renmin chubanshe, 1986), 4:366.

32. Zhang, *Zhang Taiyan quanji*, 4:367.

33. Zhang, *Zhang Taiyan quanji*, 4:367.

34. Zhang noted that some Western scholars criticize national essence because it affirms everything that a country does, even though some actions a country takes may go against humanism. Zhang explained that this theory emerged because Westerners were worried about the state stifling the rights of the individual. However, Zhang argued that this is not necessarily the case. He claimed that one needed to separate subjective and objective attitudes toward national history. In the objective moment, one records what has happened, and in the subjective one, one evaluates. Zhang, *Zhang Taiyan quanji*, 4:366.

35. Zhang, *Zhang Taiyan quanji*, 4:366.

36. Quoted in Shimada, *Pioneer of the Chinese Revolution*, 78.

37. Lin, "Zhang Taiyan," 215–16.

38. Zhang Taiyan, "Indu ren zhi guan riben" [Indian's visions of Japan], *Minbao* 20 (April 1908): 34; Zhang, *Zhang Taiyan quanji*, 4:364–65.

39. This is his argument in "On Evolution," which is discussed in detail in chapter 4 of Murthy, *The Political Philosophy of Zhang Taiyan*.

40. Zhang Taiyan, in Shimada, *Pioneer of the Chinese Revolution*, 81.

41. Zhang Taiyan, in Shimada, *Pioneer of the Chinese Revolution*, 82.

42. Zhang Taiyan, "Indu duli wei fa," *Minbao* 20 (April 1908); Zhang, *Zhang Taiyan quanji*, 4:363. Cf. Kai-wing Chow, *Xinmin yu fuxing: Jindai zhongguo sixiang shilun* [New people and revival: Interpreting modern Chinese intellectual history] (Hong Kong: Xianggang jiaoyu tushu gongsi, 1999), 220.

43. Chen Duxiu, "Jingao qingnian" [Warning the youth], in *Xin Qingnian* [The new youth], ed. Wang Zhongjiang and Wan Shuya (Zhongzhou: Zhongzhou guji chubanshe, 1999 [1915]), 29. Originally appeared in *Qingnian Zazhi*, 1:1.

NOTES TO PAGES 71–81

44. Li Dazhao, "Eguo geming zhi yuanyin jinyin" [The remote and proximate causes of the Russian Revolution], in *Li Dazhao quanji* [Complete works of Li Dazhao] (Beijing: Renmin chubanshe, 2006), 1:1.

45. Craig A. Smith, *Chinese Asianism, 1894–1945* (Cambridge, MA: Harvard University Press, 2021), 139. See also Chow, *Xinmin yu fuxing*, 15.

46. Li Dazhao, "Da yazhouzhuyi" [Big Asianism], in *Li Dazhao quanji*, 2:106.

47. Li, "Da yazhouzhuyi," 106.

48. Li, "Da yazhouzhuyi," 285. Cf. C. Smith, *Chinese Asianism*, 137–38.

49. Li, *Li Dazhao quanji*, vol. 2.

50. Li, *Li Dazhao quanji*, vol. 2.

51. Zhao Tingyang, *Tianxia tixi: shijie zhidu daolun* [The Tianxia system: An introduction to a philosophy of world order] (Jiangsu: Jiangsu jiaoyu chubanshe, 2005). For a discussion of Zhao Tingyang's work, see Viren Murthy, "Towards a New World Order: Reading Tianxia with Hegel and Marx," in *The Politics of Time in China and Japan: Back to the Future* (London: Routledge, 2022), 130–65.

52. Li, *Li Dazhao quanji*, 2:107.

53. Li Dazhao, "Dayazhouzhuyi yu xinyazhouzhuyi" [Great pan-Asianism and new pan-Asianism], in *Li Dazhao quanji*, 2:270.

54. Li, "Dayazhouzhuyi yu xinyazhouzhuyi," 2:270.

55. Li, "Dayazhouzhuyi yu xinyazhouzhuyi," 2:270.

56. Li, "Zai lun xinyazhouzhuyi" [Another discussion of new pan-Asianism], in *Li Dazhao quanji*, 3:75.

57. Chow, *Xinmin yu fuxing*, 17.

58. See C. Smith, *Chinese Asianism*, 150–83, for a detailed discussion of Sun's thought in relation to other Japanese and Chinese pan-Asianists.

59. Sun Yat-sen, "Pan-Asianism," in *Pan-Pan-Asianism: A Documentary History*, vol. 2, *1920–Present*, ed. Sven Saaler and Christopher W. A. Szpilman (Lanham, MD: Rowman and Littlefield, 2011), 78. The essay was originally published in 1924 as "Da Yazhou zhuyi."

60. Kenneth Pomeranz, *The Great Divergence: China, Europe and the Making of the Modern World Economy* (Princeton, NJ: Princeton University Press, 2000).

61. Sun, "Pan-Asianism," 2:80.

62. Sun, "Pan-Asianism," 2:79.

63. Sun, "Pan-Asianism," 2:81 (translation amended). I have replaced "rule of Might" with "way of the hegemon" and "rule of Right" with "kingly way"; these two concepts spring from the Chinese classics. The way of the hegemon refers to the use of force and is often associated with the legalists. Confucians generally preferred the kingly way to the use of punishments and force—that is, they preferred the use of rituals and education.

64. Sun, "Pan-Asianism," 2:81.

65. Sun, "Pan-Asianism," 2:81.

66. Sun, "Pan-Asianism," 2:83.

67. Sun, "Pan-Asianism," 2:85 (translation amended).

68. Sun, "Pan-Asianism," 2:84 (translation amended).

Chapter Three

1. Harry Harootunian, *Overcome by Modernity: History, Culture and Community in Interwar Japan* (Princeton, NJ: Princeton University Press, 2000).

234   NOTES TO PAGES 81–85

2. I borrow the phrase "backing into a future" from Moishe Postone, *History and Heteronomy: Critical Essays* (Tokyo: University of Tokyo Press, 2009), 82, and Moishe Postone, "Marx, Temporality and Modernity," in *East-Asian Marxisms and Their Trajectories*, ed. Joyce C. H. Liu and Viren Murthy (London: Routledge, 2017), 47.

3. Ōkawa Shūmei, *Ōkawa Shūmei dōtoku tetsugaku kōwashū* [A collection of Ōkawa Shūmei's lectures on ethics] (Tokyo: Seitō yō, 2008).

4. For a discussion of Ōkawa's life, see Cemil Aydin, *The Politics of Anti-Westernism in Asia: Visions of World Order in Pan-Islamic and Pan-Asian Thought* (New York: Columbia University Press, 2007), 112–13.

5. Cemil Aydin, "The Politics of Civilizational Identities: Asia, West and Islam in the Pan-Asianist Thought of Ōkawa Shūmei" (PhD diss., Harvard University, 2002), chap. 3; Ōtsuka Takehiro, *Ōkawa Shūmei to kindai nihon* [Ōkawa Shūmei and modern Japan] (Tokyo: Mokutakusha, 1990), 23–24.

6. Ōmori Mikihiko, *Nihon seijishisō kenkyū: Gondō Seikyō to Ōkawa Shūmei* [A study of Japanese political thought: Gondō Seikyō and Ōkawa Shūmei] (Tokyo: Seshiki shobō, 2010), 142–43.

7. Aydin, *Politics of Anti-Westernism in Asia*, 112–13.

8. Aydin, *Politics of Anti-Westernism in Asia*, 143.

9. See Timothy Brennan, "Cosmopolitanism and Internationalism," *New Left Review* 13 (January–February 2001): 75–84.

10. Ōkawa Shūmei, "Fukkō ajia no sho mondai" [Various problems concerning reviving Asia], in *Ajia shugishatachi no koe: yuzonsha to kōchisha* [The voice of Asianists: The Yuzonsha and the Kōchisha] (Tokyo: Shoshi shinsui, 2008), 145.

11. Kojima Tsuyoshi, *Kindai nihon no yōmeigaku* [Modern Japanese Yangming studies] (Tokyo: Kodansha, 2006). Wang Yangming (1472–1529) was a Confucian in the Ming dynasty who stressed the power of the heart-mind. Because of this some scholars have interpreted him as a harbinger of modern thought and the idea of subjectivity. See Shimada Kenji, *Chūgoku kindai shi ni okeru zasetsu* [The setback of modern Chinese thought] (Tokyo: Heibonsha, 2003).

12. Izutsu Toshihiko, "Isulamu no futatsu no kao: jikyoku teki kanshiin wo koeru isulamu shukyo" [Two faces of Islam: Islam beyond concerns with the current state of affairs], *Chūō kōron* 95, no. 9 (1980): 70–92.

13. Usuki Akira, "A Japanese Asianist's View of Islam," *Annals of Japan Association for Middle Eastern Studies* (January 2013): 66.

14. Aydin, *Politics of Anti-Westernism in Asia*, 113.

15. Prabha Ravi Shankar, "Henry Cotton and the Indian National Congress," *Proceedings of the Indian History Congress* 59 (1998): 775.

16. Kevin Doak, *A History of Nationalism in Modern Japan: Placing the People* (Leiden: Brill, 2007), 149.

17. Doak, *A History of Nationalism in Modern Japan*, 149–50.

18. Doak, *A History of Nationalism in Modern Japan*, 149–50.

19. Henry John Stedman Cotton, *New India or India in Transition* (London: Kegan Paul, 1885), viii.

20. The problem of "ungovernability" at this time was a global phenomenon. We can see the beginnings of Ōkawa's two-sided stance toward resistance since one could argue that Japanese fascism was precisely a response to this type of ungovernability. See Bernard S. Silberman, "The Bureaucratic State in Japan: The Problem of Authority and Legitimacy," in *Conflict in Modern Japanese History: The Neglected Tradition*, ed. Tetsuo Najita and Victor Koschmann (Ithaca, NY: Cornell University Press, 2005), 227.

NOTES TO PAGES 85–93   235

21. Manu Goswami, *Producing India* (Chicago: University of Chicago Press, 2004).

22. Ōkawa, "Fukkō ajia no sho mondai," 146.

23. Ōkawa, "Fukkō ajia no sho mondai," 147.

24. Ōkawa, "Fukkō ajia no sho mondai," 146.

25. On the relationship between sympathy and the nation in a different context, see Haiyan Lee, *Revolutions of the Heart: A Genealogy of Love in China 1900–1950* (Stanford, CA: Stanford University Press, 2010).

26. Georg Lukács, *History and Class Consciousness: Studies in Marxist Dialectics*, trans. Rodney Livingston (Cambridge, MA: MIT Press, 1971), 89.

27. Yukiko Sumi Barnett, "India in Asia: Ōkawa Shūmei's Pan-Asianism Thought and His Idea of India in Early Twentieth-Century Japan," *Journal of the Oxford University History Society* 2 (2004): 6.

28. Sho Konishi, "Translingual World Order: Language without Culture in Post-Russo-Japanese War Japan," *Journal of Asian Studies* 72, no. 1 (2013): 95.

29. See Sho, "Translingual World Order," 109.

30. On Bose's life, see H. P. Ghose's introduction to *The Two Great Indians in Japan: Sri Rash Behari Bose and Netaji Subhas Chandra Bose* by J. G. Ohsawa (Calcutta: Kusa Publications, 1954), v–xi.

31. Eri Hotta, "Rash Behari Bose and His Japanese Supporters: An Insight into Anti-colonial Nationalism and Pan-Asianism," *Interventions* 8, no. 1 (2006): 118.

32. As Mark Driscoll's recent work shows, Tōyama Mitsuru also embodies a conservative critique of capitalism that is worthy of further study. See Mark Driscoll, *The Whites Are Enemies of Heaven: Climate Caucasianism and Asian Ecological Protection* (Durham NC: Duke University Press, 2021).

33. Quoted in Hotta, "Rash Behari Bose," 121.

34. Erez Manela, *The Wilsonian Moment: Self-Determination and the Origins of Anti-colonial Nationalism* (Oxford: Oxford University Press, 2007).

35. Michael Adas, "Contested Hegemonies: The Great War and the Afro-Asian Assault on the Civilizing Mission Ideology," in *Decolonization: Perspectives from Now and Then*, ed. Prasenjit Duara (London: Routledge, 2003), 82.

36. Adas, "Contested Hegemonies," 86.

37. Jacques Bidet, *Explication et reconstruction du Capital* (Paris: PUF, 2004), 157.

38. Aydin, *Politics of Anti-Westernism in Asia*, 121.

39. Jessica Namakkal, "European Dreams, Tamil Land: Auroville and the Paradox of a Postcolonial Utopia," *Journal for the Study of Radicalism* 6 no. 1 (2012): 58–88.

40. Quoted in Aydin, *Politics of Anti-Westernism in Asia*, 122.

41. Quoted in Aydin, *Politics of Anti-Westernism in Asia*, 123.

42. Tatiana Linkhoeva, *Revolution Goes East: Imperial Japan and Soviet Communism* (Ithaca, NY: Cornell University Press, 2020).

43. Ōkawa, "Fukkō ajia no sho mondai," 147.

44. Ōkawa, "Fukkō ajia no sho mondai," 147.

45. Ōkawa, "Fukkō ajia no sho mondai," 148.

46. Usuki Akira, *Ōkawa Shūmei: isulāmu to tennō no hazama de* [Ōkawa Shūmei between Islam and the emperor] (Tokyo: Seidosha, 2010), 271.

47. Ōkawa Shūmei, "Indo jin tsuihō to Tōyama Mitsuru ō" [Exiling Indians and Tōyama Mitsuru], in *Ajia shugishatachi no koe*, 184.

48. Ōkawa, "Kakumei yōroppa to fukkō ajia," 239. See also Ōkawa's other statements, including "Our mission is to rescue the nations that have been suffering under Western oppression. . . . Together we will attain freedom, the most invaluable right of human kind, and remove Western

236 NOTES TO PAGES 94-97

oppression of our indigenous culture. The reason why we call for 'Asia for Asians' is because there can be no true Asia as long as Asia is under Western control. . . . We need to recognize that we must rescue Asia as well as the West by reforming the attitude and the spirit of the Western race. . . . The Japanese nation must prepare ourselves for our country's grand mission." Ōkawa, "Kunkoku no shimei" [Our country's mission] (published in 1916), quoted in Barnett, "India in Asia," 9; and "The light is coming from eastward." "Finally, the time comes when this old message new life, and has a new meaning. Japan, as a non-white fighter for the liberation: it has to bring a light of hope. . . . Japanese domestic political and economic reform is a starting point of world reformation." Quoted in Toshiya Kaneko, "Cultural Light, Political Shadow: Okakura Tenshin (1862–1913) and the Japanese Crisis of National Identity, 1880–1941" (PhD diss., University of Pennsylvania, 2002), 347 (Ōkawa writing in 1933). Here we see that Okawa considered Japan a fulcrum for the transformation of the world.

49. Ōkawa, "Kakumei yōroppa to fukkō ajia," 239.

50. Ōkawa, "Kakumei yōroppa to fukkō ajia," 240.

51. Ōkawa Shūmei, "Ajia no kensetsusha" [The establishers of Asia], in *Ōkawa Shūmei zenshū* (Tokyo: Ōkawa Shūmei kankōkai, 1969), 2:252. Citing from Usuki, *Ōkawa Shūmei*, 183.

52. Ōkawa, "Ajia no kensetsusha," 365–67; see also Usuki, *Ōkawa Shūmei*, 196.

53. Ōkawa, "Kakumei yōroppa to fukkō ajia," 240.

54. We will examine this document more carefully later in this chapter.

55. Ōkawa Shūmei, "Go ichi go jiken chōsho" [An investigation of the May 15 incident], in *Ajia shugishatachi no koe*, 112. The previous points are summarized in 111–12. See also Linkhoeva, *Revolution Goes East*, 72.

56. Ōkawa, "Kakumei yōroppa to fukkō ajia," 246. On the Bolshevik Revolution's impact in Japan, see Linkhoeva, *Revolution Goes East*, 72.

57. The Taishō period (1912–1925) is often considered a period when democracy emerges for a brief period in Japan before the fascist turn. However, Ōkawa criticizes the nature of this democracy.

58. Sheldon Garon, *The State and Labor in Modern Japan* (Berkeley: University of California Press, 1990), 43.

59. Garon, *The State and Labor in Modern Japan*, 45.

60. Quoted in Garon, *The State and Labor in Modern Japan*, 43.

61. Eri Hotta, *Pan-Asianism and Japan's War 1931–1945* (New York: Palgrave Macmillan, 2007), 69.

62. Ōkawa, "Kakumei yōroppa to fukkō ajia," 246. Christian Uhl has an overlapping but slightly different reading of this aspect of Ōkawa's philosophy. Christian Uhl, "Liberté—Egalité—Fraternité: Okawa Shūmei's Asia and the Romanticization of the Ideals of the French Revolution" (unpublished manuscript, 2012).

63. G. W. F. Hegel, *Phänomenologie des Geistes* (Frankfurt am Main: Suhrkamp, 1986), 44; *The Phenomenology of Spirit*, trans. Terry Pinkard (Cambridge, UK: Cambridge University Press, 2018), 27, para. 45.

64. Ōkawa, "Kakumei yōroppa to fukkō ajia," 246.

65. For Marx's argument, see "On the Jewish Question," in *The Marx-Engels Reader*, ed. Robert C. Tucker (New York: W. W. Norton, 1978), 26–46.

66. Ōkawa Shūmei, "Kita Ikki wo omou" [Remembering Kita Ikki], in *Ajia shugishatachi no koe*, 161–62.

67. Jasis Mimura, *Planning for Empire: Reform Bureaucrats and the Japanese Wartime State* (Ithaca, NY: Cornell University Press, 2011), 43.

NOTES TO PAGES 98–104

68. Quoted in Watanabe Kyōji, *Kita Ikki* (Tokyo: Chikuma gakugei bunko, 2007), 161–62.

69. Watanabe, *Kita Ikki*, 163.

70. Watanabe, *Kita Ikki*, 169. Fruitful comparisons can be made of the thoughts of Kita and Ōkawa to those of Indian philosophers of the Swadeshi movement, such as Aurobindo, who Ōkawa avidly read. As Andrew Sartori notes, "Swadeshi ideology consistently turned on the systematic opposition of substance, spiritual freedom, labor, production and wealth to form, material attachment, consumption, exchange and value." Andrew Sartori, *Bengal in Global Concept History: Culturalism in the Age of Global Capital* (Chicago: University of Chicago Press, 2008), 155. Although Ōkawa and Kita emphasized ethical substance and spirit against the material, their relation to labor was much more ambiguous. Here the figure of Saigō pulls in another direction, as he was not necessarily interested in the production of wealth.

71. Ōkawa Shūmei, "Anraku no Mon" [Gateway to comfort], in *Ajiashugi*, ed. Takeuchi Yoshimi (Tokyo: Chikuma shobō, 1963), 257.

72. Karatani Kojin, *The Structure of World History: From Modes of Production to Modes of Exchange*, trans. Michael Bourdaghs (Durham, NC: Duke University Press, 2014), 209.

73. See Wang Hui, *The End of the Revolution: China and the Limits of Modernity*, ed. Rebecca Karl (London: Verso, 2009).

74. Ōkawa, "Go ichi go jiken chōsho," 138.

75. See Louise Young, *Japan's Total Empire: Manchuria and the Culture of Wartime Imperialism* (Berkeley: University of California Press, 1998), 117–19. The Minseitō was accused of being weak by not following through with the invasion of China, while the Seiyūkai attacked the Minseitō for endangering the country.

76. Ōkawa, "Go ichi go jiken chōsho," 117.

77. Ōkawa, "Go ichi go jiken chōsho," 118.

78. The Uchimura Kanzo Incident of 1891. Uchimura Kanzo (1861–1930) was a teacher in a high school in Tokyo who was forced to resign because he did not bow to a portrait of the Meiji Emperor and the Imperial Rescript on Education.

79. State Shinto refers to the shinto that was sponsored as a state morality. At the center of this morality is the belief that the emperor is a descendent of the sun goddess. For a discussion of this, see Helen Hardacre, *Shinto and the State, 1968–1988* (Princeton, NJ: Princeton University Press, 1991).

80. Ōkawa, "Go ichi go jiken chōsho," 118.

81. Ōkawa, "Go ichi go jiken chōsho," 120.

82. Ōkawa, "Go ichi go jiken chōsho," 121.

83. Ōkawa, "Go ichi go jiken chōsho," 122.

84. Ōkawa Shūmei, "Chūyō shinchū" [New Notes on the doctrine of the mean], in *Ōkawa Shūmei dōtoku tetsugaku kōwashū* [A collection of Ōkawa Shūmei's lectures on ethics] (Tokyo: Seitō yō, 2008), 71.

85. Ōkawa Shūmei, *Shin tōyō seishin*, quoted in Usuki, *Ōkawa Shūmei*, 285.

86. Prasenjit Duara, *The Crisis of Global Modernity: Asian Traditions and a Sustainable Future* (Cambridge, UK: Cambridge University Press, 2015).

87. Duara, *The Crisis of Global Modernity*, 120. Duara is concerned with environmental crises, which were not on Ōkawa's radar.

88. Ōkawa, *Shin tōyō seishin*, quoted in Usuki, *Ōkawa Shūmei*, 286.

89. The Greater East Asia Co-prosperity Sphere refers to an ideology of pan-Asianism, which the Japanese government used to justify its imperialist practices during World War II.

90. Ōkawa, *Shin tōyō seishin*, quoted in Usuki, *Ōkawa Shūmei*, 286.

238 NOTES TO PAGES 105-110

91. Ōkawa, "Go ichi go jiken chōsho," 123.

92. Ōkawa Shūmei, "Daitōa chitsujo kensetsu" [Establishing a great Asian order], quoted in Usuki, *Ōkawa Shūmei*, 21.

93. He claims that Judaism brings together state, God, and people in a way similar to the Japanese conflation of emperor, state, and people. See Usuki, *Ōkawa Shūmei*, 216.

94. See Hegel, *Phänomenologie des Geistes*, 267.

95. Ōkawa Shūmei, "Daitōa chitsujo kensetsu," quoted in Koyasu Nobukuni, *Kindai no chōkoku to ha nanika* [What is modern China?] (Tokyo: Seidosha, 2008), 214.

96. Ōkawa, "Daitōa chitsujo kensetsu," 215.

97. Ernest Mandel, *Trotsky as Alternative*, trans. Gus Fagan (London: Verso, 1995), 108.

98. Mandel, *Trotsky as Alternative*, 107.

99. Richard Smethurst, "A Social Origin of the Second World War," in *Japan Examined: Perspectives on Modern Japanese History*, ed. Harry Wray and Hilary Conroy (Honolulu: University of Hawai'i Press, 1983), 272.

100. Mandel, *Trotsky as Alternative*, 108-9.

101. Ōkawa, "Go ichi go jiken chōsho," 112.

102. On imperialism in Manchukuo as a paradigm for understanding American imperialism, see Prasenjit Duara, *Sovereignty and Authenticity: Manchukuo and the East Asian Modern* (Lanham, MD: Rowman and Littlefield, 2004), intro.

103. Naoki Sakai, "Resistance to Conclusion: The Kyoto School Philosophy under the *Pax-Americana*," in *Repoliticizing the Kyoto School as Philosophy*, ed. Christopher Goto-Jones (London: Routledge, 2007).

104. Harry Harootunian, *Marx after Marx: History and Time in the Expansion of Capitalism* (New York: Columbia University Press, 2017); Bill Martin, *Ethical Marxism: The Categorical Imperative of Liberation* (Chicago: Open Court, 2008); Michael Löwy, *Jewish Libertarian Thought in Central Europe: A Study in Elective Affinity*, trans. Hope Heaney (Stanford, CA: Stanford University Press, 1988).

Chapter Four

1. Usuki Akira, *Ōkawa Shūmei: isulāmu to tennō no hazama de* [Ōkawa Shūmei between Islam and the Emperor] (Tokyo: Seidosha, 2010), 64.

2. Takeuchi Yoshimi, "Profile of Asian Minded Man X: Ōkawa Shūmei," *Developing Economies* 7, no. 3 (1969): 368.

3. See Richard F. Calichman, *Takeuchi Yoshimi: Displacing the West* (Ithaca, NY: Cornell University Press, 2010) and *The Coming Death: Traces of Mortality across East Asia* (Albany: State University of New York Press, 2022), chaps. 3 and 4; Lawrence Olsen, *Ambivalent Moderns: Portraits of Japanese Cultural Identity* (Lanham, MD: Rowman and Littlefield, 1992); Samuel Guex, *Entre nonchalance et désespoir: Les intellectuels japonais sinologues face à la guerre (1930-1950)* (Bern: Peter Lang, 2006); Sun Ge, *Zhuneihao de beilun* [The paradox of Takeuchi Yoshimi] (Beijing: Beijing daxue chubanshe, 2005); Okayama Asako, *Takeuchi no bungaku seishin* [Takeuchi's literary spirit] (Tokyo: Ronsōsha, 2002); and Christian Uhl, *Wer war Takuchi Yoshimis Lu Xun? Ein Annäherungsversuch an ein Monument der japanischen Sinologie* (Munich: Iudicum Verlag GmbH, 2003), for a wide array of perspectives, ranging from philosophical, literary, and historical. Sun's perspective is perhaps closest to my own, because she deals with Takeuchi's pan-Asianism. However, as we shall see, I stress the connection between Takeuchi's

NOTES TO PAGES 111–117 239

pan-Asianism and his interest in the Chinese Revolution, which meshes with a major theme of this book: socialism. As we have seen already, most pan-Asianists have in some way envisioned a community beyond capitalism.

4. Susan Buck-Morss, "Hegel and Haiti," *Critical Inquiry* 26, no. 4 (2000): 821–65; Michel-Rolph Trouillot, *Silencing the Past: Power and the Production of History* (Boston: Beacon Press, 1995).

5. Takeuchi Yoshimi, *Takeuchi Yoshimi zenshū* [The complete works of Takeuchi Yoshimi] (Tokyo: Chikuma shobō, 1982), 13:8.

6. Takeuchi, *Takeuchi Yoshimi zenshū*, 13:10. See also Oguma Eiji, *Minshu to Aikoku: sengo no nashonarisumu to kōkyūsei* [Democracy and patriotism: Postwar Japanese nationalism and publicity] (Tokyo: Shinyōsha, 2002), 396.

7. Jacques Bidet, *Explication et reconstruction du Capital* (Paris: PUF, 2004).

8. Takeuchi, *Takeuchi Yoshimi zenshū*, 5:92; Oguma, *Minshu to Aikoku*, 398.

9. Olsen, *Ambivalent Moderns*, 48.

10. Margaret Mehl, "Chinese Learning (*kangaku*) in Meiji Japan (1868–1912)," *History* 85 (2000): 48–66.

11. Kokugaku or national learning was a school of thought that emerged in eighteenth-century Japan, and one of its main goals was to decenter China and return to classical Japanese texts. Historians of Japan often interpret them as expressing Japanese proto-nationalism, which developed further during the Meiji. For a discussion, see Susan Burns, *Before the Nation: Kokugaku and the Imagining of the Community in Early Modern Japan* (Durham, NC: Duke University Press, 2003).

12. Harry D. Harootunian, "The Function of China in Tokugawa Thought," in *The Chinese and the Japanese: Essays in Political and Cultural Interactions*, ed. Akira Iriye (Princeton, NJ: Princeton University Press, 1980), 33.

13. This term was first used by Ōkuni Takamasa, an influential scholar of national learning, toward the end of the Tokugawa as part of his own effort to decenter China from a national learning perspective. See Harootunian, "The Function of China," 27.

14. On Naitō Konan, see Joshua Fogel, *Politics and Sinology: The Case of Naitō Konan (1866–1934)* (Cambridge, MA: Harvard University Press, 1984).

15. Stefan Tanaka, *Japan's Orient: Rendering Pasts into History* (Berkeley: University of California Press, 1993), 4–5.

16. Yoshikawa Kōjirō, "Honyaku jihyō" [Evaluating translation], in vol. 65 of *Chūgoku bungaku* (1941), quoted in Yamada Masaru, "Takeuchi Yoshimi: Chūgoku to iu yūmei" [Takeuchi Yoshimi: The dream called China], in *Higashiajia no chishiki jin: samazama no sengo, nihon no haisen—1950 nendai*, ed. Murata Yūjirō, Chō Kindaru, Harada Keiichi, and Yasuda Tsuneo (Tokyo: Yūshisha, 2014), 117.

17. I have dealt with Ogyū Sorai's treatment of *kundoku* and the problem of the past in "The Politics of Time in China and Japan," in *The Oxford Handbook of Comparative Political Theory*, ed. Leigh K. Jenco, Murad Idris, and Megan C. Thomas (Oxford: Oxford University Press, 2019), 191–217.

18. Takeuchi Yoshimi, "Honyaku jihyō," in *Takeuchi Yoshimi zenshū*, 14:190–91.

19. On Takeuchi and national independence, see Yamada, "Takeuchi Yoshimi."

20. Takeuchi Yoshimi, "Shina to Chūgoku," in *Takeuchi Yoshimi zenshū*, 14:167–70. Cf. Yamada, "Takeuchi Yoshimi," 118.

21. Martin Heidegger, "Origin of the Artwork," in *Poetry, Language and Thought*, trans. Albert Hofstadter (New York: Harper & Row, 1971), 47.

240   NOTES TO PAGES 117–123

22. Heidegger, *Poetry, Language and Thought*, 49.

23. Sun Wukong is the hero of the famous sixteenth-century novel *The Journey to the West*, which tells the story of a heroic excursion to India to bring back Buddhist sutras to China.

24. Sun, *Zhuneihao de beilun*, 27.

25. Takeuchi Yoshimi, "Shina wo kaku toiu koto" [Writing China], in *Takeuchi Yoshimi zenshū*, 14:285. See also Sun, *Zhuneihao de beilun*, 28.

26. Sun Ge interprets Takeuchi as expressing a general theory about the insufficiency of language. "Although the knowing subject can only have contact with reality with the help of discourse, it is precisely the lack of self-sufficiency of discourse that provides the premise of knowledge and contact with reality." Sun, *Zhuneihao de beilun*, 29. While this point is implicit in Takeuchi's work, I believe he has a more historical notion of epistemology, which is why he underscores the concept of modernity.

27. Takeuchi Yoshimi, *Takeuchi Yoshimi serekushon 1 Nihon he/kara no manazashi* [Takeuchi Yoshimi, selections, vol. 1, Looking from Japan], ed. Marukawa Tetsushi and Suzuki Masahisa (Tokyo: Nihon keizaisha, 2007), 56.

28. Takeuchi, *Takeuchi Yoshimi serekushon 1*, 54.

29. Takeuchi, *Takeuchi Yoshimi serekushon 1*, 61.

30. Takeuchi, *Takeuchi Yoshimi serekushon 1*, 53.

31. Takeuchi, *Takeuchi Yoshimi serekushon 1*, 53.

32. Takeuchi, *Takeuchi Yoshimi serekushon 1*, 56.

33. Takeuchi, *Takeuchi Yoshimi serekushon 1*, 53. The reference to nothingness and other terminology that Takeuchi uses suggests that he was influenced by Nishida Kitarō's philosophy. Nishida Kitarō (1870–1945) was the most important philosopher of the Kyoto School of philosophy, which attempted to rethink classical Japanese and Asian ideas through a profound understanding of Western, especially German, philosophy. For an in-depth discussion of the relationship between Nishida and Takeuchi, see Uhl, *Wer war Takuchi Yoshimis Lu Xun?*, and Christian Uhl, "Displacing Japan: Takeuchi Yoshimi's Lu Xun in Light of Nishida's Philosophy and Vice-Versa," *Positions: East Asia Cultures Critique* 17, no. 1 (2009): 207–38. For a more philosophical discussion of the same topic, see Calichman, *Takeuchi Yoshimi*.

34. Takeuchi, *Takeuchi Yoshimi serekushon 1*, 54.

35. Takeuchi, *Takeuchi Yoshimi serekushon 1*, 57.

36. Cited in Olsen, *Ambivalent Moderns*, 52. The original is in *Takeuchi Yoshimi serekushon 1*, 57–58.

37. Takeuchi, *Takeuchi Yoshimi zenshū*, 17:300.

38. Takeuchi Yoshimi, "Hyaku nazō" [A hundred riddles], in *Takeuchi Yoshimi zenshū*, 11:157.

39. Lin Shaoyang, "Romanticism, History and Aestheticized Politics: Yasuda Yojūrō and the Discourse of Overcoming the Modern in Wartime Japan," *Studies of Intellectual History* 13 (2011):173–214.

40. Yasuda Yojūrō, "Cogito no Shuhen," quoted in Lin, "Romanticism, History and Aestheticized Politics," 193–94.

41. Lin, "Romanticism, History and Aestheticized Politics," 193–94.

42. See Ninomiya Masayuki, *La pensée de Kobayashi Hideo: Un intellectuel japonais au tournant de l'histoire* (Geneva: Dross, 1995). For a discussion of Takeuchi's relationship to both the author of proletarian literature Nakano Shigeharu and Kobayashi Hideo, see Uhl, *Wer war Takuchi Yoshimis Lu Xun?*, 344–47.

NOTES TO PAGES 124–135 241

43. Takeuchi Yoshimi, *Rojin* [Lu Xun] (Tokyo: Noma Sawako, 2003), 38–39.

44. Quoted in Takeuchi, *Rojin*, 76.

45. Quoted in Takeuchi, *Rojin*, 77.

46. Quoted in Takeuchi, *Rojin*, 11–12.

47. Quoted in Takeuchi, *Rojin*, 60–61.

48. Quoted in Takeuchi, *Rojin*, 61.

49. Jean Laplanche, *Essays on Otherness*, trans. John Fletcher (London: Routledge, 1999), 85.

50. Christopher Fynsk, *Heidegger: Thought and Historicity* (Ithaca, NY: Cornell University Press, 1986).

51. Takeuchi, *Rojin*, 78. See also Uhl, *Wer war Takuchi Yoshimis Lu Xun?*, 290.

52. Kaji Wataru, "Takeuchi Yoshimi no bungaku shisō: rojin wo megutte" [The literary thought of Takeuchi Yoshimi: With reference to Lu Xun], *Minshu bungaku* 28 (March 1968): 75–76.

53. G. W. F. Hegel, *Elements of the Philosophy of Right*, trans. H. B. Nisbet, ed. Allen W. Wood (Cambridge, UK: Cambridge University Press, 1991), 38–39. The bracketed interpolations are in the original.

54. Takeuchi, *Rojin*, 78. See also Uhl, *Wer war Takuchi Yoshimis Lu Xun?*, 290.

55. Takeuchi, *Rojin*, 143.

56. Richard Calichman has compared Takeuchi to Derrida. See Calichman, *Takeuchi Yoshimi*.

57. Martin Hägglund, "The Autoimmunity of Religion," in *The Trace of God: Derrida and Religion*, ed. Deward Baring and Peter E. Gordon (New York: Fordham University Press, 2015), 185. Richard Calichman has recently drawn on Derrida to explain Takeuchi's idea of finitude and how this relates to his conception of identity. See Calichman, *The Coming Death*, chaps. 3 and 4.

58. Quoted in Leo Oufan Lee, "Literature on the Eve of the Revolution: Reflections on Lu Xun's Leftist Years, 1927–1936," *Modern China* 2, no. 3 (July 1977): 278.

59. Takeuchi, *Rojin*, 178.

60. Takeuchi, *Rojin*, 178.

61. Takeuchi, *Rojin*, 180–81.

62. Takeuchi, *Rojin*, 181.

63. Nishida uses the term "contradictory unity" (*mujunteki dōitsu*), as Takeuchi points out in his footnote, *Rojin*, 198. Uhl, "Displacing Japan," has argued that Takeuchi takes most of his ideas from Nishida and applies them to his reading of Lu Xun. However, Takeuchi himself says that "he does not follow the examples of Nishida's philosophy seriously." Takeuchi, *Rojin*, 198.

64. Cf. Arthur Schopenhauer, *The Essays of Arthur Schopenhauer: Studies in Pessimism*, trans. T. Bailey Saunders (University Park: Penn State Electronic Classics Series, 2005), 4:76, https://www.academia.edu/5920036/THE_ESSAYS_OF_ARTHUR_SCHOPENHAUER_STUDIES_IN_PESSIMISM_Volume_Four/.

65. Lu Xun, "The Warrior and the Flies," quoted in Takeuchi, *Rojin*, 147.

66. Lu Xun, "One Year after the Death of Sun Zhongshan," quoted in Takeuchi, *Rojin*, 149–50.

67. Takeuchi, *Rojin*, 150.

68. Takeuchi, *Rojin*, 152.

69. Takeuchi, *Rojin*, 170.

70. Takeuchi, *Rojin*, 151 (cf. 184).

71. Takeuchi, *Rojin*, 181.

72. Takeuchi, *Rojin*, 182.

73. Takeuchi Yoshimi, "Ways of Introducing Culture (Chinese Literature and Japanese Literature II) Focusing on Lu Xun," in *What Is Modernity? Writings of Takeuchi Yoshimi*, trans. Richard F. Calichman (New York: Columbia University Press, 2005), 52.

74. In the postwar period, Takeuchi claimed that Lu Xun was influenced by Japanese writers but only those who were on the margins, such as Kuriyagawa Hakuson and Arishima Takeo. See Takeuchi Yoshimi, "Bunka inyu no hōhō: Rojin to Nihon" [The method of cultural transplantation: Lu Xun and Japan], in *Takeuchi Yoshimi zenshū*, 4:121.

Chapter Five

1. Lawrence Olsen, *Ambivalent Moderns: Portraits of Japanese Cultural Identity* (Lanham, MD: Rowman and Littlefield, 1992), 55.

2. Takeuchi Yoshimi, "Kutsujo no jiken" [A shameful event], in *Takeuchi Yoshimi serekushon 1 Nihon he/kara no manazashi* [Takeuchi Yoshimi, selections, vol. 1, Looking from Japan], ed. Marukawa Tetsushi and Suzuki Masahisa (Tokyo: Nihon keizaisha, 2007), 21.

3. Takeuchi, "Kutsujo no jiken." 23.

4. Takeuchi Yoshimi, "Kaitai" [Explanation], in *Nihon to ajia: Takeuchi Yoshimi hyōron sho* [Japan and Asia: A collection of critical essays by Takeuchi Yoshimi] (Tokyo: Chikuma shobō, 1996), 443–44. Quoted in Kurokawa Midori, "Dore kara no dakkyaku wo motomete: sengo shakai no naka de" [Attempting to break free from slavery: In the midst of postwar society], in *Takeuchi Yoshimi to sono jidai: rekishigaku kara no taiwa* [Takeuchi Yoshimi and his times: Dialogues from historiography], ed. Kurokawa Midori and Yamada Satoshi (Tokyo: Yūshisha, 2018), 92–93.

5. Takeuchi Yoshimi, "Fukuin Rikki 1946" [Diary of repatriation, 1946], in *Takeuchi Yoshimi zenshū* [The complete works of Takeuchi Yoshimi] (Tokyo: Chikuma shobō, 1982), 15:405.

6. Shimizu Ikutarō, *Kichi no Ko* [Children of the military bases], quoted in Simon Andrew Avenell, *Making Japanese Citizens: Civil Society and the Mythology of the Shimin in Postwar Japan* (Berkeley: University of California Press, 2010), 59.

7. For a discussion of this idea of imperialism, see Prasenjit Duara, *Sovereignty and Authenticity: Manchukuo and the East Asian Modern* (Lanham, MD: Rowman and Littlefield, 2004).

8. Leo Panitch and Sam Gindin, *The Making of Global Capitalism: The Political Economy of the American Empire* (London: Verso, 2013).

9. Taizo Miyagi, "Postwar Japan and Asianism," *Asian Pacific Review* 13, no. 2 (2006): 5.

10. Baba Kimihiko, *Sengo nihonjin no chūgoku zō: nihon haisen kara bunkadaigakumei/nichūfukkō made* [Postwar Japanese people's image of China: From the Japanese loss in the war to the Cultural Revolution/resumption of diplomatic relations between Japan and China] (Tokyo: Shinyōsha, 2010).

11. Takeuchi Yoshimi, *What Is Modernity? Writings of Takeuchi Yoshimi*, trans. Richard F. Calichman (New York: Columbia University, 2005), 54; Takeuchi Yoshimi, *Nihon to ajia* [Japan and Asia] (Tokyo: Chikuma shobō, 2002), 13 (translation amended).

12. Takeuchi, *What Is Modernity?*, 54.

13. Moishe Postone, *Time, Labor and Social Domination: A Reinterpretation of Marx's Critical Theory* (Cambridge, UK: Cambridge University Press, 1993).

14. For a discussion of readings of Marx along these lines, see Harry Harootunian, *Marx after Marx: History and Time in the Expansion of Capitalism* (New York: Columbia University Press, 2017); Massimiliano Tomba, *Marx's Temporalities* (New York: Haymarket Books, 2014);

NOTES TO PAGES 141–151

and Gavin Walker, *The Perversion of Capital: Marxist Theory and the Politics of History in Modern Japan* (Durham, NC: Duke University Press, 2016).

15. Søren Kierkegaard, *Philosophical Fragments* (Lexington: Feather Trail Press, 2009), 13.

16. On history and sovereignty, see Constantin Fasolt, *The Limits of History* (Chicago: University of Chicago Press, 2003).

17. Takeuchi, *What Is Modernity?*, 55.

18. Takeuchi, *What Is Modernity?*, 55.

19. Takeuchi, *What Is Modernity?*, 55.

20. Georg Lukács, *History and Class Consciousness: Studies in Marxist Dialectics*, trans. Rodney Livingston (Cambridge, MA: MIT Press, 1971).

21. Takeuchi, *What Is Modernity?*, 58.

22. Takeuchi, *What Is Modernity?*, 73; *Nihon to ajia*, 45 (translation slightly amended).

23. David Bostock, *Space, Time, Matter and Form: Essays on Aristotle's Physics* (Oxford: Oxford University Press, 2006), 135.

24. Massimiliano Tomba, *Insurgent Universality: An Alternative Legacy of Modernity* (Oxford: Oxford University Press, 2019), 13.

25. See Christian Uhl, *Wer war Takuchi Yoshimis Lu Xun? Ein Annäherungsversuch an ein Monument der japanischen Sinologie* (Munich: Iudicum Verlag GmbH, 2003).

26. Lukács, *History and Class Consciousness*, chap. 3.

27. Takeuchi, *What Is Modernity?*, 74–75; *Nihon to ajia*, 47 (translation revised).

28. Martin Heidegger, *Being and Time*, trans. John Macquarrie and Edward Robinson (Oxford: Blackwell, 2001), 214.

29. Takeuchi, *What Is Modernity?*, 75.

30. Takeuchi Yoshimi, "Nihon no ajiashugi," in *Nihon to ajia*, 301. Yoshino Sakuzō (1878–1933) was a liberal political thinker during the Taisho period. Oi Kentarō (1843–1922) was a leader of the freedom and people's rights movement in the Meiji period.

31. Takeuchi, *What Is Modernity?*, 77; *Nihon to ajia*, 50.

32. Takeuchi, *What Is Modernity?*, 65; *Nihon to ajia*, 31 (translation slightly amended).

33. Takeuchi, *What Is Modernity?*, 77; *Nihon to ajia*, 50–51.

34. Takeuchi, *What Is Modernity?*, 77.

35. Nishi Junzō, *Chosakushu* (Tokyo: Uchiyama shoten, 1995), 128.

36. Takeuchi, *What Is Modernity?*, 69.

37. Lydia H. Liu, *Translingual Practice: Literature, National Culture and Translated Modernity—China, 1900–1937* (Berkeley: University of California Press, 1995), 236.

38. Takeuchi, *What Is Modernity?*, 71.

39. Zhuangzi, *Zhuangzi buzheng* (Anhui: Anhuidaxue chubanshe, 1999), 54.

40. For a discussion of this trend in Europe and in France in particular, see Stefanos Geroulanos, *An Atheism That Is Not Humanist in French Thought* (Stanford, CA: Stanford University Press, 2010).

41. G. W. F. Hegel, *Phänomenologie des Geistes* (Frankfurt am Main: Suhrkamp, 1986), 72; *The Phenomenology of Spirit*, trans. Terry Pinkard (Cambridge, UK: Cambridge University Press, 2018), 52.

42. Hegel, *Phänomenologie des Geistes*, 72; *The Phenomenology of Spirit*, 52. Robyn Marasco reads Hegel in a manner that emphasizes a politics of despair, which echoes Takeuchi's position. For example, she writes: "Hegel succeeds at those moments that the system fails to overcome despair." Robyn Marasco, *The Highway of Despair: Critical Theory after Hegel* (New York: Columbia University Press, 2015), 33.

43. Takeuchi, *What Is Modernity?*, 78–79; *Nihon to ajia*, 52–53 (translation amended).

44. Takeuchi Yoshimi, "Bungaku ni okeru dokuritsu to ha nanika," in *Takeuchi Yoshimi serekushon 1*, 226.

45. Takeuchi Yoshimi, "Nenpu" [Chronological record], in *Takeuchi Yoshimi zenshū*, 17:305.

46. See Kurokawa Midori, "Dore kara no dakkyaku wo motomete," 101.

47. Takeuchi Yoshimi, "Nihon kyōsantō he no chūbun," [Notes on the JCP], in *Takeuchi Yoshimi zenshū*, 6:204. Quoted in Kurokawa, "Dore kara no dakkyaku wo motomete," 101.

48. Takeuchi Yoshimi, *Nihon ideorogi* [Japanese ideology] (Tokyo: Koboshi bunko, 1999), 7.

49. Takeuchi, *Nihon ideorogi*, 157.

50. Takeuchi, *Nihon ideorogi*, 160.

51. Walter Lippmann, *The Phantom Public* (New York: Harcourt, 1925).

52. Takeuchi, "Hu Shi and Dewey," in *What Is Modernity?*, 102.

53. John Dewey to Albert C. Barnes, Beijing, 5 December 1920, Correspondence no. 04113, quoted in Jessica Ching-Sze Wang, *Dewey in China* (Albany: State University of New York Press, 2007), 45.

54. John Dewey to Albert C. Barnes, Beijing, 5 December 1920, 45.

55. Takeuchi, *Nihon ideorogi*, 168.

56. Takeuchi, *Nihon ideorogi*, 172.

57. Confucius, *Analects*, 14.38, in Confucius, *Lunyu yizhu, Yang Bojun yizhu* [*Analects* with notes and translation by Yang Bojun] (Beijing: Zhonghua shuju, 2002), 157.

58. Takeuchi, *Nihon ideorogi*, 178.

59. Mao Zedong, "The Foolish Old Man Who Removed the Mountains," in *Selected Works of Mao Tse-tung* (Beijing: Foreign Languages Press, 1965), 3:217–73. For the original, see Mao Zedong, "Yu Gong yi shan," in *Mao Zedong xuanji* (Beijing: Renmin chubanshe, 1991), 2:1101–4.

60. Mao, "The Foolish Old Man," 271; Mao, "Yu Gong yi shan," 1102.

61. Takeuchi, *Nihon ideorogi*, 176–77.

62. Takeuchi, *Nihon ideorogi*, 51.

63. Takeuchi, *Nihon ideorogi*, 51.

64. Takeuchi, *Nihon ideorogi*, 51.

65. Takeuchi, *Nihon ideorogi*, 146.

66. Tosaka Jun, "The Principle of Everydayness and Historical Time," trans. Robert Stolz, in *From Japan's Modernity: A Reader*, ed. Tetsuo Najita (Chicago: Center for East Asian Studies, University of Chicago, 2002), 162.

67. Takeuchi, *Nihon ideorogi*, 201.

68. Takeuchi, *Nihon ideorogi*, 142.

69. Takeuchi, *Nihon ideorogi*, 142.

70. Takeuchi, *Nihon ideorogi*, 210. Takeuchi writes here of a "drive to confess," which some might connect to indoctrination. Recently Prasenjit Duara has pointed out that as religions become confessional, they reinforce a self-other distinction and often buttress atavistic nationalisms (Prasenjit Duara, *The Crisis of Global Modernity: Asian Traditions and a Sustainable Future* [Cambridge, UK: Cambridge University Press, 2015]).To some extent, this describes Takeuchi's thinking since he was also concerned with developing a nationalist narrative. Takeuchi believed that in a world of global capitalist imperialism, one could not do away with nationalism. The nationalism he favored incorporated the intellectual into the revolutionary project, which was at once nationalist and transnational. We will return to the problem of nationalism in the next section.

NOTES TO PAGES 163–172   245

71. Michael Hardt and Antonio Negri, *Empire* (Cambridge, MA: Harvard University Press, 2001).

72. Kaoru Sugihara, "The Second Noel Butlin Lecture: Labor-Intensive Industrialisation in Global History," *Australian Economic History Review* 47, no. 2 (2007): 121–54. See also Giovanni Arrighi, *Adam Smith in Beijing: Lineages of the Twenty-First Century* (London: Verso, 2009).

73. Maruyama Masao, "Nationalism in Japan: Its Theoretical Background and Prospects," trans. David Titus, in *Thought and Behaviour in Modern Japanese Politics*, ed. Ivan Morris (Oxford: Oxford University Press, 1969), 137.

74. Maruyama, "Nationalism in Japan," 142.

75. Maruyama, "Nationalism in Japan," 142.

76. Takeuchi Yoshimi, "Kindaishugi to minzoku no mondai" [Modernism and the problem of the nation] in *Takeuchi Yoshimi serekushon 1*, 183–84. Takeuchi Yoshimi, "The Ideology of the Modern and the Problem of the Ethnic Nation," in *The Politics and Literature Debate in Postwar Japanese Criticism 1945–1952*, ed. Atsuko Ueda, Michael K. Bourdaghs, Richi Sakakibara, and Hirokazu Toeda (Lanham, MD: Lexington Books, 2017), 249 (translation amended).

77. Takeuchi, "Kindaishugi to minzoku no mondai," 186; "The Ideology of the Modern," 250.

78. Takeuchi, "Kindaishugi to minzoku no mondai," 187; "The Ideology of the Modern," 252.

79. Takeuchi, "Kindaishugi to minzoku no mondai," 189; "The Ideology of the Modern," 253.

80. Takeuchi, "Kindaishugi to minzoku no mondai," 189; "The Ideology of the Modern," 253.

81. Takeuchi Yoshimi, "Nashonarizumu to shakai kakumei," in *Nihon to ajia*, 123.

82. Takeuchi Yoshimi, "Ajia no nashonarizumu," in *Takeuchi Yoshimi zenshū*, 5:6–7.

83. Takeuchi, "Ajia no nashonarizumu," 7.

84. Takeuchi, "Ajia no nashonarizumu," 8.

85. The journal *Science of Thought* has a mission that itself has much in tune with Takeuchi's own emphasis on the everyday, to which I will return later in this chapter. For an analysis of this journal, see Adam Bronson, *One Hundred Million Philosophers: Science of Thought and the Culture of Postwar Democracy in Japan* (Honolulu: University of Hawai'i Press, 2016).

86. See Takeuchi Yoshimi, "Nihonjin no ajia kan" [Japanese visions of Asia], *Nihon to ajia* [Japan and Asia] (Tokyo: Chikuma shobō, 2002), 106. See also Takeuchi Yoshimi, "Futatsu no ajiakan: Umesao setsu to Takeyama setsu" [Two visions of Asia: Umesao's theory and Takeyama's theory], in *Nihon to ajia*, 83–90.

87. Takeuchi Yoshimi, "Nihon to ajia" [Japan and Asia], in *Nihon to ajia*, 282.

88. Takeuchi, "Nihon to ajia," 283.

89. Takeuchi Yoshimi and Umesao Tadao, "Ajia no rinen" [The idea of Asia], in *Jōkyō teki: Takeuchi Yoshimi taidan shu* [Situational: A collection of Takeuchi Yoshimi's dialogues] (Tokyo: Gadō shuppansha, 1971), 152. Umesao Tadao, *Bunmei no seitaishikan* [A theory of civilization based on ecological history] (Tokyo: Chūkō bunko, 1967). The essays were first published as a series in the journal *Chūō kōron* in 1957. For an English translation of some of these essays, see Umesao Tadao, *An Ecological View of History: Japanese Civilization in the World Context*, trans. Beth Cary, ed. Harumi Befu (Melbourne: Transpacific Press, 2003).

90. Umesao, *An Ecological View of History*, 34.

91. Umesao, *An Ecological View of History*, 34.

92. Umesao, 12.

93. Umesao, 47, 50.

94. Umesao, 51.

95. Umesao, 52.

96. Umesao, 46.

97. Umesao, 54.

98. Umesao, 55.

99. Umesao, 33.

100. Umesao, 59.

101. Umesao is probably referring to the "human wave attacks" by the Chinese during the Korean War and contends that they express a type of collective subjectivity.

102. Umesao, *An Ecological View of History*, 59.

103. Takeuchi and Umesao, "Ajia no rinen," 144.

104. Takeuchi, "Futatsu no ajiakan," 89.

105. Takeuchi, "Futatsu no ajiakan," 90.

106. See Chen Kuan-hsing, *Asia as Method: Towards De-imperialism* (Durham, NC: Duke University Press, 2010).

107. Takeuchi and Umesao, "Ajia no rinen," 145.

108. Takeuchi and Umesao, "Ajia no rinen," 146.

109. Vijay Prashad, *Darker Nations: A People's History of the Third World* (New York: New Press, 2007), xv.

110. Takeuchi, "Nihonjin no ajia kan," 100.

111. Takeuchi, "Nihonjin no ajia kan," 108.

112. Takeuchi and Umesao, "Ajia no rinen," 149.

113. Takeuchi, *Jōkyō teki*, 150.

114. Takeuchi Yoshimi, "Asia as Method," in *What Is Modernity?*, 164–65; "Hōhō to shite no Ajia," in *Takeuchi Yoshimi zenshū*, 5:114.

115. Takeuchi, *What Is Modernity?*, 165; *Takeuchi Yoshimi zenshū*, 5:114–15 (translation amended).

116. See Sasaki Takuya, *Aizenhawa: seiken no fujikomeseisaku—soren no kyōi, misairu/kuba ronsō to tōsai kōryū* [Eisenhower: The policy of the containment of political power—the Soviet threat, the debate about Cuban missiles, and East-West relations] (Tokyo: Yuhikaku, 2008). On *makikaeshi* (rollback), see 56–58.

117. Takeuchi, *What Is Modernity?*, 157; *Nihon to ajia*, 456 (translation amended).

118. Takeuchi, *What Is Modernity?*, 157; *Nihon to ajia*, 456 (translation amended).

119. Curtis Gayle, "China in the Japanese Radical Gaze, 1945–1955," *Modern Asian Studies* 43, no. 5 (2009): 1255–86.

120. Takeuchi Yoshimi, "Sensō sekinin ni tsuitei," in *Nihon to ajia*, 235–36.

121. Takeuchi Yoshimi, "Overcoming Modernity," in *What Is Modernity?*, 123.

122. Takeuchi, "Nihon no ajiashugi," 291.

123. Takeuchi, "Nihonjin no ajia kan," 95–6.

124. Takeuchi, "Nihonjin no ajia kan," 103.

125. Takeuchi, "Overcoming Modernity," 123.

126. Ashis Nandy, *The Savage Freud and Other Essays on Possible and Retrievable Selves* (Princeton, NJ: Princeton University Press, 1995), 59.

127. Nandy, *The Savage Freud*, 65.

128. Nandy, *The Savage Freud*, 79.

129. Takeuchi Yoshimi, "Sensō taiken no ippanka ni tsuite," in *Nihon to ajia*, 249.

130. For a discussion of this aspect of Hegel's thought, see Rebecca Comay, *Mourning Sickness: Hegel and the French Revolution* (Stanford, CA: Stanford University Press, 2010).

NOTES TO PAGES 184–193

131. Takeuchi, "Sensō taiken no ippanka," 249–50.

132. Takeuchi, "Sensō taiken no ippanka," 232.

133. Shirai Satoshi, *Eizoku haisenron: sengo nihon no kakushin* [A theory of perpetual defeat: The essence of postwar Japan] (Tokyo: Ohta shuppansha, 2013).

134. Takeuchi Yoshimi, *Fufukujū no isan* [Heritage of disobedience] (Tokyo: Chikuma shobō, 1961), 106–7. Quoted in Olsen, *Ambivalent Moderns*, 43–44.

135. Takeuchi, *Fufukujū no isan*, 44.

136. M. K. Gandhi, *Hind Swaraj and Other Writings*, ed. Anthony J. Parel (Cambridge, UK: Cambridge University Press, 2009), 88–89.

137. " 'Gakumon geijutsu ni jiritsusei wo' Kawabatara bunkakukakumei ni apiiru" [Towards the autonomy of scholarship and the arts: An appeal concerning the Cultural Revolution from Kawabata Yasunari and Company], *Mainichi shinbun*, March 1, 1967; citing from Baba, *Sengo nihonjin no chūgoku zō*, 260. For a general discussion of the different positions that Japanese Sinologists took with respect to the Cultural Revolution, see Onodera Shirō, *Sengo nihon no chūgokukan: ajia to kindai wo meguru kattō* [Postwar Japan's vision of China: The tensions surrounding Asia and modernity] (Tokyo: Chūō kōron shinsha, 2021), 116–43.

138. Yamada Keiji, "Labor, Technology, Humanity, 1967," quoted in Tsuchiya Masaaki, "Takeuchi Yoshimi to bunka daigakumei: eiga, yoake no kuni wo megutte" [Takeuchi Yoshimi and the Cultural Revolution: Concerning the film *The Country at Daybreak*], in *Mokugeki bunga daigakumei: eiga yoake no kuni wo yomi toku*, ed. Suzuki Hitoshi, Nakajima Takahiro, Maeda Toshiaki, and Shimozawa Kazuyoshi (Tokyo: Ohta shuppan, 2008), 24.

139. Yamada Keiji, "Chūgoku shisō ni tsuite" [On Chinese thought] (1967), quoted in Tsuchiya, "Takeuchi Yoshimi to bunka daigakumei," 23.

140. Yamada, "Chūgoku shisō ni tsuite," 24.

141. Yamada Keiji, "The Establishment of the Theory of the Commune State: It Is Right to Rebel," *Sekai* (September 1967): 114.

142. The "Shanghai Commune" refers to a worker organization modeled on the Paris Commune that promoted the ideals of self-government. It was established in January 1967 and lasted less than a month.

143. Niijima Atsuyoshi, "Chūgoku komyūn" [China commune], in *Motakuto no shiso* [Mao Zedong thought] (Tokyo: Keiso shobo shuppansha, 1968), 425.

144. Niijima, "Chūgoku komyūn," 425.

145. Niijima, "Chūgoku komyūn," 426.

146. Takeuchi Yoshimi, "Chūgoku kakumei no shinten to nichū kankei" [The development of the Chinese Revolution and China-Japan relations], in *Takeuchi Yoshimi zenshū*, 4:381.

147. Takeuchi Yoshimi, "Meiji isshin to Chūgoku kakumei" [The Meiji Restoration and the Chinese Revolution] (1967), in *Takeuchi Yoshimi serekushon 2 Ajia he/kara no manazashi* [Takeuchi Yoshimi, selections, vol. 2, Looking from Asia], ed. Marukawa Tetsushi and Suzuki Masahisa (Tokyo: Nihon keizaisha, 2007), 330.

148. Takeuchi Yoshimi, "Rekishi no naka no ajia," in *Jōkyō teki*, 212.

149. Takeuchi Yoshimi, "Shisō to jōkyō" [Thought and conditions], in *Jōkyō teki*, 74.

Chapter Six

1. Viren Murthy, "Modernity against Modernity: Wang Hui's Critical History of Modern Chinese Thought," *Modern Intellectual History* 3, no. 1 (2006): 137–65.

2. Wang Hui, *The End of the Revolution: China and the Limits of Modernity*, ed. Rebecca Karl (London: Verso, 2009), 30.

3. Wang, *The End of the Revolution*, 42–43.

4. Wang Hui, "Chaoxian bandao heping qiji yu dongbeiya tuanjie zhengzhi de keneng" [The peace in the Korean peninsula and the possibility of a politics of unity in Northeast Asia], *Wenhua zongheng* (October 2018), https://www.sohu.com/a/258976554_425345.

5. Wang, "Chaoxian bandao heping."

6. See Steven B. Smith, *Hegel's Critique of Liberalism: Rights in Context* (Chicago: University of Chicago Press, 1991).

7. See Roberto Mangabeira Unger and Cui Zhiyuan, "China in the Russian Mirror," *New Left Review* 208 (1994): 78–87.

8. Wang Hui, "The Year 1989 and the Historical Roots of Neoliberalism in China," in *The End of the Revolution*, 51.

9. V. I. Lenin, "The Right of Nations to Self-Determination," in *Collected Works* (Moscow: Progress Publishers, 1964), 20:406.

10. Wang Hui, "Twentieth-Century China as an Object of Thought: An Introduction, Part 1: The Birth of the Century: The Chinese Revolution and the Logic of Politics," *Modern China* 46, no. 1 (2020: 14–15.

11. Alfred W. McCoy, *In the Shadows of the American Century: The Rise and Decline of US Global Power* (Chicago: Haymarket Books, 2017), chap. 7.

12. McCoy, *In the Shadows of the American Century*, 195.

13. Eric Hobsbawm, *The Age of Extremes: A History of the World, 1914–1991* (New York: Vintage, 1996).

14. Hobsbawm, *The Age of Extremes*, 34.

15. Wang Hui, "Twentieth-Century China as an Object of Thought: An Introduction, Part 2: The Birth of the Century: China and the Conditions of Spatial Revolution," *Modern China* 46, no. 2 (2020): 132.

16. This culminates in Takeuchi's suggestion that Cuba could be part of Asia.

17. Wang, "Twentieth-Century China as an Object of Thought: Part 2," 140.

18. For a recent discussion of Liu Xiaofeng, see Hang Tu, "From Christian Transcendence to the Maoist Sublime: Liu Xiaofeng, the Chinese Straussians and the Conservative Revolt against Modernity," *Modern Intellectual History* (2022): 1–22.

19. G. W. F. Hegel, *The Philosophy of History*, trans. J. Sibree (Kitchener, ON: Batoche Books, 2001), 472. For a discussion of this contention, see Joachim Ritter, *Hegel and the French Revolution: Essays on the Philosophy of Right*, trans. Richard Dien Winfield (Cambridge, MA: MIT Press, 1984), and Rebecca Comay, *Mourning Sickness: Hegel and the French Revolution* (Stanford, CA: Stanford University Press, 2010).

20. G. W. F. Hegel, *Elements of the Philosophy of Right*, trans. H. B. Nisbet, ed. Allen W. Wood (Cambridge, UK: Cambridge University Press, 1991), 267–69. For a discussion of Hegel's view of colonization in relation to the sea, see Ritter, *Hegel and the French Revolution*, 71–72.

21. Wang, "Twentieth-Century China as an Object of Thought: Part 2," 141.

22. Wang, "Twentieth-Century China as an Object of Thought: Part 2," 143. The interpolation within brackets is Wang Hui's.

23. Wang, "Twentieth-Century China as an Object of Thought: Part 2," 143; Lu Xun, "Wenhua pianzhi lun" [On the extremes of cultural development], in *Lu Xun quanji* (Beijing: Renmin wenxue chubanshe), 57.

NOTES TO PAGES 203-211

24. Wang, "Twentieth-Century China as an Object of Thought: Part 2," 143–44.

25. Loren Goldman, "Left Hegelian Variations: On the Matter of Revolution in Marx, Bloch and Althusser," *Pratyka Teortyczna* 1, no. 35 (2020): 64.

26. Wang, "Twentieth-Century China as an Object of Thought: Part 2," 144.

27. Wang, "Twentieth-Century China as an Object of Thought: Part 2," 144.

28. Wang Hui, *China's Twentieth Century*, ed. Saul Thomas (London: Verso, 2016), 136–37.

29. Wang, *China's Twentieth Century*, 139–40.

30. Wang, *China's Twentieth Century*, 139–40.

31. Wang, 128.

32. Wang, 130.

33. Wang, 143.

34. Wang, 143–44.

35. See Shen Zhihua, *Mao, Stalin and the Korean War: Trilateral Communist Relations in the 1950s*, trans. Neil Silver (London: Routledge, 2012).

36. Shen Zhihua, "Revisiting Stalin and Mao's Motivations in the Korean War," Sources and Methods (blog), June 22, 2020, Wilson Center, https://www.wilsoncenter.org/blog-post /revisiting-stalins-and-maos-motivations-korean-war.

37. Shen Zhihua and Yafeng Xia, *A Misunderstood Friendship: Mao Zedong, Kim Il-Sung and Sino–North Korean Relations 1949-1976*, trans. Yafeng Xia (New York: Columbia University Press, 2018), 8.

38. See Enzo Traverso, *Left-Wing Melancholia: Marxism, History and Memory* (New York: Columbia University Press, 2017), and Viren Murthy, "Conjuring Hope Out of Leftist Melancholy: Thinking through Recent Scholarship on Neo-liberalism and the Legacy of Socialism," *Journal of Labor and Society* 21 (2018): 231–53.

39. Wang, "Twentieth-Century China as an Object of Thought: Part 2," 146.

40. Zhang Xin, "Chinese Capitalism and the Maritime Silk Road: A World-Systems Perspective," *Geopolitics* 22, no. 2 (2017): 310–31.

41. Prasenjit Duara, "The Chinese World Order in Historical Perspective: The Imperialism of Nations or Soft Power," *China and the World: Ancient and Modern Silk Road* 2, no. 4 (2020): 1–33.

42. Wang Hui, "Ershi shiji yichan yu yidai yilu" [The legacy of the twentieth century and the Belt-Road Initiative], *Wenhua zongheng* (February 2015), http://www.m4.cn/opinion/2015 -02/1263367.shtml.

43. Wang, "Ershi shiji yichan yu yidai yilu."

44. Xi Jinping, "Working Together to Forge a New Partnership of Win-Win Cooperation and Create a Community of Shared Future for Mankind," speech delivered at the United Nations, September 28, 2015, https://gadebate.un.org/sites/default/files/gastatements/70/70_ZH_en.pdf.

45. Wang Hui and Zang Xiaojia, "Zoujin 'yidai yilu': kuatixide wenming jiaohui yu lishi xushu—Interview with Professor Wang Hui" [Approaching "One Belt, One Road": Trans-systemic civilizational interaction and historical narrative], *Xibei gongye daxue xuebao* 1 (2018): 47.

46. Wang and Zang, "Zoujin 'yidai yilu,'" 46.

47. Lucian Pye, *International Relations in Asia: Culture, Nation and State* (Washington, DC: Sigur Center of Asian Studies, 1998).

48. Wang and Zang, "Zoujin 'yidai yilu,'" 46.

49. Wang and Zang, "Zoujin 'yidai yilu,'" 46.

50. Wang and Zang, "Zoujin 'yidai yilu,'" 51.

51. Radhika Desai, "The Last Empire? From Nation-Building Compulsion to Nation-Wrecking Futility and Beyond," *Third World Quarterly* 28, no. 2 (2007): 435–56.

52. Wang and Zang, "Zoujin 'yidai yilu,'" 52.

Epilogue

1. I would like to thank Zhang Ling for bringing these films to my attention.

2. Dong Kena, *Qingchun sihuo* [Youth Is Like Fire] (Beijing Film Studio, 1976).

3. For an argument that Maoist China was capitalistic, see Jake Werner, "Global Fordism in 1950s Urban China," *Frontiers of History in China* 7, no. 3 (2012): 415–41.

4. Because this is a short epilogue, I am not mentioning works in economic or social history, but for a recent intervention along these lines, see Andrew B. Liu, *Tea War: A History of Capitalism in China and India* (New Haven, CT: Yale University Press, 2020). In short, Liu uses an understanding of the abstract dynamic of capital to argue that China and India were operating under the logic of capital. (He refrains from saying that China and India were capitalist.)

5. Andrew F. Jones, *Circuit Listening: Chinese Popular Music in the Global 1960s* (Minneapolis: University of Minnesota Press, 2020), 4.

6. Jones, *Circuit Listening*, 5.

7. Michel-Rolph Trouillot, "The Anthropology of the State in the Age of Globalization: Close Encounters of the Deceptive Kind," *Current Anthropology* 42, no. 1 (2001): 128.

8. Moishe Postone, *Time, Labor and Social Domination: A Reinterpretation of Marx's Critical Theory* (Cambridge, UK: Cambridge University Press, 1993). See also Viren Murthy, "Beyond Particularity and Universality: Moishe Postone and Jewish Marxism," *Jewish Social Studies: History, Culture and Society* 25, no. 2 (2020): 127–67.

9. Viren Murthy, *The Political Philosophy of Zhang Taiyan: The Resistance of Consciousness* (Leiden: Brill, 2011).

10. Frederic Jameson, "Periodizing the 60s," *Social Text*, no. 9/10 (Spring–Summer 1984): 185.

11. Jameson, "Periodizing the 60s," 185.

12. Jameson, "Periodizing the 60s," 183. Jones's discussion of Teressa Teng also implies something like a counter-revolutionary moment, which in turn could lead to a retheorizing of "moments." Jones, *Circuit Listening*, 169–97.

13. Steven Bognar and Julia Reichert, *American Factory* (Higher Ground Productions, 2019).

14. Gopal Balakrishnan, "Swan Song of the Ultraleft," *Sublation Magazine*, May 30, 2022, https://www.sublationmag.com/post/swan-song-of-the-ultraleft.

15. Obviously, part of the reason for this is the increasing proliferation of a precariat and chronic underemployment. However, this in itself cannot explain why the unemployment rate after the pandemic is lower than before the pandemic.

16. In a forthcoming manuscript, Devin Kennedy argues that in addition to efficiency, American capitalists in the 1950s and 1960s were interested in computers because of the role they could play in planning. This was of course the role of technology in military affairs, but Kennedy shows the extent to which this was the case in business as well. Devin Kennedy, *Virtual Capital: Computing Capital in the US Economy* (New York: Columbia University Press, forthcoming).

17. Leo Panitch and Sam Gindin, *The Making of Global Capitalism: The Political Economy of the American Empire* (London: Verso, 2013).

18. Xi Jinping, "Gaoju zhongguo tese shehuizhuyi weida qizhi wei quanmian jianshe shehuizhuyi xiandaihua guojia er tuanjie fendou: zai zhongguo gongchandang di ershi ci quanguo

NOTE TO PAGE 220

daibiao dahui shang de baogao" [Raise high the great flag of socialism with Chinese characteristics to fully establish modern socialism and unite in struggle: Report at the Twentieth Annual Party Congress of the Chinese Communist Party], *Xinhuawang*, October 16, 2022, http://www.ce.cn/xwzx/gnsz/szyw/202210/25/t20221025_38192574.shtml.

19. On this point, Cui Zhiyuan's classic essay on the politics of the cultural revolution is essential reading. See Cui Zhiyuan, "Mao Zedong wenge lilun de deshi yu xiandaixing chongjian" [The good and bad points of Mao Zedong's theory of the Cultural Revolution and the reconsitution of modernity], *Wu you zhi xiang/Utopia*, September 2009, http://www.wyzxwk.com/Article/sichao/2009/09/52236.html. (The article was originally published in 1997.)

Bibliography

Adams, Nicholas. "Hegel's China: On God and Beauty." Unpublished manuscript. Accessed August 9, 2020. https://www.academia.edu/16888871/Hegels_China_on_God_and_beauty.

Adas, Michael. "Contested Hegemonies: The Great War and the Afro-Asian Assault on the Civilizing Mission Ideology." In *Decolonization: Perspectives from Now and Then*, edited by Prasenjit Duara, 78–101. London: Routledge, 2003.

Allinson, Jamie C., and Alexander Anievas. "The Uneven and Combined Development of the Meiji Restoration: A Passive Revolutionary Road to Capitalist Modernity." *Capital and Class* 34, no. 3 (2010): 469–90.

Althusser, Louis. *Lenin and Philosophy and Other Essays*. New York: Monthly Review Press, 1971.

Anderson, Kevin. *Marx at the Margins: On Nationalism, Ethnicity, and Non-Western Societies*. Chicago: University of Chicago Press, 2016.

Anderson, Mark. 2009. *Japan and the Specter of Imperialism*. New York: Palgrave Macmillan, 2009.

Arrighi, Giovanni. *Adam Smith in Beijing: Lineages of the Twenty-First Century*. London: Verso, 2009.

Avenell, Simon Andrew. *Making Japanese Citizens: Civil Society and the Mythology of the Shimin in Postwar Japan*. Berkeley: University of California Press, 2010.

Aydin, Cemil. *The Politics of Anti-Westernism in Asia: Visions of World Order in Pan-Islamic and Pan-Asian Thought*. New York: Columbia University Press, 2007.

———. "The Politics of Civilizational Identities: Asia, West and Islam in the Pan-Asianist Thought of Ōkawa Shūmei." PhD diss., Harvard University, 2002.

Baba Kimihiko. *Sengo nihonjin no chūgoku zō: nihon haisen kara bunkadaigakumei/nichūfukkō made* [Postwar Japanese people's image of China: From the Japanese loss in the war to the Cultural Revolution/resumption of diplomatic relations between Japan and China]. Tokyo: Shinyōsha, 2010.

Babicz, Lionel. "Fukuzawa Yukichi to Yono-sama: The Nostalgic Image of Korea in Modern and Contemporary Japan." Unpublished manuscript, 2006.

Balakrishnan, Gopal. "Swan Song of the Ultraleft." *Sublation Magazine*, May 30, 2022. https://www.sublationmag.com/post/swan-song-of-the-ultraleft.

Barnett, Yukiko Sumi. "India in Asia: Ōkawa Shūmei's Pan-Asianism Thought and His Idea of India in Early Twentieth-Century Japan." *Journal of the Oxford University History Society* 2 (2004): 1–22.

Bhaba, Homi K. *The Location of Culture*. London: Routledge, 2004.

Bharucha, Rustom. *Another Asia: Rabindranath Tagore and Okakura Tenshin*. Oxford: Oxford University Press, 2006.

Bhaskar, Roy. *Dialectics: The Pulse of Freedom*. London: Verso, 1994.

Bidet, Jacques. *État monde: Libéralisme, socialisme et communisme à l'échelle globale*. Paris: PUF, 2010.

———. *Explication et reconstruction du Capital*. Paris: PUF, 2004.

Bostock, David. *Space, Time, Matter and Form: Essays on Aristotle's Physics*. Oxford: Oxford University Press, 2006.

Bowman, Brady. *Hegel and the Metaphysics of Absolute Negativity*. Cambridge, UK: Cambridge University Press, 2013.

Brennan, Timothy. "Cosmopolitanism and Internationalism." *New Left Review* 13 (January–February 2001): 75–84.

Bronson, Adam. *One Hundred Million Philosophers: Science of Thought and the Culture of Postwar Democracy in Japan*. Honolulu: University of Hawai'i Press, 2016.

Buchwalter, Andrew. "Is Hegel's Philosophy of History Eurocentric?" In *Hegel and History*, edited by William Dudley, 87–110. Albany: State University of New York Press, 2010.

Buck-Morss, Susan. "Hegel and Haiti." *Critical Inquiry* 26, no. 4 (2000): 821–65.

Burns, Susan. *Before the Nation: Kokugaku and the Imagining of the Community in Early Modern Japan*. Durham, NC: Duke University Press, 2003.

Buruma, Ian, and Avishai Margalit. *Occidentalism: The West in the Eyes of Its Enemies*. New York: Penguin, 2004.

Calichman, Richard F. *The Coming Death: Traces of Mortality across East Asia*. Albany: State University of New York Press, 2022.

———. *Takeuchi Yoshimi: Displacing the West*. Ithaca, NY: Cornell University Press, 2010.

Chakrabarty, Dipesh. *Provincializing Europe: Postcolonial Thought and Historical Difference*. Princeton, NJ: Princeton University Press, 2000.

Chatterjee, Partha. "Response to Charles Taylor's Modes of Civil Society." *Public Culture* 3, no. 1 (1990): 119–32.

Chen Duxiu. "Jingao qingnian" [Warning the youth]. In *Xin Qingnian* [The new youth], edited by Wang Zhongjiang and Wan Shuya, 26–33. Zhongzhou: Zhongzhou guji chubanshe, 1999 [1915].

Chen Kuan-hsing. *Asia as Method: Towards De-imperialism*. Durham, NC: Duke University Press, 2010.

Chow, Kai-wing. *Xinmin yu fuxing: Jindai zhongguo sixiang shilun* [New people and revival: Interpreting modern Chinese intellectual history]. Hong Kong: Xianggang jiaoyu tushu gongsi, 1999.

Clark, T. J. *The Painting of Modern Life: Paris in the Art of Manet and His Followers*. Rev. ed. Princeton, NJ: Princeton University Press, 1999.

Comay, Rebecca. *Mourning Sickness: Hegel and the French Revolution*. Stanford, CA: Stanford University Press, 2010.

Confucius. *Lunyu yizhu, Yang Bojun yizhu* [*Analects* with notes and translation by Yang Bojun]. Beijing: Zhonghua shuju, 2002.

Cotton, Henry John Stedman. *New India or India in Transition*. London: Kegan Paul, 1885.

Crawford, Oliver. "Hegel and the Orient." Unpublished manuscript. Accessed August 9, 2020. https://www.academia.edu/4985405/Hegel_and_the_Orient.

BIBLIOGRAPHY

Cui Zhiyuan. "Mao Zedong wenge lilun de deshi yu xiandaixing chongjian" [The good and bad points of Mao Zedong's theory of the Cultural Revolution and the reconstitution of modernity]. *Wu you zhi xiang/Utopia,* September 2009. http://www.wyzxwk.com/Article /sichao/2009/09/52236.html.

Derrida, Jacques. *Dissemination.* Translated by Barbara Johnson. Chicago: University of Chicago Press, 2017.

Desai, Radhika. "The Last Empire? From Nation-Building Compulsion to Nation-Wrecking Futility and Beyond." *Third World Quarterly* 28, no. 2 (2007): 435–56.

Dirlik, Arif. *Anarchism in the Chinese Revolution.* Berkeley: University of California Press, 1991.

Doak, Kevin. *A History of Nationalism in Modern Japan: Placing the People.* Leiden: Brill, 2007.

Driscoll, Mark. *The Whites Are Enemies of Heaven: Climate Caucasianism and Asian Ecological Protection.* Durham, NC: Duke University Press, 2021.

Duara, Prasenjit. "The Chinese World Order in Historical Perspective: The Imperialism of Nations or Soft Power." *China and the World: Ancient and Modern Silk Road* 2, no. 4 (2020): 1–33.

———. *The Crisis of Global Modernity: Asian Traditions and a Sustainable Future.* Cambridge, UK: Cambridge University Press, 2015.

———. "The Discourse of Civilization and Pan-Asianism." *Journal of World History* 12, no. 1 (2001): 99–130.

———. *Rescuing History from the Nation: Questioning Narratives of Modern China.* Chicago: University of Chicago Press, 1995.

———. *Sovereignty and Authenticity: Manchukuo and the East Asian Modern.* Lanham, MD: Rowman and Littlefield, 2004.

Fasolt, Constantin. *The Limits of History.* Chicago: University of Chicago Press, 2003.

Fischer-Tiné, Harald. "Indian Nationalism and the 'World Forces': Transnational and Diasporic Dimensions of the Indian Freedom Movement on the Eve of the First World War." *Journal of Global History* 3 (2007): 325–44.

Fogel, Joshua. *Politics and Sinology: The Case of Naitō Konan (1866–1934).* Cambridge, MA: Harvard University Press, 1984.

Fukuzawa Yukichi. *The Autobiography of Yukichi Fukuzawa.* Translated by Eiichi Kiyooka. New York: Columbia University Press, 1966 [1899].

———. *Bunmeiron no gairyaku.* Tokyo: Iwanami bunko, 2004.

———. "Datsu-a ron" [On leaving Asia]. In vol. 10 of *Fukuzawa Yukichi zenshū,* 238–40. Tokyo: Iwanami shoten, 1952.

———. *An Outline of a Theory of Civilization.* Translated by David A. Dilworth and G. Cameron Hurst III. New York: Columbia University Press, 2009.

Fynsk, Christopher. *Heidegger: Thought and Historicity.* Ithaca, NY: Cornell University Press, 1986.

Gandhi, M. K. *Hind Swaraj and Other Writings.* Edited by Anthony J. Parel. Cambridge, UK: Cambridge University Press, 2009.

Garon, Sheldon. *The State and Labor in Modern Japan.* Berkeley: University of California Press, 1990.

Gayle, Curtis. "China in the Japanese Radical Gaze, 1945–1955." *Modern Asian Studies* 43, no. 5 (2009): 1255–86.

Geroulanos, Stefanos. *An Atheism That Is Not Humanist in French Thought.* Stanford, CA: Stanford University Press, 2010.

Ghose, H. P. Introduction to *The Two Great Indians in Japan: Sri Rash Behari Bose and Netaji Subhas Chandra Bose* by J. G. Ohsawa, v–xi. Calcutta: Kusa Publications, 1954.

Goldman, Loren. "Left Hegelian Variations: On the Matter of Revolution in Marx, Bloch and Althusser." *Pratyka Teortyczna* 1, no. 35 (2020): 51–74.

Gordon, Andrew. *Modern Japanese History*. Oxford: Oxford University Press, 2003.

Goswami, Manu. *Producing India*. Chicago: University of Chicago Press, 2004.

Guan Yun. "Pingdengshuo yu zhongguo jiu lunli de zhongtu" [The theory of equality and its conflict with the old Chinese morality]. In *Xinhai geming qian shinian jian shilun xuanji* [Selected commentations during the decade before the Revolution of 1911], vol. 2, 21–29. Beijing: Sanlian chubanshe, 1977.

Guex, Samuel. *Entre nonchalance et désespoir: Les intellectuels japonais sinologues face à la guerre (1930–1950)*. Bern: Peter Lang, 2006.

Hägglund, Martin. "The Autoimmunity of Religion." In *The Trace of God: Derrida and Religion*, edited by Deward Baring and Peter E. Gordon, 178–98. New York: Fordham University Press, 2015.

Hammond, Kelly A. *China's Muslims and Japan's Empire: Centering Islam in World War II*. Chapel Hill: University of North Carolina Press, 2020.

Hardacre, Helen. *Shinto and the State, 1968–1988*. Princeton, NJ: Princeton University Press, 1991.

Hardt, Michael, and Antonio Negri. *Empire*. Cambridge, MA: Harvard University Press, 2001.

Harootunian, Harry D. "The Function of China in Tokugawa Thought." In *The Chinese and the Japanese: Essays in Political and Cultural Interactions*, edited by Akira Iriye, 9–36. Princeton, NJ: Princeton University Press, 1980.

———. *Marx after Marx: History and Time in the Expansion of Capitalism*. New York: Columbia University Press, 2017.

———. *Overcome by Modernity: History, Culture and Community in Interwar Japan*. Princeton, NJ: Princeton University Press, 2000.

———. "Tracking the Dinosaur: Area Studies in a Time of Globalism." In *History's Disquiet: Modernity, Cultural Practice and the Question of Everyday Life*, 25–59. New York: Columbia University Press, 2000.

Hazama Naoki and Matsumoto Kennichi. "Shō heirin to meiji no 'ajiashugi'" [Zhang Binglin and Meiji pan-Asianism]. *Chishiki* (August 1990): 248–80.

Hegel, G. W. F. *Aesthetics: Lectures on Fine Art*. Vol. 1. Translated by T. M Knox. Oxford: Oxford University Press, 1988.

———. *Elements of the Philosophy of Right*. Translated by H. B. Nisbet. Edited by Allen W. Wood. Cambridge, UK: Cambridge University Press, 1991.

———. *The Encyclopaedia Logic*. Translated by T. F. Geraets, W. A. Suchting, and H. S. Harris Indianapolis: Hackett, 1991.

———. *Phänomenologie des Geistes*. Frankfurt am Main: Suhrkamp, 1986.

———. *The Phenomenology of Spirit*. Translated by Terry Pinkard. Cambridge, UK: Cambridge University Press, 2018.

———. *The Philosophy of History*. Translated by J. Sibree. Kitchener, ON: Batoche Books, 2001.

———. *The Philosophy of World History*. Translated by J. Sibree. New York: Dover, 1956.

———. *The Science of Logic*. Translated by George Di Giovanni. Cambridge, UK: Cambridge University Press, 2010.

———. *Vorlesung über die Ästhetik*. Frankfurt am Main: Suhrkamp, 1986.

———. *Vorlesung über die Philosophie der Geschichte*. Frankfurt am Main: Suhrkamp, 1986.

BIBLIOGRAPHY

Heidegger, Martin. *Being and Time*. Translated by John Macquarrie and Edward Robinson. Oxford: Blackwell, 2001.

———. "Origin of the Artwork." In *Poetry, Language and Thought*, 15–87. Translated by Albert Hofstadter. New York: Harper & Row, 1971.

Hobsbawm, Eric. *The Age of Extremes: A History of the World, 1914–1991*. New York: Vintage, 1996.

Hotta, Eri. *Pan-Asianism and Japan's War 1931–1945*. New York: Palgrave Macmillan, 2007.

———. "Rash Behari Bose and His Japanese Supporters: An Insight into Anti-colonial Nationalism and Pan-Asianism." *Interventions* 8, no. 1 (2006): 116–32.

Inaga Shigemi. "Okakura Kakuzō's Nostalgic Journey to India and the Invention of Asia." In *Nostalgic Journeys: Literary Pilgrimages between Japan and the West*, edited by Susan Fisher, 119–32. Vancouver: Institute of Asian Research, University of British Columbia, 2001.

Izutsu Toshihiko. "Isulamu no futatsu no kao: jikyoku teki kanshiin wo koeru isulamu shukyo" [Two faces of Islam: Islam beyond concerns with the current state of affairs]. *Chūō kōron* 95, no. 9 (1980): 70–92.

Jameson, Frederic. "Future City." *New Left Review* 21 (May–June 2003): 65–79.

———. "Periodizing the 60s." *Social Text*, no. 9/10 (Spring–Summer 1984): 178–209.

Jones, Andrew F. *Circuit Listening: Chinese Popular Music in the Global 1960s*. Minneapolis: University of Minnesota Press, 2020.

Kaji Wataru. "Takeuchi Yoshimi no bungaku shisō: rojin wo megutte" [The literary thought of Takeuchi Yoshimi: With reference to Lu Xun]. *Minshu bungaku* 28 (March 1968): 70–88.

Kaneko, Toshiya. "Cultural Light, Political Shadow: Okakura Tenshin (1862–1913) and the Japanese Crisis of National Identity, 1880–1941." PhD diss., University of Pennsylvania, 2002.

Kang Youwei. *Kang Youwei zhenglunji* [A collection of Kang Youwei's political writings]. Vol. 1. Beijing: Zhonghua shuju, 1981.

Karatani Kojin. *The Structure of World History: From Modes of Production to Modes of Exchange*. Translated by Michael Bourdaghs. Durham, NC: Duke University Press, 2014.

Karl, Rebecca. *Staging the World: Chinese Nationalism at the Turn of the Twentieth Century*. Durham, NC: Duke University Press, 2002.

Kawamura, Satofumi. "The National Polity and the Formation of the Modern National Subject in Japan." *Japan Forum* 26, no. 1 (2014): 25–45.

Kennedy, Devin. *Virtual Capital: Computing Capital in the US Economy*. New York: Columbia University Press, forthcoming.

Kierkegaard, Søren. *Philosophical Fragments*. Lexington: Feather Trail Press, 2009.

Kojima Tsuyoshi. *Kindai nihon no yōmeigaku* [Modern Japanese Yangming studies]. Tokyo: Kodansha, 2006.

Konishi, Sho. "Translingual World Order: Language without Culture in Post-Russo-Japanese War Japan." *Journal of Asian Studies* 72, no. 1 (2013): 91–114.

Koyasu Nobukuni. *Kindai no chōkoku to ha nanika* [What is modern China?]. Tokyo: Seidosha, 2008.

Kurokawa Midori. "Dore kara no dakkyaku wo motomete: sengo shakai no naka de" [Attempting to break free from slavery: In the midst of postwar society]. In *Takeuchi Yoshimi to sono jidai: rekishigaku kara no taiwa* [Takeuchi Yoshimi and his times: Dialogues from historiography], edited by Kurokawa Midori and Yamada Satoshi, 88–212. Tokyo: Yūshisha, 2018.

Laplanche, Jean. *Essays on Otherness*. Translated by John Fletcher. London: Routledge, 1999.

Lee, Haiyan. *Revolutions of the Heart: A Genealogy of Love in China 1900–1950*. Stanford, CA: Stanford University Press, 2010.

Lee, Leo Oufan. "Literature on the Eve of the Revolution: Reflections on Lu Xun's Leftist Years, 1927–1936." *Modern China* 2, no. 3 (1977): 277–326.

Lenin, V. I. *Collected Works*. Vol. 20. Moscow: Progress Publishers, 1964.

Li Dazhao. "Da yazhouzhuyi" [Big Asianism]. In *Li Dazhao quanji*, 2:106–8.

———. "Dayazhouzhuyi yu xinyazhouzhuyi" [Great pan-Asianism and new pan-Asianism]. In *Li Dazhao quanji*, 2:269–72.

———. "Eguo geming zhi yuanyin jinyin" [The remote and proximate causes of the Russian Revolution]. In *Li Dazhao quanji*, 2:1–10.

———. *Li Dazhao quanji* [Complete works of Li Dazhao]. 3 vols. Beijing: Renmin chubanshe, 2006.

———. "Zai lun xinyazhouzhuyi" [Another discussion of new pan-Asianism]. In *Li Dazhao quanji*, 3:74–79.

Li Zehou. *Zhongguo xiandai sixiangshi lun* [On modern Chinese intellectual history]. Anhui: Anhui chubanshe, 1991.

Lin Shaoyang. *Dingge yi wen: qingji geming yu Zhang Taiyan "fugu" de xinwenhua yundong* [Revolution by means of culture: Zhang Taiyan's new culture movement and "returning to the ancient past"]. Shanghai: Shanghai renmin chubanshe, 2018.

———. "Romanticism, History and Aestheticized Politics: Yasuda Yojūrō and the Discourse of Overcoming the Modern in Wartime Japan." *Studies of Intellectual History* 13 (2011): 173–214.

———. "Zhang Taiyan 'zizhu' de lianya sixiang" [Zhang Taiyan's ideas of independence and Asian unity]. *Quyu* 1, no. 3 (2014): 201–27.

Linkhoeva, Tatiana. *Revolution Goes East: Imperial Japan and Soviet Communism*. Ithaca, NY: Cornell University Press, 2020.

Lippman, Walter. *The Phantom Public*. New York: Harcourt, 1925.

Liu, Andrew B. *Tea War: A History of Capitalism in China and India*. New Haven, CT: Yale University Press, 2020.

Liu, Lydia H. *Translingual Practice: Literature, National Culture and Translated Modernity—China, 1900–1937*. Berkeley: University of California Press, 1995.

Liu Xi. "Kang Youwei's Journey to India: Chinese Discourse on India during the Late Qing and Republican Periods." *China Report* 48 (2012): 171–85.

Löwy, Michael. *Jewish Libertarian Thought in Central Europe: A Study in Elective Affinity*. Translated by Hope Heaney. Stanford, CA: Stanford University Press, 1988.

Lu Xun. "Wenhua pianzhi lun" [On the extremes of cultural development]. In *Lu Xun quanji*, 1:45–64. Beijing: Renmin wenxue chubanshe, 2005.

Lukács, Georg. *History and Class Consciousness: Studies in Marxist Dialectics*. Translated by Rodney Livingston. Cambridge, MA: MIT Press, 1971.

Mackinder, Halford. *Democratic Ideals and Reality*. New York: Holt, 1919.

———. "The Geographical Pivot of History." *Geographical Journal* 23, no. 4 (1904): 421–44.

Mahbubani, Kishore. *Can Asians Think?* London: Marshal Cavendish, 2009.

Mandel, Ernst. *Trotsky as Alternative*. Translated by Gus Fagan. London: Verso, 1995.

Manela, Erez. *The Wilsonian Moment: Self-Determination and the Origins of Anti-colonial Nationalism*. Oxford: Oxford University Press, 2007.

Mao Zedong. "The Foolish Old Man Who Removed the Mountains." In vol. 3 of *Selected Works of Mao Tse-tung*, 217–73. Beijing: Foreign Languages Press, 1965.

———. "Yu Gong yi shan." In vol. 2 of *Mao Zedong xuanji*, 1101–4. Beijing: Renmin chubanshe, 1991.

BIBLIOGRAPHY

Marasco, Robyn. *The Highway of Despair: Critical Theory after Hegel*. New York: Columbia University Press, 2015.

Marchand, Susan. *German Orientalism in the Age of Empire: Religion, Race, and Scholarship*. Cambridge, UK: Cambridge University Press. 2009.

Marmasse, Gilles. *L'histoire hégélienne: Entre malheur et réconciliation*. Paris: Vrin, 2015.

Martin, Bill. *Ethical Marxism: The Categorical Imperative of Liberation*. Chicago: Open Court, 2008.

Maruyama Masao. "Nationalism in Japan: Its Theoretical Background and Prospects." Translated by David Titus. In *Thought and Behaviour in Modern Japanese Politics*, edited by Ivan Morris, 135–56. Oxford: Oxford University Press, 1969.

Marx, Karl. *Capital: Volume One*. Translated by Ben Fowkes. New York: Penguin, 1990.

———. "The Manifesto of the Communist Party." In *The Marx-Engels Reader*, edited by Robert C. Tucker, 469–501. New York: W. W. Norton, 1978.

McCarraher, Eugene. *The Enchantments of Mammon: How Capitalism Became the Religion of Modernity*. Cambridge, MA: Belknap of Harvard University Press, 2019.

McCoy, Alfred W. *In the Shadows of the American Century: The Rise and Decline of US Global Power*. Chicago: Haymarket Books, 2017.

Mehl, Margaret. "Chinese Learning (*kangaku*) in Meiji Japan (1868–1912)." *History* 85 (2000): 48–66.

Mimura, Jasis. *Planning for Empire: Reform Bureaucrats and the Japanese Wartime State*. Ithaca, NY: Cornell University Press, 2011.

Mishra, Pankaj. *From the Ruins of Empire: The Intellectuals Who Remade Asia*. New York: Farrar, Straus and Giroux, 2012.

Miyagi, Taizo. "Postwar Japan and Asianism." *Asian Pacific Review* 13, no. 2 (2006): 1–16.

Mizoguchi Yūzō. *Hoho to shite no chūgoku* [China as method]. Tokyo: Tokyo daigaku shuppansha, 1989.

Murthy, Viren. "Beyond Particularity and Universality: Moishe Postone and Jewish Marxism." *Jewish Social Studies: History, Culture and Society* 25, no. 2 (2020): 127–67.

———. "Conjuring Hope Out of Leftist Melancholy: Thinking through Recent Scholarship on Neo-liberalism and the Legacy of Socialism." *Journal of Labor and Society* 21 (2018): 231–53.

———. "Imagining Asia and the Chinese Revolution: Takeuchi Yoshimi and His Transnational Afterlives." In *East-Asian Marxisms and Their Trajectories*, edited by Joyce H. Liu and Viren Murthy, 195–215. London: Routledge, 2017.

———. "Looking for Resistance in All the Wrong Places: Chibber, Chakrabarty and a Tale of Two Histories." *Critical Historical Studies* 2 (Spring 2015): 113–53.

———. "Modernity against Modernity: Wang Hui's Critical History of Modern Chinese Thought." *Modern Intellectual History* 3, no. 1 (2006): 137–65.

———. "The 1911 Revolution and the Politics of Failure: Takeuchi Yoshimi and Global Capitalist Modernity." *Frontiers of Literature in China* 6, no. 1 (2012): 19–38.

———. *The Political Philosophy of Zhang Taiyan: The Resistance of Consciousness*. Leiden: Brill, 2011.

———. "The Politics of *Fengjian* in Late Qing and Early Republican China." In *Beyond the May Fourth Paradigm: In Search of Chinese Modernity*, edited by Kai-wing Chow, Tze-ki Hon, Hung-yok Ip, and Don. C. Price, 151–82. Lanham, MD: Lexington Books, 2008.

———. "The Politics of Time in China and Japan." In *The Oxford Handbook of Comparative Political Theory*, edited by Leigh K. Jenco, Murad Idris, and Megan C. Thomas, 191–217. Oxford: Oxford University Press, 2019.

———. *The Politics of Time in China and Japan: Back to the Future.* London: Routledge, 2022.

———. "Resistance to Modernity and the Logic of Self-negation as Politics: Takeuchi Yoshimi and Wang Hui on Lu Xun." *Positions: Asia Critique* 24, no. 2 (2016): 513–54.

Nakajima Takahiro. "The Progress of Civilization and Confucianism in Modern East Asia: Fukuzawa Yukichi and Different Forms of Enlightenment." In *Chinese Visions of Progress, 1895–1949,* edited by Thomas Fröhlich and Axel Schneider, 75–99. Leiden: Brill, 2020.

Nakajima Takeshi. *Ajiashugi: sono saki no kindai e.* Tokyo: Ushio shuppansha, 2014.

Namakkal, Jessica. "European Dreams, Tamil Land: Auroville and the Paradox of a Postcolonial Utopia." *Journal for the Study of Radicalism* 6, no. 1 (2012): 58–88.

Nandy, Ashis. *The Savage Freud and Other Essays on Possible and Retrievable Selves.* Princeton, NJ: Princeton University Press, 1995.

Niijima Atsuyoshi. *Motakuto no shiso* [Mao Zedong thought]. Tokyo: Keiso shobo shuppansha, 1968.

Ninomiya Masayuki. *La pensée de Kobayashi Hideo: Un intellectuel japonais au tournant de l'histoire.* Geneva: Dross, 1995.

Nishi Junzō. *Chosakushu.* Tokyo: Uchiyama shoten, 1995.

Notehelfer, F. G. "On Idealism and Realism in the Thought of Okakura Tenshin." *Journal of Japanese Studies* 16, no. 2 (1990): 309–55.

Oguma Eiji. *Minshu to Aikoku: sengo no nashonarisumu to kōkyūsei* [Democracy and patriotism: Postwar Japanese nationalism and publicity]. Tokyo: Shinyōsha, 2002.

Ohsawa, J. G. *The Two Great Indians in Japan: Sri Rash Behari Bose and Netaji Subhas Chandra Bose.* Calcutta: Kusa Publications, 1954.

Okakura Kakuzo (Tenshin). "The Awakening of Japan." In *Okakura Tenshin Collected English Writings,* 177–239. Tokyo: Heibonsha, 1984.

———. "The Awakening of the East." In *Okakura Tenshin Collected English Writings,* 135–65. Tokyo: Heibonsha, 1984.

———. *Ideals of the East: With Special Reference to the Art of Japan.* London: John Murray, 1903.

Ōkawa Shūmei. "Anraku no mon" [Gateway to comfort]. In *Ajiashugi,* edited by Takeuchi Yoshimi, 254–322. Tokyo: Chikuma shobō, 1963.

———. "Chūyō shinchū" [New notes on the doctrine of the mean]. In *Ōkawa Shūmei dōtoku tetsugaku kōwashū* [A collection of Ōkawa Shūmei's lectures on ethics]. Tokyo: Seitō yō, 2008.

———. "Fukkō ajia no sho mondai" [Various problems concerning reviving Asia]. In *Ajia shugishatachi no koe: yuzonsha to kōchisha* [The voices of Asianists: The Yuzonsha and the Kōchisha], 145–52. Tokyo: Shoshi shinsui, 2008.

———. "Go ichi go jiken chōsho" [An investigation of the May 15 incident]. In *Ajia shugishatachi no koe,* 105–45. Tokyo: Shoshi shinsui, 2008.

———. "Indo jin tsuihō to Tōyama Mitsuru ō" [Exiling Indians and Tōyama Mitsuru]. In *Ajia shugishatachi no koe,* 178–97. Tokyo: Shoshi shinsui, 2008.

———. "Kakumei yōroppa to fukkō ajia" [Revolution Europe and revival Asia]. In *Ajiashugi,* ed. Takeuchi Yoshimi, 239–54. Tokyo: Chikuma shobō, 1963.

———. "Kita Ikki wo omou" [Remembering Kita Ikki]. In *Ajia shugishatachi no koe,* 152–78. Tokyo: Shoshi shinsui, 2008.

———. *Ōkawa Shūmei dōtoku tetsugaku kōwashū* [A collection of Ōkawa Shūmei's lectures on ethics]. Tokyo: Seitō yō, 2008.

———. *Ōkawa Shūmei zenshū.* Vol. 2. Tokyo: Ōkawa Shūmei kankōkai, 1969.

BIBLIOGRAPHY

Okayama Asako. *Takeuchi no bungaku seishin* [Takeuchi's literary spirit]. Tokyo: Ronsōsha, 2002.

Olsen, Lawrence. *Ambivalent Moderns: Portraits of Japanese Cultural Identity*. Lanham, MD: Rowman and Littlefield, 1992.

Ōmori Mikihiko. *Nihon seijishisō kenkyū: Gondō Seikyō to Ōkawa Shūmei* [A study of Japanese political thought: Gondō Seikyō and Ōkawa Shūmei]. Tokyo: Seshiki shobō, 2010.

Onodera Shirō. *Sengo nihon no chūgokukan: ajia to kindai wo meguru kattō* [Postwar Japan's vision of China: The tensions surrounding Asia and modernity]. Tokyo: Chūō kōron shinsha, 2021.

Ōtsuka Takehiro. *Ōkawa Shūmei to kindai nihon* [Ōkawa Shūmei and modern Japan]. Tokyo: Mokutakusha, 1990.

Panitch, Leo, and Sam Gindin. *The Making of Global Capitalism: The Political Economy of the American Empire*. London: Verso, 2013.

Pinkard, Terry. *Hegel's Naturalism: Mind, Nature and the Final Ends of Life*. Oxford: Oxford University Press, 2013.

Pippin, Robert. *After the Beautiful: Hegel and the Philosophy of Pictorial Modernism*. Chicago: University of Chicago Press, 2013.

Pomeranz, Kenneth. *The Great Divergence: China, Europe and the Making of the Modern World Economy*. Princeton, NJ: Princeton University Press, 2000.

Postone, Moishe. *History and Heteronomy: Critical Essays*. Tokyo: University of Tokyo Press, 2009.

———. "Marx, Temporality and Modernity." In *East-Asian Marxisms and Their Trajectories*, edited by Joyce C. H. Liu and Viren Murthy, 29–49. London: Routledge, 2017.

———. *Time, Labor and Social Domination: A Reinterpretation of Marx's Critical Theory*. Cambridge, UK: Cambridge University Press, 1993.

Prasad, Vijay. *Darker Nations: A People's History of the Third World*. New York: New Press, 2007.

Pye, Lucian. *International Relations in Asia: Culture, Nation and State*. Washington, DC: Sigur Center of Asian Studies, 1998.

Rathore, Aakash Singh, and Rimina Mohapatra. *Hegel's India: A Reinterpretation, with Texts*. New Delhi: Oxford University Press India, 2017.

Ravina, Mark. *The Last Samurai: The Life and Battles of Saigō Takamori*. New York: Wiley, 2003.

Ritter, Joachim. *Hegel and the French Revolution: Essays on the Philosophy of Right*. Translated by Richard Dien Winfield. Cambridge, MA: MIT Press, 1984.

Sakai, Naoki. "Resistance to Conclusion: The Kyoto School Philosophy under the *Pax-Americana*." In *Repoliticizing the Kyoto School as Philosophy*, edited by Christopher Goto-Jones, 183–99. London: Routledge, 2007.

———. "The West—A Dialogic Prescription or Proscription?" *Social Identities* 11, no. 3 (2005): 177–95.

Sartori, Andrew. *Bengal in Global Concept History: Culturalism in the Age of Global Capital*. Chicago: University of Chicago Press, 2008.

Sasaki Takuya. *Aizenhawa: seiken no fujikomeseisaku—soren no kyōi, misairu/kuba ronsō to tōsai kōryū* [Eisenhower: The policy of the containment of political power—the Soviet threat, the debate about Cuban missiles, and East-West relations]. Tokyo: Yuhikaku, 2008.

Schopenhauer, Arthur. *The Essays of Arthur Schopenhauer: Studies in Pessimism*. Vol. 4. Translated by T. Bailey Saunders. University Park: Penn State Electronic Classics Series, 2005. Accessed June 27, 2022. https://www.academia.edu/5920036/THE_ESSAYS_OF_ARTHUR _SCHOPENHAUER_STUDIES_IN_PESSIMISM_Volume_Four/.

Schwartz, Benjamin. *In Search of Wealth and Power: Yen Fu and the West*. Cambridge, MA: Belknap of Harvard University Press, 1964.

Shanin, Theodor. *Late Marx and the Russian Road: Marx and the Peripheries of Capitalism*. Toronto: Monthly Review Press, 1983.

Shankar, Prabha Ravi. "Henry Cotton and the Indian National Congress." *Proceedings of the Indian History Congress* 59 (1998): 775–85.

Shen Zhihua, *Mao, Stalin and the Korean War: Trilateral Communist Relations in the 1950s*. Translated by Neil Silver. London: Routledge, 2012.

———. "Revisiting Stalin and Mao's Motivations in the Korean War." Sources and Methods (blog), June 22, 2020. Wilson Center. https://www.wilsoncenter.org/blog-post/revisiting-stalins-and-maos-motivations-korean-war.

Shen Zhihua and Yafeng Xia. *A Misunderstood Friendship: Mao Zedong, Kim Il-Sung and Sino-North Korean Relations 1949–1976*. Translated by Yafeng Xia. New York: Columbia University Press, 2018.

Shimada Kenji. *Chūgoku kindai shi ni okeru zasetsu* [The setback of modern Chinese thought]. Tokyo: Heibonsha, 2003.

———. *Pioneer of the Chinese Revolution*. Translated by Joshua Fogel. Stanford, CA: Stanford University Press, 1990.

Shirai Satoshi. *Eizoku haisenron: sengo nihon no kakushin* [A theory of perpetual defeat: The essence of postwar Japan]. Tokyo: Ohta shuppansha, 2013.

Silberman, Bernard S. "The Bureaucratic State in Japan: The Problem of Authority and Legitimacy." In *Conflict in Modern Japanese History: The Neglected Tradition*, edited by Tetsuo Najita and Victor Koschmann, 226–57. Ithaca, NY: Cornell University Press, 2005.

Simpson, David, ed. *German Aesthetic and Literary Criticism: Kant, Fichte, Schelling, Schopenhauer, Hegel*. Cambridge, UK: Cambridge University Press, 1984.

Smethurst, Richard. "A Social Origin of the Second World War." In *Japan Examined: Perspectives on Modern Japanese History*, edited by Harry Wray and Hilary Conroy, 269–81. Honolulu: University of Hawai'i Press, 1983. https://www.jstor.org/stable/2052989.

Smith, Craig A. *Chinese Asianism, 1894–1945*. Cambridge, MA: Harvard University Press, 2021.

Smith, Steven B. *Hegel's Critique of Liberalism: Rights in Context*. Chicago: University of Chicago Press, 1991.

Song Nianshen. *Faxian dongya* [Discovering East Asia]. Beijing: New Star Press, 2018.

Sugihara, Kaoru. "The Second Noel Butlin Lecture: Labor-Intensive Industrialisation in Global History." *Australian Economic History Review* 47, no. 2 (2007): 121–54.

Sun Ge. *Zhuneihao de beilun* [The paradox of Takeuchi Yoshimi]. Beijing: Beijing daxue chubanshe, 2005.

Sun Yat-sen. "Pan-Asianism." In *Pan-Pan-Asianism: A Documentary History*, vol. 2, *1920–Present*, edited by Sven Saaler and Christopher W. A. Szpilman, 78–85. Lanham, MD: Rowman and Littlefield, 2011.

Takeuchi Yoshimi. "Ajiashugi no tenbō" [The vision of pan-Asianism]. In *Ajiashugi* [Pan-Asianism], edited by Takeuchi Yoshimi, 7–67. Tokyo: Chikuma shobō, 1963.

———. *Fufukujū no isan* [Heritage of disobedience]. Tokyo: Chikuma shobō, 1961.

———. *Jōkyō teki: Takeuchi Yoshimi taidan shu* [Situational: A collection of Takeuchi Yoshimi's dialogues]. Tokyo: Gadō shuppansha, 1971.

———. *Nihon ideorogi* [Japanese ideology]. Tokyo: Koboshi bunko, 1999.

BIBLIOGRAPHY   263

———. *Nihon to ajia* [Japan and Asia]. Tokyo: Chikuma shobō, 2002.

———. *Nihon to ajia: Takeuchi Yoshimi hyōron sho* [Japan and Asia: A collection of critical essays by Takeuchi Yoshimi]. Tokyo: Chikuma shobō, 1966.

———. "Profile of Asian Minded Man X: Ōkawa Shūmei." *Developing Economies* 7, no. 3 (1969): 367–79.

———. *Rojin* [Lu Xun]. Tokyo: Noma Sawako, 2003.

———. *Takeuchi Yoshimi serekushon 1 Nihon he/kara no manazashi* [Takeuchi Yoshimi, selections, vol. 1, Looking from Japan]. Edited by Marukawa Tetsushi and Suzuki Masahisa. Tokyo: Nihon keizaisha, 2007.

———. *Takeuchi Yoshimi serekushon 2 Ajia he/kara no manazashi* [Takeuchi Yoshimi, selections, vol. 2, Looking from Asia]. Edited by Marukawa Tetsushi and Suzuki Masahisa. Tokyo: Nihon keizaisha, 2007.

———. *Takeuchi Yoshimi taidanshū* [A collection of Takeuchi Yoshimi's dialogues]. Tokyo: Gōdō shuppansha, 2005 [1970].

———. *Takeuchi Yoshimi zenshū* [The complete works of Takeuchi Yoshimi]. 17 vols. Tokyo: Chikuma shobō, 1982.

———. *What Is Modernity? Writings of Takeuchi Yoshimi*. Translated by Richard F. Calichman. New York: Columbia University Press, 2005.

Tan Chung. "China jia India dengyu 'Chindia'" [China plus India equals "Chindia"]. *Guoji zhengzhi yanjiu* 3 (2005): 140–46.

Tanaka, Stefan. *Japan's Orient: Rendering Pasts into History*. Berkeley: University of California Press, 1993.

Tomba, Massimiliano. *Insurgent Universality: An Alternative Legacy of Modernity*. Oxford: Oxford University Press, 2019.

———. *Marx's Temporalities*. New York: Haymarket Books, 2014.

Tosaka Jun. "The Principle of Everydayness and Historical Time." Translated by Robert Stolz. In *From Japan's Modernity: A Reader*, edited by Tetsuo Najita, 155–65. Chicago: Center for East Asian Studies, University of Chicago, 2002.

Traverso, Enzo. *Left-Wing Melancholia: Marxism, History and Memory*. New York: Columbia University Press, 2017.

Trouillot, Michel-Rolph. "The Anthropology of the State in the Age of Globalization: Close Encounters of the Deceptive Kind." *Current Anthropology* 42, no. 1 (2001): 125–38.

———. *Silencing the Past: Power and the Production of History*. Boston: Beacon Press, 1995.

Tsou, Jung (Zou Rong). *The Revolutionary Army: A Chinese Nationalist Tract of 1903*. Translated by John Lust. Paris: Mouton, 1968.

Tsuchiya Masaaki. "Takeuchi Yoshimi to bunka daigakumei: eiga, yoake no kuni wo megutte" [Takeuchi Yoshimi and the Cultural Revolution: Concerning the film *The Country at Daybreak*]. In *Mokugeki bunga daigakumei: eiga yoake no kuni wo yomi toku*, edited by Suzuki Hitoshi, Nakajima Takahiro, Maeda Toshiaki, and Shimozawa Kazuyoshi, 18–35. Tokyo: Ohta shuppan, 2008.

Tsukiashi Tatsuhiko. *Fukuzawa Yukichi to Chōsen mondai: "Chōsen kaizō ron" no tenkai to satetsu* [Fukuzawa Yukichi and Korean problem: The development and failure of the "Discourse on the Reconstitution of Korea"]. Tokyo: University of Tokyo Press, 2014.

Tu, Hang. "From Christian Transcendence to the Maoist Sublime: Liu Xiaofeng, the Chinese Straussians and the Conservative Revolt against Modernity." *Modern Intellectual History* (2022): 1–22.

Ueda, Atsuko, Michael K. Bourdaghs, Richi Sakakibara, and Hirokazu Toeda, eds. *The Politics and Literature Debate in Postwar Japanese Criticism 1945–1952.* Lanham, MD: Lexington Books, 2017.

Uemura Kunihiko. "Fukuzawa Yukichi and Eurocentrism in Modern Japan." *Kansai University Review of Economics* 14 (2012): 1–16.

Uhl, Christian. "Displacing Japan: Takeuchi Yoshimi's Lu Xun in Light of Nishida's Philosophy and Vice-Versa." *Positions: East Asia Cultures Critique* 17, no. 1 (2009): 207–38.

———. "Liberté—Egalité—Fraternité: Okawa Shûmei's Asia and the Romanticization of the Ideals of the French Revolution." Unpublished manuscript, 2013.

———. *Wer war Takuchi Yoshimis Lu Xun? Ein Annäherungsversuch an ein Monument der japanischen Sinologie.* Munich: Iudicum Verlag GmbH, 2003.

Umesao Tadao. *Bunmei no seitaishikan* [A theory of civilization based on ecological history]. Tokyo: Chūkō bunko, 1967.

———. *An Ecological View of History: Japanese Civilization in the World Context.* Translated by Beth Cary and edited by Harumi Befu. Melbourne: Transpacific Press, 2003.

Unger, Roberto Mangabeira, and Cui Zhiyuan. "China in the Russian Mirror." *New Left Review* 208 (1994): 78–87.

Usuki Akira. "A Japanese Asianist's View of Islam." *Annals of Japan Association for Middle Eastern Studies* (January 2013): 60–84.

———. *Ōkawa Shūmei: isulāmu to tennō no hazama de* [Ōkawa Shūmei between Islam and the emperor]. Tokyo: Seidosha, 2010.

Walker, Gavin. *The Perversion of Capital: Marxist Theory and the Politics of History in Modern Japan.* Durham, NC: Duke University Press, 2016.

Wang Hui. "Chaoxian bandao heping qiji yu dongbeiya tuanjie zhengzhi de keneng" [The peace in the Korean peninsula and the possibility of a politics of unity in Northeast Asia]. *Wenhua zongheng* (October 2018). https://www.sohu.com/a/258973131_115479.

———. *China's Twentieth Century.* Edited by Saul Thomas. London: Verso, 2016.

———. *The End of the Revolution: China and the Limits of Modernity.* Edited by Rebecca Karl. London: Verso, 2009.

———. "Ershi shiji yichan yu yidai yilu" [The legacy of the twentieth century and the Belt-Road Initiative]. *Wenhua zongheng* (February 2015). http://www.m4.cn/opinion/2015-02/1263367.shtml.

———. "Twentieth-Century China as an Object of Thought: An Introduction, Part 1: The Birth of the Century: The Chinese Revolution and the Logic of Politics." *Modern China* 46, no. 1 (2020): 3–49.

———. "Twentieth-Century China as an Object of Thought: An Introduction, Part 2: The Birth of the Century: China and the Conditions of Spatial Revolution." *Modern China* 46, no. 2 (2020): 115–61.

———. *Zhongguo xiandai sixiangshi de xingqi* [The rise of modern Chinese thought]. Vol. 2. Beijing: Sanlian shudian, 2004.

Wang Hui and Zang Xiaojia. "Zoujin 'yidai yilu': kuatixide wenming jiaohui yu lishi xushu— Interview with Professor Wang Hui" [Approaching "One Belt, One Road": Tran-systemic civilizational interaction and historical narrative]. *Xibei gonyue daxue xuebao* 1 (2018): 45–53.

Wang, Jessica Ching-Sze. *Dewey in China.* Albany: State University of New York Press, 2007.

Watanabe Kyōji. *Kita Ikki.* Tokyo: Chikuma gakugei bunko, 2007.

BIBLIOGRAPHY

Weber, Max. *Economy and Society*. Translated and edited by G. Roth and C. Wittich. New York: Bedminster Press, 1968 [1921].

Weber, Thorsten. *Embracing Asia in China and Japan: Asianism Discourse and the Contest for Hegemony, 1912–1933*. Cham, Switzerland: Palgrave Macmillan, 2018.

Werner, Jake. "Global Fordism in 1950s Urban China." *Frontiers of History in China* 7, no. 3 (2012): 415–41.

Yamada Keiji. "The Establishment of the Theory of the Commune State: It Is Right to Rebel." *Sekai* (September 1967): 98–114.

Yamada Masaru. "Takeuchi Yoshimi: Chūgoku to iu yūmei" [Takeuchi Yoshimi: The dream called China]. In *Higashiajia no chishiki jin: samazama no sengo, nihon no haisen—1950 nendai*, edited by Murata Yūjirō, Chō Kindaru, Harada Keiichi, and Yasuda Tsuneo, 106–21. Tokyo: Yūshisha, 2014.

Yamamurō Shinichi. *Nichiro sensō no seiki: rensashiten kara miru nihon to sekai* [The century of the Russo-Japanese War: Looking at Japan and the world through the perspective of interconnected points]. Tokyo: Iwanami shinsho, 2005.

Yan Fu. "Tian Yan Lun xu yu an yu" [Preface and annotations to Huxley's evolution and ethics]. In *Shehui jubian yu guifan chongjian: Yan Fu wenxuan* [Social change and the reconstitution of norms], edited by Lu Yunkun, 317–40. Shanghai: Shanghai yuandong chubanshe, 1996 [1897].

Young, Louise. *Japan's Total Empire: Manchuria and the Culture of Wartime Imperialism*. Berkeley: University of California Press, 1998.

Zachman, Urs Mathias. "Blowing Up a Double Portrait in Black and White: The Concept of Asia in the Writings of Fukuzawa Yukichi and Okakura Tenshin." *Positions: Asia Critique* 15, no. 2 (2007): 345–68.

Zhang Taiyan. *Gegudingxin de zheli: Zhang Taiyan wenxuan* [The philosophy of reform and improvement]. Shanghai: Shanghai yuandong chubanshe, 1996.

———. "Guojialun" [On the state]. In vol. 1 of *Zhang Taiyan zhenglun xuanji*, 359–70. Beijing: Zhonghua shuju, 1907 [1977].

———. "Indu ren zhi guan riben" [India's visions of Japan]. *Minbao* 20 (April 1908): 34.

———. "Lun Yazhou yi zi wei chunchi." *Shiwubao* 18, no. 22 (1897): 5–8. Reproduced in *Zhang Taiyan zhenglun xuanji*, vol. 1. Beijing: Zhonghua shuju, 1977.

———. *Zhang Taiyan quanji* [The complete works of Zhang Taiyan]. 8 vols. Shanghai: Shanghai renmin chubanshe, 1982–1986.

———. *Zhang Taiyan xuanji—zhushiben* [Zhang Taiyan: Selected works, with notes]. Edited by Zhu Weizheng and Jiang Yihua. Shanghai: Shanghai renmin chubanshe, 1981.

Zhang Xin. "Chinese Capitalism and the Maritime Silk Road: A World-Systems Perspective." *Geopolitics* 22, no. 2 (2017): 310–31.

Zhao Tingyang. *Tianxia tixi: shijie zhidu daolun* [The Tianxia System: An introduction to a philosophy of world order]. Jiangsu: Jiangsu jiaoyu chubanshe, 2005.

Zhuangzi. *Chuang Tsu Basic Writings*. Translated by Burton Watson. New York: Columbia University Press, 1964.

———. *Zhuangzi buzheng*. Anhui: Anhuidaxue chubanshe, 1999.

Zou Rong. *Geming jun* [The revolutionary army]. Beijing: Huaxia chubanshe, 2002.

———. *The Revolutionary Army: A Chinese Nationalist Tract of 1903*. Translated by John Lust. Paris: Mouton, 1968.

Index

Abe Isoo, 83
Abe Kōbō, 186
Abe, Shinzo, 10
Adas, Michael, 90
Advaita Vedanta, 37, 48
"affirmative infinite" (Hegel), 40
Ah Q (Lu Xun character), 130
Alfassa, Mira, 90
"all under heaven" (*tianxia*), 52, 73
"All You Need Is Love" (Beatles), 215
Althusser, Louis, 23
American Factory (film), 214–20
American imperialism, 100, 153, 159, 176, 182, 199;
    and global capitalism, 219; and modernization
    theory, 154. *See also* imperialism
anarchist cosmopolitanism, 87–88
Anderson, Mark, 41
Andō Shōeki, 162, 200
Anesaki Masaharu, 82
Anpo movement, 184–85
anticapitalism, 12, 58, 100
anticapitalist movements, 214, 216, 217; and labor,
    220
anti-pan-Asianists, 12, 16
Asia (Orient): competing visions of, 17; and
    decentering of China, 27; Hegel on, 8–9, 16–
    20; and imperialism, 16–17, 164–65 (*see also*
    Japan: and imperialism); as "late developer,"
    16–17; and nation-states, 27; as pharmakon,
    16; resistance to West in, 25, 55, 73, 93, 143, 168,
    175, 178, 185, 211; and subjectivity, 20–21, 203;
    theocracy in, 20–21; Western imperialism in,
    16, 25, 38, 55, 73, 93, 140, 143, 168, 175, 181
Asian Solidarity Society, 59–61, 64–65, 68–69, 75,
    104; manifesto, 60–65
Asia-Pacific War, 121–22, 145, 180, 184, 187

Asō Hisashi, 96
Association for the Study of Chinese Literature,
    114, 120, 123
Atatürk, Kemal, 94, 105, 152
aufheben (Hegel), 3
Auroville ashram, 90–91
automation, 214; and postcapitalism, 218
Aydin, Cemil, *The Politics of Anti-Westernism in
    Asia,* 4

"back to the future" narratives, 5, 25, 62, 67
"bad infinity" (Hegel), 40, 43, 45
Bandung Conference (1955), 136, 167, 175–76, 206
Barakatullah, Maulavi, 87
Bayet, Albert, 90
Beatles, "All You Need Is Love," 215
Belt-Road Initiative (BRI), 192, 198, 207–8; and
    Silk Road, 208, 211; and socialism, 211; and
    tribute system, 211
Benjamin, Walter, 144
Bidet, Jacques, 23, 113
Bloch, Ernst, 203; on human agency, 203
Bolshevism, 95–96
Bose, Rash Behari, 81, 87–89
Bose, Surendra Mohan, 68
Boxer Rebellion, 53
Brennan, Timothy, 83
BRI. *See* Belt-Road Initiative (BRI)
Buck-Morss, Susan, 111

Calichman, Richard, 178
capitalism, 2, 7, 12, 17, 23, 25–26, 29, 31–32, 36, 42,
    49, 85–87, 90, 99, 108, 110, 138–39, 175, 177–78,
    187; challenges to, 7, 110, 122; crisis of, 15, 26; as
    delegitimizing itself, 196; destabilizing rem-
    nants in, 217; family/market contradiction

268   INDEX

capitalism (*cont.*)

    in, 24; and freedom, contradiction of, 23; Fuku-
zawa on, 12, 31–32; in Japan, 95, 147; Lukács on,
23, 86, 143; Marxism on, 163; and Meiji Restoration, 31; and nation-state, 29, 31–32, 55, 99;
Okakura on, 6, 36, 41–46; Ōkawa on, 6, 79, 81,
87, 95, 99, 100, 101, 106–9; and pan-Asianism,
2, 3, 5, 7–11, 46, 59; Postone on, 140–41; rise of,
in Asia, 1; and surveillance, 219; Takeuchi on,
8, 122, 135, 142–43, 157, 168, 170, 177; Umesao
on, 172–73; Zhang Taiyan on, 6, 58–59, 61–63,
65, 70, 79. *See also* anticapitalism; anticapitalist
movements; global capitalist system

Caputo, John D., 129

Castro, Fidel, 178

CCP. *See* Chinese Communist Party (CCP)

Chen Duxiu, 70–71; on Chinese feudalism, 71

Chen, Kuan-hsing, 174

Chiang Kai-shek, 147

China: changing views of, in Japan, 114–15, 137;
critiques of traditions in, 70–71; decentering of,
27; economic growth of, 197; and global capitalist economy, 193, 196, 212, 215; and market
reforms, 193–94; modernization debates in,
51; and nationalism, 54–55, 66–67, 72, 164–65;
and neoliberalism, 194; revolutionary conditions of, 148–49, 164; rise of, 2–3, 14; schools
of philosophy in, 30; and socialism, 62–63, 67,
214; as theocratic autocracy, 30; tribute system
of, 27, 52. *See also* late Qing (China); *and under*
pan-Asianism; Takeuchi Yoshimi

China Incident (1935), 106–7, 115

China's New Left, 192, 196

Chinese Communist Party (CCP), 70, 137, 147, 212;
and Korean War, 205

Chinese Esperanto Association, 88

Chinese Literature Monthly, 116, 118, 119

Chinese Revolution, 9, 13, 14, 59, 110, 135, 136, 145,
152–53, 157–58, 162, 186–87, 191, 213, 214; and pan-
Asianism, 3; Takeuchi on, 9, 110, 136, 153, 158–59,
162, 192; Wang Hui on, 192, 194, 196, 201–4

Christian culture, roots in the East, 19

Chūō kōron (journal), 71, 164

Clark, T. J., 23

"cogs in the machine" (Weber), 41

Cold War, 7, 136, 139, 154, 173–74, 196, 197, 199;
bipolarity of, 174; new, 211, 219; "Operation
Rollback," 178

Confucius, 29, 37, 60, 160; *Analects*, 158

Cotton, Henry, 86, 93; on global capitalism, 85;
New India, 84–85

Creuzer, G. F., 19

Cultural Revolution, 7, 8, 11, 14, 186–90, 194–95,
207, 210, 214, 220; Japanese Sinologists on, 187–
88; and the "people," 220

Das, Taraknath, 68

Den Kenjirō, 96

Deng Xiaoping, 193

Derrida, Jacques, on religion, 129

Desai, Radhika, 211

Dewey, John: on Japan and China, 156–57; *The
Public and Its Problems*, 156

Dharmapala, Anagarika, 87

Doctrine of the Mean, The (Confucian text), 102

Dōkai (Association of the way), 83, 87

Driscoll, Mark, 18

Duara, Prasenjit, 4–5, 18, 103–4; and "back to
the future" narratives, 5; *The Crisis of Global
Modernity*, 10; on transcendence, 5, 104

"East Is Red, The" (song), 215

East-West opposition, 70; as cultural vs. material,
61; Okakura on, 40–42, 44; in pan-Asianism,
4, 25, 79, 87–88; Takeuchi on, 140, 143; Zhang
Taiyan on, 60–63

Eisenhower, Dwight, 178

Enlightenment, 14, 34, 40, 151, 177, 202; and China,
26; and Japan, 26; and nation-state, 26

Eroshenko, Vasili, 81, 87–89

Esperanto, 88

February Revolution (Russia), 71

Fenollosa, Ernest, 35, 41; "An Explanation of Truth
in Art," 35–36; on Japanese art, 36

Frankfurt school, 107, 173

French Revolution, 8, 93, 128, 197, 202; Ōkawa
on, 102

Fukuzawa Yukichi, 17–18, 50, 53, 61–62, 69, 79,
111, 114, 176, 194, 204; as anti-pan-Asianist, 12,
16–17, 24; on Asia, 27–28; on Asia, as behind,
28, 32–33; on Asia, lack of self-reflection in, 33;
on civilization, levels of, 28–29; on civilization,
spirit of, 27–28; critique of Confucianism, 30–
31, 33; and Hegel, 27, 48–49; and imperialism,
36, 71; on Japan, as leaving Asia, 16, 32, 170; on
Korean coup of 1884, 32; "Leaving Asia," 32–33;
on linear progress, 17; on Meiji Restoration,
30–31; and Okakura, differences between,
16–18, 34–35, 45, 47, 50; *Outline of a Theory of
Civilization*, 26; on the past, 31; on the past, oppression by, 29; on the past, periods of, 28; on
progress, 12; Western orientation of, 17, 19

Fynsk, Christopher, 126

Gandhi, Mahatma, 171; *Hind Swaraj*, 185; on soul
force, 185

Garon, Sheldon, 96

Gaulle, Charles de, 148

Ghose, Aurobindo, ashram of, 90–91

Gindin, Sam, 219

INDEX

global capitalist system, 16, 85, 139, 191, 193, 212, 215–16, 219–20; and imperialism, 153, 176
Gorky, Maxim, 152
Greater East Asia War, 106, 121
Great Japanism, 74

Hägglund, Martin, 129–30
Hammond, Kelly A., 6
Harootunian, Harry, 81, 107, 109, 217, 222
Hayashi Fusao, 181
Hazama Naoki, 61
Hegel, G. W. F., 35, 82–83, 102, 111, 129, 132, 203; "affirmative infinite," 40; "amphibian," 22–23; on Asia (Orient), 8–9, 16–20, 24, 36, 39, 45, 47; *aufheben*, 3; "bad infinity," 40; critique of Hinduism, 128; critique of mathematics, 96–97; on doubt and despair, 151; *Elements of the Philosophy of Right*, 9, 20, 128; *Encyclopaedia Logic*, 18; on ethical life, 106; "ethical substantiality," 8–9; on French Revolution, 128, 197, 202; on *Geist*, 18; on Hinduism, 103; on Indian philosophy, 18; on individuality, 9, 18, 20; on Jewish philosophy, 18; *Lectures on Fine Art*, 22–23, 85; linear history in, 18; on modernity, 23, 45, 106; "moment of negativity," 8; on oppositions, reconciling, 22–23; and pan-Asianism, 3, 8–9, 17, 19, 24; on pantheism, 103; *Phenomenology of Spirit*, 19, 106, 183; *The Philosophy of World History*, 17, 19–20, 22, 202; on religious histories, 19; *Science of Logic*, 40; on secular/eternal, 21–22; on *Sittlichkeit*, 20, 29; on spirit, 27, 34, 39, 142; on the state, 66; on subjectivity, 8–9, 17–22; on substantiality, 8–9, 17–22, 29, 49, 73, 118; on substantiality, vs. negativity, 17, 20–21, 25; on the West, and subjectivity/freedom, 21–22
Heidegger, Martin, 117, 120, 126, 146
Heimin shinbun (The people's newspaper), 82, 88
Hirano Gitarō, 146
Hitler, Adolf, 194
Hobsbawm, Eric, 7, 199, 207
Hotta, Eri, *Pan-Asianism and Japan's War*, 4
Huxley, Thomas, *Evolution and Ethics*, 53

Ibn Saud, 94, 152
imperialism, 2–3, 9–10, 15, 17–18, 101, 108, 110, 143, 187, 196, 200, 202, 204–5, 208, 210; in Asia, 164–65; and nation-state, tension between, 32, 143; and the ocean, 38–39; Okakura on, 38–39, 43–44, 46–47; and pan-Asianism, 2–4, 6–8, 11, 15; Takeuchi on, 143, 179–80, 196; Western, 6, 11, 16, 69, 72, 181–82, 185, 195, 199, 211, 219. *See also* American imperialism; *and under* Japan
"imperialism against imperialism" (Takeuchi), 181–82
India House, 60

intellectual labor, 163
Inukai Tsuyoshi, 75
Ishikawa Jun, 186
Izutsu Toshikiko, 83

Japan: American occupation of, 138; as Asian leader, 29; and British imperialism, 69, 72; and fascism, 97, 107–8; and feudalism, 29; and global capitalism, 25; and imperialism, 4, 6, 8, 10, 25, 27, 49, 58, 76, 79, 91, 108, 138–39, 155, 168, 179, 180–84, 185, 196; and nation-state/nationalism, 29, 80, 108, 139, 164–65; opening of, 25; and pan-Asianism, 12, 50, 56; and postwar regionalism, 139; and Shinto, 29; shogunal system in, 29–30; subordination of, 170; *tenkō* in, 146; treaties with Britain, 58; and Western civilization, 25, 29–30, 33
Japanese Communist Party (JCP), 60, 96
Japanese Marxists, 145, 165
Japanese romantic school, 122
Japanese Sinology. See *kangaku* (traditional Japanese Sinology); *shinagaku* (new Japanese Sinology)
Japan Industrial Club, 96
JCP. *See* Japanese Communist Party (JCP)
Jones, Andrew, 215, 216

kaika (enlightenment), 26
kaishin (conversion), 145–46, 148, 151, 163
Kaji Wataru, 127; critique of Takeuchi, 127; on Lu Xun, 127
Kang Youwei, 56, 61, 64, 69, 72, 148, 211; evolutionary view of history, 54; *The Great Unity*, 51; in India, 52–55; modernization goal, 51, 53; transnational view, 52; utopian view, 51–52
kangaku (traditional Japanese Sinology), 114, 118
Kant, Immanuel, 82, 102
Kaoru Sugihara, 163
Karl, Rebecca, 59
Katayama Sen, 36, 45
Katsura Tarō, 84
Kawabata Yasunari, 186
Kierkegaard, Søren, 141
Kishi Nobusuke, 139
Kita Ikki, 97–99; and Bushido ethics, 98; *The Theory of the Body Politic and Pure Socialism*, 97
knight-errant, in China and Japan, 86
Kobayashi Hideo, 123
Kojiki (Japanese compiled text), 101
Kojima Tsuyoshi, 83
Korean coup of 1884, 32
Korean War, 153; and pan-Asianism, 205
Kotoku Shusui, 83, 84, 88
Kropotkin, Peter, 88

270 INDEX

kundoku (Japanese method of reading Chinese), 116

Kyoto school philosophers, 145

Laplanche, Jean, 126

Last Samurai, The (Ravina), 26

late Qing (China), 26, 31, 32, 51, 52, 64, 73, 147, 149, 216; and Japan, 65; modernization debates in, 51, 55, 65; and nationalism, 54–55; revolutionaries in, 53–54, 86

League of Nations, 90

left Hegelians, 106

Lenin, Vladimir, 44, 63, 152, 158; on awakening of Asia, 200; on national self-determination, 198; on 1905 Revolution, 198

Li Dazhao, 12, 50, 53, 70–72; China focus of, 71–73; on Chinese nationalism, 72–73; on global alliance, 74; "Great Pan-Asianism," 71–73; on Japan, 74; on "New Asianism," 74; "New Chinese Republican Nationalism," 72; pan-Asianism of, 71–74; on Republic of China, 72

Li Hongzhang, 32

Li Zehou, 26

Liang Qichao, 53

Liezi (Daoist text), 159

Lin Shaoyang, 61, 68

linear infinity, 40

Linkhoeva, Tatiana, 91

Lippmann, Walter, 156

literature, autonomy of, 132

Liu, Lydia, 150

Löwy, Michael, 109

Lu Xun, 9, 13, 88, 111, 117, 120, 130, 142, 144, 148, 151, 201–2, 208; conversion experience of, 124–25; despair in, 150; in Japan, 124; literature and politics in, 127–28, 131; "Mr. Fujino," 124; *Na Han* (Screaming), 123–25; on perpetual (eternal) revolution, 133–34, 145; as "poet of the people," 135; on power of the will, 203; on revolutionary literature, 131; on Sun Yat-sen, 133–34; transcendent experience, 125; turn to writing, 124, 128; "The Wise Man, the Fool, and the Slave," 144, 149

Lukács, György, 23, 86, 143, 145; on capitalism, 23, 86, 143

Luohan, Ben, 68

MacArthur, Douglas, 138

Mackinder, Halford, 38–39, 198

MacLeod, Josephine, 37

Mahayana Buddhism, 92

Mahbubani, Kishore, *Can Asians Think?*, 7

maki kaeshi (rollback), double meaning of, 177–78

Mandel, Ernest, 107; on fascism, 107–8

Manela, Erez, 90

Manet, Édouard, *Olympia*, 23

Mao Zedong, 7–11, 14, 98–99, 128, 137, 148, 151, 157, 162–63, 169, 188–90, 194, 195, 199–200, 206–8, 210, 214; and "ancient utopianism," 169; on Korean War, 206; "mass line," 205; "New Democracy," 202; and pan-Asianism, 8; parable of the foolish old man, 158–59; on revolutionary base areas, 169; and Third Worldism, 169

Maoism, 86, 169, 215; as future beyond capitalism, 215

Marchand, Susan, 19

Martin, Bill, 109

Maruyama Masao, 167, 185, 205; on Chinese revolution, 164–65; on imperialism in Asia, 164–65; on nationalism, 164–65; "Nationalism in Japan," 164

Marx, Karl, 11, 23, 43, 62, 106, 143, 167, 169, 203, 216, 218; *Capital*, 32, 43; on capitalist civil society, 97; on capitalist expansion, 142; *Communist Manifesto*, 42; critique of Hegel's *Philosophy of Right*, 158; ideal society of, 218; on socialism without industrialization, 11; on subsumption of labor, 216

Marxism, 5, 11, 14, 42, 86, 109, 123, 141, 188, 222; and aesthetics, 123; and Asian revolutionary development, as contradicting, 230; depiction of Asia, 81; and pan-Asianism, 11, 14; Takeuchi on, 136, 161, 169, 177. *See also* Japanese Marxists

Masuda Wataru, 127

McCoy, Alfred, 39; on the rise of China, 199

Mehl, Margaret, 114

Meiji Restoration, 24–25, 27, 32, 34, 114, 147; as "back to the future," 25; and capitalism, 31; and Confucianism, 30; contradictions in, 25–26; and Enlightenment, 26; and nation-state, 26

Michi (journal), 86

Minbao (The people's journal), 58, 59, 60, 68

Mishima Yukio, 186

Mitsukawa Kametarō, 99

Miyazaki Tōten, 75

modernism/modernity, 7, 23, 25, 34, 41, 54, 56, 58, 59, 66, 87, 108, 111, 122, 135, 151, 155; alienation in, 18, 23–24; antinomy of, 41; education in, 23–24; and fascism, 13, 107–8; ideology of, 165; and metrics of quantity and speed, 144; Ōkawa on, 81–82, 94, 104–6; and rationalization, 143, 145; and reification, 143–44; structures of, 23; Takeuchi on, 13, 111–13, 117–22, 136–37, 139–44, 146–47, 154–55, 157–58, 162, 165–67, 170, 174–75, 180, 190; Umesao on, 173

modernization theory, 24, 154, 165, 166, 170, 212

Modi, Narendra, 10

Mohapatra, Rimina, 18

Naitō Konan, 115

Nakamuraya, 87–88

Nandy, Ashis, 182

INDEX

nationalism, 167; and China, 54, 72–73, 164; and civilization, 4; and Japan, 29, 80, 108, 139, 164–65; Lenin on, 198; Maruyama on, 164–65; Okakura on, 47; Ōkawa on, 80–81, 83, 86, 92, 101; and pan-Asianism, 4–5, 10, 59, 64, 74, 87, 164; Takeuchi on, 136, 152, 160, 163–69, 176, 211; Umesao on, 170; Wang Hui on, 200, 202, 206; Yasuda on, 123; Zhang Taiyan on, 58–59, 61, 65–69. *See also* nation-state

nation-state, 26; and capitalism, 29, 31–32; and Enlightenment, 26; and imperialism, tension between, 32; and Meiji Restoration, 26; and ocean/land dichotomy, 26. *See also* nationalism

New Text Confucians, 52

New Youth (journal), 71

Niijima Atsuyoshi, 187, 191; "China Commune," 188; on Cultural Revolution, 189; on Shanghai Commune, 189

1911 Revolution (China), 70, 71, 75, 132, 134, 140, 144, 147, 155, 165, 205

Nishi Junzō, "Confucianism and Chinese Thought from Now On," 149

Nishida Kitarō, 132

North Korea, 196

Nosaka Sanzō, 96, 137

October Revolution (Russia), and Japanese workers' movements, 95–96

Oda Takeo, 127

Ogyū Sorai, 116

Ōi Kentarō, 146

Okakura Tenshin, 3, 12, 23, 33, 51, 58, 77, 79, 80, 81, 190, 198; on anti-imperialism, 44; "Asia is one," 94; on Asian culture, 6, 34, 37–39, 45; on Asian culture, and freedom/liberty, 39–40, 45, 49; "The Awakening of the East," 40, 46, 48; background of, 34–35; circle/line in, 40; East/West opposition in, 61, 215; East/West opposition in, and individuality, 40–42, 44; and Fukuzawa, differences between, 16–18, 34, 45, 47, 50; and Hegel, 34, 36, 45–49; *Ideals of the East,* 37, 45; on imperialism, 39; in India, 36–38; on Japan, 47–48; on linear infinity, 40; and Marx, similarities and differences between, 42–44; on money, problem of, 42–43; on monotony, 41, 44–45; on nationalism and unity, 47; as pan-Asianist, 3, 16–18, 24, 34, 43, 47–49; philosophical influences on, 35; on religious fervor, 44; on substantiality and negativity, 18, 215; "Theory of Art," 35; on universality, 37–38; on Western imperialism, 38, 43–44, 46–47

Ōkawa Shūmei, 3, 10, 24, 41, 75, 79, 91, 135, 152, 154, 187, 190; and anarchism, 88; as anticolonial, 85–86; anti-imperialism of, paradoxical, 100, 106–8; arrest of, 85, 95, 99; on Asian culture, 6; on Asian heroes, 94; background of, 82–83; and

Bose, 89; on capitalism, 6, 79, 81, 87, 95, 99, 101, 106–9; on China Incident, 106–7; and Christianity, 83; and class, 108; and Confucianism, 82, 102–3; on contemplative thought, 86–87; cosmopolitanism of, 82–83; Cotton's influence on, 84–85, 92; coup attempts of, 99; critique of democracy, 96–98; on the emperor, 101; *The Establishers of Asia,* 94; and fascism, 80–81, 95, 101, 107–8; on French Revolution, 102; Hegelian themes in, 103–5; and imperialism, 101, 108, 110; inclusive vision of Asia, 13, 94, 104; and India, 84, 90, 92, 104, 107; and Indian nationalists, 92; and Indian philosophy, 82, 84; and Islam, 83, 92–94, 104–5; on Japan, 105–6; "The Japanese and Their Road," 92; on Japanese capitalism, 95; in Japanese wartime, 13; as knight-errant, 86; and Mahayana Buddhism, 92; on Manchuria, 99–100; on Meiji Restoration, 100–101; on militarism, 100; and modernity, 81, 94, 105–6; "Mystical Mohammedanism," 83; as nationalist, 80–81, 83, 86, 92, 101; *The New Spirit of Asia,* 103; and pan-Asianism, 3, 13, 24, 80, 82–83, 89, 104, 107, 110; politicization of, 84–86; "Problems Concerning Reviving Asia," 83, 94; on religion and state unity, 104–5; on religious transcendence, 99, 101, 103–5, 109; "Revolutionary Europe and the Revival of Asia," 92–93, 95; and Richard, 92; on Russian Revolution, 95; on Saigō, 98; and Shinto, 101; on spiritual freedom in Asia, 91; on state and religion unity, 104–6; statism of, 95–96, 108; synthesis efforts in, 84; utopian views of, 87, 92, 99, 100, 102, 105, 107, 109

Ōkuma Shigenobu, 69

Opium War, 27, 52, 114

Osaka Industrial Association, 96

Ōsugi Sakae, 60

"overcome by modernity" (Harootunian), 81

"overcoming modernity" (Kyoto school), 187

Ōya Sōichi, on Cultural Revolution, 186

Pal, Radhabinod, on Tokyo war crimes trials, 182

pan-Asianism, 1–4, 12–15, 28, 32, 50–51, 53–55, 63, 68, 80–81, 88, 91, 103, 216; academic approach to, 1, 4, 6; and alienation, 24; as anti-colonial, 8, 87; and anti-imperialism, 2, 6–8, 11, 55, 59, 64, 80, 91; and anti-Westernism, 4, 87; as "back to the future" narrative, 6–7; as "better future," 3–4, 7, 79; and capitalism, 2, 3, 5, 7–11, 46, 59; and capitalist automation, 14–15; and capitalist crisis, 26; and China, 12, 14, 50–51, 53–56, 78–79, 164; and Chinese Revolution, 3, 110; and colonialism, 6; contemporary, 192; and critique of capitalism, 2–3, 6, 13; and critique of linear time, 17; and culture, 2, 6–7; East-West opposition in, 4, 25, 79, 87–88; emergence, context

pan-Asianism (*cont.*)
of, 16; and Eurocentrism, 6, 8, 81, 110; and
fascism, 13; and geography, 2, 12; and global
capitalism, 153; and Hegel, 3, 8–9, 17, 19, 24;
and imperialism, 2–4, 6–8, 11, 15; and India, 58;
and individuality, 9; and Japan, 12, 50, 56–57,
68, 180–81, 183; and Japanese imperialism, 4, 6,
8, 10, 58, 79, 180–81, 183; and Korean War, 153;
as liberatory, 4; and Mao, 8; and Marxism, 11,
14; and Meiji Restoration, 25; and modernization theory, 24; and nationalism, 4–5, 10, 59,
64, 74, 87, 164, 168, 181; popular approach to, 1;
postwar, 111; prewar, 111; reactionary dimension
of, 80; right-wing, 9; and Russia, 91, 198; and
Russo-Japanese War, 69; and socialism, 11, 12,
15, 59, 79; and subjectivity, 9; and *tenkō*, 146–47;
and Third World, 2, 6, 11, 136, 168, 191; and
transnational unity, 4–5; and WWI, 90. *See also
under* Li Dazhao; Okakura Tenshin; Ōkawa
Shūmei; Sun Yat-sen; Zhang Taiyan
pan-Islamism, 4
Panitch, Leo, 219
Pearl Harbor, 121, 122
People's War, 204–5
Perry, Matthew, 25
"phantom public" (Lippmann), 156
Pinkard, Terry, 23–24
Plato, 23
Plekhanov, Georgi, 198
Pomeranz, Kenneth, 76
Postone, Moishe, 43, 216, 218; on capital, 140–41
Potsdam Declaration, 137
Prashad, Vijay, 48, 175
Pye, Lucian, 210

Rai, Lala Lajpat, 92
Rao, Rama, 182
Rathore, Aakash Singh, 18
Republican Revolution of 1911 (China). *See* 1911
Revolution (China)
Revolutionary Army, The (pamphlet), 54
revolutionary base areas, 169
"revolution follows heaven" (*shun tian*), 55
Richard, Paul, 87, 90–91; on Japan, 91; on Russia,
91; Wilsonian thought in, 91
Richet, Etienne, 90
"rise of China," question of, 2–3, 14
Riza, Ahmad, 57, 76
rollback (*maki kaeshi*), double meaning of,
177–78
Rousseau, Jean Jacques, 54–55
Russian Revolution (1917), 59, 91, 95. *See also* Feb-
ruary Revolution (Russia); October Revolution
(Russia), and Japanese workers' movements
Russo-Japanese War, 42, 58, 69, 76–77, 80, 94, 124,
198, 199; and anarchism, 87–88; and critique of

West, 57–58; importance of, 56–57; and pan-
Asianism, 57, 69, 76
ryōshin (conscience), 146

Saigō Takamori, 26, 98
Sakai Toshihiko, 60, 83
Satsuma Rebellion, 26
Schelling, Friedrich, 46
Schlegel, Friedrich, 19
Schopenhauer, Arthur, 133
Schwartz, Benjamin, 31–32
Science of Thought (journal), 169
Shen, Bao, 68
Shen Zhihua, on Mao, 206–7
Shidehara Kijūrō, 99, 100
Shimuzu Ikutarō, 138
shinagaku (new Japanese Sinology), 114–15, 118
Shirai Satoshi, *A Theory of Perpetual Defeat*, 184
Shiratori Kurakichi, 115
Shivaji, 68, 69
Sho Konishi, 87
shokuzai (atonement), 126
"short twentieth century" (Hobsbawm), 7, 199–
200, 207
Showa Restoration, 99
shun tian (revolution follows heaven), 55
Silk Road, 1, 208, 211
Sino-Japanese War, 65, 114, 199
Sinology, Japanese. See *kangaku* (traditional
Japanese Sinology); *shinagaku* (new Japanese
Sinology)
Sittlichkeit (Hegel), 20, 29
Smith, Adam, 59
Smith, Craig A., *Chinese Asianism*, 4
Sōma Aizō, 88
Sōma Kokko, 88
Sōma Toshiko, 89
Spencer, Herbert, 35
Spengler, Oswald, *The Decline of the West*, 90
Spinoza, Baruch, 18, 21, 103
Stalin, Joseph, 148
"sublate" (Hegel), 3
Sun Wukong, 118
Sun Yat-sen, 3, 12, 53, 79, 91, 132, 143, 151, 152, 171,
202, 208; on Asian resistance, 76–77; Confucian
perspective of, 75, 77; East-West opposition
in, 77–78; as eternal revolutionary, 132–34, 135;
on imperialism, 76–77; and Japan, 6, 12, 75–78;
nationalism of, 10; and pan-Asianism, 3, 50,
76, 78, 80, 94; on Russia, 12, 76, 78, 168, 198; on
tribute system, 77

Tagore, Rabindranath, 92, 152, 171, 177
Taishō crises, 84
Takeuchi Yoshimi, 4, 75, 80, 88, 107, 109, 115, 192–
93, 200, 205–7, 210–11, 215, 217, 220; on ancient

utopianism, 169; as anticapitalist, 13–14; on "Asia," concept of, 136–37, 152, 167, 169, 173, 175–76; "Asia as Method," 14, 177–79, 201, 212; on Asian collaboration, 179; on Asia-Pacific War, 121–22, 178; on atonement and sin, 126, 128–29; and autonomy, 113; background of, 112–13; on bureaucratic culture, 135, 143; on capitalism, 142–43, 147, 168; on China, 9, 13–14, 110–14, 117, 120, 136–37, 139–40, 151, 156–57, 159–60, 168, 178–79, 186; and China and Japan, comparison of, 147–48, 150, 155; on Chinese Communist Party (CCP), 157; on Chinese intellectuals in countryside, 162; and Chinese Revolution, 9, 110, 136, 153, 162; on conscience, 146; on Cuba, as part of Asia, 175–76; on Cultural Revolution, 11, 14, 186, 189–90; on decolonization, 14; on democracy, 156, 160; on despair, 150, 158; on Dewey, 156–57; "Diary of Repatriation," 138; earth in, 117–18; on East-West opposition, 140, 143–45, 152, 168, 175, 177, 201; "elemental groan," 120, 129; on Enlightenment, 172; on Eurocentrism, 13; on freedom, 142; "The Generalization of War Experience," 183–84; "The Greater East Asia War and Our Resolution (A Manifesto)," 121; on "honor student" culture, 146, 150; on humanism, 151; on imperialism, 143, 196; "imperialism against imperialism," 179–80; "infinite instants," 141; on intellectual labor, 163–64; on Japan, 137, 147–48, 150, 153, 155–57, 160, 179; on Japan, as leaving Asia, 170–71; on Japanese Communist Party (JCP), 10, 131, 153–57, 161; on Japanese constitution, 160–61; *Japanese Ideology*, 154, 157, 160, 164; on Japanese imperialism, 180–83; "Japanese romantics," 166; on Lenin, 158; on liberation, 150; on literature, 118–21, 123; on literature, and politics, 131–32; on literature, and religion, 129; on Lu Xun, 111, 113–14, 117–18, 120, 122–26, 128–35, 150, 163, 201; on *maki kaeshi*, 178; in Manchuria, 113; and Mao, 8–10, 137, 148, 157–58, 169, 185; on Marx, 158; and Marxism, 136, 141, 161, 169, 177; on Marxist cosmopolitanism, 166–67; on modernity, 13, 111–13, 117–22, 136–37, 139–42, 146–47, 151, 154, 157, 165–66; on morality, 160; on movements of history, 144; on nationalism, 152, 160, 163–69, 176, 211; on nationalism/modernity dichotomy, 166; on nation-state, sovereignty of, 173; on negativity, 158; on 1911 Revolution, 140, 165; "On Asian Nationalism," 164; on Oriental capitalism, 142; on perpetual/eternal revolution, 132–34, 139, 186; philosophy of endless revolution, 132–34; and postwar period, 138–39; on reification, 132, 135, 143; on religion, foundation of, 129; on religious conversion, 126, 162–63; resignation of, 160, 185; on revolution, and the everyday, 161–62, 189–90; on revolution, endless, 132–34, 139, 189;

on revolutionary China, 10–11, 157–59, 161–62; *Rojin*, 111, 123, 126, 136; scholarship on, 136; on secularization, 120, 126–27; on separation of mental and manual labor, 162–63; on Soviet Union, 155; on the state, naturalist view of, 184; on subjectivity, 9, 13, 111–12, 117–18, 136, 141, 155, 158, 190–91; on subjectivity, and awareness of history, 183; on substantiality, 118; on teleology, 136; on *tenkō*, 145–47; on Third World nationalization, 137, 168; on transcendence, 130, 141; on translating Chinese, 116; on universality, 177; on war memory, 183–85; on Western modernity, 140–44; on Western nationalism, 168; "What Is Modernity?," 13, 139–40, 142, 144, 147, 152, 155, 158, 162, 170, 174–75, 180, 190
Takeyama Michio, 194; hierarchy in, 174; on history, 174; on "leaving Asia," 170
tenkō (ideological reversal), 83, 145–48, 166
tianxia (all under heaven), 52, 73
Tibet, 209
Tōjō Hideki, 148
Tōma Seita, 153
Tomba, Massimiliano, 144, 217
Tosaka Jun: *On Japanese Ideology*, 154, 161; principle of everydayness, 161
Tōyama Mitsuru, 75, 89
Tōyama Saburō, 83
Toynbee, Arnold, 175
Toyotomi Hideyoshi, 86
Treaty of Versailles, 74
Trotsky, Leon, 107–8
Trouillot, Michel-Rolph, 111; on global capitalist economy, 215
Trump, Donald, 10
Tsuda Sōkichi, 115
Tsukiashi Tatsuhiko, 32
Tsune (Okakura's guardian), 34

Umesao Tadao, 169–70; on Asia, 171, 174, 176; on despotic empires, 172; on development, as not uniform, 172; everydayness in, 171; on feudalism, 172–73; on history, 174; on Japan, 171; on modernity, 173; on nationalism, 170; theory of ecological zones, 171–72
Union of Asian Peoples, 89

Vivekananda, Swami, 37
Voltaire, 19

Wakamiya Unosuke, "What Is Great Pan-Asianism?," 71–72
Wang Hui, 7–8, 14–15, 23, 73, 191, 212–13, 220; on American hegemony, 195–97; on Asian revolutionary nationalisms, 200, 202; on awakening of Asia, 199; background of, 193; on Belt-Road Initiative (BRI), 198, 207–12; on Bloch, 203–4;

Wang Hui (*cont.*)
  on China, and land/sea dichotomy, 200–201,
    208, 210–11, 215; on China, as multicultural,
    209–10; on China, as nation-state, 210; on
    China, loss of revolutionary consciousness in,
    195–96; on China, 1989 social movement in,
    193; on China, rise of, 199–200, 207; on Chinese
    Communist Party (CCP), 207; on Chinese
    neoliberals, 193; on Chinese Revolution, 192,
    194, 196–97, 199, 201–4; on Cold War, 195, 197;
    on Cultural Revolution, 194; on East-West
    dichotomy, 209; on ideals of freedom and
    equality, 202; "The Legacy of the Twentieth
    Century and the Belt-Road Initiative," 208; on
    Lu Xun, 201–2; on nationalism, 200, 202, 206;
    on nonrevolutionary revolutionary, 192, 197; on
    pan-Asianism, and subjectivity, 201; on People's
    War, 204–5, 213–14; as postmodern, 204; on
    principle of self-determination, 206; on revolu-
    tionary potential, 198; *Rise of Modern Chinese
    Thought*, 210; on Russia's October Coup, 197;
    on Russo-Japanese War, 198; on specter of
    communism, 196; "temporal tendency," 204;
    and Third Worldism, 14
Wang Yangming, 83, 104
Washington, George, 54–55
Watanabe Kyōji, 98, 99
Weber, Max, 41
Whitman, Walt, 54
Wilson, Woodrow, 90

Xi Jinping, 1, 207–9, 220
Xinjiang, 209

Yamada Keiji, 191; on China, as commune, 187–88;
  on Cultural Revolution, 187–88; on modern
  division of labor, 187
Yamakawa Hitoshi, 60
Yamamurō Shinichi, 56

Yan Fu, 31, 32, 53
Yan'an revolutionary base, 169
Yasuda Yojūrō, 113, 122–23; on Marxism, 123; on
  modernity, 122; on nationalism, 123; on politi-
  cized literature, 123
Yoshikawa Kojirō, 115, 118
Yoshimoto Takaaki, 190
Yoshino Sakuzō, 146
Youth Is Like Fire (film), 214–16, 219
Yūzonsha (Japanese political party), 95

Zasulich, Vera, 11
Zhang Ji, 60
Zhang Taiyan, 12, 53–56, 76, 78, 79; as anti-
  Manchu, 56; on Asian culture, 6; background
  of, 55; on Britain, 69–70; and Buddhism, 65,
  69; and capitalism, 59, 61–63; and diversity,
  64; East-West opposition in, 60–63, 65, 67; on
  equitable field system, 63; and imperialism,
  61–62, 67–68; on India-China alliance, 68;
  "Indians in Japan," 69; "Interpretation of the
  Equalization of Things," 65; on Japan, 65, 69,
  107; on linear time, 50; on modernity, 66; on
  "national essence," 67; "The National Essence
  Movement in India," 67; on nationalism, 58–59,
  61, 65–69; on nationalization of land, 59; "On
  the Five Negations," 66; and pan-Asianism, 50,
  54, 56, 58–61, 63–65, 70, 80; prison sentence,
  56, 58; and socialism, 59, 62–63; on statism, 66;
  temporality in, 67; on Western morality, 65
zhantuoruo (evil), 65
Zhao Tingyang, 73
Zhou Enlai, 137
Zhuangzi, "Discussion of the Equalization of
  Things," 150
Zou Rong, 53–54; as anti-Manchu, 55–56; on
  China, race in, 54; nationalism of, 54–55; and
  pan-Asianism, 54–55; *The Revolutionary Army*,
  54

Printed and bound by CPI Group (UK) Ltd, Croydon, CR0 4YY
02/02/2025

14636546-0002